"Remarkably wide-ranging and undeniably riveting, *Consumer Culture Theory in Asia* offers a deep dive into the socio-cultural, ideological, and experiential consumption underlying precarity and power in the world's fastest-growing region. In excavating the impact of neo-colonial development on vulnerable populations, the authors plead for socially sustainable consumer culture."

Annamma Joy, *Professor of Marketing,*
The University of British Columbia, Canada.

"*Consumer Culture Theory in Asia* presents chapters from active researchers who address Asian consumption from a rich variety of historical and theoretical perspectives. Their work will engage the Consumer Culture Theory community as well as students and scholars from the humanities and social sciences."

Terrence H. Witkowski, *Professor Emeritus of Marketing,*
California State University, Long Beach, USA.

"This volume contains cutting-edge scholarship that traverses myriad historical and contemporary consumption contexts in Asia. Curating work by an interdisciplinary group of scholars, it will prove to be an invaluable resource for those interested in this vital, vibrant area of the globe typified by changes and challenges in the marketplace."

Cele Otnes, *Anthony J. Petullo Professor of Business*
Administration, Gies College of Business,
University of Illinois at Urbana-Champaign, USA.

"People around the world are grappling with how issues of diversity and inclusion impact consumption. Studies in this book contemplate these issues in the marketplace with a focus on vulnerable consumers in Asia—a generally underrepresented region in marketing scholarship."

Tonya Williams Bradford, *University of California, Irvine, USA.*

Consumer Culture Theory in Asia

We live in times of increasing world uncertainty. Consumer culture in Asia has embodied such precariousness, with their unprecedented states of both prosperity and vulnerability.

Works in this volume examine the consumer cultures that exist in today's precarious Asia. They do this through culturally oriented, critical consumer research. How deeply has the consumer precariousness in Asia been intertwined with the sociohistorical patterning of consumption including class, gender, and other social categories? How do these problematics affect consumers' identity projects, consumer rituals, and marketplace cultures? How is consumer precariousness aggravated by the governmentality of the superpower? How does the changing landscape of inter-Asian and global popular culture impact consumer culture in these nations? Together, the authors in this volume attempt to answer these questions through consumer research within the paradigm known as consumer culture theory (CCT). Since most CCT inquiry has been in Western contexts, this volume augments the existing knowledge. It presents the most current, critical, historical, and material consumer studies focused on Asia.

This volume will be of interest to seasoned CCT researchers and academics, for anyone new to CCT, and for postgraduate students interested in CCT or writing a consumer culture-related thesis.

Yuko Minowa is Professor of Marketing in the School of Business at the Brooklyn Campus of Long Island University in New York, United States.

Russell Belk is York University Distinguished Research Professor and Kraft Foods Canada Chair in Marketing, Schulich School of Business, York University, Canada.

Routledge Frontiers in the Development of International Business, Management and Marketing
Series Editors: Marin Marinov and Svetla Marinova

1. **Economic Transition and International Business**
   Managing Through Change and Crises in the Global Economy
   Edited by Eric Milliot and Sophie Nivoix

2. **Value in Marketing**
   Retrospective and Perspective Stance
   Edited by Marin A. Marinov

3. **Cross-cultural Challenges in International Management**
   Edited by Bruno Amann and Jacques Jaussaud

4. **Covid-19 and International Business**
   Change of Era
   Edited by Marin A. Marinov and Svetla T. Marinova

5. **Open Internationalization Strategy**
   Edited by Nadine Tournois and Philippe Very

6. **Philosophy of Marketing**
   The New Realist Approach
   Matteo Giannasi and Francesco Casarin

7. **Business Models and Firm Internationalisation**
   Edited by Christian Nielsen, Svetla T. Marinova and Marin A. Marinov

8. **Consumer Culture Theory in Asia**
   History and Contemporary Issues
   Edited by Yuko Minowa and Russell Belk

For more information about this series, please visit: www.routledge.com/business/series/RFDIBMM

Consumer Culture Theory in Asia
History and Contemporary Issues

Edited by
Yuko Minowa and
Russell Belk

First published 2022
by Routledge
605 Third Avenue, New York, NY 10158

and by Routledge
2 Park Square, Milton Park, Abingdon, Oxon, OX14 4RN

Routledge is an imprint of the Taylor & Francis Group, an informa business

© 2022 selection and editorial matter, Yuko Minowa and Russell Belk; individual chapters, the contributors

The right of Yuko Minowa and Russell Belk to be identified as the authors of the editorial material, and of the authors for their individual chapters, has been asserted in accordance with sections 77 and 78 of the Copyright, Designs and Patents Act 1988.

With the exception of Chapter 13, no part of this book may be reprinted or reproduced or utilised in any form or by any electronic, mechanical, or other means, now known or hereafter invented, including photocopying and recording, or in any information storage or retrieval system, without permission in writing from the publishers.

Chapter 13 of this book is available for free in PDF format as Open Access from the individual product page at www.routledge.com. It has been made available under a Creative Commons Attribution-Non Commercial-No Derivatives 4.0 license.

Trademark notice: Product or corporate names may be trademarks or registered trademarks, and are used only for identification and explanation without intent to infringe.

Library of Congress Cataloging-in-Publication Data
Names: Minowa, Yuko, editor. | Belk, Russell W., editor.
Title: Consumer culture theory in Asia : history and contemporary issues / edited by Yuko Minowa and Russell W. Belk.
Description: 1 Edition. | New York, NY : Routledge, 2022. | Series: Routledge frontiers in the development of international business, management and marketing | Includes bibliographical references and index.
Identifiers: LCCN 2021040052 (print) | LCCN 2021040053 (ebook) | ISBN 9780367629496 (hardback) | ISBN 9780367629502 (paperback) | ISBN 9781003111559 (ebook)
Subjects: LCSH: Consumer behavior—Asia. | Consumption (Economics)—Asia.
Classification: LCC HF5415.33.A78 C667 2022 (print) | LCC HF5415.33. A78 (ebook) | DDC 658.8/342095—dc23/eng/20211018
LC record available at https://lccn.loc.gov/2021040052
LC ebook record available at https://lccn.loc.gov/2021040053

ISBN: 978-0-367-62949-6 (hbk)
ISBN: 978-0-367-62950-2 (pbk)
ISBN: 978-1-003-11155-9 (ebk)

DOI: 10.4324/9781003111559

Typeset in Sabon
by Apex CoVantage, LLC

To our mothers, Chieko Minowa (1931–2020) and Betty Belk (1923–2021)

Contents

List of Illustrations	xi
List of Contributors	xii
Acknowledgments	xx

1 Introduction   1
YUKO MINOWA AND RUSSELL BELK

SECTION I
History of Consumerism in Asia   17

2 The Long March of the Commodity in China   19
ALISON HULME

3 Consumerism in Early Modern Japan: Food, Fashion,
and Publishing   33
KAZUO USUI

SECTION II
Consumer Identity Projects   61

4 Century of Humiliation and Consumer Culture:
The Making of National Identity   63
I-CHIEH MICHELLE YANG, JULIANA FRENCH, AND
CHRISTINA LEE

5 Predicting a Mother's Role in Investing in Children's
Education: A Study on Autonomy and Empowerment
From India   82
AKSHAYA VIJAYALAKSHMI, MENG-HSIEN (JENNY) LIN,
AND SARAH RICKS

x   *Contents*

SECTION III
Consumer Rituals

103

6   Gift-Giving and Kinship-Making: *Male Phoenix* in China
JIA CONG AND XIN ZHAO

105

7   Solitary Death Is Elsewhere: The Making of Memorial
Community in Japan
YUKO MINOWA

118

8   The Work of Culture in Thai Theravāda Buddhist
Death Rituals
RUNGPAKA AMY HACKLEY

138

SECTION IV
Governance and Sustainability in Consumption Practices

157

9   Utopia and Dystopia: Consumer Privacy and China's
Social Credit System
ERIC PING HUNG LI, GUOJUN (SAWYER) HE, MAGNUM MAN
LOK LAM, AND WING-SUN LIU

159

10   The Thanatopolitics of Neoliberalism and Consumer Precarity
ROHIT VARMAN AND DEVI VIJAY

179

11   Cold Chains in Hanoi and Bangkok: Changing Systems of
Provision and Practice
JENNY RINKINEN, ELIZABETH SHOVE, AND MATTIJS SMITS

202

SECTION V
Body, Technology, and Mass-Mediated Marketplace Ideologies

223

12   Market Versus Cultural Myth: A Skin-Deep Analysis of
the Fairness Phenomena in India
ANOOP BHOGAL-NAIR AND ANDREW LINDRIDGE

225

13   Haptic Creatures: Tactile Affect and Human–Robot
Intimacy in Japan
HIROFUMI KATSUNO AND DANIEL WHITE

242

Index

263

Illustrations

Figures

3.1	A high-quality cooking teahouse, Yaozen, in Sanya, Edo, drawn in a woodblock print by Hiroshige Utagawa. (c. 1840)	36
3.2	A soba/udon noodles restaurant in Edo (1753)	37
3.3	A Nightjar Soba Seller (1817) drawn in a woodblock print (a part extracted)	38
3.4	The kanbun pattern shown in the Early Sample Book (1667)	41
3.5	Restored kimono designed by Kōrin Ogata (18th century)	43
3.6	Secret fashion in linings of kimono (c. 1789–1801)	45
3.7	A lady wearing kimono with the pattern of vertical stripes (1857)	46
3.8	The shop front of a famous publisher in Edo (1834)	49
3.9	A facing page in a popular yellow-covered book (1785)	51
4.1	Thematic map	69
13.1	Qoobo, by Yukai Engineering	243
13.2	LOVOT, by Groove X	244
13.3	AIBO, by Sony	249
13.4	Paro, by AIST	254
13.5	Tactile interaction with Qoobo, by Yukai Engineering	255

Tables

5.1	Key Descriptive and Measurements Used for Study 1	88
5.2	Regression Results for Study 1 (Autonomy and Education Expenditures[a])	89
5.3	Details of the Participants for Study 2	91
6.1	Participants' Demographic Profiles	108

Contributors

Russell Belk is York University Distinguished Research Professor and Kraft Foods Canada Chair in Marketing, Schulich School of Business, York University. A fellow, past president, and Film Festival co-founder in the Association for Consumer Research, he has a number of awards, including the Paul D. Converse Award, and two Fulbright Fellowships. He is a fellow in the Royal Society of Canada and has received the Sheth Foundation/*Journal of Consumer Research* Award for Long-Term Contribution to Consumer Research. He is prolific and has over 700 publications. His research involves the extended self, meanings of possessions, collecting, gift-giving, sharing, digital consumption, and materialism.

Anoop Bhogal-Nair is Senior Lecturer in Marketing and Consumption at Leicester Castle Business School, UK. Anoop's research interests center upon understanding how consumers negotiate and consume both their sense of physical being and their self-identity within the spaces they occupy. To date, her work has focused upon Indian female consumers, religious minorities, and marginalized groups. Anoop is currently a coinvestigator for a British Academy–funded project which looks to address marginalization, discrimination, and access to employment and skills for rural women in India. Much of Anoop's research takes an interdisciplinary perspective—cultural studies, sociology, history, and religion—focusing on the challenges, threats, and opportunities consumers experience in their daily lives as individuals.

Jia Cong is a PhD candidate at the Department of Marketing at Lancaster University Management School, UK. Her principal interests are consumer culture theory, gift-giving, and social mobility. She is interested in qualitative research methods, mainly involving ethnography and netnography. Her work appears in *Advances in Consumer Research Conference*. Jia also participated in the research of Chinese national social mobility research.

Juliana French is a senior lecturer and the head of department (marketing) at Monash Business School, Malaysia. Her research interests lie in the

Contributors xiii

area of consumption experiences and behavior, specifically the influence of culture on consumption behavior. These include the intersections of culture and marketplace, sociohistorical patterning of consumption, consumption and identity, gender, and vulnerable communities. Juliana utilizes and specializes in a range of interpretive qualitative research. Her previous industry background includes advertising, which then led her to become a television consultant for children's educational programs. During this time, she worked closely with the Ministry of Education and program sponsors. She went on to manage and market professional golfers on the Asian PGA before settling comfortably into academia

Guojun (Sawyer) He, PhD, is Assistant Professor of Marketing at SKEMA Business School, Lille, France. Prior to his move to France, Sawyer started his PhD program in England and earned his doctoral degree from HEC Montréal, Quebec, Canada. Sawyer held multiple teaching/research positions at the University of Bath, HEC Montréal, and Bishop's University. His research focuses on consumer culture theory, branding, material culture studies, and politics of consumption. Sawyer has a dozen of accepted, under-review, and published peer-reviewed papers, which honor him to serve as a frequent reviewer for the *Journal of Business Research* and for various conferences organized by the American Marketing Association, Association for Consumer Research, Consumer Culture Theory Consortium, and Administrative Sciences Association of Canada. Sawyer holds several coauthorships of research projects funded by the Social Sciences and Humanities Research Council, Canada, and is currently working on several manuscripts for other peer-reviewed journals and books.

Alison Hulme is Senior Lecturer in International Development at the University of Northampton, UK. Her work focuses on consumerism and alternatives and often focuses on China. Her publications include monographs *On the Commodity Trail* and *A Brief History of Thrift*. She supervises PhD students in the area of consumerism and alternative growth. Alison used to be a radio presenter and has presented much of her work on national media. She is the Chair of the Global Studies Association, UK.

Hirofumi Katsuno is Associate Professor of Anthropology and Media Studies in the Faculty of Social Studies at Doshisha University, Kyoto, Japan. He obtained a PhD degree in anthropology from the University of Hawaii. His primary research interest consists of the sociocultural impact of new media technologies, specifically focusing on the formation of imagination, agency, and presence in technologically mediated environments in the age of AI and robotics. Since 2018, he has co-organized an ethnographic research project called Model Emotion. In xiv *Contributors*

this project, he is particularly interested in the development of robotics and AI technologies in the entertainment field, analyzing the complex nexus of touch, emotion, and technology in new sociotechnical contexts. His publications, podcasts, and other projects can be found at www.modelemotion.org.

Magnum Man Lok Lam is currently Teaching Associate at Hong Kong Design Institute and a visiting scholar at the Faculty of Management, University of British Columbia—Okanagan, Canada. His research interests include consumer moralism, sustainable consumption behaviors, symbolic consumption and identity, and experiential learning. His works have been published in a number of academic journals, including *Resources, Conservation & Recycling, International Journal of Consumer Studies, The Design Journal, Fashion, Style & Popular Culture,* and *Journal of Global Fashion Marketing.* He recently received the "Junior Researcher Award" at the International Foundation of Fashion Technology Institutes (IFFTI) Annual Conference.

Christina Lee is Professor of Marketing and Dean of Federation Business School, Federation University of Australia. Her specializations in consumer research and marketing provide the basis of her business consulting and research experience. Her academic research on sustainable consumption, decision-making, and identity has been presented at international conferences and published in marketing journals, such as *Journal of Macromarketing, Journal of Business Research, Journal of Service Marketing, European Journal of Marketing, Journal of Behavioral Finance, Journal of Strategic Marketing,* and *International Journal of Consumer Studies.*

Eric Ping Hung Li is Associate Professor at the Faculty of Management of the University of British Columbia—Okanagan campus, Canada. His research focuses on international marketing, fashion and culture, and experiential learning. Dr. Li's research interests include social enterprise and social innovation, not-for-profit marketing, pro-social behavior, multicultural marketing and consumption, consumer well-being, health promotion, consumer privacy, food economy and market system, fashion and popular culture, and digital marketing and social media marketing. His work has been published and presented in a number of academic journals and conferences such as the *International Marketing Review, American Behavioral Scientist, Qualitative Research in Organizations and Management, Management Decision, Consumption Markets & Culture, International Journal of Consumer Studies* as well as conferences such as the Association for Consumer Research annual conference, the American Marketing Association annual conference, Academy of Management Conference, and the Consumer Culture Theory Conference.

Contributors xv

Meng-Hsien (Jenny) Lin is Associate Professor of Marketing at California State University Monterey Bay, United States. She received her MBA and PhD in marketing from Iowa State University. Her research focuses on consumer psychology, sensory marketing, neuromarketing, and more recently green consumption behaviors. She also examines the empowering role of social media on mothers and parental influence on children's processing of online advertising. Jenny's work has been published in the *Journal of Advertising, European Journal of Marketing, Journal of Consumer Affairs, Journal of Macromarketing, Frontiers in Psychology,* and other outlets. She is a two-time winner of the *Journal of Advertising* best paper award in 2018 and 2020, respectively. She is also an avid mentor for undergraduate researchers and McNair Scholars and has won best mentor award in 2020.

Andrew Lindridge is Reader in Marketing at Newcastle University Business School, UK. Andrew's research interests focus on the marginalized consumer, that is, consumers who feel unable or unwilling to identify with the consumer market or who the market intentionally excludes owing to cultural, economic, political, religious, or social reasons. An interest that has led to researching marginalized consumers in Britain, China, France, India, and the United States on a variety of consumption topics ranging from: ethnic minorities and alcoholism, intergenerational rifts within ethnic minorities, and how David Bowie fans use his music to reimagine their own past. Andrew is a currently principal investigator for a British Academy–funded project which looks to address marginalization, discrimination, and access to employment and skills for rural women in India.

Wing-sun Liu is Lecturer at the Hong Kong Polytechnic University. His research focuses on fashion and subcultural studies, symbolic meanings of consumption, and branding. He is in the editorial board of the *Journal of Global Fashion Marketing* and *Fashion, Style and Popular Culture.* He has published and presented in a number of academic journals and conferences such as the *Journal of Consume Behaviour, International Journal of Consumer Studies, The Design Journal, Fashion Theory, Fashion, Style and Popular Culture* as well as conferences such as the Association for Consumer Research annual conference and the Global Marketing Conference.

Yuko Minowa is Professor of Marketing in the School of Business at the Brooklyn Campus of Long Island University in New York and a former visiting scholar in The Jerome A. Chazen Institute of Global Business/Graduate Business School of Columbia University, United States. Her research involves a theoretical study of consumption phenomena and consumer behavior with a focus on consumption rituals, interpretive research methods, semiotic analysis of cultural media, and historical

xvi *Contributors*

research in marketing and consumer behavior. Her research is published in the *Marketing Theory, Journal of Business Research, Journal of Macromarketing, Consumption, Markets & Culture,* and *Visual Communications Quarterly,* and in edited volumes, *Brand Mascots* and *Global and Multinational Advertising.* She published the book *Gifts, Romance, and Consumer Culture* (Routledge 2019) edited with Russell Belk.

Sarah Ricks is a graduate student at California State University Monterey Bay (CSUMB), in the Master of Instructional Science and Technology program, United States. She received her BS in Business Administration from California State University, with a concentration in Marketing and Information Systems. She was an undergraduate researcher at CSUMB in the Undergraduate Research Opportunities Center (UROC) and conducted research investigating the relationship between social media use (passive versus active) and the psychological empowerment of mothers in India in relation to spending on their children's education. As a UROC researcher, she presented her research at the 44th Annual Social Science Student Symposium 2019, Society for Marketing Advances Annual Conference 2019, and the 2020 American Marketing Association Winter Academic Conference.

Jenny Rinkinen is a postdoctoral researcher in the Consumer Society Research Centre at the University of Helsinki, Finland. She is particularly interested in the evolution of energy-intensive practices related to dwelling, food provision, and urban development, and much of her research deals with the relations between materials, objects, and practices and their implications for resource demand. Jenny's books include *Energy Fables* (Routledge, 2019), co-edited with Elizabeth Shove and Jacopo Torriti and *Conceptualising Demand* (Routledge, 2020) written with Elizabeth Shove and Greg Marsden.

Rungpaka Amy Hackley is Senior Lecturer in Marketing at Birkbeck, University of London, UK. Prior to this, she was Lecturer in Marketing at Queen Mary, University of London, Durham University, and before that at University of Surrey. Dr. Hackley obtained her PhD degree from Royal Holloway, University of London, where she also worked as a teaching and research associate. Her PhD entailed a cross-cultural study of young consumers' experiences of TV product placement, and her first publication from her PhD research was the only UK paper cited by the ITV companies in their response to the UK government's first consultation on UK TV product placement regulation. She is a known international authority on Asian perspectives in interpretive consumer research. Her work has generated unique insights into Asian cultures, values, and contradictions from a consumer perspective and also into digital sociology, promotional strategy, media regulation, and creative production in international markets.

Contributors xvii

Elizabeth Shove is a professor in the Department of Sociology, Lancaster University, and was the PI of the DEMAND (Dynamics of Energy, Mobility and Demand) Research Center, UK (www.demand.ac.uk). She is best known for her work on social theories of practice and everyday consumption. Elizabeth's current research includes work on time, flexibility, and energy demand and an ambitious project demonstrating the relevance of practice theory for conceptualizing large-scale social issues such as climate change, the rise in obesity, digitally enabled forms of communication and business; social inequalities; the accumulation of wealth and changing theories of health and well-being. Recent books include *Infrastructures in Practice* (Routledge 2018), edited with Frank Trentmann, and *The Nexus of Practices: Connections, Constellations, Practitioners* (Routledge 2017), edited with Allison Hui and Ted Schatzki.

Mattijs Smits works as Assistant Professor at the Environmental Policy group at Wageningen University and Research, the Netherlands. He is a human geographer interested in social practices, energy and climate transitions, renewable energy policy and politics, and development issues and inequalities. Much of his work has focused on the Global South through detailed case studies in various Southeast Asian countries. Some of this work is consolidated in the book *Southeast Asian Energy Transitions: Between Modernity and Sustainability* and a forthcoming edited volume on climate governance in Southeast Asia. More recently, Mattijs has expanded this scope to include renewable energy transitions in Europe, notably in the field of (urban) wind energy and public engagement.

Kazuo Usui is a Doctor of Commerce and Professor at Saitama Gakuen University (Japan), Professor Emeritus at Saitama University (Japan), and an honorary professor at the University of Edinburgh, UK. He is a recipient of Japan Society for Distributive Sciences (JSDS), Best Publication Award in 2014 and 1999. He is a Board Member of CHARM, JSDS (Japan Society for Distributive Sciences). His research focus is historical research in marketing, comparative study of marketing in Japan, the UK, and the United States and knowledge management in marketing from a critical perspective. He is the author of *Marketing and Consumption in Modern Japan*, Abington: Routledge, 2014; *The Development of Marketing Management: The Case of the USA c.1910–1940*, Aldershot: Ashgate, 2008; "The role of newly emergent wholesalers in the food and drink industry in Japan, c.1880 to 1940: Focusing on the case of Kokubu," *Journal of Marketing Channels*, 2018, 25(4), 211–35; "Precedents for the 4Ps idea in the USA: 1910s—1940s," *European Business Review*, 2011, 23 (2), 136–53.

xviii *Contributors*

Rohit Varman is Professor of Marketing and Consumption at the University of Birmingham, UK. His research interests are broadly in the fields of critical marketing and consumer culture. He uses interpretive methodologies, and his current research focuses on corporate violence, marketization, and vulnerability. He has published in leading journals in marketing and management, including *Journal of Consumer Research, Organization Science, Human Relations*, and *Journal of Retailing*. He has recently co-edited books published by Cambridge University Press on alternative organizations in India and on critical marketing published by Routledge.

Akshaya Vijayalakshmi is Assistant Professor of Marketing at the Indian Institute of Management Ahmedabad, India. She completed her PhD in Marketing at Iowa State University, United States. Her research interests broadly lie in the intersection of media and gender, children, and violence. Her work has implications for the field of marketing and public policy. Akshaya was the co-chair of the Asia Pacific Association for Consumer Research 2019 Conference. Her research papers have appeared in the *Journal of Advertising* (won the best paper award), *Journal of Marketing Communications, Journal of Marketing Management, Journal of Consumer Affairs,* and others. She has won international and national grants to pursue her research. Akshaya continuously attempts to make her research accessible by writing for the public in mass media outlets and has published in the *World Advertising Research Centre, Forbes*, and *Wall Street Journal (Asia)*, among others.

Devi Vijay is Associate Professor at the Indian Institute of Management Calcutta, India. Her research spans questions of inequality, institutions, and collective action, with a specific focus on the healthcare sector. She has co-edited, *Alternative Organizations in India: Undoing Boundaries* (Cambridge University Press, 2017) and has published in journals, including *Journal of Business Ethics, Journal of Service Research, Gender Work & Organization, Public Management Review, Marketing Theory, M@n@gement*, and *Journal of Marketing Management*.

Daniel White is Senior Research Associate in the Department of Social Anthropology at the University of Cambridge, UK. He is trained in cultural anthropology (PhD, Rice University), international relations (MA, Waseda University), and Japanese literature (MA, University of Hawai'i). He currently researches the social and political dimensions of affect, artificial intelligence, and affective computing in Japan and the UK. Since 2018, he has co-organized an ethnographic research project called Model Emotion, working across disciplines with anthropologists, psychologists, computer scientists, and robotics engineers to trace and critique how theoretical models of emotion are built into machines

Contributors xix

with artificial emotional intelligence. The project adopts a comparative perspective, integrating work across Japan, the United Kingdom, and the United States. His publications, podcasts, and other projects can be found at www.modelemotion.org.

I-Chieh Michelle Yang is a lecturer and the department coordinator (Marketing) at Monash Business School, Malaysia. Her main research interest lies in the area of Asian consumer culture and tourism marketing, specifically the interplay of macro- and microinstitutional forces (political, sociohistorical, and cultural) in shaping consumption experiences and consumer identities. Her doctoral dissertation explored how consumer agency during the construction of national identity is constrained by the macroinstitutional logics in China. Her research works have been presented at international conferences, such as Consumer Culture Theory Conference and published in tourism marketing, such as *Annals of Tourism Research* and *Current Issues in Tourism*.

Xin Zhao is Senior Lecturer in Marketing at Lancaster University Management School, UK. His research focuses on consumption rituals, gift-giving, politicized consumption, sociocultural aspects of brands, semiotics, digital consumption, and the consumption of space. His work on Chinese consumer culture and market development has been published in the *Journal of Consumer Research, Journal of Retailing, Journal of Advertising, Journal of Advertising Research, Journal of Macromarketing*, and *Journal of Consumer Affairs*, among others.

Acknowledgments

Some chapters in this volume are based on papers presented at the Consumer Culture Theory Conference in Odense, Denmark, in 2018 and Montreal, Canada, in 2019. Some other chapters originated in conversations with the contributors at the Association for Consumer Research Conference in Atlanta, Georgia, in 2019. This book was made possible by the authors who prepared manuscripts with enthusiasm during the challenging period of the COVID-19 pandemic in 2020.

Each chapter was reviewed by two to three scholars in the field of consumer culture and history. We are particularly grateful to the following external reviewers who kindly contributed their valuable time: Adam Arvidsson, Noah Castelo, Julien Cayla, Penelope Francks, Alessandro Gandini, Karl Gerth, Aditya Gupta, Annamma Joy, John McCreery, Ruth McManus, Krittinee Nuttavuthisit, Stephanie O'Donohoe, Yupin Patarapongsant, Per Skålen, and Jeff Wang.

In preparing the book proposal and the chapters for publication, we would like to acknowledge the substantial help provided by the staff at Francis & Taylor. In particular, we thank the editor Brianna Ascher for believing in this project and the editorial assistant Naomi Round Cahalin for providing us with invaluable help as the process of organizing the volume progressed.

Finally, we would like to thank our families and friends for their continued love and support.

Yuko Minowa
Russell Belk
June 2021

1 Introduction

Yuko Minowa and Russell Belk

We live in times of increasing world uncertainty. The Asian tigers of the late 20th century have now been overtaken by the lions of China and India as kings of the jungle in Asia and the world more generally. But China and India have also embodied precariousness, with an unprecedented state of both prosperity and vulnerability. While Asia has emerged as the world's largest and fastest growing region with its nearly 5 billion people and 2,301 spoken languages in 53 countries, its remarkable economic growth and poverty reduction have mostly worsened gaps between the rich and the poor in terms of income, access to education, health care, employment, and other life-sustaining infrastructure and services. These disparities unduly affect the vulnerable segments of society, including women and the elderly. They also debilitate inclusive growth, hamper social cohesion, and lead to unsustainable consumption patterns. Meanwhile, these vulnerable consumers in Asia are exposed and "bare," under the surveillance and social control exercised by a clique of sovereignty. A fog of anxiety hangs in precarious Asia.

Works in this volume examine consumer culture in today's precarious Asia through culturally oriented, critical consumer research. Precariousness may be defined as a human condition that is risky, unpredictable, and uncertain. Consumer culture refers to "a social arrangement in which the relations between lived culture and social resources, between meaningful ways of life and the symbolic and material resources on which they depend, are mediated through markets" (Arnould 2006, 605). Another definition of consumer culture is "a culture in which the majority of consumers avidly desire (and some noticeable portion pursue, acquire and display) goods and services that are valued for non-utilitarian reasons, such as status seeking, envy provocation, and novelty seeking" (Belk 1988b, 105). Consumer research pursuing this paradigm investigates the sociocultural, ideological, symbolic, and experiential aspects of consumption.

How deeply has the consumer precariousness in Asia been intertwined with the sociohistorical patterning of consumption, such as class, ethnicity, gender, and other habituated social categories? How have wars, colonialism, and ideological movements affected current precarity? How are

DOI: 10.4324/9781003111559-1

2   Yuko Minowa and Russell Belk

these problematics affecting consumers' identity projects, consumption practices, rituals, and marketplace activities? How is consumer precariousness assuaged or aggravated by the governmentality of the superpowers? How has the changing landscape of global popular culture, digital media, and technology been positively or negatively impacting the consumer precariousness as they create and shape new consumer cultures?

The authors in this volume attempt to answer these questions through consumer research that is underpinned through roughly the four broad streams of consumer research programs in consumer culture theory (CCT) proposed by Arnould and Thompson (2005). They are consumer identity projects, marketplace cultures, the sociohistorical patterning of consumption, and mass-mediated marketplace ideologies and consumers' interpretive strategies. Consumer culture theory is heteroglossic and embraces epistemological, ontological, and theoretical diversity (Arnould and Thompson 2007; Thompson, Arnould, and Giesler 2013). Inquiry within CCT has been predominantly in the Western context, with some exceptions (e.g., Arnould 2006). This volume aspires to augment extant knowledge with the most current, critical, historical, material, and experiential consumer studies in the Asian context.

Previous studies of consumer culture in the Asian context include identity formation in Indian branded wellness centers (Annavarapu 2018); Kafkaesque hardships for the poor in India (Belk and Ghoshal 2017); technology consumption at the bottom of the pyramid in India (Bhattacharyya and Belk 2018, 2019); the creation of Asian brands and transregional imagined community (Cayla and Eckhardt 2008); acceptance and rejection of Western brands to claim Chinese national identity (Dong and Tian 2009); the consumer culture of coffee in Japan (Grinshpun 2014); gift-giving and cultural values in Hong Kong (Joy 2001); anti-corruption and middle-class politics affecting consumption in India (Khandekar and Reddy 2015); the role of civil society actors in green food consumption in China (Leggett 2020); identity projects and material lifestyles by Indians and Indian immigrants (Mehta and Belk 1991); romantic gift-giving of mature consumers in Japan (Minowa and Belk 2019); harmonization in Vietnamese wedding rituals (Nguyen and Belk 2013); sociomaterial life and experiential aspects of national and global brands in China (Tran 2016); marketplace tensions in consuming mountain climbing in Nepal (Tumbat and Belk 2011); the impact of media on subaltern groups of consumers in India (Varman and Belk 2008); nationalist ideology in an anticonsumption movement in India (Varman and Belk 2009); vulnerable consumers and the failure of a BOP marketing initiative in India (Varman, Skålén, and Belk 2012); exploitation, coercion, and normative violence in India (Varman, Skålén, Belk, and Chowdhury 2020); the impact of marketization and sharing on destabilizing status hierarchy in India (Vikas, Varman, and Belk 2015); future global dominance of Chinese brands (Wu, Borgerson, and Schroeder 2013); the shaping of

Introduction 3

authenticity in globalizing handcraft markets in Thailand (Wherry 2006); the reselling of Western luxury by Chinese women as gendered transnational prosumption (Zhang, L. 2017); the role of culture in consumption decision-making strategies in contemporary China (Zhang, W. 2017); the growth of gated communities in India (Chadhuri and Jagadale 2021); and the appropriation of a communist ideology during a period of transition in China (Zhao and Belk 2008). While these works offer theoretical advances in understanding Asian consumer culture context, they do not necessarily focus on precariousness in contemporary Asia.

The authors in this volume, on the other hand, interrogate consumer culture of vulnerable populations as they are related to sociological problems of migration, poverty, inequality, and governmentality in precarious Asia. They problematize the legitimacy of the neocolonial development paradigm, inadequate population management, and the grossly disproportionate distribution of Asian wealth. The studies in this volume address the need to ensure socially sustainable consumer culture in which consumers are assured of security and privacy, extended social protections, emotional support, decent education and jobs, and universal health care for addressing severe poverty and inequality.

Consumer Culture Theory in Asia: History and Contemporary Issues consists of five parts, ranging over several social scientific disciplines, reflecting the many faces of macro- and microissues in consumer culture. Part I focuses on the history of consumerism in Asia, highlighting China and Japan. Part II focuses on consumer identity projects. Part III focuses on consumer rituals. Part IV focuses on governance and sustainability in consumption practices. Finally, Part V interrogates intersections of body, technology, and mass-mediated marketplace ideologies.

History of Consumerism in Asia

According to Arnould and Thompson (2005, 875), "Consumption is a historically shaped mode of sociocultural practice that emerges within the structures and ideological imperatives of dynamic marketplaces." Historically, it was China, followed by Japan and Korea, in which consumers formulated their goals in life through the acquisition of goods beyond subsistence and for more than traditional display (Clunas 1991; Nishiyama 1997). Consumerism has played a vital role in modern history, not only in the West, but also in Asia (Stearns 2001). How has consumer desire and zeal risen, developed, and contributed to generating consumer culture in Asia? Has consumer precariousness impeded consumerism, fostered resistance, or stimulated consumer culture? Two chapters in this section provide historical exploration of consumerism and consumer culture in China and Japan, focusing on the period from early modern times to our time.

In Chapter 2, "The Long March of Commodity in China," Alison Hulme maps a concise history of consumerism in China, comparing and

4   *Yuko Minowa and Russell Belk*

contrasting the key eras in China's history. The chapter begins with an exploration of the role of Confucianism in the Dynastic era (1600 BCE–1912). It considers Confucianism's apparent restraint in encouraging propriety and nonmaterial aspirations. The chapter analyzes consumerism in the Republican era (1912–1949) and the national products movement in particular. Hulme provides a nuanced understanding of China's consumerist desires and behaviors during the Mao era (1949–1976). During the Reform era (1978–present), she proceeds to explain how Deng Xiao-ping exploited the lineage between Confucianism and Maoism in order to substantiate the opening up policies of 1978. In doing so, he encouraged not only the creation of wealth but also the spending it on consumption. The final section of the chapter addresses the most recent two decades of the reform period during which consumerism has become a stated ambition within China's economic plans. In sum, the chapter critically assesses the interweaving of different strands of Chinese culture in its history as an unsteady gestation period for its consumer society, rather than the smoother path often depicted by many Western scholars.

In Chapter 3, entitled "Consumerism in Early Modern Japan: Food, Fashion, and Publishing," Kazuo Usui explores popular culture and consumerism in early modern Japan: the Edo Period under the *Pax Tokugawa* (1603–1868). His chapter discusses three fields of consumerism: culinary culture focusing on dining out of sushi and noodles, fashion trends in kimono, and popular illustrated novels. He shows that consumerism during the Edo period was characterized by a rapid growth in consumption and strict class hierarchy. The market economy started to pervade everyday life and consumption styles—sometimes restricted by the sumptuary laws, yet nurtured by the trickle-down effect—became the identity of Edoites. The author discusses the effect of consumerism in the late period of early modern Japan and in the subsequent period. Following the Meiji Restoration (1868), there was an opening up of Japan and an infusion of Western influences. Then, the mixture of Japanese styles with Western styles in consumption occurred. This was aided by the rapid industrialization and Westernization of the late 19th century. As a result of the Western influences, Japanese consumer culture became to comprise two layers: "authentic" commodities from early modern and hybridized commodities in modern Japan. The chapter concludes with a discussion about the place of *manga, kawaii* (cute culture), and fake uniform pastiche fashion in the escapist consumer culture of problematic contemporary Japan, all of which suggests a resemblance to the development of consumer culture in early modern Japan.

Consumer Identity Projects

Consumers are identity makers and seekers. The marketplace is a major source of mythic and symbolic resources through which consumers, including those who lack resources to fully participate in the market,

Introduction 5

construct narratives of identity (Arnould and Thompson 2007). Consumer identity projects include extended self (Belk 1988a), identity play, body image, self-presentation, gender performativity, negotiating cultural contradictions, and experiential aspects of consumption. Possessions may play a more extensive role than might be imagined in the construction of the self in the "Third World consumer culture" (Belk 1988b). Material lifestyles and possessions are also used to construct and reconstruct the identity of consumers in transition. For example, a migrant negotiates the self of multiple—often dissimilar—cultures (Joy and Dholakia 1991; Mehta and Belk 1991). Immigrant consumers, with ideological tensions in a new world, may also use commodified cultural symbolic mediators to construct and reaffirm their identities and quietly resist the dominant order (Jafari and Goulding 2008). Mass-mediated marketplace ideologies powerfully contribute to these projects. The stream of research in this area is interested in consumer motivations and goals.

In Chapter 4, "Century of Humiliation and Consumer Culture: The Making of National Identity," I-Chieh Michelle Yang, Juliana French, and Christina Lee illustrate the multiplicity of emergent identity positions produced by Chinese travelers within their humiliation discourse. China's astounding economic development in the last several decades has fostered a vigorous consumer culture. However, as China remains as an authoritarian government, the contradictory consumer culture obscures the evolution of Chinese national identity. Meanwhile, literature on how Chinese consumers draw on market resources for identity projects is limited. Based on the results from an ethnographic study, the authors argue that consuming international tourism provides a potent platform for Chinese people to negotiate their national identity—what it means to be Chinese today by interacting with foreign cultures and people. The authors contend that international tourism functions as the platform for the Chinese to affirm their achievements and demonstrate to the world their economic prowess and the modern Chinese identity.

In Asia and elsewhere, disparity of wealth is to a large extent the consequence of inequalities in opportunities, including access to quality education. In consumer culture, an autonomous mother, being a key decision-maker for her child, plays a significant role for her children's educational status that also leads to their identity construction. She imparts consumer socialization. She is responsible for the child's consumer enculturation. In Chapter 5, "Predicting a Mother's Role in Investing in Children's Education: A Study on Autonomy and Empowerment from India," Akshaya Viayalakshmi, Meng-Hsien (Jenny) Lin, and Sarah Ricks examine the influence of a mother's level of autonomy in spending on her children's education and investigate the relationship between a mother's level of autonomy and psychological empowerment. By using a large-scale survey database in India, the authors investigate the influence of four categories of "autonomy" on her child's educational spending.

6   *Yuko Minowa and Russell Belk*

The study revealed that women with strong natal relations—one dimension of autonomy—seem to have only a slightly positive influence on investing in her children's education. However, autonomy is a complex concept largely influenced by the societal and cultural context within which women exercise their freedom. Based on in-depth interviews conducted with Indian mothers, they then find that psychological empowerment, instead of autonomy, tends to better reflect a mother's impact on her children's educational investments.

Consumer Rituals

Consumers are culture bearers and makers. The market serves as the locus of cultural production. It is in this context that consumers participate in rituals of solidarity grounded in traditional sociality as well as shared ideologies and common lifestyles. Consumer rituals are practices that follow established procedures, ranging from individual habitual activities to family celebrations, cultural holidays, and religious rites. Both the material objects and actions involved in rituals communicate symbolic meanings (Rook 1985). Since human experience is a negotiation of culturally constructed symbols, culture mediates the interpretation of consumers' ritual experiences (Tharp and Scott 1990). In the age of globalization, rituals can also migrate from one nation to another via globalizing media and through expatriates (Minowa 2012). Traditional consumer rituals in Asian nations, such as henna-night weddings in India and Turkey (Üstüner, Ger, and Holt 2000) and death rituals in China (Zhao and Belk 2007), illustrate the hybridization of foreign ritual influences and the ubiquitous materialism of postmodern consumer culture. In this section, three chapters examine consumer rituals—gift-giving in China and death rites and rituals in Japan and Thailand.

In Chapter 6, "Gifts-Giving and Kinship-Making: *Male Phoenix* in China," Jia Cong and Xin Zhao investigate the role of gifts in bridging sociocultural differences in marriage and family life and in the process of kinship formation. In contemporary China, the *"male phoenixes"* signify urban male migrants who grow up in rural villages, attain higher education in cities, and wed into urban families. They are often denounced in Chinese society and incline to participate in lavish compensatory gift-giving practices among their kinship networks. On the basis of ethnographic fieldwork with in-depth interviews in Shandong Province and Shanghai, the authors investigate how gifts are employed to fill the gap of class disparity within the family and to compete for status in matrimonial relationship. The results of their study reveal that gifts play critical roles in resolving struggles within rural–urban marriage and family relations. They show, however, such gifts do not necessarily maintain social relations through imposing obligations for gift reciprocity.

Introduction 7

Due to rising life expectancy and declining mortality and fertility, Asian populations are aging at an unprecedented pace. Creating social protection systems, to ensure affordable consumption and its rituals over the extended lifespan and in older age, is a serious concern. In Chapter 7, "Solitary Death Is Elsewhere: The Making of Memorial Community in Japan," Yuko Minowa examines end-of-life activities (*shūkatsu*) and death rituals of the elderly in super-aged Japan. Threatened by solitary death, those consumers preplan their death rites and prepay to be interned in a shared burial site. They participate in a supportive network while alive, call each other "tomb friends," and conduct mass memorial services at an institution—often a Buddhist temple—for the repose of departed souls. Minowa investigates the making of this community, utilizing actor–network theory as the analytical approach. She discusses the attempts by various actors to make the shūkatsu practice more accessible for a larger group of heterogeneous and mature senior consumers. She argues that sacralized material objects, such as human remains, and sanctified natural and religious artifacts, constitute the sources of material semiotics and act as a symbolic bridge between social and natural entities.

On the other hand, in Chapter 8, "The Work of Culture in Thai Theravāda Buddhist Death Rituals," Rungpaka Amy Hackley explores the Theravāda Buddhist tradition of death rituals in Thailand. Her focus is on the everyday experience of religious belief as they manifest in Thai death ritual practices. These rituals explicitly illustrate how death and related rituals are potentially beneficial sources for consumer cultural insight. Hackley assesses Ricoeur's and Obeyesekere's "cultural hermeneutics" and "the work of culture" within the context of Thai death rituals and death consumption. These death rituals echo a feeling of immortality, identity, and continuity as part of collective cultural identities that connect the living with the dead. By using an autoethnographic practice theory perspective, the author shows how the death rituals involve the symbolic exchange between the living and the deceased within the liminal spaces of death rituals. We consider death as a culturally prescribed conception assuming the ontological irrevocability and finality. But Hackley argues that Thai death rituals and the language related to them contribute to the consumer's sense of self-consciousness and identity and are a critical part of their consumer culture. She concludes that, by engaging with death through these rituals, the cultural identity of the deceased is sustained.

Governance and Sustainability in Consumption Practices

Moving from microlevels and mesolevels to macrolevels, this section first addresses questions of social system requirements versus consumer's rights and needs. It is underpinned by critical theories: the post-structural perspective on systems of knowledge and the structure and distribution of power by Michel Foucault (1975); and the establishment of sovereign

8   *Yuko Minowa and Russell Belk*

power and political order through the exclusion of *homo sacer*, or bare human life without rights, by Giorgio Agamben (1998). How do macroforces, such as the power of sovereignty and government policies involving population management, create segments of vulnerable consumers in precarious Asia? Research in this stream focuses on the violence involved in the governmentality of superpowers and the social sustainability of consumers and their cultures. By applying the concept of neoliberal governmentality, for example, Varman et al. (2012) examine conflicting goals of poverty alleviation and economic profitability in a BOP (bottom of the Pyramid) initiative.

Governments, often backed by powerful elites and corporations, are increasingly resorting to various apparatuses of concealed and unconcealed surveillance and violence and targeted mass displacement in order to manage their populations. For example, Myanmar is accused of the genocide of the Rohingya. Governmental techniques of power maintenance—surveillance, intimidation, oppression, imprisonment, expulsion, genocide—are effective. The first two chapters in this section discuss governmentality of the population through surveillance with big data and the social credit system in China, and the violent and manipulative, biopolitical control of the bare life in the context of healthcare in India.

The sustainability of modern energy, including electricity, is another concern of Asian governments. Energy is basic infrastructure. Access to energy, along with clean water and safe sanitation, is considered as a human right. Equal access should be ensured to provide everyone with a life of dignity. Its benefits for the environment, society, and economy are inestimable. Access to energy accelerates productivity and aids sustainable development, while it enhances social cohesion and promotes consumption. Electricity—modern energy—is a prerequisite for functioning at home and school, accessing information, and conditioning adequate hygiene and health. However, there exists disparity, and those precariat are without ready access to electricity. Governments are a sociotechnical regime responsible for governance of sustainable social arrangements (Schatzki 2011). They have been utilizing new technologies to explore the ways to generate affordable, reliable, and efficient energy services as well as to exploit clean and safe energy generation. They manage market structures in partnership with private sectors to arrange public goods, such as telecommunications and transportation in addition to energy. From a social practice theoretical perspective (Schatzki 2011; Warde 2005), the third chapter in this section discusses how electricity and its appliances shape consumption practices and global food system in Thailand and Vietnam.

In Chapter 9, "Utopia and Dystopia: Consumer Privacy and China's Social Credit System," Eric Ping Hung Li, Guojun (Sawyer) He, Magnum Man Lok Lam, and Wing-sun Liu examine the new social credit system that the Chinese government launched in early 2010s to monitor

Introduction 9

citizens' and businesses' behavior through trustworthiness scores affecting their access to goods and services. Citizens with low social credits (social scores) may receive punishments through deprivation of free consumption, such as travel bans, limited access to entertainment facilities, slow internet connection, and exclusion from luxury hotels. Punishments also include restraining them from applying for the government positions and attending private schools. Deviants with low scores are registered on "blacklists." In this chapter, the authors discuss how the Chinese government has converted its governance mechanism to control citizens' everyday behaviors and create what Michel Foucault (1975) calls "docile bodies." They illustrate how digital devices and technologies, as well as algorithms, become instruments for maintaining the social and market order. The authors conclude the chapter with an open dialogue about the intersectionality of consumer privacy and governance under the new state-operated social credit system.

In Chapter 10, "The Thanatopolitics of Neoliberalism and Consumer Precarity," Rohit Varman and Devi Vijay interrogate the politics of death: how the neoliberal system of profiteering conceals and uses the disruptive death of the precariat. They illustrate the incident involving the shortage of oxygen supply at a medical hospital in India and discuss how such a spectacle reveals and conceals the ongoing nature of violence against the precarious. The authors then examine three cases of encephalitis in the poor region that expanded over a period of ten years. The catastrophe of an epidemic among the precarious due to the oxygen shortage became a media spectacle. The authors build on the works of Giorgio Agamben to argue that systemic violence against the bare lives is utilized to further the instruments of neoliberal capitalism that harms them. The authors believe that precariat will need to dismantle the dominant corporate order to terminate the ongoing violence. Through the analysis of concealment of structural violence, the authors add to existing understandings of thanatopolitics, neoliberal capitalism, and consumer precarity.

In Chapter 11, "Cold Chains in Hanoi and Bangkok: Changing Systems of Provision and Practice," Jenny Rinkinen, Elizabeth Shove, and Mattijs Smits (2019) focus on the energy consumption and social practices that implicate the sustainability of the food system. Patterns of domestic consumption are situated within larger systems of provision and show that material objects such as home appliances create assemblages between practices of daily culinary routines and rising global systems of food marketing and consumption. By examining the utilization of fridge freezers in Bangkok and Hanoi as expressions of complex and evolving processes of urbanization and food provisioning, the authors offer fresh insight into how particular configurations and constellations of consumption take place and how they diverge and evolve. They contend that there are two functions of changing systems and practices: one is to show how household strategies reflect and contribute to more extensive transformations;

10   *Yuko Minowa and Russell Belk*

another is to illustrate how these strategies are shaped by enduring tensions between new and established forms of urban food supply and accompanying concepts of food security.

Body, Technology, and Mass-Mediated Marketplace Ideologies

Through socioculturally dynamic market-mediated networks and the embedded consumption, mass-mediated marketplace ideologies are fostered, involving consumption subcultures, brand communities, and microcultures (Arnould and Thompson 2007). Research streams in this domain focus on discursive, imagistic, and material representations of consumerist ideologies in the marketplace. Dong and Tian (2009) found that Chinese consumers respond to Western brands as a reflection of sociohistorical forces that motivate them to political action tied to nation making. Cayla and Eckhardt (2008) argue that transnational imagined community, in this case imagined Asia as a globalized, hyper-urban, multicultural common experience, may be mutually fostered and reinforced by brands and consumers with various cultural referents. This contrasts with an earlier study that found distinct consumer cultures across Asian nations (Tse, Belk, and Zhou 1989). Varman and Belk (2008) interrogated the relationship between media, consumer culture, and, specifically, television's impact on the quotidian lives of socially subordinate—subaltern—consumers in India. Their consumer culture was delineated by dialects of unrest and tranquility. In another study, Varman and Belk (2009) found that the repeatedly appropriated use of the nationalist ideology of swadeshi propelled a new anticonsumption movement in India where global brands were perceived as anti-national icons of oppression. The research program in these areas examines materiality, the meanings of objects, and how these objects work in the social construction of memory and expectations.

In Chapter 12, "Market Versus Cultural Myth: A Skin-Deep Analysis of the Fairness Phenomena in India," Anoop Bhogal-Nair and Andrew Lindridge identify an array of extensively circulated narratives about Indian women and skin color found in traditional Hindu texts and historical narratives surrounding colonialism as well as in the marketplace. By interrogating a variety of Indian skin lightening cream advertisements and data collected from 27 informants, the authors then demonstrate how Indian women are socialized to believe that lighter skin tones are sign of female beauty, and moreover, they believe such a norm unwillingly or unconsciously. Skin color narratives reveal that there is little understanding of historical and religious narratives on Indian ideal of fairness cultivated over millennia apart from colonial rule. The authors argue that the legitimacy of the myth of fairness depends on how effectively its meaning is socially shared and its social practice embedded in India's collective memory and shared unconscious, while the changing

Introduction 11

representations in mythology help to reinforce the image of ideal womanhood evolved through collective history and reimagined and penetrated in the marketplace.

As the study by Bhogal-Nair and Lindridge illustrates, consumer's body images are a pervasive part of his or her self-concept. They are subjective and culturally construed. The body has been investigated from sociological, psychological, and ontological perspectives. This domain of CCT is concerned with consumer's confrontation with a culture of increasingly enhanced physiques driven by ideal body, body decoration, and body mutilation. Consumers use technology, such as cosmetic surgery and tattoos, to cope with their body anxiety, express ideologies, and transform their self (Roux and Belk 2019). The consumer's negotiation with the body and his or her performances to communicate it with others can take place at private as well as communal and religious rituals (Schouten 1991; Scott, Cayla, and Cova 2017). These bodily ideals are also articulated in a variety of everyday practices in areas such as the home, food, and clothing (Daniels 2010; Nützenadel and Trentmann 2008; Pham 2015; Watson and Caldwell 2005; Wu and Chee-beng 2001).

Furthermore, the body is an indispensable part of consumer's understanding the world (Falk 1994). Skin is one sensory receptor that responds to sensation. We interpret the meanings of sensory data selectively. In marketplace, in the era of sensory marketing, brands compete for unique sensory qualities. Such brands evoke different associations and generate distinctive experiences, which differentiate themselves from their competitors. Consumer's optimal feelings are translated into design elements of many products, including robots (Nevett 2018; Robertson 2007). On the other hand, anthropologists of sensory research suggest that our tactile experiences resemble a primal language that we acquire prior to written or spoken language (Howes 2005). The meaning of touching—and sensation—is socioculturally construed (Cranny-Francis 2011; Low 2012). It may mean affection, care, connection, engagement, power, charisma, tangency, status, differentiation, confidence, and so on. Touching creates social categories such as "touchable" and "untouchable" people (Alex 2008). It has the power to sacralize (Belk, Wallendorf, and Sherry 1989). It has healing properties. Today, the meanings—and their embodiment—can be deployed by technologies (Cranny-Francis 2011).

In Chapter 13, "Haptic Creatures: Tactile Affect and Human–Robot Intimacy in Japan," Hirofumi Katsuno and Daniel White situate the advancement of robots with the capacity to interact with humans in Japan. They focus on *haptic creatures*: robot companions that are intended to provide a feeling of comfort through a combination of their movement and a sensation of healing touch. Since the 1990s, Japanese institutions have developed robot companions (or social robots) with affect and emotion as a result of collaborations between entertainment industries and artificial intelligence researchers. These robot companions are designed to provide comfort, healing (*iyashi*), and intimacy to alleviate stress partly stemming from socioeconomically problematic contemporary Japanese society. Many of these robots with "artificial emotional intelligence" have capacities—although primitive—to understand human emotion through facial expression recognition and the similar mechanisms. Haptic creatures are, however, another category of companion robots that are also revolutionary. On the basis of historical analysis and ethnographic studies on new users of these robots, focusing specifically on the cushion robot called Qoobo, the authors contend that these haptic creatures are designed as experimental robots that can generate unanticipated pleasures of affective care unique to human–robot relationships. The authors argue that differentiating the two types of robots is important for understanding and evaluating how firms can try to use human–robot affect as a way to market care to consumers while also searching for and developing new markets.

Conclusion

The Belt and Road Initiative, the largest coordinated infrastructure investment plan in human history, is perceived as a sign of the beginning of an Asian-led world order (Khanna 2019). This Asian-initiated and led project involves 68 countries representing two-thirds of the world's population and half its GDP. Driven by the large fast-growing economies of China and India, a new regional consciousness, the "Asianization of Asia," is emerging. This uniquely transnational Asian idea about world order is believed to be the spirit of a plan to solidify Asia's economic power in the globalized marketplace. We might therefore ask, is the "Asianization of World" a possible motif for this century, following the Europeanization of the 19th century and the Americanization of the 20th century? Although facets of Asian consumer culture—from yoga and K-pop to sushi and anime—pervade consumer practice and culture in the West, for such a legacy to truly materialize in the 21st century, inclusive economic growth, technocratic pragmatism, and geopolitical stability in the homeland are imperative.

Whatever the 21st century holds has been cast in uncertainty by the COVID-19 pandemic. This too is something that began in Asia. Its impact on global health is written in life and death. Its impact on global economies is no less important as it affects the life and death of businesses and consumption as we know it. Who lives and who dies, where they live, and what new economic structures emerge are yet to become known as we write this. Will the world contract into isolation as is occurring during the crisis or will the global economy arise from the ashes? Will the aftermath rein-in Asia's global ambitions or strengthen them? We are reminded of the Chinese curse: may you live in interesting times. To this, we would only add: be careful what you wish for.

Introduction 13

References

Agamben, Giorgio (1998), *Homo Sacer: Sovereign Power and Bare Life*, Palo Alto, CA: Stanford University Press.

Alex, Gabriele (2008), "A Sense of Belonging and Exclusion: 'Touchability' and 'Untouchability' in Tamil Nadu," *Ethnos*, 73 (4), 523–43 (https://doi.org/10.1080/00141840802563956).

Annavarapu, Sneha (2018), "Consuming Wellness, Producing Difference: The Case of a Wellness Center in India," *Journal of Consumer Culture*, 18 (3), 414–32 (https://doi.org/10.1177/1469540516682583).

Arnould, Eric J. (2006), "Consumer Culture Theory: Retrospect and Prospect," in *European Advance in Consumer Research*, Vol. 7, ed. Karin M. Ekstrom and Helene Brembeck, Göteborg, Sweden: Association for Consumer Research, 605–07.

Arnould, Eric J. and Craig J. Thompson (2005), "Consumer Culture Theory (CCT): Twenty Years of Research," *Journal of Consumer Research*, 31 (4), 868–82 (https://doi.org/10.1086/426626).

——— (2007), "Consumer Culture Theory (and We Really Mean Theoretics): Dilemmas and Opportunities Posed by an Academic Branding Strategy," in *Consumer Culture Theory, Research in Consumer Behavior*, Vol. 11, ed. Russell Belk and John F. Sherry Jr., Oxford: Elsevier, 3–22.

Belk, Russell (1988a), "Possessions and the Extended Self," *Journal of Consumer Research*, 15 (2), 139–68 (https://doi.org/10.1086/209154).

——— (1988b), "Third World Consumer Culture," in *Marketing and Development: Towards Broader Dimensions*, ed. Erdoğan Kumku and Fuat Firat, Greenwich, CT: JAI, 103–27.

Belk, Russell and Tanuka Ghoshal (2017), "The Kafka Quagmire for the Poor in India," *Journal of Marketing Management*, 33 (17/18), 1159–69 (https://doi.org/10.1080/0267257X.2017.1318939).

Belk, Russell, Melanie Wallendorf, and John F. Sherry, Jr. (1989), "The Sacred and the Profane in Consumer Behavior: Theodicy on the Odyssey," *Journal of Consumer Research*, 16 (1), 1–38 (https://doi.org/10.1086/209191).

Bhattacharyya, Arundhati and Russell Belk (2018), "Technology Metaphors and Impediments to Technology Use Among the Involuntarily Poor," in *Cultural Change from a Business Anthropology Perspective*, ed. Maryann McCabe and Elizabeth Brody, Lexington, MA: Lexington Books, 143–64.

——— (2019), "Consumer Resilience and Subservience in Technology Consumption by the Poor," *Consumption, Markets and Culture*, 22 (5/6), 489–507 (https://doi.org/10.1080/10253866.2018.1562686).

Cayla, Julien and Giana M. Eckhardt (2008), "Asian Brands and the Shaping of a Transnational Imagined Community," *Journal of Consumer Research*, 35 (2), 216–30 (https://doi.org/10.1086/587629).

Chadhuri, Himadri and Sujit Jagadale (2021), "Normalized Heterotopia as a Market Failure in a Spatial Marketing System: The Case of Gated Communities in India," *Journal of Macromarketing*, 41 (2), 297–314 (https://doi.org/10.1177/0276146720957382).

Clunas, Craig (1991), *Superfluous Things: Material Culture and Social Status in Early Modern China*, Cambridge: Polity.

14   Yuko Minowa and Russell Belk

Cranny-Francis, Anne (2011), "Samefulness: A Social Semiotics of Touch," *Social Semiotics*, 21 (4), 463–81 (http://doi.org/10.1080/10350330.2011.591993).

Daniels, Inge (2010), *The Japanese House: Material Culture in the Modern House*, Oxford: Berg.

Dong, Lily and Kelly Tian (2009), "The Use of Western Brands in Assessing Chinese National Identity," *Journal of Consumer Research*, 36 (3), 504–23 (https://doi.org/10.1086/598970).

Falk, Pasi (1994), *The Consuming Body*, London: Sage.

Foucault, Michel (1975), *Discipline & Punish: The Birth of the Prison*, New York: Vintage Books.

Grinshpun, Helena (2014), "Deconstructing a Global Commodity: Coffee, Culture, and Consumption in Japan," *Journal of Consumer Culture*, 14 (3), 343–64 (https://doi.org/10.1177/1469540513488405).

Howes, David, ed. (2005), *Empire of the Senses: The Sensual Culture Reader*, Oxford: Berg.

Jafari, Aliakbar and Christina Goulding (2008), "'We Are Not Terrorists!' UK-based Iranians, Consumption Practices and the 'Torn Self'," *Consumption, Markets and Culture*, 11 (2), 73–91 (https://doi.org/10.1080/10253860802033605).

Joy, Annamma (2001), "Gift Giving in Hong Kong and the Continuum of Social Ties," *Journal of Consumer Research*, 28 (2), 239–56 (https://doi.org/10.1086/322900).

Joy, Annamma and Ruby Roy Dholakia (1991), "Remembrances of Things Past: The Meaning of Home and Possessions of Indian Professionals in Canada," *Journal of Social Behaviour and Personality*, 6 (6), 385–403.

Khandekar, Aalok and Deepa S. Reddy (2015), "An Indian Summer: Corruption, Class, and the Lokpal Protests," *Journal of Consumer Culture*, 15 (2), 221–47 (https://doi.org/10.1177/1469540513498614).

Khanna, Parag (2019), *The Future Is Asian: Commerce, Conflict, and Culture in the 21st Century*, New York: Simon & Schuster.

Leggett, Angela (2020), "Bringing Green Food to the Chinese Table: How Civil Society Actors Are Changing Consumer Culture in China," *Journal of Consumer Culture*, 20 (1), 83–101 (https://doi.org/10.1177/1469540517729009).

Low, Kelvin E.Y. (2012), "The Social Life of the Senses: Charting Directions," *Sociology Compass*, 6 (3), 271–82 (https://doi.org/10.1111/j.1751-9020.2011.00451.x).

Mehta, Raj and Russell Belk (1991), "Artifacts, Identity, and Transition: Favorite Possessions of Indians and Indian Immigrants to the United States," *Journal of Consumer Research*, 17 (4), 398–411 (https://doi.org/10.1086/208566).

Minowa, Yuko (2012), "Practicing *Qi* and Consuming *Ki*: Folk Epistemology and Consumption Rituals in Japan," *Marketing Theory*, 12 (1), 27–44 (https://doi.org/10.1177/1470593111424185).

Minowa, Yuko and Russell Belk (2019), "Romantic Gift-Giving of Mature Consumers: A Storgic Love Paradigm," in *Gifts, Romance, and Consumer Culture*, ed. Yuko Minowa and Russell Belk, New York: Routledge, 37–64.

Nevett, Joshua (2018), "Sex Robot WORLD DOMINATION: China Cyborgs Go GLOBAL as 'Sin Investors' Back Asia Over US," *Daily Star*, May 18 (www.dailystar.co.uk/news/latest-news/sex-robot-doll-china-action-17138916).

Nguyen, Thuc-Doan T. and Russell Belk (2013), "Harmonization Processes and Relational Meanings in Constructing Asian Weddings," *Journal of Consumer Research*, 40 (3), 518–38 (https://doi.org/10.1086/671464).

Nishiyama, Matsunosuke (1997), *Edo Culture: Daily Life and Diversions in Urban Japan, 1600–1868*, Honolulu: University of Hawai'i Press.

Nützenadel, Alexander and Frank Trentmann, eds. (2008), *Food and Globalization: Consumption, Markets and Politics in the Modern World*, Oxford: Berg.

Pham, Minh-Ha (2015), *Asians Wear Clothes on the Internet: Race, Gender, and the Work of Personal Style Blogging*, Durham, NC: Duke University Press.

Rinkinen, Jenny, Elizabeth Shove, and Mattijs Smits (2019), "Cold Chains in Hanoi and Bangkok: Changing Systems of Provision and Practice," *Journal of Consumer Culture*, 19 (3), 379–97 (https://doi.org/10.1177/1469540517717783).

Robertson, Jennifer (2007), "Robo Sapiens Japonicus: Humanoid Robot and the Posthuman Family," *Critical Asian Studies*, 37 (3), 369–498 (https://doi.org/10.1080/14672710701527378).

Rook, Dennis W. (1985), "The Ritual Dimension of Consumer Behavior," *Journal of Consumer Research*, 12 (December), 251–64 (https://doi.org/10.1086/208514).

Roux, Dominique and Russell Belk (2019), "The Body as (Another) Place: Producing Embodied Heterotopias Through Tattooing," *Journal of Consumer Research*, 46 (3), 483–507 (https://doi.org/10.1093/jcr/ucy081).

Schatzki, Theodore R. (2011), "Where the Action Is (on Large Social Phenomena Such as Sociotechnical Regimes). Sustainable Practices Research Group," *Working Paper 1* (www.sprg.ac.uk/uploads/schatzki-wp1.pdf).

Schouten, John W. (1991), "Personal Rites of Passage and the Reconstruction of Self," in *Advances in Consumer Research*, Vol. 18, ed. Rebecca H. Holman and Michael R. Solomon, Provo, UT: Association for Consumer Research, 49–51.

Scott, Rebecca, Julien Cayla, and Bernard Cova (2017), "Selling Pain to the Saturated Self," *Journal of Consumer Research*, 44 (1), 22–43 (https://doi.org/10.1093/jcr/ucw071).

Stearns, Peter N. (2001), *Consumerism in World History: The Global Transformation of Desire*, 2nd edition, New York: Routledge.

Tharp, Marye and Linda M. Scott (1990), "The Role of Marketing Processes in Creating Cultural Meaning," *Journal of Macromarketing*, 10 (2), 47–60 (https://doi.org/10.1177/027614679001000204).

Thompson, Craig J., Eric Arnould, and Markus Giesler (2013), "Discursivity, Difference, and Disruption: Genealogical Reflections on the Consumer Culture Theory Heteroglossia," *Marketing Theory*, 13 (2), 149–74 (https://doi.org/10.1177/1470593113477889).

Tran, Van Troi (2016), "Thirst in the Global Brandscape: Water, Milk and Coke at the Shanghai World Expo," *Journal of Consumer Culture*, 16 (3), 677–98 (https://doi.org/10.1177/1469540514553713).

Tse, David K., Russell Belk, and Nan Zhou (1989), "Becoming a Consumer Society: A Longitudinal and Cross-Cultural Content Analysis of Print Ads From Hong Kong, the People's Republic of China, and Taiwan," *Journal of Consumer Research*, 15 (March), 457–72 (https://doi.org/10.1086/209185).

Tumbat, Gülnur and Russell Belk (2011), "Marketplace Tensions in Extraordinary Experiences," *Journal of Consumer Research*, 38 (1), 42–61 (https://doi.org/10.1086/658220).

16   Yuko Minowa and Russell Belk

Üstüner, Tuba, Güliz Ger, and Douglas B. Holt (2000), "Consuming Ritual: Reframing the Turkish Henna-Night Ceremony," in *Advances in Consumer Research*, Vol. 27, ed. Stephen Hoch and Robert Meyer, Provo, UT: Association for Consumer Research, 209–15.

Varman, Rohit and Russell Belk (2008), "Weaving a Web: Subaltern Consumers, Rising Consumer Culture, and Television," *Marketing Theory*, 8 (3), 227–52 (https://doi.org/10.1177/1470593108093555).

——— (2009), "Nationalism and Ideology in an Anticonsumption Movement," *Journal of Consumer Research*, 36 (4), 686–700 (https://doi.org/10.1086/600486).

Varman, Rohit, Per Skålén, and Russell Belk (2012), "Conflicts at the Bottom of the Pyramid: Profitability, Poverty Alleviation, and Neoliberal Governmentality," *Journal of Public Policy and Marketing*, 31 (1), 19–35 (https://doi.org/10.1509/jppm.10.026).

Varman, Rohit, Per Skålén, Russell Belk, and Himadri Chowdhury (2020), "Normative Violence in Domestic Service: A Study of Exploitation, Status, and Grievability," *Journal of Business Ethics*, 171, 645–65 (https://doi.org/10.1007/s10551-020-04444-1).

Vikas, Ram Manohar, Rohit Varman, and Russell Belk (2015), "Status, Caste, and Market in a Changing Indian Village," *Journal of Consumer Research*, 42 (3), 472–98 (https://doi.org/10.1093/jcr/ucv038).

Warde, Alan (2005), "Consumption and Theories of Practice," *Journal of Consumer Culture*, 5 (2), 131–53 (https://doi.org/10.1177/1469540505053090).

Watson, James and Melissa Caldwell, eds. (2005), *The Cultural Politics of Food and Eating: A Reader*, Malden, MA: Blackwell.

Wherry, Frederick F. (2006), "The Social Sources of Authenticity in Global Handicraft Markets: Evidence From Northern Thailand," *Journal of Consumer Culture*, 6 (1), 5–32 (https://doi.org/10.1177/1469540506060867).

Wu, David and Tan Chee-beng, eds. (2001), *Changing Chinese Foodways in Asia*, Hong Kong: Chinese University Press.

Wu, Zhiyan, Janet Borgerson, and Jonathan E. Schroeder (2013), *From Chinese Brand Culture to Global Brands*, New York: St. Martin's Press.

Zhang, Lin (2017), "Fashioning the Feminine Self in 'Prosumer Capitalism': Women's Work and the Transnational Reselling of Western Luxury Online," *Journal of Consumer Culture*, 17 (2), 184–204 (https://doi.org/10.1177/1469540515572239).

Zhang, Weiwei (2017), "No Cultural Revolution? Continuity and Change in Consumption Patterns in Contemporary China," *Journal of Consumer Culture*, 17 (3), 639–58 (https://doi.org/10.1177/1469540515611201).

Zhao, Xin and Russell Belk (2007), *Money to Burn: Consumption by the Dead in China*, 23 min., video, Upper Saddle River, NJ: Pearson Prentice Hall.

——— (2008), "Politicizing Consumer Culture: Advertising's Appropriation of Political Ideology in China's Social Transition," *Journal of Consumer Research*, 35 (2), 231–44 (https://doi.org/10.1086/588747).

Section I

History of Consumerism in Asia

2 The Long March of the Commodity in China[1]

Alison Hulme

Introduction

From a dynasty of spectacular things, so desired by Western consumers, to the "factory of the world" of today, the commodity has loomed large in China's economic history, even if the path of consumerism has been far from smooth in terms of both economic growth and conceptual continuity. By the way of illustration, the Tang dynasty (618–906) is generally known as a golden age for Chinese innovation and commodity production, during which it was viewed as a spectacular land of wonders by foreigners. As Timothy Brook points out, the scholar Chen Yao complained in the 1570s (Ming dynasty, 1368–1644) that, no longer content with the customary light silk gauze, young men in China's villages had begun to lust for Suzhou embroideries, long skirts and wide collars, and broad belts and narrow pleats, in a quest to obtain 'the look of the moment (*shiyang*)' (Brook 1998, 220). Antonia Finnane argues a similar interest in fashion existed in the late Qing dynasty and continued to do so into the era of the Kuomintang's Republic of China[2] (Finnane 2007). Wu Juanjuan asserts that even in the earlier part of the Mao era (1949–1976), certain small differences in clothing were tolerated; differences that amounted to fashion. For example, she describes how minor details in women's and men's wear, such as the number of buttons and pockets, did exist, and how women often put the collar of their inner shirt over that of their outer shirt so that the pattern could be seen or wore different styles of scarf (Wu 2009, 37–38). This was not the case, however, during the Cultural Revolution period (1966–1976).[3] Similarly, Schrift argues that Mao badges, of which there were a variety, were used to gain a sense of uniqueness (Schrift 2001). So, while Western scholars often find it tempting to posit a sudden leap in consumer society following the end of the Mao era in 1976, this rather ignores the elements of consumer society that were present pre-Mao and perhaps even in minor ways during the Mao era. This is, of course, not to suggest that the sweeping Economic Reform (often referred to as the "opening up policies") introduced by Deng Xiao Ping from 1978 onward was not very sudden and impactful, but rather,

DOI: 10.4324/9781003111559-3

20   *Alison Hulme*

that what followed was not born out of thin air. As Zhao and Belk argue, consumer society in China was not a sudden onslaught of consumerism with no backstory (Zhao and Belk 2008). In fact, it relied heavily upon elements from the pre-Mao eras of China's history, not least the reappropriation of elements of Confucianism.

This chapter will chart a brief history of consumerism in China, comparing and contrasting the established key eras in China's history.[4] It will begin with the Dynastic era (up until 1912) which spans from the first known dynasty[5] (the Shang dynasty 1600–1050 BCE) to the fall of the last dynasty (the Qing dynasty) in 1912. This section will explore how part of the reason dynastic China is often imagined as a nonconsumerist entity is the perceived role of Confucianism in encouraging propriety and nonmaterial aspirations. The chapter will then analyze consumerism in the Republican era (1912–1949) that followed. In particular, movements such as the national products movement that Karl Gerth's work explores and how the distrust of the West continued to inform China's consumption and its burgeoning consumer culture. A brief synopsis of the Mao era (1949–1976) will follow and attempt to insist on a nuanced understanding of what happened to China's consumerist desires and behaviors during this period. The next section will tackle the Reform era (1978[6]–present) specifically analyzing the aforementioned preexisting lineage between Confucianism and aspects of Maoism and how Deng Xiao-ping utilized this in order to substantiate the opening up policies of 1978 onward and encourage not only the creation of wealth but also, crucially, the spending of it. The final section of the chapter will address the most recent two decades of the reform period up to the present. It will note how consumerism has become a stated ambition within China's economic plans. Specifically, it will look at how consumerism began to be promoted not only to soak up excess production, especially following the 2008–2009 financial crisis, but also to create domestic waste that could be reused as raw materials[7] for production. The conclusion evaluates the bumpy path to a consumer society in China and discusses the socioeconomic and cultural reasons for the way in which the onset of consumerism has not been, and continues not to be, straightforward in China.

In plotting this brief history of the formation of consumer society in China, this chapter hopes to challenge the idea that China has essentially followed a smooth economic trajectory in which it has progressed from preindustrial to industrial to consumer society. It also seeks to incite a more nuanced understanding of the conceptual shifts that have taken place, confronting the idea that the Mao era was an "historical blip" in a trajectory toward consumer society, and indeed, the idea that the Mao era itself provided seamless continuity, when in fact just prior to the Cultural Revolution consumption was encouraged by the Party (see Riskin 1987). Rather, this chapter acknowledges that continuities and ruptures run throughout China's history informing its iterative processes

The Long March of the Commodity in China 21

of change. This is to insist on the specificity of China's history and indeed the uniqueness of its present.

Dynasties and Desires

China's dynastic period spans thousands of years and it is of course impossible to analyze such a long historical period in a few hundred words, and anyway information about the extent of consumerism in early China is scant. However, there are two key features of the Dynastic era that are known and are highly relevant to an overview of consumerism in China. The first is the fact that China was an incredible producer of beautiful products and that as a result the West was desperate to trade with China as soon as explorers, missionaries, and merchants began to travel there. Crucially, for the large part, China was disinterested or actively protectionist (not without a good reason). The second is the role of Confucianism up until the fall of the last dynasty in 1911 and the creation of the Republic of China in 1912. Therefore, what follows will focus on these two aspects of consumer culture within the dynastic period.

From its early dynasties, China began producing sophisticated and beautiful products, such as silks and ceramics. Early accounts of exploration in China detail its scale and wealth. Pliny the Elder (AD 23–79) describes chariots of gold and silver—the China he describes is one of the exotic riches and dominated Western imaginations of China for many centuries (Pliny quoted in Yule and Cordier 1913, 198). Marco Polo (1254–1324)[8] too was impressed by China's size, richness, and prosperity; its flourishing commerce and interregional trade; and its splendid cities—especially Kinsai (present-day Hangzhou). In fact, Richard Humble argues it was Polo's account that caused China to be seen as synonymous with Eldorado (Humble 1975, 35). The Portuguese soldier, sailor, and merchant adventurer, Galeote Pererira (16th century), emphasizes the size and commerce of China in his accounts (in Boxer 1953, 13). Gonzalez de Mendoza's (1545–1618) hugely influential *History*[9] impresses upon the reader the size of China and the beauty of its cities (De Mendoza 1588), and the Jesuit explorer Matteo Ricci (1552–1610) also emphasized the scale of China and the abundance of food, clothing, and other delicacies within it (Ricci 1953/1583–1610). Finally, and perhaps most influentially, Du Halde (1674–1743) in his *General History of China* relates the enormity and prosperity of China (despite never having set in foot on Chinese soil).[10] This work was relied upon by so many later writers, including Montesquieu, de Guignes, the Encyclopedistes, Rousseau, Voltaire, Hume, and Goldsmith.

As a result, Western traders quickly became extremely keen to enter into the exchange of goods with China. This is famously illustrated by the well-known episode of the McCartney embassy, named after its leader—George McCartney—who was sent to China in 1793 at the request of

22   *Alison Hulme*

the then King of England—George the Third. The embassy aimed to convince the Qing dynasty via the Chinese Emperor—Qianlong—to ease restrictions on trade. China at this time used the "Canton System"[11] to control trade with the West. The system forced any nondomestic trade through the area of Canton (current-day Guangzhou) and thus through one of the 13 factories managed by Chinese merchants known as "hongs" (see Carroll 2010). The British traders found this restrictive, and therefore, the McCartney embassy asked Emperor Qianlong for (1) a permanent embassy in Beijing, (2) possession of "a small unfortified island" for British traders to live on and store goods, and (3) reduced tariffs on Western traders in Canton. They showed the Emperor various British products they felt would be desirable and induce him to be more open toward trade with them. Yet, despite these advances, the Chinese remained ambivalent toward trade with the West, the Qianlong emperor writing to George 111 in 1793 to say "We possess all things. I set no value on objects strange or ingenious, and have no use for your country's manufactures" (Qianlong quoted in Cheng, Lestz, and Spence 2013). Despite this, the official report by George Leonard Staunton (1797) was, on the whole, a eulogy of China and the Chinese. McCartney himself wrote an account at the time that was also relatively positive about the Chinese. He criticized Britain as well as China and found many positive aspects in the Chinese culture, calling the Chinese "a strong hardy race, patient, industrious" (McCartney quoted in Barrow 1807). It was clear that despite being a nation that had skills and pride in producing products for consumption, the Qing leaders had no interest in growing that consumer market through engaging with Western players. However, it is important not to interpret this reticence toward trade with the West, as a more general isolationist stance. China did trade very actively, in certain eras of dynastic rule, with its Asian neighbors. For example, as Craig Clunas details, during the earlier Ming dynasty, there were vibrant trade relations in painting and ceramics (including the famous blue-and-white porcelain of the period), weapons, architecture, textiles, and books (Clunas 2007). Indeed, Clunas argues that the Ming-era manuals of taste[12] show how important consumption was as a vehicle for connoisseurship and the showing of good taste. Clunas describes the manuals as part of an elite consensus for "the way things ought to be" in terms of what constituted the refined versus the vulgar (Clunas 1991, 53).

This kind of elite consensus must be viewed within the context of an all-pervasive Confucianism and the accompanying social mores about appropriate behavior (including consumptive behavior). Indeed, it is perhaps all too easy to imagine China as a nonconsumerist entity in this period due to the perceived role of Confucianism in encouraging propriety and nonmaterial aspirations. Put very briefly, the central tenets of Confucian belief are (1) personal and governmental morality, correctness of social relationships, justice, and sincerity; (2) the valuing of hierarchy in both political and social spheres and the accompanying assertion that

The Long March of the Commodity in China   23

in the political sphere citizens were not and should not be equal; (3) the valuing of intellect—the scholar—and the notion that only those who worked with their minds were fit to rule; (4) the idea of propriety and "proper behavior according to status" (*li*); and (5) filial piety—the idea that the "lesser" party—son, wife, student, and subject—must show loyalty and obedience to the father/husband who must deliver assistance (Confucius 1998). This emphasis on correct behavior and knowing one's own status played out in terms of what was consumed and by whom. As Stearns describes, under Confucian ethics, "ordinary people should not plan on material indulgence at all, for this would contradict appropriate social ranking" (Stearns 2001, 5). He goes on to posit Confucianism as "a climate in which consumerism would nevertheless clearly be rejected" (Stearns 2001, 5).

However, as Geir Sigurdsson points out, wealth, under Confucian thought, although not an acceptable goal in its own right with frugality presented as a commendable virtue, was not considered "wrong" per se (Sigurdsson 2014). He goes on to argue that Confucians "would not see anything wrong as such with material wealth as it simply provides conditions for good living" (Sigurdsson 2014, 132). Similarly, in contrast to those who associate Confucianism with a strict moral framework, Ruiping Fan sees this acceptance of wealth on the condition that it is not the sole aim, as a pragmatic vein running through Confucianism, which presents wealth as legitimate when it is the source of family and individual well-being (Fan 2010, 233). This perhaps explains why trade and consuming, although not considered the highest form of lived expression under Confucian ethics, was thriving throughout many of the later dynasties. Indeed, Sigurdsson argues that despite having a generally negative view of the commercial class, "Confucian scholar-officials produced favourable economic policies during the imperial period in China," their pragmatism enabling them to distinguish between economic policies and economic attitude (Sigurdsson 2014, 128). Therefore, while it might be reasonable to assume that Confucianism tempered any material excesses, it did not curtail consumerism in any direct way and as mentioned previously, the work of Clunas and others shows very clear how rich a material culture existed throughout much of the Dynastic era.

Republicanism, Nationalism, and Westernism

By the late 19th century, China was growing increasingly dissatisfied with its dynastic leaders. The Qing dynasty had, it was felt, been weak in the face of foreign invasion, and the emperors (and empress) were blamed for the foreign domination of ports and the opium crisis (1839–1842 and 1856–1860). A growing nationalist sentiment abounded, fed by the dislike of foreigners, yet ironically coupled with the desire for precisely the wealth and political power witnessed in the West. In addition, there were

24   Alison Hulme

frustrations with Confucianism, in particular its emphasis on hierarchy, obedience, and what had come to be seen as "useless" intellectualism (i.e., intellect that had no application in real life). Indeed, China had also begun to generate images of its *Confucian* self as lazy, and there was a widespread acknowledgment, popular among left wing thinkers of the time, of the way in which dynastic rule and Confucian thought had apparently held back the nation and created gaping inequalities between the rich and the poor. Through writers such as Lu Xun,[13] Confucianism came to be associated with privilege and laziness. The literary stereotypes created at the time remain part of popular imagination and common parlance today. A classic example is Lu Xun's character Kong Yi Ji—a Confucian failed scholar who typifies laziness by being an unemployed alcoholic and who possesses arcane knowledge that is irrelevant to a modernizing China. In the eponymously titled short story, Kong Yi Ji regularly drinks as a specific bar, where he often owes money on his tab, and spends his time quoting erudite texts to anyone who will listen. His pomposity and use of archaic phrases are portrayed as only serving to maintain a rigid class system and therefore being truly oppressive. Lu Xun's creation of this character was a reaction against the norms of Confucian scholarship and the traditions and privileges that came along with it (see Jameson's interpretation of the character, 1986). In the story, Kong has his legs broken and is forced to beg for a living, being seen around less and less and eventually presumed dead. If one accepts Fredric Jameson's (1986) view that Lu Xun writes characters as allegories for China (or parts of Chinese culture), it is plausible to interpret what happens to the character of Kong as representing the breaking of Confucian norms and the disintegration of the privileges associated with dynastic rule. Such cultural changes challenging the privileged few and questioning Confucian social norms paved the way for the end of dynastic rule and the beginning of the Republic of China under Sun Yat Sen [1866–1925].

Sun Yat Sen was of course a nationalist and had come to power not least as a result of nationalist sentiment, so the nationalist context cannot be ignored when attempting to consider China's history of consumerism. Particular attention should be drawn to movements such as the national products movement that Karl Gerth's work explores and how the distrust of the West continued to inform China's consumption and its burgeoning consumer culture. In fact, the consumer became, more than ever before, a vehicle for fighting nationalistic battles. The major concern during the Republic of China period was that the Chinese should consume products created by themselves, rather than those supplied by foreign forces (see Gerth 2003). Consumption, in other words, was entirely embedded in nationalism. As is always the case though, the consumer was unruly. The fact that in many cases, the consumer became a vehicle for nationalism did not mean that this was true evenly across the board. For example, Frank Dikötter's landmark study into material objects in modern China

The Long March of the Commodity in China   25

asserts at every turn the frequency and plenitude with which foreign goods could be found in the China of the 1930s (Dikötter 2006). Furthermore, as Gerth admits, obstacles such as the lack of a tariff economy and genuine sovereignty, not to mention the strong association of foreign goods with modernity, and allegiances to lineage and clan as much as to nation, allowed imports to pour into China, making the success of nationalistic consumption a challenge to say the least (Gerth 2003, 355). As Gerth says, "in short, the movement [national product movement] did not instil product-nationality as the pre-eminent attribute of a commodity" (Gerth 2003, 355–56).

However, as Gerth concedes, the national product movement did filter into Chinese culture in a way that provided many legacies that would come to the fore throughout the 20th century. It is difficult to consider the anti-Japanese boycotts of the mid-1980s, the "war of the chickens," between KFC and domestic competitors, or indeed the success of the famous *China Can Say No*, without returning to the Republican era sentiments of consumer patriotism that were more subtly embedded in Chinese culture. Indeed, from the Republican era onward, there has been a strong element of nationalism in China's consumerism. Whether the Republican desires to protect Chinese markets from Western products, the Maoist urges to develop through domestic production, or the reformist determination to catch up with the West through exports and latterly through consumerism itself, nationalism has never been entirely off the agenda.

Mao and the Great Provision

Under Mao, consumerism became provision, and it was the vision of a wonderful provision for all that became the hook for national loyalty. The good life under Mao was specifically based on the idea of provision, and it was this guarantee of having enough that motivated the industriousness of the Mao era. The promise of the "iron rice bowl" was extremely attractive to a populace who had suffered extreme poverty at the hands of past leaders who enabled a hierarchical distribution of resources. Mao promised the provision of resources and services for all according to their personal circumstances and needs—it was about *provision* in a fair system. This was part of being comradely—the sharing of effort and the sharing of the results of effort. And, as Vladislav Todorov argues, it was precisely this sharing of production processes (as depicted in the posters) in condensed spaces (such as factories), which created "technological togetherness" and led to a "fellowship of collaboration" that would come to be known as comradeship (Todorov 1995, 48). Industriousness then created the way of the comrade, and its reward was a mutual enjoyment of the gains.

Mao built on the thinking of left-wing writers such as Lu Xun and was to ban Confucianism, largely due to its emphasis on accepting hierarchy (see Leese 2011). Not only did its insistence on the legitimacy and

26   *Alison Hulme*

positive impact of hierarchy sit in direct opposition to his stance on social equality, but he also blamed its traditionalism for China's "backwardness" in terms of science and development. This backdrop of righteous frustration with the state China was in its "humiliation," and the desire to quash any tradition that maintained social inequalities added force to Mao's rhetoric of industriousness in order to gain a "happy life for all." "Catching up" with the West was of the utmost importance according to him and was to be gained through the physical exertions and incredible labor capacity of the population—which was proudly celebrated. The industriousness of the masses was China's great blessing and would be its salvation, enabling the creation of a world of plentiful provision for all, in which comradely relations and the lack of concerns about life's necessities would provide the basis for a new utopia—the communist "happy life." It was via this powerful rhetoric and the positing of this utopian vision that Mao was able to galvanize the population despite their exhaustion following extended periods of global and domestic war and unrest. And so, the twin paradigms of industriousness and its reward—the good life—were born, and they would continue with greater or lesser influence throughout Mao's reign.

Despite the outlawing of Confucianism, elements of it found their way into the Mao era in unlikely ways. For example, the Confucian view of miserliness is perhaps more aligned to the Marxist one than would at first appear obvious. Under Confucianism, frugality that leads to miserliness is seen as deplorable in much the same way as Marx depicts early traders in 18th century Manchester (England) as "old misers" with "a passion for wealth as wealth," who, in order to accumulate, exercised extreme parsimony and "were far from consuming even the interest on their capital" (Marx 1976, 741). In addition, the exemplary person under Confucianism is willing to financially help those in need but always tries not to increase the wealth of those who are already rich (see Analects 6.4; 11.17). The concern, according to Confucius, ought to lie with wealth distribution— "the ruler of the state or the head of a household does not worry that his people are poor, but that wealth is inequitably distributed . . . For if the wealth is equitably distributed, there is no poverty" (Analects 16.1). Similarly, for both Marx and Mao, the concern was with equality and the distribution of wealth.

Despite the anti-consumerist times, certain goods were purchased and coveted under Mao—bicycles and wrist watches for example. And, as Wu Juanjuan claims, even in the Mao era, certain small differences in clothing were tolerated; differences that amounted to fashion. She describes how minor details in women's and men's wear, such as the number of buttons and pockets, did exist, and how women often put the collar of their inner shirt over that of their outer shirt so that the pattern could be seen or wore different styles of scarf (Wu 2009, 37–38). So, as previously argued, there were elements of consumer society that were present pre-Mao and

The Long March of the Commodity in China   27

perhaps even in minor ways during the Mao era. This is, of course, not to suggest that the changes introduced by Deng Xiao Ping in from 1978 onward were not very sudden and impactful, but rather, that what followed not born out of thin air. Consumer society in China was not a sudden onslaught of consumerism with no backstory. In fact, it relied heavily upon elements from the pre-Mao eras of China's history.

Reform and the Coming of the Market

In 1978, Deng Xiaoping became leader of the Chinese Communist Party (hereafter, the CCP) and began his now famous policies of "opening up" China to the rest of the world. Initially, this comprised the creation of special economic zones (SEZs) most notably that of Guangzhou in which trade with the West could take place. (It is no coincidence of course that this is the same area that had housed the "hongs" under the Canton system and been a treaty port from the latter half of the 19th century enabling it to already have the infrastructures and practices in place for economic success.) The SEZs meant that suddenly China was open to trade and there was a huge influx of products that would previously have been deemed too "bourgeois" and/or too Western. In addition, Deng encouraged the setting up of small business and "leaping into the sea" (giving up one's State employment and becoming an entrepreneur). This ideological change and the cultural changes among many Chinese people that it led to were as much of a revolution as the officially recognized "Communist revolution" that had come before it. Daily life was unrecognizable. Thus, cultural reassurance was necessary as, despite the desire for change from both populace and much of the Party at the time, Deng could not simply instigate such enormous changes without some kind of continuity with the past that would convince, or at least appease, those more conservative Party members who were skeptical of his plans. This continuity was achieved by requisitioning aspects of China's past attitudes toward consumerism, in order to legitimize a plan for its future. Confucianism, via Maoism, was rebranded for the market.

This was achieved by the state taking specific "Confucian values" and positing them as the necessary ingredients for the new economic aims of entrepreneurialism and wealth generation. As Sigurdsson argues, a Confucian work-ethic, family-based loyalty, sense of duty, and attitude toward thrift, all began to be celebrated as quasi-Protestant qualities necessary for market development (Sigurdsson 2014, 129). Deng actively encouraged this reappropriation of Confucianism in the new context of business entrepreneurship, for example, by emphasizing the importance of family ties and encouraging would-be business people to borrow money from relatives in order to cover their start-up costs and provide them with initial capital. This was to position the family as the basis of profit-oriented entrepreneurialism in exactly the way that Mao had been concerned about

28   *Alison Hulme*

as he felt it could lead to spontaneous capitalistic urges. Deng, in fact, wanted nothing more than to utilize these capitalistic urges in the name of a communism that was almost unrecognizable to that of Mao's. In the process, he managed to attach Confucianism to industriousness, via the notion of family responsibility, whereas Mao (and the preceding generation of authors and thinkers) had attached it firmly to laziness, unearned privilege, and lack of efficiency. Importantly, the reward for industriousness this time around was not provision, but the ability to consume. After the avowed anti-consumerism of the Cultural Revolution, consumerism was back—legitimate in Confucian terms as it was part of providing well-being for one's family and was not "for its own sake"; and in Communist terms because it helped "share the wealth" in order that an improved standard of living could be achieved alongside greater economic equality. This idea of wealth creation for individuals as beneficial to all members of society loomed large. It was posited as Confucian pragmatism, but could just as easily be seen as the promotion of trickle-down economics—the idea that the enrichment of the upper income levels will benefit poorer members of society by improving the economy as a whole. Deng's faith in the trickle-down effect was in effect the philosophical outcome of him having been the first Chinese leader to look into Western classic economics to inform the country's economic policy. However, Deng made trickle-down more palatable to those with nationalistic and/or Maoist sentiments by presenting it as a form of equal distribution of wealth, thus maintaining the Maoist ideal and continuing the revolutionary path.

Conclusion—The Politics of Consumption in Present-Day China

Since Deng Xiaoping's death in 1997, Chinese leaders have actively supported the creation and promotion of a consumer society in China. It has become a stated ambition within China's economic plans, first emerging in the 2011 "12th Five Year Plan," which called for the continued expansion of domestic demand in order to enable continued economic growth (China's Twelfth Five Year Plan 2011). At the time, this was of course most necessary, as global exports had decreased during the 2008/2009 financial crisis, and domestic consumption in China was still low when considered as a proportion of GDP—only 34%, compared to 60% in Japan, 64% in the United Kingdom, and 72% in the United States (The World Bank 2013). Subsequent Five-Year Plans have continued to place emphasis on domestic consumption.

As part of this emphasis on consumer society, successive leaders have concerned themselves with the creation and expansion of a middle class or *xiaokang*. (It is important to note that this middle class ought not perhaps to be read in the same way as one might read the British middle class or indeed the American middle class, both of which have

The Long March of the Commodity in China   29

their own specific connotations not to mention wealth levels.) Deng Xiao-ping used the term xiaokang in 1979, positing it as the ultimate goal of Chinese modernization. The suggestion was that the enabling of all to reach this state would involve wealth distribution and create the desired "balance" and "harmony" within Chinese society. Creating a xiaokang was also part of Hu Jintao's "scientific development" theory, which emphasized sustainable development and social welfare in pursuit of a "socialist harmonious society." In perusing this harmonious society, Hu chose to return to the Confucian language of balance and modesty using the term xiaokang, meaning "basically" or "functionally" well-off or middle class but without huge wealth, living comfortably but ordinarily. Similarly, the xiaokang is fundamental to Xi Jinping's notion of the "Chinese Dream"[14]—an aspirational society in which building oneself a good life is entirely possible for all.

The attitudes and consumer behavior of the younger end of the xiaokang have been of particular interest to China analysts and academics. The appeal of products to the younger generations in China is very much about them taking up their ability to assert their own personalities and individuality, and how this is seen as part of being "modern" and extends to other choices such as taking part in certain protests. (See Hulme 2018 for an explanation of how products have become linked to asserting one's individuality.) This has seen the biggest generational rift yet witnessed in Chinese culture, as well as the increased polarization of rich and poor, and urban and rural. As Li Conghua states, "the first generation of single-child consumer, or the s-generation, is now entering adulthood and assuming the real-life responsibilities" (Li 1998, 6). And this is not without its complexities. There are vast generational attitudinal differences in terms of life priorities, the importance (or not) of saving, and ideas about what is "enough." Successive changes in welfare policy in China, such as the improvement of health and pension provision, have been geared toward providing a greater safety net for Chinese citizens, and this has in no small part been about convincing them to part with their savings and spend. "Golden week" holidays have been created specifically to provide time for travel to cities in which one might wish to consume things one could not in one's own local area. In addition, emphasis has somehow become placed on the consumption of certain types of goods and experiences (often those with a classic European "pedigree") in order to gain *suzhi* (quality) as a person.

Overall, the encouragement of consumerism has not been, and continues not to be, straightforward in China. As this chapter has shown, the interweaving of different strands of Chinese culture has provided an unsteady gestation period for China's consumer society. The Chinese citizen has not been easily convinced of the delights of consumerism, or indeed his or her duty to engage with it. While consumerism is mainstream and highly prevalent across most of China now, it has indeed been a long march.

30 *Alison Hulme*

Notes

1. The 'long march'; is the term used to describe the 6000-mile trek across rural China from 1934–35 which resulted in the relocation of the communist revolutionary base from south-eastern to north-western China and saw Mao emerge as the Communist Party leader. The heroism attributed to the long march inspired many young Chinese to join the Chinese Communist Party during the late 1930s and early 1940s.
2. The Republic of China existed from 1912 to 1949 under the Nationalist government of the Kuomintang (KMT). This is not to be confused with the Peoples Republic of China from 1949 to the present which is specific to the Communist Party's governance of China.
3. The Cultural Revolution (1966–1976) was the period where Mao reasserted his control and encouraged the "Red Guards" to enforce strict adherence to the Party line, punishing any behavior deemed to be remotely capitalist or celebrate capitalist influences.
4. Chinese Studies have typically separated Chinese history into certain eras, and it is these that are used within this chapter. They are the dynastic era, the Republic of China era/Republican era, the Mao era, and the reform era (which continues to this day).
5. Some historical accounts cite the Xia Dynasty (c. 2070–1600 BC) as the first dynasty. However, as no contemporary sources exist, very little is known about the Xia period. For this reason, some scholars believe it to be mythical or quasi-legendary, and therefore, it is standard practice to consider the Shang dynasty as the first dynasty.
6. The Mao era is considered to have ended in 1976 when Mao died. However, the Reform era is not considered to have started until 1978 when Deng Xiaoping came to power. The intervening period between 1976 and 1978 saw China ruled by an interim leader Hua Guofeng who essentially continued Mao's policies.
7. See the author's own work *On the Commodity Trail* (2015) in which she explores the buying in of domestic waste from the West in order to gain cheap raw materials for production.
8. Marco Polo dictated *The Travels of Marco Polo* to a fellow captive while being held as a prisoner of war from 1298 to 1299. It is thought to be inaccurate and wildly exaggerated. Many historians believe that Marco was never in China. Regardless, the *Travels* had a huge impact on the Western imagination of China.
9. According to Boxer, *History* was the point of departure for all later works on China written in Europe before the 18th century. (See Boxer)
10. All du Halde's writing is from his editing of the *Lettres edifiantes et curieuses* (1709–43).
11. The Canton System existed from 1757 to 1842. It was eventually challenged by the Opium Wars in which Britain forced opium upon China in order to gain access to the products it wanted (namely tea), and as a result of which certain "Treaty Ports" including Hong Kong were leased to Britain and other foreign powers.
12. Clunas refers specifically to Ming-era manuals such as those written by Gao Lian, Tu Long, and Wen Zhenheng, whose "Treatise on Superfluous Things" provides the inspiration for the title of Clunas's own book.
13. Lu Xun (1881–1936) was a famous Chinese author best known for "Diary of a Madman" and "The Real Story of Ah Q." His work has been seen as presenting many allegorical characters that represent China as a nation (see Fredric Jameson's "Third World Literature in the Era of Multi-National Capitalism" on this point). Lu Xun was part of a left-wing writer's scene in

The Long March of the Commodity in China   31

Shanghai and has been entirely appropriated by the CCP in the contemporary era despite certain anomalies in his own thought which meant he never joined the Communist Party.

14. In 2013 began promoting the phrase "Chinese Dream" as a slogan, leading to its widespread use in the Chinese media. Xi describes the dream as "national rejuvenation, improvement of people's livelihoods, prosperity, construction of a better society and military strengthening." Some believe the slogan to have come from Helen Wang's 2010 book—*The Chinese Dream*—which is based on over 100 interviews of members of the new middle class in China. She did not define the Chinese Dream (but could have provided the idea).

References

Barrow, John (1807), *Some Account of the Public Life and a Selection from the Unpublished Writings of the Earl of Macartney*, Vol. 2 (www.rct.uk/collection/1020628/some-account-of-the-public-life-and-a-selection-from-the-unpublished-writings-of).

Boxer, Charles R., ed. (1953), *South China in the Sixteenth Century: Being the Narratives of Galeote Pereira, Fr. Gaspar da Cruz, O.P. [and] Fr. Martín de Rada, O.E.S.A. (1550–1575)*, London: The Hakluyt Society.

Brook, Timothy (1998), *The Confusions of Pleasure: Commerce and Culture in Ming China*, Berkeley, CA: University of California Press.

Carroll, John M. (2010), "The Canton System: Conflict and Accommodation in the Contact Zone," *Journal of the Royal Asiatic Society Hong Kong Branch*, 50, 51–66.

Cheng, Pei-Kai, M. Lestz, and J.D. Spence, eds. (2013), *The Search for Modern China*, New York: W. W. Norton & Company.

China's Twelfth Five Year Plan (2011), British Chamber of Commerce in China/China Britain Business Council (www.britishchamber.cn/content/chinas-twelfth-five-year-plan-2011-2015-full-english version).

Clunas, Craig (1991), *Superfluous Things: Material Culture and Social Status in Early Modern China*, Chicago: University of Illinois Press.

——— (2007), *Empire of Great Brightness: Visual and Material Cultures of Ming China, 1368–1644*, London: Reaction Books.

Confucius (1998), *The Analects of Confucius: A Philosophical Translation*, trans. Roger T. Ames and Henry Rosemont, Jr., New York: Ballantine Books.

De Mendoza, Juan Gonzales (1588), *History of the Great and Mighty Kingdom*, London: The Hakluyt Society.

Dikötter, Frank (2006), *Things Modern: Material Culture and Everyday Life in China*, London: Hurst & Company.

Fan, Ruiping (2010), *Reconstructionist Confucianism: Rethinking Morality After the West*, Dordrecht, The Netherlands: Springer Verlag.

Finnane, Antonia (2007), *Changing Clothes in China: Fashion, History, Nation*, New York: Hurst.

Gerth, Karl (2003), *China Made: Consumer Culture and the Creation of the Nation*, Cambridge, MA: Harvard University Asia Center.

Hulme, Alison (2015), *On the Commodity Trail*, London: Bloomsbury.

——— (2018), "Greening the Chinese City: Young People, Environmental Activism and ChinaNet," in *Chinese Urbanism: Critical Perspectives*, ed. Mark Jayne, London: Routledge.

32 Alison Hulme

Humble, Richard (1975), *Marco Polo*, New York: G.P. Putnum's Sons.

Jameson, Fredric (1986), "Third-world Literature in the Era of Multinational Capitalism," *Social Text*, No. 15, 65–88 (https://doi.org/10.2307/466493).

Leese, Daniel (2011), *Mao Cult: Rhetoric and Ritual in China's Cultural Revolution*, Cambridge: Cambridge University Press.

Li, Conghua (1998), *China: The Consumer Revolution*, New York: Wiley and Sons.

Marx, Karl (1976), *Capital*, Vol. 1, London: Penguin Books.

Ricci, Matteo (1953/1583–1610), *China in the Sixteenth Century: The Journals of Matthew Ricci: 1583–1610*, trans. Louis J. Gallagher, New York: Random House.

Riskin, Carl (1987), *China's Political Economy: The Quest for Development since 1949*, Oxford [Oxfordshire] and New York: Oxford University Press.

Schrift, Melissa (2001), *Biography of a Chairman Mao Badge: The Creation and Mass Consumption of a Personality Cult*, New Brunswick, NJ: Rutgers University Press.

Sigurdsson, Geir (2014), "Frugalists, Anti-Consumers and Prosumers: Chinese Philosophical Perspectives on Consumerism," in *The Changing Landscape of China's Consumerism*, ed. Alison Hulme, Oxford: Elsevier, 125–49.

Staunton, George (1797), *An Authentic Account of an Embassy from the King of Great Britain to the Emperor of China*, London: G. Nicol.

Stearns, Peter (2001), *Consumerism in World History: The Global Transformation of Desire*, London: Routledge.

The World Bank (2013), *World Development Indicators, Household Final Consumption Expenditure, etc. (% of GDP)* (http://datanank.worldbank.org/data/views/reports/tableview.aspx). [Accessed 10/19/2013]

Todorov, Vladislav (1995), *Red Square, Black Square: Organon for Revolutionary Imagination*, Albany, NY: State University of New York Press.

Wu, Juanjuan (2009), *Chinese Fashion: From Mao to Now*, Oxford and New York: Berg.

Yule, Henry and Henri Cordier (1993), *The Travels of Marco Polo*, New York: Dover Publications.

Zhao, Xin and Russell Belk (2008), "Politicizing Consumer Culture: Advertising's Appropriation of Political Ideology in China's Social Transition," *Journal of Consumer Research*, 35 (2), 231–44 (https://doi.org/10.1086/588747).

3 Consumerism in Early Modern Japan

Food, Fashion, and Publishing

Kazuo Usui

Early modern Japan, a preindustrial society, has nevertheless been described as "a world of economic vitality and growth" (Gordon 2012, 486, see also Hanley and Yamamura 1977; Hayami, Saitō, and Toby 2004; Smith 1988). There was a wide demand and distribution of commodities such as rice, salt, crops like ginned cotton, various processed agricultural products, iron and other metal products, and cotton and silk cloth (Hanley and Yamamura 1977, 78; see also Miyamoto 1971; Shimbo and Hasegawa 2004; Usui 2018). An "economic society" developed (Hayami 2004, 9), where both the providers of goods and services and their consumers act to the greatest degree on the basis of economic values. Correspondingly, urban consumerism developed with an increased enthusiasm for goods and services in the marketplace. This chapter will feature three typical fields, that is, eating out rather than eating at home, mass fashion trends in *kimono*, and popular pictorial novels, and explore this development and its Japanese characteristics.

An Analytical View of Consumerism in Early Modern Japan

Before the exploration, two analytical points of view in this chapter, that is, commodification and the class structure, should be explained.

First, the term commodification refers to the transformation of goods and services that had never been traded into objects of trade, or the social process by which something comes to be apprehended as a commodity (Radin 2005, 81). Although this term is often used in critical contexts such as the fetishism of the world of commodities (e.g., Brownlie 2015; Ertman and Williams 2005; Song 2003), this chapter recognizes commodification as the development of monetization in an economy (Duffy and Yamamura 1971) or market economy in preindustrial contexts. As Storey (2017, 105–06) insisted, not only expansion of production but also a rapid growth in consumption served to prepare for the rising dominance of capitalism (see also Bermingham 1995). In addition, as trading in the

DOI: 10.4324/9781003111559-4

34   *Kazuo Usui*

market place gained momentum, some consumers began to display their identities by what they consumed.

The second point is the three-tier class structure of consumers: first, the warrior or high-end culture (Nishiyama 1983b, 235–41, 1997, 33–35). At first, the warriors tried to emulate the traditional court culture as new *samurai* nobilities. For instance, when the new capital Edo (now Tōkyō) was constructed, the reigning *shōgun* and all local lords (*daimyō*), who were forced to reside in Edo in alternative years, built their residences in Edo. Many of them preferred to revive the dynastic style developed in the ancient capital Kyōto, such as Japanese landscape gardens inside their residences. In due course, courtiers, monks, artists, and scholars joined the warrior culture and created many aesthetic objects and activities such as architecture, gardens, folding screens, paintings and calligraphic works, craft works, tea sets and tea ceremonies, scented incense, poetry. Although analysis of this high culture should be fascinating as "consumption of culture [or art]" (Bermingham 1995), this is not the focus in this chapter.

The consuming agents that this chapter will focus on are not people in the warrior class, but the townspeople (*chōnin*), who were composed of merchants and artisans residing in metropolises and towns. However, they were also widely divided into the class structure. On the upper side, there existed wealthy merchants, often much better-off than the lower-ranked warriors, while below, there were many middle and lower class of the townspeople, some of whom had fled from rural areas. They usually lived in tenements in the back alleys and worked in carpentry, plastering, scaffolding, peddling of various goods, bearing palanquins, etc.

Wealthy merchants can be categorized as the second type; their behaviors tended to emulate warrior culture, typically in the luxurious costume of merchants' wives (Baba 2008, 243; Ikegami 2005, 273–74), an example of conspicuous consumption and the trickle-down model in fashion development.

The focus of analysis in this chapter is the third type of culture, that is, consuming culture by the middle class or even the lower class of the townspeople, in other words, popular culture in early modern Japan. This type of culture became clear in the latter half of the 18th century to the early half of the 19th century,[1] and flourished mainly in Edo, rather than the old capital Kyōto and nearby Ōsaka.[2] As everyday-life goods and services were commodified, consumers had to navigate a course between their lifestyle ambitions and the restrictions of sumptuary and publication laws.

A leading cultural historian, Matsunosuke Nishiyama (see 1997), noted that "behavioral culture" was recognizable as an explosive phenomenon in Edo city but had long been growing throughout Japan (Nishiyama 1972, 34–36, 1981, 171–77, 1983a, 41–44, 1983b: 162–66; see also Francks and Hunter 2012, 7–8). Behavioral culture encouraged pilgrimages on foot to distant sacred sites and hot springs, despite the authorities'

Consumerism in Early Modern Japan 35

travel restrictions. More local visits, to special openings of temples and shrines, which were permitted, were also popular, together with *kabuki* theaters, *sumō* wrestling, and *bon* festival dances. Many townspeople raised beautiful potted floral displays at home, such as morning glories. Trips became popular to view cherry blossoms, moonlight, and snow and visits to hear insects singing. Commerce naturally followed, in sales of woodblock prints (*ukiyoe*) and travel booklets and novels to boost tourism, tickets to events, gardening goods like seeds and seedlings. Fairs sold gifts and souvenirs; sacred sites offered promises such as longer life extension, fulfilment of a vow, safe childbirth, safety from fire. Nishiyama (1972, 33–34, 1981, 174, 1983a, 41) called these phenomena "commodification of behaviors," emphasizing that the townspeople did not develop subversive revolutionary activities against political and social oppressions, but instead found release in a varied leisure culture. The following sections will feature eating out, fashion, and light novels.

Consumerism in Culinary Culture

Early modern Japan saw widespread of eating out as opportunities grew to buy food services.

Development of Cooking Teahouses

The universal choice for eating out in early modern Japan was the general restaurant with wide menu: the "cooking teahouse (*ryōri chaya*)," despite the existing inns and teahouses (*chaya*, serving green tea) (Ishige 2011, 120; Nishiyama et al. 1994, 269–70).

The early cooking teahouses mainly served cheap cooking rice with green tea and black and red beans (Matsushita 2009, 352), but they attracted wide attention (Nishiyama et al. 1994, 270) and developed in various formats including high-end catering from the mid-18th century for wealthy merchants (Ishige 2011, 121; Nihon Fūzokushi Gakkai 1978, 400). An encyclopedia of metropolitan customs, *Morisada Mankō*, published from 1837 (Kitagawa [n.d.] 1996, 208–09), noted, "serving tea-ceremony dishes has disseminated since the early Tempo Years [1831–1845]." *The Small Guidebook of Famous Eating and Drinking Places in Edo* published in 1848 introduced 120 cooking teahouses offering tea-ceremony dishes, compared with 149 which did not (Anon. 1848).

Figure 3.1 shows a cooking teahouse, Yaozen, which *Morisada Mankō* (Kitagawa [n.d.] 1996, 209) introduced as "the top, renowned in Edo." The picture suggests that the main customers of these establishments were the warriors, but they remained an aspiration for middle- and lower-class townspeople, who often used small-sized specialty restaurants, stalls, and street vendors.

Figure 3.1 A high-quality cooking teahouse, Yaozen, in Sanya, Edo, drawn in a woodblock print by Hiroshige Utagawa. (c. 1840)

Source: Utagawa, Hiroshige (c. 1840), "Sanya."

Retrieved from the National Diet Library Digital Collections, https://dl.ndl.go.jp/info:ndljp/pid/1308393

Eating Out of Soba Noodles

A good example was *soba* noodles. Soba, meaning buckwheat, not wheat, had been eaten since ancient times as grains, buckwheat dumplings, or baked buckwheat doughs. However, eating it in the form of noodles was relatively new at that time. It is generally believed that the first of the new "*kendon* soba noodle restaurants" appeared as early as 1664 in Edo (Shinmi n.d.; also see Brau 2018, 66; Kasai 2001 65; Nihon Fūzokushi Gakkai 1978, 30; Niijima 1975, 63–64; Nishiyama et al. 1994, 262).

In early days, *udon* noodle restaurants (*udonya*) were commonly used because udon noodles (made of wheat, not buckwheat) had existed earlier than soba noodles and were eaten by the noble class (Iwasaki 2003, 31). Soba noodles began to be served alongside udon (Nihon Fūzokushi Gakkai 1978, 30). Figure 3.2 gives an example. In due course, independent soba noodle restaurants (*sobaya*) became popular around the end of the 1750s (Nishiyama et al. 1994, 263). *The Complete Book of Soba Noodles* (*Soba Zensho*) written in 1751 (Nisshinsha 1751/2006) already carried a list of 78 famous soba noodle restaurants in Edo.

From then on, the number of these restaurants grew remarkably. The encyclopedia *Morisada Mankō* (Kitagawa [n.d.] 1996, 205) reported that

Consumerism in Early Modern Japan 37

Figure 3.2 A soba/udon noodles restaurant in Edo (1753)
Source: The illustration extracted from Nishimura and Suzuki (n.d.), Ehon Edo Miyage [The souvenir picture book of Edo], Edo: Kikuya Yasubei.
Retrieved from the National Diet Library Digital Collections, https://dl.ndl.go.jp/info:ndljp/pid/2551548?tocOpened=1

as of 1860, the number of restaurants in Edo (except the "nightjar soba sellers" below) reached 3,763 when they gathered to talk about taking measures against rising prices of buckwheat. Amazingly, this number was almost the same as the current number in Tōkyō, as shown by the data 3,765 soba/udon restaurants in 2016 (Statistics Bureau of Japan 2016). While the competition among these restaurants led to diversification of recipes for soba noodles (Hanabusa 2018, 26–37; Iwasaki 2003, 49–52; Kitagawa [n.d.] 1996, 204–05), soba sauce came to mean dark soy sauce originating from around Edo instead of Ōsaka/Kyōto (Iwasaki 2007, 58–64) which encouraged local consumers' preferences.

A unique feature was the night street vendors serving soba noodles. They shouldered portable stalls and their customers ate the noodles while standing up as "fast food." As they conducted their business from evening to dawn, they were often called "nightjar soba-sellers (*yotaka-soba*)" as shown in Figure 3.3. The "nightjars" had the connotation of streetwalking prostitutes, and the figure suggests the female customers eating soba noodles may also be "nightjars."

They served only one type of soba noodles, *kakesoba* (boiled soba in hot soup). A minority wishing to differentiate themselves began to hang a

Figure 3.3 A Nightjar Soba Seller (1817) drawn in a woodblock print (a part extracted)

Source: Utagawa, Kunisada (Toyokuni III) (1817), "Kan'nazuki: Hatsuyuki no Sōka" [The 10th month: Streetwalkers in the first snowfall].

Reproduced with courtesy of Japan Ukiyoe Museum

wind-chime (*fūhrin*) on their stalls to attract attention from potential customers and gradually came to be called "wind-chime soba sellers (fūhrin soba)." They used beautiful containers and served soba noodles with some supplementary ingredients, apparently targeting much higher ranked customers than those of the "nightjars" (Niijima 1975, 90). Later, however, many nightjar soba sellers followed the practices more typical of wind-chime soba sellers, so that the distinction between these eventually faded.

It should be noted that as a result of these developments, eating out of soba noodles was becoming a feature of the identity of "Edoite (*Edokko*)." While the meaning of Edoite has been much debated (see Nishiyama 1980, 1–29, 1997, 41–43), this chapter uses it for townspeople born and raised inside Edo city for a few generations, including people of both the middle class and the lower class. As a famous comic *haiku* (*senryū*) observed, "It is the Edo's features that are haiku and soba-eating belly" (Michian Shujin 1933, 13), consumption of soba noodles became the identity of the townspeople in Edo, as expressed in many comic haiku and stories (*rakugo*) (Hanabusa 2018, 138–83). Eating soba noodles was often considered to express the Edoite's "chic (*iki*)" (Hanabusa 2018; Iwasaki 2007).

Marketing of Sushi

Another example was *sushi*. The internationally most famous types are the hand formed with topping of seafood (*nigirizushi*) and rolled sushi (*makizushi*), which were invented late in the modern period, although the history of sushi can be traced back much further to ancient times.

It is believed that sushi originated in the mountainous areas of Southeast Asia in order to preserve fish flesh through the natural fermentation of rice (Shinoda 1970, 20). The process took from a few months to two years, fermented fish-meat could be eaten only after the gruel-state fermented rice was scraped off (Hibino 2001, 15; Matsushita 2009, 49). Between the 14th and 16th centuries, half-fermented fish-meat called "halfway fermented (*namanare*) sushi" developed to shorten the fermentation period, and rice began to be eaten with fish-meat (Hibino 2001, 16–17; Matsushita 2009, 48; Shinoda 1970, 50). In the early years of early modern Japan, the so-called "*hayazushi* (speedy sushi)" appeared (Matsushita 2009, 42; Shinoda 1970, 208). This was cooked by vinegarization of fish-meat and rice, instead of the natural fermentation process, relying on progress in the production of vinegar.

At the time, the square boxes in which fish-meat and rice were enclosed with a lid, called "boxed sushi (*hakozushi*)" or "pushed sushi (*oshizushi*)," became popular in both Kyōto/Ōsaka and Edo. Also, sushi rolls (makizushi), vinegarized rice, and some ingredients like dried gourd rolled in laver seaweed, appeared. Sushi restaurants, stalls, and peddlers of these types of sushi became widespread. However, it was not until around the 1820s that the world-famous form of sushi, "nigirizushi,"

40   *Kazuo Usui*

which is vinegarized rice topped with basically raw fish, emerged. It is generally believed (e.g., Nihon Fūzokushi Gakkai 1978, 211; Nishiyama et al. 1994, 259–62; Matsushita 2009, 50; Shinoda 1970, 91–92) that this was invented by Yohei Hanaya, who was a sushi chef and owner of a famous sushi restaurant in Edo. This type came to be called the "Edo-style (*Edomae*)," the word originally representing sushi with seafood from the sea in front of the city of Edo.[3] "Nigirizushi," rooted in Edo style, rapidly became the representative form (Shinoda 1970, 18). The encyclopedia *Morisada Mankō* described that while "sushi pushed into a box (oshizushi) had been popular in all three major cities," this type "became obsolete and was almost replaced by nigirizushi at some stage" particularly in Edo (Kitagawa [n.d.] 2001, 107).

The number of sushi shops rapidly increased. It was served at restaurants, some of which attached counters for stand-up eating at the front of stores, at stalls without eat-in space, and by street vendors. *Morisada Mankō* (Kitagawa [n.d.] 2001, 109–10) suggested the number of sushi shops was rather larger than that of soba noodles, noting, "there were extremely many sushi shops [restaurants plus stalls] in Edo, that is, one or two sushi shops every *cho* [one block: usually about 120 meters long], while one soba noodles shop every one or two cho."

Other culinary specialties, such as *tempura* (deep-fried seafoods and vegetables) and eels (*unagi*), particularly in the form of broiled eel (*kabayaki*), also spread widely in early modern Japan through restaurants and street vendors. Especially in the case of eels, keenly competitive marketing by restaurants succeeded in establishing the mid-summer "Day of the Ox" as a special day for eating eels, so that the *Meiwa Record* (*Meiwa-shi*), which collected historical events occurring around 1808, indicated "recently we eat eels on the Ox Day. . . . This . . . began around Meiwa to Tenmei Years [1772 to 1789]" (Aoyama [1822] 1916, 15). This commercial custom is still current in eel restaurants and supermarkets in the current Japan.

Fashion Trends Linked to the Regulations

Culinary culture progressed rather smoothly, reflecting the commodification or commercialization of food services. In the case of fashion trends in clothing, they were more or less in a state of tension with regulations repeatedly issued by the government (Tokugawa Shōgunate) such as the thrift ordinances and the sumptuary laws (Nishimura 1979a, 1979b, 1979c). Fashion trends developed with attempts to slip through these regulations.

Early Fashion Trends in Kimono Wearing

Early modern Japan saw widespread adoption of the shape of *kosode* kimono (e.g., Izutsu 2015, 166; Kanazawa 1962, 39; Kitamura 1973, 115–16; Maruyama 1999, 223, 2008, 48). In contrast to the traditional court kimono with wide sleeve openings, kosode kimono had narrow sleeve openings, which had been the underwear for the court people in medieval Japan. This was signified by one-piece clothing fastened at the waist by a broad belt (*obi*). Fashion trends in kimono developed as the patterns decorating the single piece of cloth from the top to the hem (Maruyama 1999, 217).

The first fashion trends appeared naturally among the warrior class. What is known as the "Keichō patterns" were flamboyant asymmetric designs of birds, grasses, and landscapes mainly in reddish black colors by using *shibori* tie-dyeing called *kanoko* (dappled patterns like deer spots), embroidery and glued gold or silver foil (Maruyama 2007, 20–21, 2008, 589). The so-called "Kanbun patterns," spread around 1661–1673, tended to have unexpected dynamic asymmetric designs, being half blank decorated by kanoko shibori tie-dyeing and golden-colored threads instead of glued gold foil (Maruyama 2007, 22; see also Saito 1935, 10–12).

In 1667, a pattern book, *The New Selection of Sample Patterns* (*Shinsen On-Hiinagata*), was published in Kyōto, the center of dyeing technology, to exhibit the "Kanbun patterns," as Figure 3.4 shows. Following this book,

Figure 3.4 The kanbun pattern shown in the Early Sample Book (1667)

Source: A page extracted from Asai, Ryoi (1667), Shinsen On-Hiina-gata [The new selection of sample patterns].

Retrieved from the National Diet Library Digital Collections, https://dl.ndl.go.jp/info:ndljp/pid/2541138

42   *Kazuo Usui*

more than 120 books were published by the early 19th century (Maruyama 2007, 80–81; see also Fūzoku Hakubutsukan 1998; Izutsu 2015, 170), enabling the tailored kimono to be made to order (Koike M. 1999, 235–36). These pattern books became the sources of fashion trends in kimono. Ikegami (2005, 272) described them as the basis of mass fashion at the time. Actually, the new type of large-sized retail stores (*ōdana*) of kimono started their business in Edo and are seen as the predecessors of modern department stores in Japan. Echigoya (now Mitsukoshi Department Store) introduced the new marketing method of cash sales at the shop to target random town shoppers as early as 1676, rather than the traditional home sales visits to the house of high-ranked warrior class people. The number of this type of stores reached 47 by 1735 in Edo (Usui 2014, 76–77).

From the late 17th to the early 18th centuries, the "Genroku patterns" spread among wealthy townspeople as well as the warrior class. These were known as the gorgeous patterns with kanoko shibori tie-dyeing and embroidery covering almost all parts without any blank gaps (Maruyama 2008, 69). At the time, fashion trends spilled over from the warrior class to the wealthy merchants. Actual costume comparisons (*ishō kurabe*) were sometimes held between housewives of wealthy merchants (Baba 2008, 243; Ikegami 2005, 273–74), as luxury fashion reached from the warrior class—a trickle-down effect in fashion.

The Relationship Between Fashion and the Sumptuary Laws

This effect led to government regulations in fashion. In early modern Japan, the Tokugawa Shogunate and local lords frequently issued dress regulations to maintain the social ranking system. The regulations applied to all classes including the warrior, the peasant, and the townspeople and were defined in detail according to the social position. In the case of the peasant class, for instance, the village heads (*shōya*) and their wives and children were allowed to wear kimono made of silk and pongee (*tsumugi*), while ordinal people were only allowed cotton and hemp (Nishimura 1979a, 11). In the case of the townspeople, the merchants were allowed plain silk and pongee, but not allowed high-quality silk and woolen cloth (*rasha*), while their apprentices wore only cotton and hemp (Hayashi 1992, 13).

Most regulations were directed to the townspeople because they tended to indulge in luxury. One well-known ban was issued in 1683 (called *Tenwa no Kinrei*), which prohibited townspeople from using *kinsha* (woven with golden-colored threads), embroidery, and *kanoko shibori* tie-dyeing for their kimono (e.g., Baba 2008, 243; Maruyama 2007, 24–25, 2008, 155–56; Saito 1935, 14).

However, as the skill of *yūzsen* dyeing was developing, embroidery and shibori tie-dyeing were going out of fashion. Yūzsen was a hand-drawn dyeing with various colors using the protecting agent made from amber-colored sticky rice. As a result, the patterns in kimono became pictorial designs painted with myriad colors. As this skill penetrated the industry, the fashion trends of kimono progressed in a few significant directions.

One was the development of "picture drawing (*kakie*)," picturesque designs drawn on kimono with pigments, black ink, and dyestuffs (Maruyama 2007, 32). Some woodblock print artists became involved, and many specialized kimono artists appeared and published their designs in pattern books (Maruyama 2007, 33). The artist Moronobu Hishikawa (1618–1694), known as the originator of woodblock prints, published his pattern book in 1684 and changed his designs with quite large patterns scattered across all parts of the kimono in order to conform to the 1683 regulation (indicated by Maruyama 2008, 152–57).

In the early half of the 18th century, "Kōrin's patterns" by the artist Kōrin Ogata (1658–1716) became extremely popular among townspeople (see Maruyama 2007, 42–43, 2008, 184–87). The "*Rinpa*" art school, named much later, is permanently associated with his work, signifying bold designs of plants, animals, and human figures often with gold or silver ground. Figure 3.5 shows kimono drawn by Kōrin, which showed largely stylized waves or plants such as plums, chrysanthemums, bellflowers, pines, and maples. Maruyama (2008, 184–85) indicates the reason why Kōrin's work became popular was that the townspeople wanted to

Figure 3.5 Restored kimono designed by Kōrin Ogata (18th century)

Left figure: Photo from the front of Kimono

Right figure: Photo from the back of Kimono

Source: "Kosode: Shiro Ayaji Akikusa Moyō [Kosode with Autumn Grass Pattern on the White Cloth]," hand-painted by Korin Ogata.

Retrieved from Colbase, https://colbase.nich.go.jp/collection_items/tnm/I-721?locale=ja

44   *Kazuo Usui*

differentiate themselves by his patterns while superficially pretending to be frugal.

The few other fashion trends explored below progressed by going through the restrictions of sumptuary laws. These trends became popular among the middle- and lower-class townspeople especially from the latter half of the 18th century in Edo.

Subtle Aesthetic in Fashion

One trend was patterns inside the linings of kimono (Maruyama 2008, 76–77; see also Ikegami 2005, 279). This trend ostensibly conformed to the regulations of the sumptuary laws, but out of sight, enjoyed using expensive textures or flamboyant designs in linings. As shown by Figure 3.6, people began to express their identities secretly in fashion with these internal patterns and skirted the regulations (see also Maruyama 2007, 26).

The other trend was development of hem patterns, first encouraged by the progress of *obi* belts for kimono as a decorative detail. Obi belts were becoming wider, longer, and more varied in quality of cloth, colors and patterns, and the style of knotting (Maruyama 2007, 150–51). This development led to greater division between the upper and lower areas of the kimono, and the decorative patterns tended to be pushed downward to the hem. Such hem patterns were also considered appropriate in accordance with the sumptuary regulations (Maruyama 2007, 26–27).

The third, but the most important trend, was development of simple abstract patterns. Townspeople, especially in Edo, began to prefer restricted patterns such as vertical strips (*shima*), splashed patterns called *kasuri* (Takatsukasa 1979, 33), checked patterns like stone pavements (called "Ichimatsu patterns" after the name of a Kabuki theater actor) (Maruyama 2007, 28–29 and 36–37), and delicately fine patterns called *komon*, which looked like plain colors from a distance but were actually small and beautiful patterns when seen up close (Mizukami 2008, 269; Maruyama 2008, 199–205).

The fine patterns were suitable for silk cloth, whereas the strip designs were for cotton. After the middle period of early modern Japan, cotton spread among the townspeople as it was easily dyed (Koike M. 1999, 234–35) and developed as the everyday fabric for the working population (Ikegami 2005, 283). They often bought their kimono from second-hand shops or peddlers (Takatsukasa 1979, 34). Figure 3.7 shows a working waitress for serving foods and tea at the cooking teahouse Kyōwaro in Edo, who wore kimono with the striped pattern.

Among the "preferences in Edo city (*Edo-gonomi*)" (Takatsukasa 1979), these simple abstract patterns were enthusiastically welcomed by

Consumerism in Early Modern Japan 45

Figure 3.6 Secret fashion in linings of kimono (c. 1789–1801)
Source: Kitagawa, Utamaro (c. 1789–1801), "Seirō Jūni Toki: U no Koku" [A Day in a Brothel: Morning].
Reproduced with courtesy of Iwashita Shoten (Yokohama).

Figure 3.7 A lady wearing kimono with the pattern of vertical stripes (1857)

Source: Utagawa, Kunisada (Toyokuni III) and Kunihisa Utagawa (1857), "Edo Meisho 100-nin Bijo, Meguro Ryūsenji" [100 Beautiful Ladies in Famous Places in Edo City: Meguro Ryūsenji Temple].

Retrieved from the National Diet Library Digital Collections, https://dl.ndl.go.jp/info:ndljp/pid/1311359

Consumerism in Early Modern Japan 47

middle- and lower-class townspeople. Ikegami (2005, 279–84) explained this aesthetic sense could be called "urban chic (*iki*)." Interestingly, along with this development, pictorial pattern books were gradually falling into disuse (Maruyama 2008, 187). Mizukami (2008, 268) emphasized that these simpler aesthetic values were not created as a trickle-down effect, but as an observance of sumptuary decrees: again slipping through the regulations, rather than opposition, is a recognizable fashion development.

Commercialized Publication and Pictorial Light Novels

Two Types of Publishers Based in Kyōto and Edo

Early modern Japan saw the emergence of commercialized publication of books and paintings (see Berry 2006; Ikegami 2005, Ch.11; Kornicki 2001). Many townspeople as well as warriors enjoyed these printed materials, which played an important role in the commercialization of "behavioral culture" as mentioned previously. These products were a medium to spread knowledge and images of popular places, events, and stories.

First, it should be noted that literacy levels in early modern Japan were not low (Dore [1965] 2011, Rubinger 2007). Education in reading and writing was provided not only for children of the warrior class at the domain schools (*hankō*) that were officially managed by the local daimyō lords but also for townspeople's children at what were privately run basic writing schools (*tenaraijo*) or temple schools (*terakoya*). This suggests that some townspeople, as well as warriors, could buy books. Even so, Japanese phonetic syllabaries (*hiragana* characters) were much easier to read than *kanji* characters, so popular books and booklets were written mainly in them.

Many books in early modern Japan were not printed with letterpress machines, but with woodblocks (*hangi*) (e.g., Imada 1977, 26; Kamisato 1965, 191; Nakano 2015, 9), on which the engravers carved the letters and printed them on paper. Pictures too were produced by the woodblock method, although the printing techniques for the woodblock prints independently progress from black-and-white printings, via two colors with black (Uchida 2007, 21), to the multicolor printings called "*nishi-kie*" from 1764 when the artist Harunobu Suzuki (c.1725–1770) and the publisher Kyōsen published these for the first time (Ishii 1929, 9; Uchida 2007, 30). Skills in picture printing also developed to include making gradations (*bokashi-zuri*) and embossing (*kara-zuri*), and different carvers and printers were employed in books and for picture preparation (Ishii 1929, 123).

These whole printing processes were controlled by the publishers. They drew up plans with authors and/or painters, arranged carvers and rubbers of the woodblocks, and sold the books and/or the pictures (Nihon Ukiyoe Kyōkai 1982, 134). There were basically two different types of publishers

48   *Kazuo Usui*

in early modern Japan: "the book publisher (*shomotsu-don'ya*)" and "the Edo-native publisher (*jihon-don'ya*)."

First to appear were the book publishers (shomotsu-don'ya). They emerged in Kyōto and published traditional or scholarly books such as Buddhist texts, classical novels like *Genji Story*, and Chinese classics like Confucian writings (Imada 1977, 30–31; Ōkubo 2013, 14). In due course, they began to publish the popular entertainment books called "*kana-zōshi*," written in easy hiragana characters combined with some *kanji* characters. After the books of amorous stories by the author Saikaku Ihara (c.1642–1693) were extremely well received, these books became known as "*ukiyo-zōshi* (the books of fleeting world stories)." In order to publish these popular stories, new publishers were established in Ōsaka (Imada 1977, 39–40). Then, the publishers in Kyōto/Ōsaka entered the newly growing market in Edo through sales by their affiliated publishers there who were allowed to use the original woodblocks for books (Imada 1973, 113–16) or through sharing the woodblocks between them (Imada 1977, 53).

However, as the market in Edo was growing, the second type of publishers, the Edo-native publishers (jihon-don'ya), emerged and developed in the late period of early modern Japan, unconnected with the book publishers in Kyōto/Ōsaka. It was these Edo-native publishers that produced and distributed various types of printing materials very widely in Edo, both full-colored woodblock prints and various kinds of entertaining books and booklets. Historical research has been conducted to identify the names and the trading marks of these publishers (Inoue K. 1916; Inoue T. 1982; Ishii and Hirose 1920), and Nihon Ukiyoe Kyōkai (1982, 143–48) made a list of 1,022 such publishers in Edo.

Figure 3.8 depicts the shop front of a famous publisher, Tsuruya Kiemon. They published both books and colored woodblock prints. As is shown by this case, many eminent publishers had their own retail shops. Unique trade customs existed between the publishers and the shops: a "book exchange (*hon-gae*)," meant that middlemen mediated the exchange of pictures and books among different publishers' stores in order to expand the assortment in each shop (Ōkubo 2013, 51 and 83–85; Suzuki T. 2010, 92). In addition to these direct shops, there were many small-sized retail shops (Nihon Ukiyoe Kyōkai 1982, 120; Ōkubo 2013, 51–53; Suzuki T. 2010, 16), and there were also many street vendors who mainly rented books (Imada 1977, 152–57) as many readers preferred to borrow rather than buy. As a result of these distribution systems, woodblock prints, books, and booklets were enthusiastically welcomed by the townspeople in Edo.

From a marketing point of view, production and sales of woodblock prints and books/booklets were slightly different, although many Edo-native publishers dealt with both. With woodblock prints, product turnover was quick. The pictures typically sold out in around two months;

Consumerism in Early Modern Japan   49

Figure 3.8 The shop front of a famous publisher in Edo (1834)

Source: Hasegawa, Settan ([1834] 1928), Edo Meisho Zukai, Maki 1 [The famous places described in pictures in Edo City, Vol. 1]. Reprint by Saito, Yukio ed., Tōkyō: Yoshikawa Kōbunkan, 76–77.

Retrieved from the National Diet Library Digital Collections, https://dl.ndl.go.jp/info:ndljp/pid/1176676

and after this, these pictures could no longer be found (Ōkubo 2013, 45). The three major genres of colored woodblock prints were the pictures of actors of *kabuki* theaters, beautiful ladies, and popular tourist landmarks (*meisho-e*). The pictures of kabuki actors had the shortest product lifespan: these could be only sold within the period of performance that related to the kabuki titles; therefore, these pictures were usually exhibited prominently at the front of stores, while those of popular places/landscapes were at the back of the stores (Ōkubo 2013, 60 and 70–79). Regarding the number of printings, 200 copies were usually produced per colored woodblock print as the first printing unit, and then, many more were printed according to expected sales estimates (Ōkubo 2013, 30). A usual practice was to produce 1,000–1,500 copies and 2,000 copies in the case of good sales. A successful case was a set of three pictures which sold 8,000 copies each (Ōkubo 2013, 47).

In the case of books and booklets, it was reported that the first printed runs were usually 300 copies per book, and if a book became popular,

50   *Kazuo Usui*

the reprints could reach 2,000 copies or more (Kamisato 1965, 215). When a book reached 1,000 copies, "a celebration of publishing 1,000 copies (*sen-bu burumai*)" was often held (Imada 1973, 119). The Edo-native publishers created popular items as suggested below, which could be tremendously popular with the townspeople.

Popular Pictorial Booklets Kusa-zōshi: A Precedent of Manga

The Edo-native publishers began to publish popular books and booklets that originated in Edo city. These included *kusa-zōshi* (booklets of illustrations with stories written chiefly in *hiragana* characters), *kokkei-bon* (funny stories in easily spoken words), *ninjō-bon* (depicting love affairs), *share-bon* (depicting lives in brothels), and *yomi-bon* (narrating mysterious stories with many letters rather than pictures) (Nishiyama et al. 1994, 430–32 and 438–45). These genres were lumped together and called "amusement literature (*gesaku*)," and the authors of these genres were called popular novelists (*gesaku sakka*).

Among these popular writings, the pictorial booklets kusa-zōshi are worth consideration. These booklets were featured as large-sized illustrations with easy narrations written chiefly in hiragana characters. Each booklet typically had ten pages (five pieces of paper folded in half) and were sold as a set (one story) in two or three volumes (Nishiyama et al. 1994, 441). At first, these booklets were published for the new year sales but gradually changed to being published all year round (Kamisato 1965, 160–62).

The pictorial "red-covered booklets (*aka-bon*)" were the first to appear, around 1661–1751, containing mainly fairy tales for children (Kato 2006; Nishiyama et al. 1994, 441). The so-called five major classical fairy tales (Momotarō, Crack mountain, Monkey crab battle, Tongue-cutting sparrow, and Old man making flowers bloom) were published for the first time on a commercial basis (Koike T. 1961a, 22–26) although the stories themselves had emerged long before.

This expanded to "the black-covered or blue-covered booklets (*kuro-bon, ao-bon*)" between 1775 and 1806, which contained much more varied and complicated narratives for adults such as religious stories, love affairs, sightseeing stories, happy events, legends, tales of older times, summaries of puppet plays, and arranged dramas from theaters (Koike T. 1961a, 36; Kuroishi 2006; Nishiyama et al. 1994, 442–43).

Then, "the yellow-covered booklets (*ki-byōshi*)" appeared from 1775 (Nishiyama et al. 1994, 444). These contained stories describing the real world with humor and satire, producing laughter by a combination of illustrations and narrations (Suzuki N. 2015, 15). Figure 3.9 shows a two-page spread in a best-selling yellow-covered booklet, *Edo Umare Uwaki no Kabayaki* (*Playboy Roasted à la Edo*), by a popular writer,

Figure 3.9 A facing page in a popular yellow-covered book (1785)

Source: Santō, Kyōden (1785/1938) Edo Umare Uwaki no Kabayaki [Playboy, roasted à la Edo], Reprint by Tōkyō: Yoneyamadō.
Retrieved from the National Diet Library Digital Collections, https://dl.ndl.go.jp/info:ndljp/pid/1072450

Kyōden Santō (1761–1816) (see Koike T. 1935, 191; Mizuno 1991; Satō 2009). As the figure demonstrates, the illustrations were the main body of the booklets while the narrations were written vertically, primarily from right-to-left in easy hiragana characters to fill the spaces within the pictures.

The yellow-covered booklets developed into "combined books (*gōkan*)" from c.1807, single volumes for longer stories (Nishiyama et al. 1994, 445). Every year around 50–70 volumes of these pictorial booklets were published (Nishiyama 1983b, 154), and the best sellers were reported to have sold more than 10,000 copies (Nishiyama et al. 1994, 430).

In the meantime, Tokugawa Shōgunate repeatedly enforced censorship over publications in order to maintain social order, so that the commercial publications were often under tension with these regulations. This was the case with popular novelists (gesaku sakka) (Satō 2017), as well as with ukiyoe painters, scholars, and political activists, because they tended to be contrary to what the government regarded as "preferred order and ethics."

An example was the case of the popular novelist Kyōden Santō in 1791 (e.g., Inoue Y. 2013, 34 and 51; Koike T. 1935, 53–61, 1961b,

52   *Kazuo Usui*

97–100; Mizuno 1991, 44; Satō 2009, 96–100, 2017, 68–112). The government exposed Kyōden Santō and his publisher Tsutaya because they were "villains" who published three-volume share-bon, profligate stories of brothels. Kyōden Santō's punishment was to have to wear handcuffs on the wrists for 50 days, and the publisher Tsutaya had half of his estate confiscated along with the books. In addition, the two judges in the censorship, who decided to permit the publication of this book, also had their rights of publishing revoked and were expelled from Edo.

Under these circumstances, the authors, the artists, and the publishers had to work to circumvent censorship. This frequently led to the development of indirect expressions such as using a lot of metaphors, changing dramatis personae and the times of political or scandalous events, mocking idiots in place of the ruling class, and horror stories of ghosts taking revenge on arrogant warriors (Inoue Y. 2013; Nishiyama 1972). Many townspeople would see through such satire and insinuation.

As Kimura (2009, 2) suggested, the huge number of commercialized *kusa-zōshi* publications could be recognized as a substantial precedent of the current *manga* culture, although the handwritten picture scrolls, "*Chō Jū Giga*" (Caricature of animals and humans) in the 12th and 13th centuries, were generally recognized as the precursor of modern *manga* (Hosobara 1924, 8–31; Ishiko 1979, 20) and the pictorial booklets were often ignored. Consumption of such pictorial booklets was a significant feature of consuming culture in early modern Japan.

Concluding Remarks: The Changed and the Unchanged

As explored thus far, enthusiastic consumption of soba noodles and sushi outside homes, simple abstract patterns in kimono like fine, delicate designs and vertical strips, and light pictorial novels typically delivered by the yellow-covered booklets were part of the explosive consuming phenomena centered on Edo city in the late period of early modern Japan. As eating soba noodles and sushi became the identity of the Edoite, as simple abstracted patterns in kimono were called "preferences in Edo city" and showed the sense of "chic," and as pictorial booklets by popular novelists were published by the Edo-native publishers, purchasing and consuming these commodities became part of the identity of the townspeople in Edo.

After the Meiji Restoration in 1868, the social and political structure was fundamentally changed from that of early modern Japan. As Usui (2014) delineated, a vital feature in consuming culture was the rapid progress of westernization, which was essentially a combination of traditional Japanese factors and new western ones. This way of westernization was welcomed as modernization and industrialization by many Japanese consumers. Nevertheless, it is only natural that the traditional habits

Consumerism in Early Modern Japan 53

created in early modern Japan were, directly or indirectly, inherited by modern Japan.

Regarding food, eating out of soba noodles and sushi became firmly rooted in national culinary culture, although some new recipes joined the national diet resulting from a combination of Japanese and Western recipes, such as *korokke* (modified from French dish croquette), *curry rice* (curry with rice, created with the curry powder made by the British company Crosse and Blackwell), and *tonkatsu* (deep fried pork rather than sautéed, adapted from French cutlet recipes). Thus, Japanese culinary culture became composed of two strata: the recipes from early modern Japan and those created in modern Japan.

In the case of fashion, wearing kimono continued even in early periods in modern Japan, but was totally discontinued after the Second World War (Usui 2014). Nowadays, kimono is worn only on very limited occasions, and kimono with the fine patterns (komon) were used in some casual situations. However, the legacy of fashion in kimono is generally very indirect. For instance, the world-class Japanese designers, such as Kenzō Takada, Issei Miyake, and Kansai Yamamoto, made the formal Western-style suits much more loose-fitting by introducing some aspects of kimono (Across Henshūbu 1995, 200–05).

As for the pictorial light novels, the legacy can be said to have developed into the world-famous manga culture, as already indicated. Popular culture among current Japanese youngsters, such as manga, cute culture, and fake school uniforms (assembled from various components of different school uniforms) (e.g., Ōsaki 2013), has also developed in the tension with social pressures and regulations that current Japanese society imposes, such as too strict school disciplines and awful entrance examination ordeals. Avoiding direct conflict with these pressures, but slipping through them into areas without regulations, resembles the development of consumer culture in early modern Japan.

Notes

1. Culture in this period is referred to the Kasei Culture.
2. Initially in early modern Japan, the cultural center still remained in Kyōto and Ōsaka. This was the case with the famous Genroku Culture (this term was coined later in modern Japan), which was in full bloom from the late 17th to early 18th centuries. Although this was often called culture by the townspeople (Bitō 1975, 18), the main actors were not only them but also the warriors, the court nobles, and the monks. From around the 1720s to the 1770s, the so-called "eastward movement of the center of culture" was identifiable (Kabuki Gakkai 1998, 14; Tanaka 2002, 1), then the new metropolis Edo began gaining a more influential position in culture.
3. The term "Edomae" was originally used for eels taken from the rivers in front of the Edo Castle to differentiate these from the eels from other areas and brought into Edo called "traveled eels (*tabi unagi*)" (Nihon Fūzokushi Gakkai 1978, 31).

54 *Kazuo Usui*

References

Across Henshūbu (Editorial Office of Across), ed. (1995), *Sutorīto Fassyon 1945–1995 (Street Fashions 1945–1995)*, Tōkyō: Parco.

Anon. (1848), *Edo Meibutsu Shuhan Tebikigusa* [*The Guidebook of Famous Eating and Drinking Places in Edo*], Edo: Kurasakidō (https://dl.ndl.go.jp/info:ndljp/pid/2533095).

Aoyama, Hakuho (1822/1916), *Meiwa-shi* [*Meiwa Record*], Reprint in *Sohaku Jisshu, Dai 2* [*Collections of Valuable Things, Vol. 2*], ed. Engyo Mitamura, Tōkyō: Kokusho Kankōkai (https://dl.ndl.go.jp/info:ndljp/pid/1767733).

Baba, Mami (2008), "Chōnin no Kimono, 1. Kanbun kara Edo Chūki made no Kimono" [Kimono for the Townspeople, No. 1, Kimono from Kanbun Years to the Middle of the Edo Era], *Sen'i Gakkaishi* [*Journal of Fiber Science and Technology*], 64 (7), 242–44.

Bermingham, Ann (1995), "The Consumption of Culture: Image, Object, Text," in *The Consumption of Culture 1600–1800: Image, Object, Text*, ed. Ann Bermingham and John Brewer, London: Routledge, 1–20.

Berry, Mary Elizabeth (2006), *Japan in Print: Information and Nation in the Early Modern Period*, Berkeley and Los Angeles: University of California Press.

Bitō, Masahide (1975), *Nihon no Rekishi, 19, Genroku Jidai* [*History of Japan, Vol. 19, The Genroku Age*], Tōkyō: Shōgakukan.

Brau, Lorie (2018), "Soba, Edo Style," in *Devouring Japan: Global Perspectives on Japanese Culinary Identity*, ed. Nancy K. Stalker, New York: Oxford University Press, 65–76.

Brownlie, Douglas (2015), "Commodification and Consumption," in *Routledge Companion to Philosophy in Organization Studies*, ed. Raza Mir, Hugh Willmott and Michelle Greenwood, London: Routledge, 301–08.

Dore, Ronald P. (1965/2011), *Education in Tokugawa Japan*, Abingdon: Routledge.

Duffy, William J. and Kozo Yamamura (1971), "Monetization and Integration in Tokugawa Japan: A Spectral Analysis," *Explorations in Economic History*, 8 (4), 395–423.

Ertman, Martha M. and John C. Williams, eds. (2005), *Rethinking Commodification: Cases and Readings in Law and Culture*, New York and London: New York University Press.

Francks, Penelope and Janet Hunter (2012), "Introduction: Japan's Consumption History in Comparative Perspective," in *The Historical Consumer: Consumption and Everyday Life in Japan, 1850–2000*, ed. Penelope Francks and Janet Hunter, Basingstoke Hampshire and New York: Palgrave Macmillan Co., 1–23.

Fūzoku Hakubutsukan [Costume Museum] (1998), "Shiryō Nippon fūzokushi" [Materials for Costume History in Japan] (www.iz2.or.jp/fukushoku/f_disp.php?page_no=0000115).

Gordon, Andrew (2012), "Consumption, Consumerism, and Japanese Modernity," in *The Oxford Handbook of the History of Consumption*, ed. Frank Trentmann, Oxford: Oxford University Press, 485–504.

Hanabusa, Takenori (2018), *Iki o Shokusu* [*Eating Iki*], Tōkyō: Temjin.

Hanley, Susan B. and Kozo Yamamura (1977), *Economic and Demographic Change in Preindustrial Japan 1600–1868*, Princeton, NJ: Princeton University Press.

Consumerism in Early Modern Japan   55

Hayami, Akira (2004), "Introduction: The Emergence of 'Economic Society'," in *The Economic History of Japan: 1600–1990*, ed. Akira Hayami, Osamu Saitō, and Ronald P. Toby, Oxford: Oxford University Press, 1–35.

Hayami, Akira, Osamu Saitō, and Ronald P. Toby, eds. (2004), *The Economic History of Japan: 1600–1990*, Oxford: Oxford University Press.

Hayashi, Reiko (1992), "Haruka-nari Men no Michi" [Far and Away, the Cotton Road], in *Nihon no Kinsei, 5. Shonin no Kastudō [The Early Modern Period in Japan, Vol. 5. The Activities of Merchants]*, Tokyo: Chuō Kōronsha, 9–42.

Hibino, Terutoshi (2001), *Sushi no Jiten [Encyclopedia of Sushi]*, Tōkyō: Tōkyōdō Shuppan.

Hosobara, Seiki (1924), *Nihon Manga-shi [History of Manga in Japan]*, Tōkyō: Yūzankaku.

Ikegami, Eiko (2005), *Bonds of Civility: Aesthetic Networks and the Political Origins of Japanese Culture*, Cambridge: Cambridge University Press.

Imada, Yōji (1973), "Edo no Shuppan Shihon" [The Publishing Capital in the Edo Era], in *Edo Chōnin no Kenkyu, Dai 3 Kan [Research in Townspeople in Edo, Vol. 3]*, ed. Matsunosuke Nishiyama, Tōkyō: Yoshikawa Kōbundo, 109–95.

—— (1977), *Edo no Honya-san [The Bookshops in the Edo Era]*, Tōkyō: NHK Books.

Inoue, Kazuo (1916), *Keichō Irai Shobai Shūran [The Overview of Book Publishers From Keichō Years]*, Kyōto: Shūbundō (https://dl.ndl.go.jp/info:ndljp/pid/1870968).

Inoue, Takaaki (1982), *Kinsei Shorin Hanmoto Sōran [The Overview of Book Publishers in the Kinsei Era]*, Tōkyō: Seirindō Shoten.

Inoue, Yasushi (2013), *Edo no Hakkin Bon: Yokubō to Yokuatsu no Kinsei [Banned Books in the Edo Era: Concupiscence and Suppression in Kinsei]*, Tōkyō: Kadokawa Shoten.

Ishige, Naomichi (2011), *The History and Culture of Japanese Food*, London and New York: Routledge.

Ishii, Kendō (1929), *Nishikie no Hori to Suri [Carving and Rubbing Techniques in Nishikie]*, Tōkyō: Geisōdō.

Ishii, Kendō and Kikuo Hirose (1920), "Jihon Nishikie Ton'ya Fu" [Records of Ton'ya of Jihon and Nishikie] (https://dl.ndl.go.jp/info:ndljp/pid/11445826).

Ishiko, Jun (1979), *Nihon Manga-shi, Jōkan [History of Manga in Japan, Vol. 1]*, Tōkyō: Ōtsuki Shoten.

Iwasaki, Shinya (2003), *Sobaya no Keizu [A Genealogy of Soba Restaurants]*, Tōkyō: Kōbunsha Shinsho.

—— (2007), *Edokko wa Naze Soba nanoka [Why Did the Edoite Prefer to Eat Soba Noodles?]*, Tōkyō: Kōbunsha Shinsho.

Izutsu, Masakaze (2015), *Nihon Fukusō-shi, Josei-hen [Japanese History of Clothing: Female Edition]*, Tōkyō: Kōson Suiko Shoin.

Kabuki Gakkai (Kabuki Society), ed. (1998), *Kabuki no Rekishi: Atarashii Shiten to Tenbō [History of Kabuki: A New Perspective and Prospective]*, Tōkyō: Yūzankaku.

Kamisato, Haruo (1965), *Edo Shosekishō-shi [History of Book Merchants in the Edo Era]*, Tōkyō: Meicho Kankōkai.

Kanazawa, Yasutaka (1962), *Edo Fukusō-shi [The History of Clothing in the Edo Era]*, Tōkyō: Seiabō.

56   *Kazuo Usui*

Kasai, Toshiya (2001), *Soba: Edo no Shoku-bunka* [*Soba: Eating Culture in Edo*], Tōkyō: Iwanami Shoten.

Kato, Yasuko (2006), "Aka-hon Gaisetsu" [An Overview of the Red-covered Booklets], in *Kusa-zōshi Jiten* [*The Dictionary of Kusa-zōshi*], ed. Sō no Kai, Tōkyō: Tōkyōdo Suppan, 1–5 and 355–61 (in Japanese and English).

Kimura, Yaeko (2009), *Kusa-zōshi no Sekai: Edo no Shuppan Bunka* [*The World of Kusa-zōshi: Publication Culture in the Edo Era*], Tōkyō: Pelican Books.

Kitagawa, Morisada (n.d./1996), *Morisada Mankō, Kan 5* [*Morisada Mankō, Vol. 5*] (https://dl.ndl.go.jp/info:ndljp/pid/2592394). Rev. by Usami, Hideki, 1996, Tōkyō: Iwanami-bunko.

—— (n.d./2001), *Morisada Mankō, Kōshū Kan 1* [*Morisada Mankoh, Latter Part, Vol. 1*] (https://dl.ndl.go.jp/info:ndljp/pid/2592417). Rev. by Usami, Hideki, 2001, Tōkyō: Iwanami-bunko.

Kitamura, Tetsurō (1973), *Nihon Fukushoku-shi* [*History of Clothing in Japan*], Tōkyō: Ifuku Seikatsu Kenkyū-kai.

Koike, Mie (1999), "Monyō o Yomu" [Reading the Designed Patterns of Kimono], in *Edo Mōdo Zukan: Kosode Monyō nimiru Bi no Keifu* [*Edo à la Mode: Aesthetic Lineages Seen in Kosode Kimono Motifs*], ed., Kokuritsu Rekishi Hakubutsukan [National Museum of History and Folklore], Tōkyō: NHK Promotions, 225–40.

Koike, Tōgorō (1935), *Santō Kyōden no Kenkyū* [*Research in Kyōden Santō*], Tōkyō: Iwanami Shoten.

—— (1961a), *Aka-bon, Kuro-bon, Ao-bon ni Tsuite* [*On the Red-covered, the Black-covered and the Blue-colored Books*], Tōkyō: Dai-Tōkyū Memorial Library.

—— (1961b), *Santō Kyōden, Jinbutsu Sōsho* [*Kyōden Santō, A Series of Biographies*], Tōkyō: Yoshikawa Kōbundō.

Kornicki, Peter (2001), *The Book in Japan: A Cultural History from the Beginning to the Nineteenth Century*, Honolulu: University of Hawai'i Press.

Kuroishi, Yōko (2006), "Kuro-bon Ao-bon Gaisetsu [An Overview of the Black-Covered and the Blue-Covered Booklet]," in *Kusa-zōshi Jiten* [*The Dictionary of Kusa-zōshi*], ed. Sō no Kai, Tōkyō: Tōkyōdo Suppan, 5–8 and 349–54 (in Japanese and English).

Maruyama, Nobuhiko (1999), "Fukusō-shi no nakano Kosode: Naze Kimono ni Monyō ga Arunoka" [*Kosode* in the History of Clothing: Why Were the Patterns Shown on *Kimono*?], in *Edo Mōdo Zukan: Kosode Monyō nimiru Bi no Keifu* [*Edo à la Mode: Aesthetic Lineages Seen in Kosode Kimono Motifs*], ed. Kokuritsu Rekishi Hakubutsukan [National Museum of History and Folklore], Tōkyō: NHK Promotions, 217–30.

——, ed. (2007), *Edo no Kimono to Seikatsu* [*Kimono and Clothing Life in the Edo Era*], Tōkyō: Shōgakukan.

—— (2008), *Edo Mōdo no Tanjō: Monyō no Ryukō to Sutā Eshi* [*Birth of the Mode of Edo: Vogues in Patterns and Drawers as Stars*], Tōkyō: Kadokawa Gakugei Shuppan.

Matsushita, Sachiko (2009), *Zusetsu Edo Ryōri Jiten* [*Encyclopedia of Edo Cuisines With Pictures*], Tōkyō: Kashiwa Shobō.

Michian Shujin (1933), *Senryū Soba no Hana* [*Comic Haiku: Flowers of Soba*], Tōkyō: Nichigetsuan Yabutada (https://dl.ndl.go.jp/info:ndljp/pid/1103630).

Consumerism in Early Modern Japan   57

Miyamoto, Mataji (1971), *Gaisetsu Nihon Shōgyō-shi* [*The Outline of Japanese History of Commerce*], Tōkyō: Ōhara Shinseisha.

Mizukami, Kayoko (2008), "Chōnin no Kimono, 2. Edo Kōki kara Meiji Shoki no Kimono" [Kimono for the Townspeople, No. 2, Kimono from the Latter Half of Edo Era to the Early Meiji Era], *Sen'i Gakkaishi* [*Journal of Fiber Science and Technology*], 64 (8), 268–71.

Mizuno, Minoru (1991), *Santō Kyōden Nenpukō* [*A Chronological Record of Kyōden Santō*], Tōkyō: Pelicansha.

Nakano, Mitsutoshi (2015), *Edo no Ita-hon* [*Board-Shaped Books in the Edo Era*], Tōkyō: Iwanami Shoten.

Nihon Fūzokushi Gakkai [The Japan Society for Historical Research of Manners and Customs], ed. (1978), *Zusetsu Edo-Jidai Syoku-seikatsu Jiten* [*Encyclopedia of Diet in the Edo Era With Illustrations*], Tōkyō: Yūhzankaku.

Nihon Ukiyoe Kyōkai [Japan Ukiyoe Association], ed. (1982), *Genshoku Ukityoe Dai-Hyakka Jiten, Dai 3-kan, Yoshiki, Hosuri, Hanmoto* [*The Large-Sized Encyclopedia of Ukiyoe in Primary Colors, Vol. 3, Styles, Carvings and Publishers*], Tōkyō: Taishūkan Shoten.

Niijima, Shigeru (1975), *Sobashi-kō* [*A Consideration on the History of Soba*], Tōkyō: Kinseisha.

Nishimura, Yasuko (1979a), "Bakuhan Taisei-ka niokeru Fukusō Kisei" [The Regulations Against Clothing Under the System of Tokugawa Shōgunate], *Fukoso Bunka* [*Clothing Culture*], 161, 3–19.

―――― (1979b), "Bakuhan Taisei-ka niokeru Fukusō Kisei: Zoku" [The Regulations Against Clothing Under the System of Tokugawa Shogunate, No. 2], *Fukoso Bunka* [*Clothing Culture*], 162, 12–31.

―――― (1979c), "Bakuhan Taisei-ka niokeru Fukusō Kisei no Taiyō" [The Situations of Regulations Against Clothing in the Edo Era], *Fukoso Bunka* [*Clothing Culture*], 163, 18–29.

Nishiyama, Matsunosuke (1972), "Edo Chōnin Sōron" [General Discussions of Edo Chōnin], in *Edo Chōnin no Kenkyū* [*Research in Townspeople in Edo, Vol. 1*], ed. Matsunosuke Nishiyama, Tōkyō: Yoshikawa Kōbunkan, 1–42.

―――― (1980), *Edokko, Edo Sensho 1* [*Edoite, Selective Books of Edo, Vol. 1*], Tōkyō: Yoshikawa Kōbunkan.

―――― (1981), *Ōedo no Bunka* [*Culture of Great Edo*], Tōkyō: NHK.

―――― (1983a), *Edo no Seikatsu Bunka, Nishiyama Matsunosuke Chosakushū 3* [*Everyday Culture in Edo, The Collective Works of Matsunosuke Nishiyama, Vol. 3*], Tōkyō: Yoshikawa Kōbunkan.

―――― (1983b), *Kinsei Bunka no Kenkyū, Nishiyama Matsunosuke Chosakushū 4* [*Research in Early Modern Culture, The Collective Works of Matsunosuke Nishiyama, Vol. 4*], Tōkyō: Yoshikawa Kōbunkan.

―――― (1997), *Edo Culture: Daily Life and Diversions in Urban Japan, 1600–1868*, trans. and ed. Gerald Groemer, Honolulu: University of Hawai'i Press.

―――― et al., eds. (1994), *Edo-gaku Jiten* [*Encyclopedia of Edo-ology*], Tōkyō: Kōhbundō.

Nisshinsha, Yūkyōshi (1751/ 2006), *Soba Zensho* [*The Complete Book of Soba Noodles*], trans. to modern language by Kazuo Fujimura, Tōkyō: Hāto Shuppan.

Ōkubo, Junichi (2013), *Ukiyoe Shuppan Ron* [*Explorations of Ukiyoe Publishing*], Tōkyō: Yoshikawa Kōbunkan.

58 *Kazuo Usui*

Ōsaki, Tomohiro (2013), "Fake School Uniforms: Let Some Turn Back the Clock," *Japan Times*, May 1.

Radin, Margaret Jane (2005), "Contested Commodities," in *Rethinking Commodification: Cases and Readings in Law and Culture*, ed. Martha M. Ertman and John C. Williams, New York and London: New York University Press, 81–95.

Rubinger, Richard (2007), *Popular Literacy in Early Modern Japan*, Honolulu: University of Hawai'i Press.

Saito, Ryūzō (1935), *Kinsei Jiyō Fūzoku* [*The Fashion and Customs in Kinsei*], Tōkyō: Sanseidō.

Satō, Yukiko (2009), *Santō Kyōden, Kokkei Share Daiichi no Sakusha* [*Kyōden Santō: The Top Author of Kokkei and Share Books*], Kyōto: Minerva Shobō.

―――― (2017), *Edo no Shuppan Tōsei: Dan'atsu ni Honrō sareta Gesakushatachi* [*Controls of Publications in the Edo Era: Popular Novelists Messed with Repressions*], Tōkyō: Yoshikawa Kōbundō.

Shimbo, Hiroshi and Akira Hasegawa (2004), "The Dynamics of Market Economy and Production," in *The Economic History of Japan: 1600–1990*, ed. Akira Hayami, Osamu Saitō, and Ronald P. Toby, Oxford: Oxford University Press, 159–91.

Shinmi, Masatomo (n.d.), "Mukashi-mukashi Monogatari" [Stories Long Time Ago] (https://archive.wul.waseda.ac.jp/kosho/ri05/ri05_05049/ri05_05049.pdf).

Shinoda, Osamu (1970), *Sushi no Hon* [*The Book of Sushi*], Tōkyō: Shibata Shoten.

Smith, Thomas S. (1988), *Native Sources of Japanese Industrialization, 1750–1920*, Los Angeles: University of California Press.

Song, Edward (2003), "Commodification and Consumer Society: A Bibliographic Review," *The Hedgehog Review: Critical Reflection on Contemporary Culture* (https://hedgehogreview.com/issues/the-commodification-of-everything/articles/commodification-and-consumer-society-a-bibliographic-review).

Statistics Bureau of Japan (2016), "Economic Census 2016," (www.e-stat.go.jp/dbview?sid=0003215480).

Storey, John (2017), *Theories of Consumption*, London and New York: Routledge.

Suzuki, Nao (2015), "Kyōden Kibyōshi no Zanshō: Bunka Makki ni okeru Gōhon o Chūshin ni" [The Afterglow of Kyōden's Yellow-covered Booklets: Considering the Combined Books in the End of Bunka Years (1804–1818)], Chiba University, *Gobun Ronsan* [*The Japanese Language and Literature Review*], 30, 15–34.

Suzuki, Toshiyuki (2010), *E-Zōshiya, Edo no Ukiyoe Shop* [*E-Zōshiya: Retail Shops of Ukiyoe in Edo City*], Tōkyō: Heibonsha.

Takatsukasa, Rinko (1979), "Edokko to Kōki Fūzoku" [The Edoite and Costume in the Late Edo Era], *Fukuso Bunka* [*Clothing Culture*], 163, 30–39.

Tanaka, Katsuyoshi (2002), "Toshi Edo no Seiritsu: Ippanshi teki Haikei," [Establishment of Edo City: Backgrounds in General History], *Keiō Gijuku Daigaku Shakai Kagaku Kenkyū Kiyō* [*Keiō Gijuku University, Studies in Sociology, Psychology and Education*], 54, 1–11.

Uchida, Keiichi (2007), *Edo no Shuppan Jijō* [*The Publishing Conditions in the Edo Era*], Kyōto: Seigen-sha.

Usui, Kazuo (2014), *Marketing and Consumption in Modern Japan*, London and New York: Routledge.

———— (2018), "The Role of Newly Emergent Wholesalers in the Food and Drink Industry in Japan, c.1880 to 1940: Focusing on the Case of Kokubu," *Journal of Marketing Channels*, 25 (4), 211–35 (https://doi.org/10.1080/10466 69X.2019.1658013).

Section II

Consumer Identity Projects

4 Century of Humiliation and Consumer Culture

The Making of National Identity

I-Chieh Michelle Yang, Juliana French, and Christina Lee

Introduction

Since the late 19th century, China is said to be enmeshed in a profound national identity crisis (Gries 2004; Guo 2004). Major historical events such as the Opium War, the Sino-Japanese War, and a series of foreign invasions has adversely affected China's internal stability and self-image. From an imperial power with five thousand years of civilization, decades of foreign invasions have resulted in China's downfall. The protracted hardship faced by the Chinese is commonly discussed as the hundred years of national humiliation discourse (*bainian guochi*) to the Chinese, as they question how the descendants of the dragon were reduced to become the Sick Man that is bullied and humiliated by foreign powers (Scott 2008). More recently, too, events such as the US international uproar of the Tiananmen massacre in 1989, the continual Sino-Japanese disputes over territories, and China's unsuccessful bid for the 2000 Olympics further aggravated the Chinese sense of victimhood and strengthened the humiliation discourse. Scott (2008) underscores that China's contemporary national identity is defined in a nationalistic perspective of contemporary Chinese history, in which China is positioned as victim of the hostile West. The humiliation discourse is often used for the making of Chinese national identity which is also increasingly reconstructed in the broader context of modernity and globalization.

Nevertheless, since the reform and open policy in 1978, the influx of foreign investments into China has created immense opportunity for economic growth and employment. Further, the opening of the country's doors and growing economic affluence have also provided Chinese citizens the ability to consume luxury goods or services, such as traveling abroad (Shambaugh 2013). Parenthetically speaking, the opening of China's doors has also propelled the growth of consumerism and consumer culture in the country (Dong and Tian 2009). With more foreign companies and commodities entering China, the growing economic affluence has also provided Chinese citizens the ability to consume luxury goods or services

DOI: 10.4324/9781003111559-6

64   I-Chieh Michelle Yang et al

(Dong and Tian 2009). The advent of consumerism and more importantly consumer culture is cited as an instrumental avenue for Chinese people to exhibit their restored dignity and identity expression (Gerth 2003), allowing them to identify themselves as citizens of a powerful and modern nation (Dong and Tian 2009). It is, however, vital to note that despite the symbolic opening of China's doors and embracement of consumer culture that was developed in the West, China remains an authoritarian state with a tightly censored public sphere. State apparatuses such as Patriotic Education and Central Leading Group for Propaganda and Ideology have remained pervasive and forceful in influencing how Chinese citizens identify as members of their nation. More importantly, despite consumer culture being associated with freedom and emancipation to consume, China's unique socialist system has rendered its consumer culture a paradoxical one. As such, the ways in which Chinese consumers engage in national identity projects in a tightly controlled institutional environment proffers an invaluable analytical ground to advance theoretical understanding of consumer culture. Anchoring these arguments, this chapter seeks to explore how the national identity project is facilitated by the parallel forces of China's humiliation discourse and growing consumer culture. The following part of this chapter delves into the review of extant literature, focusing on how the notion of national identity is increasingly regarded as a postmodern identity crisis and how consumer culture instigates a revival of national identity.

Consumer Culture and International Tourism in China

Consumer culture and consumerism are perhaps instrumental avenues for Chinese people to exhibit their restored dignity. As Gerth (2003) argues, the emergence of Chinese consumer culture has in its way shaped modern Chinese identity. Importantly, he contended that nationalism and Chinese consumer culture are "parallel social forces" that mutually define each other (Gerth 2003, 125). Featherstone (2007) highlights that China's dramatic economic growth since the opening of its doors to foreign investments has also precipitated the growth of consumer culture in the socialist state. Economic reforms led by Deng Xiaoping have reintroduced foreign brands and investments into the country (Chao and Myers 1998); urbanization in key development states, such as Shanghai and Beijing, has similarly introduced modern and Western architecture and influences into the country, providing fertile grounds for consumer culture.

Further, the expanding middle and upper classes in China are said to have an "insatiable appetite for travel," as they see it as an avenue to express their class identities (Hsu and Kang 2009, 704). As the world's greatest source of outbound tourists with the largest tourism spending, Chinese tourists are currently the most sought-after market segment to tourism-dependent nations. With an estimate of 100 million outbound

Chinese tourists traveling internationally by 2020, it is indubitable that China is set to transform the world's tourism landscape (Li 2016). Ong (1997) further asserts that Chinese national identity is no longer confined to the parameters of the country's territory or political ideology, as modernity in China has transformed national identity to one that is mobile and international. Therefore, international tourism may be used as a site for national identity negotiation. This argument seems valid, as Gries (2004) illuminates, national identities evolve through international relations, and in the specific case of China, Chinese national identity is negotiated through its interaction with the world. Guo (2004) further avows that Chinese national identity provides a moral compass for its people and an interpretation of themselves on the world stage and defines how Chinese citizens conduct themselves collectively.

National Identity—A Postmodern Identity Crisis

Hall (1992) notes that identities are increasingly fractured. Modernity and social progress have paved ways for "new identities" to be formed. Accordingly, the growing diversity and fragmentation of cultural landscapes, such as those of social class, gender, sexuality, ethnicity and nationality, have precipitated the "crisis of identity" of individuals—wherein individuals become increasingly active in constructing their respective identities. Nevertheless, Pratt (2003) underscores that as an individual encounters conflicting identities and such fragmentation, they would actively negotiate their identities until they are able to construct an identity that would remain stable. The premise of identity negotiation resonates with the discursive approach which sees the process of identification as a construction, one process that is never complete, as individuals relentlessly seek to construct their identities (Hall 1996). Consumption, in particular, is perceived as an important activity that facilitates identity negotiation. Lamont (2000) avows that the increasing popularity and accessibility of the marketplace offers individuals an alternative channel to perform, affirm, and transform their identities. Therefore, consumption constitutes a felicitous lens and context to examine how collective identity and membership can be acquired in symbolic communities (Lamont and Molnár 2001). It is vital to note that the notion that consumption influences the identity negotiation process has its roots in consumer culture theory (CCT). As a prominent theory in marketing literature, CCT is an overarching theoretical framework that focuses on the relationship between consumer behavior, the marketplace, and cultural meanings (Arnould and Thompson 2005). Parenthetically speaking, consumer culture is constituted by social arrangements in which the relations between culture and social resources or the ways of life and the symbolic interaction with resources are both mediated through markets (Arnould and Thompson 2005).

Consumer Identity Projects

As a principal pillar in CCT, consumer identity projects accentuate the co-constitutive co-productive ways that consumers adopt, along with marketer-generated materials to forge a sense of self (Arnould and Thompson 2005; Belk, Ger, and Askegaard 2003). A plethora of studies have established that consumption plays a significant role in consumers' role and identity negotiation projects (Price, Arnould, and Curasi 2000). Individuals attach symbolic meaning to consumption and possession of goods, which resultantly facilitates identity negotiation and allows individuals to construct their respective narratives of identity (Belk 1988; Price et al. 2000). Further, extant studies on consumer identity projects have explored identity works vis-à-vis material possessions and experiential consumption. On the one hand, the premise that material possession is symbolically used for identity works has its roots in Belk's (1988) venerable conception of the extended self and possession. Based on the proposition that *"we are what we have,"* several studies have explored how different possessions allow individuals or collectives to navigate their identity projects. For instance, a panoply of studies have shown that the identity crisis faced by young people (due to age transitions) has propelled them to rely on material possessions to construct and define their identities (Gabriel and Lang 2006). Piacentini and Mailer (2004) found that young people are compelled to communicate their "maturity and adultness" to others through material possessions (Piacentini and Mailer 2004, 253). Accordingly, teenagers seek to purchase clothes that allow them to fit in with the groups they belong to, and clothing is used to symbolize a link between the individual and their collectivity.

Similarly, material possession also facilitates the negotiation of collective identities. The symbolic meaning of a consumption can be used to reflect a person's affiliation or connection to a collectivity or to allow a collectivity to express themselves (Piacentini and Mailer 2004). As postulated by Baudrillard (1998), the consumption practice of a person is often motivated by a need to exemplify his belonging to his own group. To illustrate, Mehta and Belk (1991) found that a shift in environment would alter the importance of certain possessions to individuals being placed in a foreign environment may engender some form of identity crisis, for example, fundamental differences between Indian and American societies have propelled Indian migrants to be more proactive in consuming items that would allow them to connect with "mother India." Artifacts such as ancestor photographs, heirloom furniture, and traditional clothing are essential anchors to affirm Indian identity. Subsequent studies (Lamont and Molnár 2001) have similarly found how material consumptions allow one to affirm their collective identity.

On the other hand, a growing strand of research has explored how experiential consumption, that is, intangible lived consumption experiences facilitate identity projects (Gilovich, Kumar, and Jampol 2015). Notably, this approach seeks to move forward from Belk's contention that we are the sum of all our possessions and proposes that *"we are what we do, not what we have"* (Carter and Gilovich 2012). Brands, for instance, emerge as a dominant stream of research in understanding experiential consumption. To exemplify Allen, Fournier, and Miller (2008), the experience derived from consumption does not always stem from the products or services; instead, it comes from the meaning attached to the brands, and consumers draw on the symbolic meaning of the brands to negotiate their identities (Ahuvia 2005). In addition, the act of shopping has a symbolic experiential value which allows for one to construct identity (Hammad and El-Bassiouny 2018). Grocery shopping is perceived as a social practice where consumers engage in a "sharing" experience with their loved ones, such as family or partners. It also offers an experience where homemakers feel that they are "in control" as they are able to complete their roles and have the autonomy to choose from a grocer (Woodruffe-Burton and Wakenshaw 2011).

Recently, too, the consumption of leisure activities has also gained traction in the study of consumer identity projects (Dimanche and Samdahl 1994). Various leisure activities such as golfing and tourism have been conceptualized as an important symbolic consumption to express a person's identity. As Sirgy (1982) noted, sign value is an important component in experiential consumption, and leisure activities tend to carry significant sign values, wherein individuals would be motivated to seek experiences that will enhance their identity and self-construct. Hummon (1988) exposited that tourism involves consumption outside one's normalized life; therefore, the symbolic representation of travel is significant for status display in the "socially invisible of everyday life" (Hummon 1988, 180). The following section seeks to expound on the extant literature on identity negotiation and tourism.

Identity Negotiation and Tourism

Tourism entails consumption outside of one's regular social environment; the opportunity that tourism offers for identity expression and symbolic representations is often more conspicuous and preferred (Hummon 1988). Munt (1994) was among the first to discuss how tourism consumption is used for identity construction. He was particularly interested in how postmodern tourists (new middle class) construct their new middle-class identities by traveling to "Third World" destinations such as Ghana and Latin American countries. Accordingly, the new middle class is characterized by a "hegemonic struggle" for cultural and class superiority (Munt 1994, 110), and tourism offers a platform for them to negotiate with

68 *I-Chieh Michelle Yang et al*

their authentic identities. Particularly in less developed destinations, the travel experiences produced a feeling of "uniqueness" (Munt 1994, 108), allowing these individuals to assert their middle-class identities. Scholarly exploration on how tourism facilitates identity works is certainly not novel, research on heritage tourism and diaspora tourism have demonstrated how tourism offers the avenue for experiential consumption and sign value for the identity projects.

On the one hand, research on heritage tourism focuses on how the development of historical heritage sites allows citizens to affirm their cultural identity. Henderson (2001), for instance, explores how the development of heritage sites for inbound tourism in Hong Kong has facilitated identity negotiation for Hong Kong residents. Specifically, the unique circumstance faced by Hong Kong residents, such as being a former British colony and the recent reunification with Mainland China, has resulted in an identity crisis (Lau 1997). Therefore, the development of heritage sites based on its colonial history is seen as an effort to protect "culture and heritage" (Lau 1997, 235) and reminds Hong Kong citizens of their colonial history and affirms their cultural identity. Similarly, Palmer (2005) discusses how sites such as Battle Abbey have allowed English citizens to affirm their Englishness as they are reminded of the values and discourses of the British Nationhood. On the other hand, diaspora tourism refers to the return of migrants to their ancestors' lands. This form of tourism is essential to one's identity making, especially when one is unable to feel a sense of belonging to identity affirmation in the host country (Hall and Williams 2002). As Bandyopadhyay (2008) enumerates, the homeland is conceived as an important place for identity security, as members of a diaspora often experience identity conflict and a dearth of sense of belonging in the host country. Both heritage and diaspora tourism have provided sacrosanct evidence to establish the fruitfulness of tourism in identity works. Nevertheless, there is limited exploration on how international tourism and related experience facilitates the negotiation of one's national identity. Therefore, this study aims to address this gap by understanding how Chinese citizens negotiate their national identity during their international travels. The following section delves into the methodology adopted in this study.

Methodology

This study adopted constructivist grounded theory (Charmaz 2006) as the methodology which posits that the development of theory is grounded in the data that are collected from the field, specifically, "the action, interactions or processes through interrelated categories of information based on data collected from individuals" (Creswell 2007, 63). The lead researcher led the field work from January to December 2018, initially going on three group tours with Chinese tourists traveling around Malaysia as a participant observer. The first two tours consisted of older retirees and the third tour group has a good mixture of tourists of different ages. A couple of tour guides who were personal friends helped her recruit her initial interview candidates and it snowballed from there. She conducted 28 interviews in Mandarin during or after tours or tourist site visits in hotels or neighboring cafes with informants aged 21–72. In addition to this, she also went to independent tourist sites frequented by Chinese tourists to observe and add on to her field notes. All interviews were audio-taped with permission granted by the informants and transcribed verbatim in Chinese and subsequently translated to English. The findings are based on approximately 9 hours of interviews that resulted in 310 pages of transcripts and field notes. Initial open coding and idiographic analyses of field notes and transcripts were performed after every fieldwork. The data were analyzed using a hermeneutic and iterative approach (Spiggle 1994; Thompson 1997) moving between theory and data to identify different codes and categories (Fischer and Otnes 2006) until our themes emerged.

Findings

The analysis identified three themes associated with the identity negotiation of Chinese tourists—a reminder of the past humiliation, rising from the ashes, and surpassing the former enemies. The following section will be discussed vis-à-vis the respective themes. In addition, a thematic map (Figure 4.1) is also developed on the basis of the findings to better illustrate the key themes and how they address the research question.

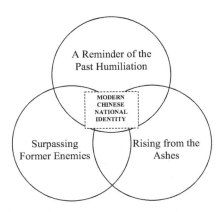

Figure 4.1 Thematic map

70 I-Chieh Michelle Yang et al

A Reminder of the Past Humiliation

This theme illustrates how traveling to another country allows Chinese citizens to be reminded of their past humiliation:

> Sometimes you would see our antiques being displayed in the museums of these countries, it is beautiful, but at the same time, it is also hurtful because it belongs to us, yet to see it, you have to travel to another country. It is saddening.
>
> (Informant N, 28)

According to Informant N, the reminder of Western invasion and hostility during the 19th century becomes prominent when one travels abroad and witnesses the display of Chinese artifacts in foreign museums. The display of the artifacts, which symbolizes the "rape of China," is hurtful to Chinese citizens. Owing to patriotic education and politically engineered history lessons in school, the painful memories of being invaded by foreign powers is etched in the minds of Chinese, even among the young generations. To further exemplify, the recent unfortunate burning of Notre Dame in Paris evokes global sympathy for the French people; however, in China, some netizens consider the incident to be a payback for the French's burning of the Old Summer Palace. Comments such as "this easily reminded of the Yuanming Yuan being burned down by the British and French armies, which was more valuable than Notre Dame. There is a karmic cycle" and "I find it hard to sympathize with the French people" were published on Weibo (the largest microblogging site in China) (Zhuang 2019). These evidences conclusively reflect the ingrained distrust of the French among the Chinese, even when France is a popular travel destination for Chinese.

France has also been singled out by many informants as an unfriendly nation to the Chinese. Both Informant I and Informant C shared that there were several reports of Chinese tourists being treated with hostility.

> I have not been to France, but I heard that French people are really hostile to Chinese, I was not there to experience it, but I have heard from my friends who have been there.
>
> (Informant I, 55)

Informants shared that some countries, particularly western countries, have been less than friendly with Chinese tourists. Some informants have shared that they experienced unfriendliness or hostility from foreigners during travel or have heard from fellow Chinese comrades about the hostility they have experienced. For instance, after traveling to Singapore for her studies, Informant P, a young student in her early 20s observes that "I feel that foreigners don't seem to think highly of Chinese people."

Century of Humiliation and Consumer Culture 71

Correspondingly, Informant T shares that when he was living in Australia for his doctoral studies, both he and his friend had experienced attacks due to their nationality. On one occasion, his friend, who also came from China, had pizza thrown at him while walking on the street. For Informant T, a white Australian student deliberately startled him when he was walking home from university. When asked what the reasons for such hostility could be, he responded that Chinese people are developing too well and that they are too hardworking, and it results in growing jealousy of foreigners. To him, such hostility is "normal" and inevitable as China continues its quest to become a world leader.

Informant T further discusses the constant reporting of misbehavior of Chinese tourists, which is commonly regarded as a politically motivated move by foreign media to tarnish the image of China and Chinese citizens.

> The media is always exaggerating, for example, those kids peeing on the street or garden in foreign countries. What is the big deal? It is not even such a big deal to make it to the headlines, what are you trying to achieve with that?
>
> (Informant T, 34)

To the informant, as well as otherwise expressed by others, it is a norm and common sight in China where children are allowed to urinate on the streets. However, when the same behavior is repeated when Chinese citizens travel abroad and subsequently reported on in the media, Chinese citizens often become defensive. As can be seen in his excerpt, "what are you trying to achieve with that," the informants ascribe the reporting of Chinese tourist misbehavior as a form of a politically motivated move to taint the reputation of China. In 2014, a Chinese tourist was seen instructing her child to pee on a street in Hong Kong. When called out by a local resident, the Chinese couple became enraged and defensive. The video and news report subsequently made it back to China, where netizens expressed outrage over this incident. Their anger, however, was not directed at the parents of the child, but Hong Kongers for "their perceived lack of empathy." Many of them advocated for the boycott of Hong Kong as the Chinese believe that they are god because they are the consumers and that Hong Kong people would "come begging us to go back" (Wong 2014). Informant T's comment, along with such reports, further illustrates how Chinese people believe they are wrongly perceived by others and experience uncalled-for hostility.

Rising From the Ashes

This core category of "rising from the ashes" illustrates the extent to which China has been restored from its previous downfall and of China's economic growth since the reform.

72　I-Chieh Michelle Yang et al

I feel that Chinese people have higher income now and many would like to travel abroad to enjoy themselves. It is a good thing for our people to go out to see and experience other cultures and observe the differences, to experience different places, it is better for them actually.

(Informant U, 26)

As shown in the excerpt, China's economy has successfully revived and citizens enjoy a higher income and have greater economic freedom to engage in luxurious consumption such as international tourism. More importantly, traveling abroad allows Chinese tourists to clearly observe China's economic revival by comparing it with another country. Informant X (30) shares his travel experience in Vietnam and noted that the Southeast Asian nation was parallel to China prior to the reform. "The current Vietnam looks very much like China a few decades ago, with a lot of motorcycles on the street, China used to look like that." Notably, to compare Vietnam and China's current development allowed him to understand how far China has come.

Since the reform, our GDP and national income have all increased. Especially if you look at the exchange rate now, our Chinese Yuan is appreciating against the Singapore dollar. For our currency to constantly appreciate, it shows that China is becoming more powerful on many levels.

(Informant V, 54)

Informant V discussed China's economic revival relative to the country's strong exchange rate against other currencies. She associated China's economic development as a form of power. A plausible interpretation of this excerpt is that when Chinese citizens travel to another country, like Singapore, and observe the difference in the exchange rate, it provides them a sense of economic advantage. The mention of Singapore is perhaps a conscious and deliberate comparison as Singapore has achieved remarkable economic development in recent decades. As the key financial center in Asia, Singapore is officially recognized as a developed country by OECD. However, to know that the Chinese currency is appreciating, especially against a developed Asian country, further affirms their ideal-identity image that China is rejuvenating economically.

Prior to the reform in 1978, China suffered various wars and failed economic plans. For instance, the country's great leader Mao inaugurated various economic plans such as the infamous Great Leap Forward (GLF) in 1958 with hopes of hastening China's pace of modernization (Song 2009). However, wrong plantation methods along with natural disasters led to a drastic decline in agricultural harvest and nationwide famine. The famine, which is also known as the worst man-led famine in human history, had

Century of Humiliation and Consumer Culture   73

calamitous impacts on China's economy (Callahan 2010). Subsequently, the Cultural Revolution in 1966 further deteriorated China's economy. For decades, Chinese citizens suffered from starvation and unemployment. Thus, when Chinese economy began to improve with the reform, Chinese people's hope for national restoration began to sprout. The ability to travel and the massive Chinese tourism market in foreign countries, for instance, have instantiated the recovery of Chinese economy since the reform.

Further, in recent years, China has gradually transformed into a cashless society with the adoption of mobile payment systems such as Alipay or WeChat Pay, the technology which has been subsequently adopted in foreign countries to cater to Chinese tourists.

Some of our informants expressed surprise in seeing the Chinese payment system in foreign countries. They talked about Chinese technology is "advancing" globally. For instance, during a visit to a Mexican restaurant, a country that is geographically far away from China, seeing how companies such as WeChat helped symbolize the extensiveness of China's technological modernization.

In addition to payment methods, our informants commented on the level of technological advances in other areas as well. Specifically, many of our informants expressed confidence in using Chinese-made products during travel, as it would provide them with a greater sense of security. As Informant E contends, Chinese products are made with superior quality, including Chinese airplanes, which has a solid safety record. Informant E has recently retired from the workforce. He has traveled abroad previously, and he shared that he has used different airlines to know that the standard of Chinese airlines is higher than others. The complete trust in Chinese airlines also seems to suggest a collective display of confidence in Chinese technologies.

Surpassing the Former "Enemy"

Under this theme, the informants have shared about how international tourism has allowed them to "realize" that China is developing well and has surpassed former "enemies"—specifically America and Japan.

> I would not deliberately compare, but sometimes, you would not have this revelation that, wow, Shenzhen also has this, or you would feel that Shenzhen is actually better than this place. . . . Sometimes I would feel really proud, because Shenzhen is not just a good and developed city within China, but it is also really good as compared to cities in other countries . . . those big and famous cities such as Tokyo and London, they all have their unique cultures that their people are proud of. It is really admirable, but on other aspects, you will also realize that they are not as good as those in China.
>
> (Informant Q, 22)

74 *I-Chieh Michelle Yang et al*

Alluding from this excerpt, traveling abroad has allowed Informant Q to recognize Shenzhen as a global city that is comparable to Tokyo and London. Informant Q perceives China to be better than countries such as Japan and the United Kingdom. No matter how great these global cities are, they are still unable to offer what cities in China do. While he expresses a genuine unintentional comparison, he is subconsciously looking at the world with the preconceived notion that China is still better than others. More importantly, the others that were mentioned coincidentally are the countries that were involved in wars with China. The First Opium War was with Britain and the First Sino-Japanese War with Japan in the 19th century. These two industrialized countries have been constantly mentioned in Chinese history classes to remind Chinese citizens of how they humiliated and bullied China. This could be interpreted as an internalized and heightened sense of enmity with other countries especially when one travels abroad.

Some informants have noted that China has a growing global power that can exert substantial influence in the region and in the world.

> Well, at least someone is able to compete with America now. . . . America is seeking to be the center of the universe and that everything revolves around their country. That is why China is rising from the third world nations to compete with America economically.
>
> (Informant S, 28)

First, Informant S highlights the form of hegemony that America seeks to obtain by stating that "America is seeking to be the center of the universe"; however, his statement can be interpreted as a form of disdain toward America. To most Chinese, America's global dominance is seen by Chinese people as a form of undesirable hegemony. In addition, about China, he also mentioned "at least someone is able to compete with America now" to signify the extent of China's rejuvenation—that it is now able to compete with the former world leader, America. More importantly, the statement can be further inferred as a sense of Chinese heroism and altruism. Chinese people see their rejuvenation not only as a benefit for China but also that China's growing power can be extended to as far as Africa.

Discussion

The findings demonstrate that as Chinese citizens navigate and define their national identity during their international travels, they are nevertheless bound by the humiliation discourse. It is vital to understand that humiliation is an integral part in Chinese national identity. Under the theme of "a reminder of the past humiliation," the informants have revealed how their travel experiences have reminded them of China's past "humiliation." Through visiting countries such as France, which was a part of the

Western coalition that invaded China, Chinese citizens have reportedly been treated poorly, reflecting and reliving the previous hostility that Chinese people experienced by the Western powers. Notably, the rising cases of Chinese tourists being victims of criminal activities such as robbery in European countries, as well as the exhibition of Chinese artifacts strongly reminded the informants about their humiliating past and how they were bullied by the West. Further, some informants have also discussed being discriminated against during travel, further amplifying a sense of victimhood where Chinese people are despised and treated poorly by Westerns. To further illustrate, the inauguration of "National Humiliation Day" in 2004 is a deliberate political engineering of CCP to remind the population of the country's past. This important holiday, which is commonly known as the 918 day to the Chinese, falls on September 18 of each year, commemorating Japan's invasion, and conquest of Manchuria in 1931. The slogan, "never forget national humiliation" (*wuwang guochi*) is repeated by every Chinese leader. Along with other initiatives, such as the Patriotic Education program where all Chinese students are required to take history classes and visit historical sites (such as the ruins of the Old Summer Palace), the CCP has successfully imbued a strong logic of humiliation among Chinese citizens. This study demonstrates how international tourism, similar to state apparatus such as education, reinforces the unpleasant national history of foreign invasion.

The theme "rising from the ashes," on the other hand, shows how the act of traveling abroad is a way to show that the country has overcome hardship, as people are now affluent and can afford travel (Hsu, Cai, and Wong 2007). Following the conclusion of the Second World War in 1945 and China's economic development since 1979, Chinese people seem more eager to engage in consumption as well as to demonstrate to the world China's present developments. As Oakes (1998) explains, China's national identity is largely shaped by the collective aspirations to restore their pride and dignity as the descendants of the Yellow Emperor (*yan huang zi sun*) and Dragon and to obtain wealth and power. These aspirations are etched in the collective memories of Chinese citizens and embedded in national identity making. Chinese citizens are inherently proud of their nation's civilization and past glory, along with its rapid economic developments, Chinese people are seemingly eager to demonstrate to the world their national identity in various ways.

Moreover, traveling abroad also gives Chinese citizens a chance to visit other countries to draw comparisons with China. These comparisons allow them to observe how China is progressing relative to other countries, such as Malaysia and the United States. As Wang (2014) notes, the concept of revival is ingrained in China's national experience and collective memory, representing the desire to be "strong, prosperous and free of foreign invasion," and it is an integral constituent to a successful construction of China's modern national identity (Wang 2014, 11). In addition, the spending propensity of the Chinese and desire to consume luxury products has resulted in major tourism destinations adopting Chinese online payment systems, such as WeChat and Alipay. More importantly, the adoption of Chinese systems is perceived by the Chinese as the rising importance of Chinese people, further confirming China's revival from past downfall.

Further, as exemplified in the final theme, "surpassing the former enemy," Chinese citizens have capitalized on their travel experiences to affirm how they have surpassed rival countries. Importantly, to advance the humiliation discourse and to lead the Chinese population to experience a sense of victimhood, a common enemy is required. The United States and Japan appear to be two countries that are in constant dispute with China. Recently, too, events such as the US bombing of the Chinese embassy in Belgrade, the international uproar of the Tiananmen massacre in 1989, the continual Sino-Japanese disputes over territories, and China's unsuccessful bid for the 2000 Olympics have further aggravated the Chinese's sense of victimhood (Guo 2004). More importantly, it further validates CCP's constant ideological agenda of painting CCP as the savior of the Chinese nation who are devoted to restoring the Middle Kingdom. Having a national enemy, specifically when these countries did invade China, is proven to be useful in mobilizing the Chinese population to advance the political agenda of the CCP. As demonstrated in this study, the informants have drawn upon history with these countries, as well as the ongoing political disputes to illustrate their national identity. More to the point, with the younger generations (including the younger informants in this study) becoming cognizant of the country's sad history, CCP has been able to harness and retain its political power and achieve legitimacy (Wang 2014).

To wit, China's contemporary national identity is defined in a nationalistic perspective of contemporary Chinese history, in which the Chinese Communist Party has positioned China as victim of the hostile West (Callahan 2010; Scott 2008). More importantly, the discourse of humiliation can be seen as an outcome of the continuous interplay between historical trajectories and political engineering. Specifically, the Chinese government under Mao's leadership had capitalized on the "national humiliation" (guochi) discourse in the country's identity politics. Through national education and propaganda, Chinese citizens are constantly reminded of atrocities committed by Western imperialists (including Japan) and how China was labeled as the "Sick Man of East Asia" by these evil enemies (Tang and Darr 2012). To the Chinese, the profound sense of humiliation was particularly directed at the Western powers for being evil and jealous of China's ancient civilization and cultural superiority. These historical impressions have precipitated greater anti-western nationalism in China, specifically in recent decades, when China's development and aspiration to rejuvenate are met with obstruction from the same Western powers.

Century of Humiliation and Consumer Culture 77

To this end, these national discourses engineered by the CCP continue to influence how consumer culture is developed in China (Dong and Tian 2009; Zhao and Belk 2008), and how Chinese consumers negotiate their national identity through consumption.

To summarize, international tourism provides an opportunity to compare China with other nations. Several informants have lived through hardship, such as the widespread famine and Cultural Revolution under Mao's regime. Decades, or even centuries of hardship, have created the general perception of China as the "Sick man of East Asia" (Gries 2004, 71). The open-door policy in the late 1980s, however, has greatly alleviated China's protracted economic and social predicaments. The experience and participation in the country's growth, from past difficult times to the current economic status, has given these informants a sense of attachment to the nation. The communist party has also devoted considerable effort to instill patriotism by creating a Chinese national identity. National humiliation and victimhood have been used by the government as a discourse in Chinese identity politics (Wang 2014, 2).

Conclusion

In essence, this study has demonstrated the ways in which Chinese tourists use tourism as a consumption instrument to negotiate their identity, predominantly by affirming and expressing what it means to be a Chinese in the modern world. Evidently, the Chinese tourists in this study have shown conspicuous efforts to negotiate their national identities during their travels, exemplified in their proclivities to compare themselves with the quality of life in the destination country, or to believe that countries depend heavily on Chinese tourists. More specifically, it allowed them to invalidate the humiliating "Sick Man of East Asia" narrative by exhibiting their international and economic influences through traveling. Traveling abroad has allowed Chinese citizens to recognize their country as the "Strong Man of East Asia." This first scholarly attempt to examine how Chinese citizens negotiate their national identity in the tourism context has uncovered important findings that are unique to the Chinese consumer culture context. Given that Chinese people are known to be economically affluent and generous consumers, future research can be initiated to investigate identity negotiation of Chinese national identity in relation to other aspects of consumer culture, such as how branding is influenced by the Chinese national identity and how social media plays a role in shaping national discourse among younger citizens. Further, the cases of hostility toward Chinese tourists deserve further scholarly exploration—particularly with the increasing bilateral tension between China and the Western countries. How political circumstances or even race politics propagate negative attitudes toward Chinese tourists need to be further unpacked.

References

Ahuvia, Aaron C. (2005), "Beyond the Extended Self: Loved Objects and Consumers' Identity Narratives," *Journal of Consumer Research*, 32 (1), 171–84 (https://doi.org/10.1086/429607).

Allen, C.T., Susan Fournier, and F. Miller (2008), "Brands and Their Meaning Makers," in *Handbook of Consumer Psychology*, ed. C.P. Haugtvedt, P.M. Herr, and F.R. Kardes, London: Lawrence Erlbaum Associates, 781–822.

Arnould, Eric J. and Craig J. Thompson (2005), "Consumer Culture Theory (CCT): Twenty Years of Research," *Journal of Consumer Research*, 31 (4), 868–82 (https://doi.org/10.1086/426626).

Bandyopadhyay, Ranjan (2008), "Nostalgia, Identity and Tourism: Bollywood in the Indian Diaspora," *Journal of Tourism and Cultural Change*, 6 (2), 79–100 (https://doi.org/10.1080/14766820802140463).

Baudrillard, Jean (1998), *The Consumer Society: Myths and Structures*, London: Sage.

Belk, Russell (1988), "Possessions and the Extended Self," *Journal of Consumer Research*, 15 (2), 139–68 (https://doi.org/10.1086/209154).

Belk, Russell, G. Ger, and Soren Askegaard (2003), "The Fire of Desire: A Multisited Inquiry Into Consumer Passion," *Journal of Consumer Research*, 30 (3), 326–52 (https://doi.org/10.1086/378613).

Callahan, William A. (2010), *China: The Pessoptimist Nation*, Oxford: Oxford University Press.

Carter, Travis J. and Thomas Gilovich (2012), "I Am What I Do, Not What I Have: The Difference Centrality of Experiential and Material Purchases to the Self," *Journal of Personality and Social Psychology*, 102 (6), 1304–17 (https://doi.org/10.1037/a0027407).

Chao, Linda and Ramon H. Myers (1998), "China's Consumer Revolution: The 1990s and Beyond," *Journal of Contemporary China*, 7 (18), 351–68 (https://doi.org/10.1080/10670569808724319).

Charmaz, Kathy (2006), *Constructing Grounded Theory: A Practical Guide Through Qualitative Analysis*, London: Sage.

Creswell, John W. (2007), *Qualitative Inquiry and Research Design: Choosing Among Five Approaches*, 2nd edition, Thousand Oaks: Sage.

Dimanche, Frédéric and Diane Samdahl (1994), "Leisure as Symbolic Consumption: A Conceptualization and Prospectus for Future Research," *Leisure Sciences*, 16 (2), 119–29 (https://doi.org/10.1080/01490409409513224).

Dong, Lily and Kelly Tian (2009), "The Use of Western Brands in Asserting Chinese National Identity," *Journal of Consumer Research*, 36 (3), 504–23 (https://doi.org/10.1086/598970).

Featherstone, Mike (2007), *Consumer Culture and Postmodernism*, 2nd edition, London: Sage Publications.

Fischer, Eileen and Cele Otnes (2006), "Breaking New Ground: Developing Grounded Theories in Marketing and Consumer Behaviour," in *Handbook of Qualitative Methods in Marketing*, ed. Russell Belk, Northampton, MA: Edward Elgar, 19–30.

Gabriel, Yiannis and Tim Lang (2006), *The Unmanageable Consumer*, London: Sage.

Gerth, Karl (2003), *China Made: Consumer Culture and the Creation of the Nation*, Cambridge, MA: Harvard University Press.

Gilovich, Thomas, Amit Kumar, and Lily Jampol (2015), "A Wonderful Life: Experiential Consumption and the Pursuit of Happiness," *Journal of Consumer Psychology*, 25 (1), 152–65 (https://doi.org/10.1016/j.jcps.2014.08.004).

Gries, Peter H. (2004), *China's New Nationalism: Pride, Politics and Diplomacy*, Los Angeles: University of California Press.

Guo, Yingjie (2004), *Cultural Nationalism in Contemporary China: The Search for National Identity Under Reform*, London: Routledge Curzon.

Hall, Colin M. and Allen M. Williams (2002), *Tourism and Migration*, Dordrecht: Springer.

Hall, Stuart (1992), "The Question of Cultural Identity," in *Modernity and Its Futures*, ed. Stuart Hall, David Held, and Tony McGrew, Cambridge: Polity Press, 274–323.

—— (1996), "Who Needs Identity," in *Questions of Cultural Identity*, ed. Stuart Hall and Paul du Gay, London: Sage, 1–17.

Hammad, Hadeer and Noha El-Bassiouny (2018), "'I Shop Therefore I Am': Social and Psychological Transformations in Conspicuous Consumption," *Luxury Research Journal*, 1 (4), 303–24 (https://doi.org/10.1504/LRJ.2018.090974).

Henderson, Joan (2001), "Heritage, Identity and Tourism in Hong Kong," *International Journal of Heritage Studies*, 7 (3), 219–35 (https://doi.org/10.1080/13527250120079402).

Hsu, Cathy H.C., Liping A. Cai, and Kevin K.F. Wong (2007), "A Model of Senior Tourism Motivation: Anecdotes From Beijing and Shanghai," *Tourism Management*, 28 (5), 1262–73 (https://doi.org/10.1016/j.tourman.2006.09.015).

Hsu, Cathy H.C. and Soo K. Kang (2009), "Chinese Urban Mature Traveller's Motivation and Constraints by Decision Autonomy," *Journal of Travel & Tourism Marketing*, 26 (7), 703–21 (https://doi.org/10.1080/10548400903284537).

Hummon, D.M. (1988), "Tourist Worlds: Tourist Advertising, Ritual and American Culture," *The Sociological Quarterly*, 29 (2), 179–202 (https://doi.org/10.1111/j.1533-8525.1988.tb01250.x).

Lamont, Michèle (2000), *The Dignity of Working Men: Morality and the Boundaries of Race, Class, and Immigration*, Cambridge, MA: Harvard University Press.

Lamont, Michèle and Virág Molnár (2001), "How Blacks Use Consumption to Shape Their Collective Identity: Evidence From Marketing Specialists," *Journal of Consumer Culture*, 1 (1), 31–45 (https://doi.org/10.1177/146954050100100103).

Lau, Siu-Kai (1997), "Hongkongese or Chinese: The Problem of Identity on the Eve of Resumption of Chinese Sovereignty Over Hong Kong," in *Social Development and Political Change in Hong Kong*, ed. Siu-Kai Lau, Hong Kong: Chinese University Press.

Li, Xiang (2016), *Chinese Outbound Tourism 2.0*, Oakville: Apple Academic Press.

Mehta, Raj and Russell Belk (1991), "Artifacts, Identity, and Transition: Favourite Possessions of Indians and Indian Immigrants to the United States," *Journal of Consumer Research*, 17 (4), 398–411 (https://doi.org/10.1086/208566).

80   I-Chieh Michelle Yang et al

Munt, Ian (1994), "The 'Other' Postmodern Tourism: Culture, Travel and the New Middle Classes," *Theory, Culture and Society*, 11 (3), 101–23 (https://doi.org/10.1177/026327694011003005).

Oakes, Tim (1998), *Tourism and Modernity in China*, London: Routledge.

Ong, Aihwa (1997), "Chinese Modernities: Narratives of Nation and of Capitalism," in *Undergrounded Empires: The Cultural Politics of Modern Chinese Transnationalism*, ed. A. Ong and Donald Nonini, London: Routledge, 171–202.

Palmer, Catherine (2005), "An Ethnography of Englishness: Experiencing Identity Through Tourism," *Annals of Tourism Research*, 32 (1), 7–27 (https://doi.org/10.1016/j.annals.2004.04.006).

Piacentini, Maria and Greig Mailer (2004), "Symbolic Consumption in Teenagers' Clothing Choices," *Journal of Consumer Behaviour: An International Research Review*, 3 (3), 251–62 (https://doi.org/10.1002/cb.138).

Pratt, Michael G. (2003), "Disentangling Collective Identities," in *Identity Issue in Groups*, Vol. 5, ed. Jeffrey T. Polzer, West Yorkshire: Emerald Publishing Limited (https://doi.org/10.1016/S1534-0856(02)05007-7).

Price, Linda, Erick J. Arnould, and Caroline F. Curasi (2000), "Older Consumers' Disposition of Special Possessions," *Journal of Consumer Research*, 27 (2), 179–201 (https://doi.org/10.1086/314319).

Scott, David (2008), *China and the International System: 1840–1949*, New York: State University of New York Press.

Shambaugh, David (2013), *China Goes Global*, Oxford: Oxford University Press.

Sirgy, Joseph M. (1982), "Self-Concept in Consumer Behaviour: A Critical Review," *Journal of Consumer Research*, 9 (3), 287–300 (https://doi.org/10.1086/208924).

Song, Shige (2009), "Does Famine Have a Long-Term Effect on Cohort Mortality? Evidence form the 1959–1961 Great Leap Forward in China," *Journal of Biosocial Science*, 41 (4), 469–91 (https://doi.org/10.1017/S002193 2009003332).

Spiggle, Susan (1994), "Analysis and Interpretation of Qualitative Data in Consumer Research," *Journal of Consumer Research*, 44 (1), 491–503 (https://doi.org/10.1086/209413).

Tang, Wenfang and Benjamin Darr (2012), "Chinese Nationalism and Its Political and Social Origins," *Journal of Contemporary China*, 21 (77), 811–26 (https://doi.org/10.1080/10670564.2012.684965).

Thompson, Craig J (1997), "Interpreting Consumers: A Hermeneutical Framework for Deriving Marketing Insights from the Texts of Consumers' Consumption Stories," *Journal of Marketing Research*, 34 (4), 438–55 (https://doi.org/10.2307/3151963).

Wang, Zheng (2014), "The Chinese Dream: Concept and Context," *Journal of Chinese Political Science*, 19 (1), 1–13 (https://doi.org/10.1007/s11366-013-9272-0).

Wong, Hiufu (2014), "Chinese Call for Boycott of Hong Kong after Urine Incident," (https://edition.cnn.com/travel/article/chinese-boycott-hk-urine-incident/index.html).

Woodruffe-Burton, Helen and Susan Wakenshaw (2011), "Revisiting Experiential Values of Shopping: Consumers' Self and Identity," *Marketing Intelligence & Planning*, 29 (1), 69–85 (https://doi.org/10.1108/02634501111102760).

Zhao, Xin and Russell Belk (2008), "Politicizing Consumer Culture: Advertising's Appropriation of Political Ideology in China's Social Transition," *Journal of Consumer Culture*, 35 (2), 231–44 (https://doi.org/10.1086/588747).

Zhuang, Pinghui (2019), "Notre Dame Fire Attracts Wave of Sympathy in China, But Some Web Users Revive Old Grievances Over Destruction of Old Summer Palace," *South China Morning Post* (www.scmp.com/news/china/society/article/3006409/notre-dame-fire-attracts-wave-sympathy-china-some-web-user).

5 Predicting a Mother's Role in Investing in Children's Education

A Study on Autonomy and Empowerment From India

Akshaya Vijayalakshmi, Meng-Hsien (Jenny) Lin, and Sarah Ricks

Introduction

Educational status is viewed as a critical factor in an individual's identity construction. This chapter explores the connection between investment in children's education and a mother's autonomy. We focus on education since it plays a pivotal role in upward mobility (Asher, Novosad, and Rafkin 2018). Given that India's per capita income is still low compared to the western economies (World Bank 2019), the cost of educating children is likely to take up a relatively high share of a family's resources and monthly spending. The decision to allocate a higher percentage of the budget to children's education is challenging yet promises a better future for families. Research in economics and psychology disciplines addressing this topic suggests that a mother's autonomous status is a critical determinant of investment in children's future (Mencher 1988). The investments made in advancing children's education are believed to lead to future generations' enhanced well-being. In this chapter, we aim to achieve the following: (a) consider the impact of a mother's level of autonomy on her children's educational expenditures and (b) differentiate the construct of autonomy from psychological empowerment.

We examine the mother, a key player in family decision-making, and her impact on her children's educational expenditure. Previous research shows that the independent status of a woman plays a key role in many consumption decisions made at home pertaining to the family and children (Amin and Becker 1998). For example, a mother's autonomous status has a substantial influence on a child's educational attainment (Korupp, Ganzeboom, and Lippe 2002), survival (Fantahun, Berhane, Wall, Byass, and Högberg 2007), and health condition (Senarath and Gunawardena 2009). We extend the decision domain from educational attainment to educational investments and postulate that all forms of a woman's autonomy are likely to impact educational expenditures.

DOI: 10.4324/9781003111559-7

Mother and Children's Education Investment   83

This chapter is set in India, a country with the largest youth population today, with close to 400 million people under the age of 14. Some researchers have observed that India has the potential to reap a large demographic dividend because of its population profile and by providing quality education that will help improve the next generations' ability to contribute to the society (Aiyar and Mody 2013). Previous studies have empirically substantiated the link between various dimensions of a mother's autonomy and their investments in their children's well-being (Korupp et al. 2002; Fantahun et al. 2007; Senarath and Gunawardena 2009). First, we consider: *what is the link between a mother's autonomy and children's educational investments?* The measures for autonomy capture few behaviors of the woman. These behavioral measures, however, do not provide insights into how the individual feels about their sense of empowerment from these arrangements, which we argue is key to driving change in gender roles. Hence in this chapter, we also ask the question: *what is the relationship between a mother's level of autonomy and psychological empowerment?* Psychological empowerment is a multidimensional construct which includes intrapersonal and interactional empowerment as its dimensions (Zimmerman 1995; Zimmerman 1990). Intrapersonal empowerment is seen as a component or trait of someone's character that strongly impacts one's control over their decision-making (Zimmerman 1995). Interactional empowerment is based on having awareness and understanding of your sociopolitical environment and knowing how you fit into your community and ways by which you can bring about change (Zimmerman 1995). For the rest of this chapter, we refer to psychological empowerment as its entirety when empowerment is mentioned.

We used a mixed-method approach consisting of analysis of a nationwide survey data, followed by qualitative interviews conducted with Indian mothers. One key recommendation from our study is that psychological empowerment, rather than a level of responsibility-based autonomy, may better capture a woman's influence on her children's educational investments.

Overall, our study while focusing on women and their level of autonomy and empowerment could inform related fields of study such as the role women play in a patriarchal society; children and their education competing for family resources; and a system of children's education that is deficient and requires families to opt for higher-cost alternatives. This study is timely given the renewed focus of the Indian government on education, especially for girls (*Beti Bachao, Beti Padhao* Save the Daughter, Educate the daughter 2015 campaign) and concerns about falling labor force participation rates for women in India (The Economist 2018). This research should be of potential interest to researchers working on vulnerable consumers and emerging markets, interest groups empowering women, and corporations taking a social marketing approach.

84 *Akshaya Vijayalakshmi et al*

Autonomous Women

In the last several decades, consumer research has considered the changing nature of gender roles and decision-making within families (Venkatesh 1980). The majority of such gender research has focused on Western nations and assumes that a wife/mother could assert her autonomy and identity at will. The assumption of equal choice and independence as a commodity for all women, however, is questionable. There are several constraints on women's autonomy in India. For instance, women perform worse than men on several counts—literacy rate (68% versus 86%), being married before the age of 18 years (27% versus 20%), or having comprehensive knowledge of HIV (21% versus 33%) (see the National Family Health Survey 2015–16). Even products as ubiquitous as a mobile phone are only owned and used by 46% of women. Dyson and Moore (1983) go to the extent to say that understanding women's social status is the most vital factor in comprehending India. Given the heterogeneity in women's autonomy, we study the possible significant impact of this difference on decision-making related to children and their education.

Hirschmann (1997) coined the phrase women as agents and characterized them as self-reliant and independent individuals. Similarly, Nobel Laureate Amartya Sen (1999) argued that a woman's well-being is dependent on her agency to bring about change. In marketing, consumer behavior researchers have mainly studied the influence of autonomy on consumers' decisions and decision-making ability (Palan, Gentina, and Muratore 2010). Research across several fields—philosophy, psychology, economics, and others—has recognized the importance of one's autonomy (in our context, the women's) to achieve their potential, which in turn can contribute to their individual and societal well-being (Ryan and Deci 2006).

If autonomy is essential for an individual's well-being, how do we nurture autonomy? Autonomy thrives when an individual has opportunities to make meaningful choices (Ryan and Deci 2006). An autonomy-supporting environment allows independent critical thinking and decision-making (Soenens and Beyers 2012). Conversely, autonomy is stifled in the presence of enticing rewards or coercive conditions such as surveillance, punishment, and threats. Another means by which autonomy is minimized is conditional regard, that is, affection or regard that is contingent on meeting certain expectations (Ryan and Deci 2006). For example, parents' use of conditional regard can reduce self-esteem and increase feelings of rejection and shame in children (Assor, Roth, and Deci 2004). Overall, research concludes that an autonomy-supportive environment is likely to enhance individuals' performance and well-being (Ryan and Deci 2006).

Several definitions of autonomy have been proposed, and the most common definition is that it reflects the ability of a woman to make decisions for herself and others (Palan et al. 2010). In more specific terms, "the ability . . . to obtain information and to use it as the basis for making decisions about one's private concerns and those of one's intimates" (Dyson and Moore 1983, 45). In general, it is believed that a woman with higher autonomy can make better and perhaps more informed choices on events in her life, even if her husband and/or other family members may disagree with her decision (Bloom, Wypij, and Das Gupta 2001). Dixon-Mueller (2013) links autonomy to the degree of access to and control over material and social resources within the family. In sum, autonomy is defined by (a) access to resources (such as material, information, and knowledge) and (b) the extent of voice or agency in the use of such resources in matters affecting oneself and one's families (Bloom et al. 2001). Agency gives women the ability to formulate strategic choices and decisions, for themselves or others, that affect important life outcomes. In the context of children's education, we examine women's role as an agent having direct influence on decisions related to providing resources for their children's pursuit of education. Hence, we posit that women with autonomy are better positioned to negotiate domestic expenditure demands, thus increasing spending on their children's education.

The different forms of resources over which a woman could exercise her agency include cash, household income, assets, welfare receipts, and participation in paid employment, whereas nonmaterial forms include information and knowledge. Access to these resources can enhance the ability of women to exercise choice. Lloyd and Blanc (1996) found that household resource allocation toward children's education is higher when women have more control over the family's resources. Another study on household data from Asian and African countries found that when the wife, compared to the husband, had control over assets, significant expenditures were allocated toward education, health, and clothing (and less on luxury consumption or tobacco) (Roushdy 2004). Further, women who engaged in the workforce and have an independent source of income are likely to have higher control over resources although some have argued that women may work out of necessity (Hoodfar 1990, 1997; Early 1993) and that their income-earning activity may not provide them complete control over the resources they generate (Nawar, Lloyd, and Ibrahim 1994).

In an instrumental role, women with autonomy are more likely to use the resources available to them for their children's benefit (Quisumbing 2003). Overall, maternal altruism is suggested to lead to better household outcomes (Desai and Johnson 2005). Because the majority of India has a patrilineal structure, we define autonomy for this study as the extent to which women have a voice in matters affecting themselves and their families and have some control over the allocation of family resources (Amin and Becker 1998). In this study, we aim to demonstrate that a woman's autonomy is not just beneficial for personal growth but also has a positive influence on future generations through financial investment in children's

86   *Akshaya Vijayalakshmi et al*

education. We expect and hypothesize that *a mother's autonomy is positively related to her children's education expenditures.*

Study 1: Autonomy and Educational Expenditures

Data Description

A nationwide, large-scale survey dataset from the India Human Development Survey (IHDS) 2011–12 (Desai and Vanneman 2015) was used for study 1. We consider the autonomy variables from this survey, which is also widely used by economists and development studies scholars (Barik, Desai, and Vanneman 2018; Basu and Desai 2016). IHDS comprises a nationally representative sample of 41,152 Indian households from 1,503 villages and 971 urban neighborhoods in India. Given our interest in educational spending for children, we screened the data to include only women with school-age children, which resulted in 36,662 qualifying women. The survey covered several topics, including questions related to income and social capital, education and health, and women's role in household decision-making and gender relations. Other relevant questions include household spending on various purchases, including expenditures for their children's education. The calculated total expenditures made for each child consist of the total amount spent on his/her school fees, private tuition fees, and expenditure on books and uniforms annually.

Participants

The mean age of the sample is 37.12 years (SD = 9.49). Seventy-three percent of these women were in the age range of 28–50 years. The average age of the women at marriage was 17.93 years (SD = 3.72). Forty percent of the women surveyed were illiterate, with only 5.5% of them having received a Bachelor's degree or above. Almost 88% of women were not educated beyond 10th grade. The average number of children the women had was 2.75 (SD = 1.43); 67% of the women were from rural parts of the country, and the remaining 33% lived in urban areas. The majority (34.7%) of these women had two children, while 24.9% had three children. The average annual income of the family was ₹ 123,114.

Women's personal life decisions, current work status, and financial freedom are fundamental to the understanding of a woman's level of autonomy. We first conducted a descriptive analysis of pertinent background information of the women. Sixty-two percent of the women who believed that they would be allowed to work if a suitable job was available. Majority of the women participated in arranged marriage, indicating that they did not have a say in choosing their husband, while only 14% of women had an opportunity to talk to their future husbands on the phone

Mother and Children's Education Investment   87

before their marriage. The percentage of women who had a bank account was 54%, and only 15% had homeownership or a rental with their name on it. More than 85% of the women surveyed expected to stay with their son (versus daughter) when they become old. The average percentage of household expenditure on education expenses was 6.3%. We also found that women who had been to college (above 12th grade) spent more on children's education than those who had not received college-level schooling (₹ 22,081 versus ₹ 4,518; $p < .01$).

Measurement of Autonomy and Education Spending

Past studies have identified four dimensions of autonomy: mobility, realized (financial) autonomy, natal family relations, and influence on child-related decisions (Amin and Becker 1998). To operationalize autonomy in the traditional sense, we followed Amin and Becker's (1998) procedure and used these four dimensions of autonomy from the IHDS survey to create an index score for women's autonomy. Mobility autonomy was measured in the survey with the question, "Please tell us whether you have to ask permission from your husband or a senior family member to do the following: visit the doctor, visit relatives, visit the store and travel short distances by train or bus." Realized (financial) autonomy was measured with the help of four questions: "Do you have a say in land/property purchase?" "Is your name on the house rental?" "Do you have cash in hand for household expenditures?" and "Is your name on the bank account?" The responses to the questions were recorded on a nominal scale of yes/no. Natal family relational autonomy, which is seen as an indicator for the level of freedom an Indian woman has, since traditionally women live with their husband's family after the wedding and occasionally visit their natal family for short durations. Natal family relation was measured by the following questions: "How often do you visit your natal family?" "How often do members from your natal family visit you?" "How often do you speak to someone on the phone from your natal family?" The three items were answered on a 5-point ordinal scale, where 1 was "daily/weekly" and 5 was "less than once a year." To capture parenting and child-related decisions, we used the following questions from the survey on who in the family decides "the number of children to have," "what to do when a child falls sick," and "whom should your child marry."

A descriptive analysis of these four dimensions of autonomy, including the items used to measure the dimensions, has been provided in Table 5.1. A factor analysis of the items further confirmed that the items fall onto the four identified dimensions—mobility, realized (financial) autonomy, natal family relations, and child-related decisions. The Kaiser-Meyer-Olkin test was significant ($p < .01$), with the measure of sampling adequacy being .68.

88   *Akshaya Vijayalakshmi et al*

Table 5.1 Key Descriptive and Measurements Used for Study 1

	N	Mean	Std. deviation
Natal family autonomy	36,662	.51	.15
Visit natal	36,662	.41	.20
Natal visits	36,662	.41	.21
Speak natal	36,662	.65	.22
Mobility autonomy	36,662	.18	.26
Visit doctor	36,662	.14	.31
Visit relative	36,662	.21	.36
Visit store	36,662	.27	.40
Short distance	36,662	.11	.27
Realized (financial) autonomy	36,662	.59	.24
Land/property decision	36,036	.74	.44
Cash in hand	36,662	.91	.29
Name in bank account	25,737	.54	.50
Name in rental	36,662	.15	.36
Child decision autonomy	36662	.86	.26
Number of children	36,662	.92	.27
Child falls sick	36,662	.85	.36
Child marriage	39,523	.82	.39

In the IHDS-II dataset, educational expenditure was measured at the household level. Given the typical multihousehold family structure in India, we controlled for household size. We ran two models for this study. The first model had just the independent variables and the second model included the control variables. Previous studies have found variables such as income, rural/urban location, religion, caste, parent's education, and age to impact educational expenditures (Kugler and Kumar 2017; Menon 1998). Hence, similar control variables were included in the analysis.

Regression Results

To address our research question, we estimated the impact of women's autonomy on the educational expenditure within the household (expressed as a percentage of the household income). As expected, the prediction model, including control variables, had a significant impact on the educational spending of the family ($F(4, 34,907) = 278.57, p < .01$). Among the four dimensions of autonomy, natal relations had a partially significant positive relationship with children's education expenditure ($\beta = .01, p < .10$) while realized autonomy had an insignificant positive relationship ($\beta = .00, p > .05$). Interestingly, mobility ($\beta = -.01, p < .01$)

Mother and Children's Education Investment 89

and noneducational child-related decisions ($\beta = -.01$, $p < .05$) had a significant negative impact on educational expenditures, going against our expectations.

The *F* values in the models with and without control variables indicate that the control variables account for a much larger proportion of variance in the dependent variable. Among the control variables, income ($\beta = .16$, $p < .01$), education of mother ($\beta = .19$, $p < .01$), number of children in the household ($\beta = -.07$, $p < .01$), and age of mother ($\beta = .09$, $p < .01$) have a significant impact on children's educational expenditure. Families living in urban areas ($\beta = .06$, $p < .01$), in comparison to those living in rural areas, spend more on their children's education. Religion, whether being Hindu ($\beta = -.02$, $p > .05$) or Christian ($\beta = .00$, $p > .05$), did not have a significant impact on children's education expenditure. However, Muslim mothers ($\beta = -.04$, $p < .05$) did not have a significant positive say on their children's education expenditure. Further details of the results are provided in Table 5.2.

Table 5.2 Regression Results for Study 1 (Autonomy and Education Expenditures[a])

	Model 1			Model 2		
	β	t-value	p-value	β	t-value	p-value
Autonomy						
Mobility	−.01	−2.04	.04	−.01	−2.66	.01
Realized autonomy	.00	.82	.41	.00	.90	.37
Natal family	.06	10.60	.00	.01	1.67	.09
Children decision	−.01	−2.55	.01	−.01	−2.13	.03
Control variables						
Education				.19	30.49	.00
Number of children				−.07	−12.10	.00
Age				.09	14.99	.00
Income				.16	30.02	.00
Urban				.06	10.98	.00
Hindu				−.02	−1.13	.26
Muslim				−.04	−2.79	.01
Christian				.00	.04	.97
Sikh				.04	4.70	.00
Brahmin				.01	.97	.33
Forward				.01	.57	.57
OBC				−.03	−1.41	.16
SC				−.02	−1.91	.06
ST				−.05	−3.04	.00

a. Dependent Variable: Education expenditure (in Rupees)

Discussion

In contradiction to our expectations that autonomy should play an important role in predicting education investments, the results of study 1 offered a strong signal that women's autonomy may not fully explain the phenomenon of interest. We find that an increase in a woman's mobility and her involvement with noneducation-related decision-making for her children are associated negatively rather than positively with family expenditure on children education. Similarly, Chatterji (2018) found no association between a mother's decision-making and investments in her children's education when also using the same IHDS database. Looking at the other two dimensions, natal relations only marginally predicted the family's spending on a child's education; and financial autonomy was not related to educational spending at all.

Several explanations can be offered for these findings. First, could it be possible that women's autonomy does not matter in the education investment decision? However, this does not appear to be a reasonable explanation as Indian women generally take an active role in shaping their children's future (Kaur and Singh 2006). Second explanation is that the autonomy scale used in the study may have generalizability issues. The four dimensions of the autonomy scale—mobility, financial autonomy, natal relations, and decision autonomy—reflect a general state of autonomy that may not apply to all contexts, including the one examined in this study. The items in the autonomy scale focus on capturing a woman's ability to run a household (e.g., make grocery purchases) but do not pay much attention to emotions and decisions related to herself (Basu and Koolwal 2005). Third, the wording of the autonomy questions could have made the role or identity of the "wife" becomes salient, prioritizing women's household responsibilities over other personal identities (Hein et al. 2016). Basu and Koolwal (2005) suggest that autonomy measures should instead focus on women exercising choice and freedom, rather than focusing on gender-centered roles and responsibilities of the wife and mother as expected by the social conventions. Instead, the autonomy measure should also capture self-indulgent and nonproductivity-based activities, such as media consumption or going out to meet a friend. Finally, it is also possible that the women being surveyed may not fully understand the meaning of autonomy as presented in local Indian languages (Jeffery and Jeffery 1997).

At the least, there appears to be some operationalization issues to this rather popular autonomy scale, possibly resulting in the unexpected findings. To investigate this possibility further, we conducted in-depth interviews with Indian mothers in the next study to gain a deeper understanding of what other factors may influence women's role in their children's education.

Mother and Children's Education Investment   91

Study 2: Understanding Autonomy in Modern India

Methods and Participants

Five mothers living in Ahmedabad, Gujarat, India, were interviewed by one of the authors. The women were asked questions regarding their employment, social status, media usage, and children's education. The interviews were conducted in Hindi (a language in which the interviewer and participants could speak fluently), and each lasted between 20 and 45 minutes. All participants interviewed were recruited via convenience sampling and had at least one school-attending child between ages of 10 and 15. The interviews were conducted at a place of convenience for the participant, such as their homes or close to their work location (see Table 5.3 for more details about the participants). While the sample size is small, we got an opportunity to discuss various issues in depth, thus gaining quality information.

Findings and Themes From the Interviews

Significance of Children's Education

All five women felt that educating their children (compared to achieving other life goals such as their careers or buying a home, etc.) was of utmost importance. The women were willing to take up additional jobs to increase their resource base or leave their current jobs to devote more

Table 5.3 Details of the Participants for Study 2

Pseudonym	Employed	Children (grades)	Age	Children taking private tutorials	School type	Owns smart-phone
Geetha	Yes	Boy (10th) Boy (8th)	25–35	Yes	Run by a private charitable trust	Yes
Varsha	Yes	Girl (3rd), Boy (kindergarten)	25–35	Yes	Private	Yes
Bhuvana	Yes	Girl (12th), Girl (8th)	35–45	No	Private	Yes
Srividya	No	Girl (10th), Boy (5th)	35–45	Yes	Private	Yes
Nithya	Yes	Girl (12th)	25–35	No	Government	Yes

92   Akshaya Vijayalakshmi et al

time to their children and sacrifice vacations or family get-togethers to get their children a good quality education.

For example, Bhuvana says she has tried to give her children the best possible education as it will help them climb up the social ladder. She works from 9 AM to 2 PM and then again from 5 PM to 8 PM, traveling to six houses to cook their lunch or dinner. She works six days a week. Bhuvana said she has to work hard in order to educate her children well. Her husband is a cook at a restaurant and takes up additional odd jobs such as cleaning cars. He works from 6 AM to 10 AM and then from 4 PM to 2 AM. The story was no different for the other participants, working long and hard hours. The participants believed that only through their hard work they can contribute to improving their child's educational status, which for them reflected their commitment to their children's development.

Moreover, all the children of the participants interviewed attended private schools. Some of the main reasons noted were that it is widely believed that private schools provided a better-quality education, their teacher absenteeism was low, and English was the medium of instruction. Additionally, three of the mothers interviewed had enrolled their children in private tutoring to supplement their school education. In fact, Geetha, one of the participants said that she moved her son from free to paid tuition when he started tenth grade. She believed that "paid tuition" meant that her son would get better quality education. Overall, parents appear to believe that spending more on education was the way to achieve superior educational performance.

Safety Concerns May Mask the Impact of Mobility

All interviewed women had high realized autonomy. That is, they had their bank accounts, worked out of home for income, and traveled to work independently. Although all five women had financial freedom, they relied on their husbands to travel everywhere, including within the city. The women considered it safe to travel with their husbands rather than being on their own, which according to the typical indicators of autonomy, would appear as if women had low levels of freedom. Further, if the participants traveled alone (again, even within the city grounds), they usually consulted with their family members before doing so. We found that this was primarily for safety reasons.

> "I go with my husband to malls, hospital, or clinic. I don't travel alone. The only time I travel alone is when I take the standard route to work or when I have done some grocery shopping."
>
> (Varsha)

Public transportation is reported to be unsafe for women, and several instances of harassment have been reported (Shah, Viswanath, Vyas, and

Gadepalli 2017). Recent research using data from Google Maps and a travel app, Borker (2018) found that 25% of women (versus 5% men) in Delhi were willing to attend a lower-quality institution for the reason that the commute between home and school was safer. In fact, women were also willing to pay 16 times more than men for a more reliable commute (Borker 2018). In the same study, close to 90% of female college students reported incidents of harassment during their commute to school. In such an unsafe society, it is not surprising to find that even the most autonomous women prefer to rely on their male family members to travel within and outside the city. Similar scenes played out when our participants visited their families in different towns/villages. They usually traveled with their husbands to visit their parents because of safety concerns. Because the travels were longer, they were required to consult with their husband to plan the trip. This could explain why the mobility dimension of the autonomy construct in the previous study negatively correlated with educational expenditures, countering our expectations.

In sum, women in India with high realized autonomy rarely travel on their own due to external factors such as societal safety concerns. Thus, reflecting what we found in study 1, women with low mobility still exhibit high levels of autonomy, playing a critical role in decisions related to their children's educational plans.

Financial Concerns May Weaken the Relevance of Autonomy

Similar to travel, women consulted their husbands when making significant household purchase decisions as they wanted to be cautious about their expenditures. Many of them had tight monthly budgets to spend on daily purchases, which limited their freedom to spend on big-ticket items without any discussion with their spouse. Therefore, women said they consulted their husbands in most major purchase decisions except daily grocery purchases.

> Our incomes are such that we have to survive on hand-to-mouth existence every month. That means we have to spend every *paisa* (penny/ cent) carefully. So my husband and I discuss every expenditure, be it school fees or books or clothes for our boys' birthdays.
>
> (Geetha)

Availability of resources often has higher priority than women's autonomy on educational spending decisions. Especially, since the data in study 1 reflected actual spending and not intentions to spend. Take the case of Geetha whose sons study in a private school run by a trust. According to her, the school was expensive for her family and was located farther away from home, but she feels that it is the right choice for her children's future. Geetha mentioned that she has taken up sewing so that she can earn a little bit

94 Akshaya Vijayalakshmi et al

more to pay for her son's private tuition. She also occasionally sells clothes to acquaintances to supplement her monthly income. Similarly, Bhuvana and her husband recently started delivering home-cooked food to various families, in addition to the jobs they do. They want to make sure that their wards receive college education and attain better jobs than the ones the parents themselves hold. This is similar to what we found in study 1, showing income plays a significant role in educational spending.

Collective Family Decision-Making

Being part of a collectivistic culture, it made sense that Indian families made decisions on most things collectively. Varsha mentioned that she and her husband make decisions together when they are buying clothes for themselves or the family. Geetha mentioned that when it comes to daily household decisions, she decides on her own. However, for other significant decisions, she consults her husband. Extended families have tight-knit relationships. Geetha visits her mother and extended family of brothers and sisters-in-law on a daily basis. During these visits, everyday matters are discussed and advice on various issues are jointly considered. What we find is that women have the habit of consulting their husbands, if not the extended family, on most matters. Similarly, Varsha mentioned that she and her husband together decide which school their children should study in. However, this does not necessarily mean that the women lack autonomy. The joint decision-making is the cultural way-of-life.

What Empowers a Woman?

According to the qualitative interviews, women's equality in the partner-ship is likely to depend on the extent to which they feel empowered in the relationship. A woman is expected to feel empowered when she considers herself to be a significant actor of change rather than merely being a recipient of change (Mishra and Tripathi 2011); autonomy makes no such demands of the individual. Thus, a woman can be autonomous (e.g., free to travel) but still not feel empowered. From the interviews, we find that even if a woman is capable and free to lead her life on her terms, she might depend on others for her safety and well-being.

Overall, the interviews help shed light on what seems like the traditional measures of autonomy are in opposition to women's development and well-being, especially when social norms and cultural expectations are considered. When autonomy is juxtaposed against everyday life's complex reality from safety concerns to limited financial resources, we conclude that the current measure of autonomy appears to fall short. On the basis of the two studies, we reach upon a conclusion that autonomy is a complex construct that is much more nuanced, often influenced and dependent on the cultural and societal circumstances. Hence, the field standard form of autonomy measures do not fully provide the theoretical basis for predicting families' investments in children's education in India. External social conditions and internal resource issues limit the relevance and exercise of autonomy by women within Indian families. Instead, these factors are reflected in a stronger emphasis on the partnership between the man and the woman, especially when making essential spending decisions.

To address this deficiency in the current measure, we propose that focusing on psychological empowerment may better capture feelings of power and freedom, accounting for cultural and societal realities. According to Zimmerman (1995), psychological empowerment is a multidimensional construct—intrapersonal empowerment (measured by self-efficacy, perceived competence, and control) and interactional empowerment (measured by collective action and interpersonal relationships). Together, these two components of psychological empowerment may provide a better explanation for the role of empowerment on a mother's spending on educational resources, hence more relevant than autonomy.

Psychological empowerment focuses on how people gain personal skills, confidence, and community support to achieve their goals (Zimmerman 1995). Parents with intrapersonal empowerment (a component of psychological empowerment) were more likely to mediate the impact of social media influencers on their children (Lin, Vijayalakshmi, and Laczniak 2019). We believe that the women we interviewed felt certain about helping their children reach certain levels of education (i.e., psychological empowerment) even if they did not exercise personal liberties such as travel or purchase (i.e., autonomy) without consulting and getting approval from their husbands. For instance, Geetha, Varsha, and Bhuvana mentioned that they would take up additional jobs to fund their children's education. This determination and certainty demonstrates self-belief and competence rather than lack of autonomy. We find that a lack of autonomy, as traditionally measured by travel etc., does not necessarily mean a woman is less empowered. Future studies could further confirm this proposition about the impact of psychological empowerment on educational expenditures.

General Discussion

The primary objective in this chapter is to understand how mothers' level of autonomy affects allocation of resources for children's education. We focus on mothers since their beliefs and views have a more significant impact on decisions for their children (Vijayalakshmi, Lin, and Laczniak 2018; Lin et al. 2019). To investigate this relationship, we examined autonomy in its original form and measurement and evaluated its relevance to a family's resource allocation decision. The context of our study takes place in India, where we find that psychological empowerment, rather than autonomy, has more significant implications for furthering

96 Akshaya Vijayalakshmi et al

children's future and well-being. In this chapter, small but essential steps were taken to promote the need for more balanced gender roles, especially mothers and their critical role in enhancing the well-being and quality of life for their future generations.

Contradicting our expectations, we find that not all dimensions of autonomy necessarily lead to increased educational expenditure. This could well be one of the possible reasons why researchers have not ventured down this path of examining the relevance of women's autonomy in critical decisions such as educational expenditure. However, we were able to provide insights into these counterintuitive findings presented in study 1 by using a qualitative interview approach in study 2. Based on the interviews conducted with mothers, it appears that autonomy could be perceived as responsibilities or, in some instances, not indicative of societal limitations (e.g., freedom to travel is worthless if the roads are not safe for women). The qualitative analysis identified that what appears to be critical is a woman's *perceptions* of being free and powerful (i.e., the focus of empowerment) rather than merely the freedom she has to conduct certain activities (i.e., the focus of autonomy). Further, our results suggest that merely granting women the freedom to travel or freedom to visit their natal families has no bearing on educational spending decisions. Instead, we find that educational spending is related to *feelings* of power and capacity for change. The psychological sense of empowerment is critical for the well-being of the self and family. Therefore, we suggest that empowerment (versus autonomy) better predicts positive educational expenditure.

It should be noted that we are not suggesting that the onus for family welfare be entirely on the woman. Given the differences in social norms between India and other western countries, unless societal norms and attitudes change in India, women's autonomy may not have the same impact it has seen in different societies and contexts. As demonstrated in our studies, even highly empowered women living in patriarchal societies like India may find their power reduced and their decisions vetoed. A woman will need societal freedom to exercise her empowered feelings (Wathieu et al. 2002). Khader (2016, 128) states that "transformations in (an) individual's psychic capacities do not simply vanish structural barriers." Therefore, despite the focus on the woman in the household in this study and others, there is an equal and urgent need to bring about structural changes to the current patriarchal setup in society and families such as ones in India.

Research in marketing has mostly considered education in two contexts—educating the consumer or effectively teaching marketing at the university level. We expand the current boundaries by examining factors related to expenditure on secondary schooling. Through findings from our studies, we show methods by which marketers could play a role in this life-changing consumption decision—investing in a child's education. By borrowing key constructs from economics and psychology, we also contribute to them by reimagining them in a newer light.

Mother and Children's Education Investment   97

Limitations and Future Research

Findings from the studies are tempered by the data and design limitations. One aspect to keep in mind is that the study was conducted in a collectivistic and patriarchal cultural setting. While the results could be generalized cautiously to 1.2 billion people, the question of external validity for other countries might be a difficult one to answer. Future research should replicate the study in individualistic and less patriarchal cultures, perhaps even beyond women to include men. Further, while study 1 had a representative sample, study 2 was limited to urban cities. Future research should consider and extend the results to rural settings. Another significant limitation of the study, which is beyond the scope of this chapter, is that we have not considered the role of fathers/husbands in supporting children/wives. Their voice in the education spending decision-making process is not observed, but we believe it is critical for future studies building on this research to take that into account. To better understand how (and whether there is societal change), a longitudinal study could also be conducted by comparing IHDS-I survey data with IHDS-II to help develop more robust insights into this topic.

The women interviewed in this study indicated they did not have the time to watch TV programs as they were preoccupied with their jobs and household chores. However, they owned smartphones and relied on them for communication, entertainment, and social interaction purposes. "When my regular phone stopped working, my daughters insisted that I get a smartphone. I use WhatsApp on it now to communicate with friends and family. . . . I hardly have any time to watch TV. I watch a little TV, some serial (family drama) when I go home in the afternoon, mostly to fall asleep (Bhuvana)." Research suggests that social media enables participation, which increases feelings of empowerment. Bucy and Gregson (2001) found that mere involvement in social media, even if it did not involve decision-making, induced empowerment. Researchers studying gender-related issues suggest the need for social media groups, which through online interactions facilitate learning, reflection, analysis, and action (Khader 2016). Social media such as Facebook or WhatsApp groups provide such a space, where the latter has become a dominant social media platform in India. Finally, other forms of research approaches such as experiments could be conducted to establish causal relationships between social media use, empowerment, and decision-making.

Data Collection Information

The data for study 1 are from a publicly available database—Indian Human Development Survey. The second author analyzed the data for this study. The data for study 2 were collected primarily by the first author in December 2019. The data were analyzed jointly by the first and second

98　*Akshaya Vijayalakshmi et al*

authors. The data are currently stored in the personal computers of the first and second authors.

Acknowledgments

We would like to thank Dr. Sridhar Ramaswami (professor, Iowa State University) and Dr. Shwadhin Sharma (associate professor, California State University Monterey Bay) for their help with the paper.

References

Aiyar, Shekhar and Ashoka Mody (2013), "The Demographic Dividend: Evidence from the Indian States," *India Policy Forum, National Council of Applied Economic Research*, 9 (1), 105–48.

Amin, Ruhul and Stan Becker (1998), "NGO-promoted Microcredit Programs and Women's Empowerment in Rural Bangladesh: Quantitative and Qualitative Evidence," *Journal of Developing Areas*, 32 (2), 221–36 (https://doi.org/10.2307/4192755).

Asher, Sam, Paul Novosad, and Charlie Rafkin (2018), "Intergenerational Mobility in India: Estimates from New Methods and Administrative Data," *World Bank Working Paper* (www.dartmouth.edu/~novosad/anr-india-mobility.pdf).

Assor, Avi, Guy Roth, and Edward Deci (2004), "The Emotional Costs of Parents' Conditional Regard: A Self-Determination Theory Analysis," *Journal of Personality*, 72 (1), 47–88 (https://doi.org/10.1111/j.0022-3506.2004.00256.x).

Barik, Debasis, Sonalde Desai, and Reeve Vanneman (2018), "Economic Status and Adult Mortality in India: Is the Relationship Sensitive to Choice of Indicators?" *World Development*, 103, 176–87 (https://doi.org/10.1016/j.worlddev.2017.10.018).

Basu, Alaka and Sonalde Desai (2016), "Hopes, Dreams and Anxieties: India's One Child Families," *Asian Population Studies*, 12 (1), 4–27 (https://doi.org/10.1080/17441730.2016.1144354).

Basu, Alaka and Gayatri B. Koolwal (2005), "Two Concepts of Female Empowerment—Some Leads From DHS Data on Women's Status and Reproductive Health," in *A Focus on Gender—Collected Papers on Gender Using DHS Data*, ed. Unita Kishor, Calverton, MD: ORC Macro, 15–33.

Bloom, Shelah S., David Wypij, and Monica Das Gupta (2001), "Dimensions of Women's Autonomy and the Influence on Maternal Health Care Utilization in a North Indian City," *Demography*, 38 (1), 67–78 (https://doi.org/10.1353/dem.2001.0001).

Borker, Girija (2018), "Safety First: Perceived Risk of Street Harassment and Educational Choices of Women," *Job Market Paper* (https://data2x.org/wp-content/uploads/2019/11/PerceivedRiskStreetHarassmentandEdChoicesofWomen_Borker.pdf).

Bucy, Erik P. and Kimberly S. Gregson (2001), "Media Participation: A Legitimizing Mechanism of Mass Democracy," *New Media and Society*, 3 (3), 357–80 (https://doi.org/10.1177/1461444801003003006).

Chatterji, Sangeeta (2018), "Like Mother like Daughter: Mothers' Education and Investment in Daughters' Education in India," PhD dissertation, Rutgers Uni-

Mother and Children's Education Investment 99

versity-School of Graduate Studies (https://rucore.libraries.rutgers.edu/rutgers-lib/58951/PDF/1/).

Desai, Sonalde and Kiersten Johnson (2005), "Women's Decision-Making and Child Health: Familial and Social Hierarchies," in *A Focus on Gender*, ed. Sunita Kishor, Calverton, MD: ORC Macro.

Desai, Sonalde and Reeve Vanneman (2015), "India Human Development Survey-II (IHDS-II) 2011–12," *ICPSR36151-v2*, Ann Arbor, MI: Inter-university Consortium for Political and Social Research [distributor], 31.

Dixon-Mueller, Ruth B. (2013), *Rural Women at Work: Strategies for Development in South Asia*, New York: Routledge.

Dyson, Tim and Mick Moore (1983), "On Kinship Structure, Female Autonomy, and Demographic Behavior in India," *Population and Development Review*, 9 (1), 35–60 (https://doi.org/10.2307/1972894).

Early, Evelyn A. (1993), *Baladi Women of Cairo: Playing With an Egg and a Stone*, Boulder, CO: Lynne Rienner.

Economist, The (2018), "Why India Needs Women to Work," (www.economist.com/leaders/2018/07/05/why-india-needs-women-to-work).

Fantahun, Mesganaw, Yemane Berhane, Stig Wall, Peter Byass, and Ulf Högberg (2007), "Women's Involvement in Household Decision-making and Strengthening Social Capital—Crucial Factors for Child Survival in Ethiopia," *Acta Pædiatrica*, 96, 582–89 (https://doi.org/10.1111/j.1651-2227.2007.00147.x).

Hein, Aung, Kyan Htoo, L. Seng Kham, Myat Thida Win, Aye Mya Thinzar, Zaw Min Naing, Mi Win Thida, Ni Lei, Lu Min, and Naw Eh Mwee (2016), "Rural Livelihoods in Mon State, Myanmar: Evidence from a Representative Household Survey," *Feed the Future Innovation Lab for Food Security Policy*, 1–136 (https://doi.org/10.22004/ag.econ.259064).

Hirschmann, Nancy J. (1997), "Eastern Veiling, Western Freedom?" *The Review of Politics*, 59 (3), 461–88 (https://doi.org/10.2307/1408548).

Hoodfar, Homa (1990), "Survival Strategies in Low Income Households in Cairo," *Journal of South Asian and Middle Eastern Studies*, 13 (4), 22–41.

—— (1997), *Between Marriage and the Market: Intimate Politics and Survival in Cairo*, Berkeley, CA: University of California Press.

Jeffery, Roger and Patricia Jeffery (1997), *Population, Gender and Politics: Demographic Change in Rural North India*, Cambridge: Cambridge University Press.

Kaur, Pavleen and Raghbir Singh (2006), "Children in Family Purchase Decision Making in India and the West: A Review," *Academy of Marketing Science Review*, 8, 1–30.

Khader, Serene (2016), "Beyond Autonomy Fetishism: Affiliation with Autonomy in Women's Empowerment," *Journal of Human Development and Capabilities*, 17 (1), 125–39 (https://doi.org/10.1080/19452829.2015.1025043).

Korupp, Sylvia E., Harry B. Ganzeboom, and Tanja Van Der Lippe (2002), "Do Mothers Matter? A Comparison of Models of the Influence of Mothers' and Fathers' Educational and Occupational Status on Children's Educational Attainment," *Quality and Quantity*, 36 (1), 17–42 (https://doi.org/10.1023/A:1014393223522).

Kugler, Adriana D. and Santosh Kumar (2017), "Preference for Boys, Family Size, and Educational Attainment in India," *Demography*, 54 (3), 835–59 (https://doi.org/10.1007/s13524-017-0575-1).

100 *Akshaya Vijayalakshmi et al*

Lin, Meng-Hsien, Akshaya Vijayalakshmi, and Russell N. Laczniak (2019), "Toward an Understanding of Parental Views and Actions on Social Media Influencers Targeted at Adolescents: The Roles of Parents' Social Media Use and Empowerment," *Frontiers in Psychology*, 10, 2664 (https://doi.org/10.3389/fpsyg.2019.02664).

Lloyd, Cynthia B. and Ann K. Blanc (1996), "Children's Schooling in sub-Saharan Africa: The Role of Fathers, Mothers, and Others," *Population and Development Review*, 22 (2), 265–98 (https://doi.org/10.2307/2137435).

Mencher, Joan (1988), "Women's Work and Poverty: Women's Contribution to Household Maintenance in South India," in *A Home Divided: Women and Income in the Third World*, ed. Judith Bruce and Daisy Dwyer, Stanford, CA: Stanford University Press, 99–119.

Menon, Maria Eliophotou (1998), "Factors Influencing the Demand for Higher Education: The Case of Cyprus," *Higher Education*, 35 (3), 251–66 (https://doi.org/10.1023/A:1003047014179).

Mishra, Nripendra Kishore and Tulika Tripathi (2011), "Conceptualising Women's Agency, Autonomy and Empowerment," *Economic and Political Weekly*, 26 (11), 58–65 (www.jstor.org/stable/41151972).

National Family Health Survey (NFHS-4) (2015), *Ministry of Health and Family Welfare*, Assam, India (www.dhsprogram.com/pubs/pdf/FR338/FR338.AS.pdf).

Nawar, Laila, Cynthia B. Lloyd, and Barbara Ibrahim (1994), "Women's Autonomy and Gender Roles in Egyptian Families," Presented at the *Population Council Symposium on Family Gender and Population Policy: International Debates and Middle Eastern Realities*, Cairo, Egypt.

Palan, Kay M., Elodie Gentina, and Isabelle Muratore (2010), "Adolescent Consumption Autonomy: A Cross-cultural Examination," *Journal of Business Research*, 63 (12), 1342–48 (https://doi.org/10.1016/j.jbusres.2010.01.001).

Quisumbing, Agnes R. (2003), "Social Capital, Legal Institutions, and Property Rights: Overview," in *Household Decisions, Gender and Development: A Synthesis of Recent Research*, Washington, DC: International Food Policy Research Institute, 139–44.

Roushdy, Rania (2004), "Intra Household Resource Allocation in Egypt: Does Women's Empowerment Lead to Greater Investments in Children?" *Population Council, West Africa and North Asia Region*. Working Paper 041011, 306–26, (http://paa2011.princeton.edu/papers/110550.)

Ryan, Richard M. and Edward L. Deci (2006), "Self-regulation and the Problem of Human Autonomy: Does Psychology Need Choice, Self-determination, and Will?" *Journal of Personality*, 74 (6), 1557–86 (https://doi.org/10.1111/j.1467-6494.2006.00420.x).

Sen, Amartya (1999), *Development as Freedom*, New York: Anchor Books.

Senarath, Upul and Nalika Sepali Gunawardena (2009), "Women's Autonomy in Decision Making for Health Care in South Asia," *Asia Pacific Journal of Public Health*, 21 (2), 137–43 (https://doi.org/10.1177/1010539509331590).

Shah, Sonal, Kalpana Viswanath, Sonali Vyas, and Shreya Gadepalli (2017), "Women and Transport in Indian Cities: A Policy Brief," *Institute for Transportation and Development Policy* (www.researchgate.net/profile/Sonal_Shah11/publication/322330719_Women_and_Transport_in_Indian_Cities/links/5b7f9f134585151fd12e7a0d/Women-and-Transport-in-Indian-Cities.pdf).

Mother and Children's Education Investment   101

Soenens, Bart and Wim Beyers (2012), "The Cross-Cultural Significance of Control and Autonomy in Parent—Adolescent Relationships," *Journal of Adolescence*, 35 (2), 243–48 (https://doi.org/10.1016/j.adolescence.2012.02.007).

Venkatesh, Alladi (1980), "Changing Roles of Women—A Life-Style Analysis," *Journal of Consumer Research*, 7 (2), 189–97 (https://doi.org/10.1086/208806).

Vijayalakshmi, Akshaya, Meng-Hsien Jenny Lin, and Russell N. Laczniak (2018), "Managing Children's Internet Advertising Experiences: Parental Preferences for Regulation," *Journal of Consumer Affairs*, 52 (3), 595–622 (https://doi.org/10.1111/joca.12177).

Wathieu, Luc, Lyle Brenner, Ziv Carmon, Amitava Chattopadhyay, Klaus Wertenbroch, Aimee Drolet, John Gourville, A.V. Muthukrishnan, Nathan Novemsky, Rebecca K. Ratner, and George Wu (2002), "Consumer Control and Empowerment: A Primer," *Marketing Letters*, 13 (3), 297–305 (https://doi.org/10.1023/A:1020311914022).

World Bank (2019, May 5), "GDP Per Capita—India," (https://data.worldbank.org/indicator/NY.GDP.PCAP.CD?locations=IN).

Zimmerman, Marc A. (1990), "Taking Aim on Empowerment Research: On the Distinction Between Individual and Psychological Conceptions," *American Journal of Community Psychology*, 18 (1), 169–77 (https://doi.org/10.1007/BF00922695).

———— (1995), "Psychological Empowerment: Issues and Illustrations," *American Journal of Community Psychology*, 23 (5), 581–99 (https://doi.org/10.1007/BF02506983).

Section III
Consumer Rituals

6 Gift-Giving and Kinship-Making

Male Phoenix in China

Jia Cong and Xin Zhao

Introduction

Male rural migrants seeking upward social mobility in urban China are often referred to as "male phoenix": they grows up in rural areas but obtains higher education and settle in major cities through their own efforts, talent, and diligence (Wu and Treiman 2004). In Chinese society, their marriages into urban families are widely perceived as inappropriate and often stigmatized because of different values and practices that each class embraces. The challenges of such interclass marriages can be seen in a post in the popular Chinese social media platform *Douban: I am a local Shanghainese girl, with an HR job in a foreign company. . . . I have a partner in a stable/serious relationship, and he is smart and works really hard. . . . My parents are strongly against this relationship. My boyfriend wanted me to go to his rural home and have a family dinner with his extended family. I agreed, but when I arrived in his hometown, I was astonished to see the terrible circumstance and I cannot bear his family's lifestyle. I just wanted to go back to Shanghai at that time and I am now thinking whether I should end this relationship (Douban 11 February 2016).* Although the male phoenix is portrayed negatively in popular culture representations, countercultural narratives emphasize their hardworking and self-made characters. Gift-giving plays important roles in bridging and integrating these social differences.

The widespread phenomenon of the male phoenix in contemporary China provides a rich theoretical context to study kinship-making through gift-giving and other consumption practices in a modern society, in which indigenous kinship systems are often jeopardized by rapid social changes and social mobilities. In this chapter, we examine how modern kinship is made through gifts among these male phoenixes, their wife, and their extended families. We regard kinship-making as an important mode of relating in the social worlds (Sahlins 2011), so is gift-giving (Sherry 1983). Our findings suggest that marriage does not necessarily legitimize the bonding connection of affinity and that gifts help to consolidate the conflicting relationships between urban and rural extended families and

DOI: 10.4324/9781003111559-9

106 *Jia Cong and Xin Zhao*

to bridge the sociocultural differences between the male phoenix and
the urban girl in contemporary Chinese society. The mixed reciprocities within the extended family that we have found here extend Sahlin's
(1972) notions of generalized, balanced, and negative reciprocity based
on kinship distance. In this small social world of extended families, gifts
play more active roles in constructing and integrating social relationships
than what Cheal (1988) may have suggested in his work on the role of
gifts in the moral economy.

Gift-Giving and Kinship-Making

Gift-giving is among the most important instruments in establishing and
maintaining social relationships, especially in courtships and marriages,
and among family members (Belk 1996; Caplow 1982; Cheal 1988; Mauss
1925/1990). In their study of gifts exchange among different case hierarchy
in India, Vatuk and Vatuk (1971) found that people from a lower caste are
not expected to return gifts received from those of a higher caste. Yan's
(1996) work suggested that it might not be the case in China, where gift-
giving from a lower social class to a higher social class is probably more
normal. Marriage is regarded as one of the most important ritualized gift-
giving occasions in China (Cohen 1976), in which such hierarchical gift-giving can be observed (Yang 1989, 1994). Marriage gift may attain nuanced
meanings when the groom is from a lower social status in comparison to
the bride's family. In this study, we focus on examining how both ritualized
and nonritualized gifts integrate interclass marriages of *the male phoenix.*

Kinship refers to "mutuality of being, or people who are intrinsic to
one another's existence of life itself" (Sahlins 2011, 2). It is created not
only by procreation or a collective arrangement of common descents,
but more importantly by social construction and performance (Schneider
1980). For instance, the Iñupiat in Alaska create and expand their kinship
through names and naming. Children are named after the dead and made
members of namesakes' families. A brand community also suggests such
a loose sense of symbolic kinship. Within the small social worlds that
are dominated by a moral economy (Cheal 1988), gifts help to create a
sense of mutuality, or a sense of the "intersubjective belonging" (Sahlins
2011, 2). Similarly, mutual help and a sense of community are common
among members of strong brand community. The intentional practice of
gift-giving in order to produce beneficial effects also resonates with other
modes of relating in the social world. The symbolic act of sharing food
also generates a sense of kinship as seen in New Guinea Highlands. Kinship is thus important for us to understand a variety of consumer behavior
in contemporary society. In consumer culture theories, gift-giving has
been examined in various family contexts and gifting occasions (Joy 2001;
Otnes, Lowrey, and Kim 1993). However, it remains to be theorized
how gift-giving establishes and sustains a family, an extended family,

Gift-giving and Kinship-making 107

or a kinship network. To a certain extent, extended kinship network is more important in sustaining social solidarity in collectivist societies than nuclear families in individualist countries in which most previous gifting studies have been conducted.

On the basis of kinship distance, Sahlins (1972) differentiates generalized, balanced, and negative reciprocity. Generalized reciprocity aims at giving assistance, and values are expected to balance over time. Reciprocation is influenced by what the receiver needs, rather than self-interested calculation of gains and losses. Generalized reciprocity sustains one-way flow for an extended period of time, in which the failure to reciprocate may not stop the giver from giving. Balanced reciprocity expects a fair return, and the reciprocation is an equivalent exchange without delay. It resembles an economic exchange in which the gifts of commensurate value are exchanged within a short term. Negative reciprocity is an exchange in which both gift givers and receivers seek to gain from the transaction and to maximize each other's own interests at the other's expense. Sahlins (1972) contended that close kinship relations are more likely to invite generalized reciprocity. As we move away from kinship relations, equivalence in exchange becomes more compulsory. The farther away from home and kinship, the more likely gifts exchange will take the form of negative reciprocity. Reciprocity is also influenced by social rank (Gouldner 1960).

However, in such notions of reciprocity, kinship is already established. We study how gift-giving and reciprocity may help to establish kinship in the context of a modern consumer society. We also examine how failed reciprocity may renounce kinship. In particular, we explore how the male phoenix uses gifts to manage relationships within extended families and regain a sense of respect from stigmatized identity in contemporary China through ethnographic approach.

Methods

The data for this study were collected over a two-year period in both Northern and Southern China, Shandong province and Shanghai. Ethnographic in-depth interview and ethnographic observation (Elliott and Jankel-Elliott 2003) were adopted for data collection. Interviews were conducted during in informants' homes or coffee shops by participants' choices.

The fieldwork and in-depth interview took place with 25 participants in the Houbanmiao Village and Shanghai Marriage Market (see Table 6.1). The choice of the two different areas was to obtain cultural-historical variations in order to understand different gift exchange. Houbanmiao Village, located in the southwest of Shandong province, is a moderate farming community that grows mostly garlic and millet, known as "the land of garlic." The first author conducted fieldwork and interviewed 10 *male phoenixes* and their parents from the village. Due to social norms, such as face, Renqing, shame, and modesty, the participants are naturally

108 *Jia Cong and Xin Zhao*

Table 6.1 Participants' Demographic Profiles

Pseudonym	Age	Sex	Occupation	Education	Status	Family background
Shenhao	24	M	Student	Master	Girlfriend	Business owner
Dongdong	30	M	Project manager	Master	Girlfriend	Doctor/business owner
Guopeng	26	M	Uni lecturer	PhD	Single	Government agency staff
Huqiang	25	M	Student	PhD	Girlfriend	Manual worker
Yangyang	32	M	Middle manager	BA	Married	Military
Jiaxing	32	M	Chemical researcher	BA	Married	Farmer
Jiangjie	40	F	Business owner	BA	Married	State-owned enterprise CEO
Wangchen	40	M	Teacher	BA	Married	Worker
Yangfan	33	M	Photographer	College	Divorced	Worker
Liran	25	M	Researcher	PhD	Girlfriend	Farmer
Liangxiao	24	M	Project manager	BA	Girlfriend	Doctor/uni lecturer
Lulu	29	M	Uni lecturer	PhD	Married	Farmer
Mahui	36	M	Associate professor	PhD	Married	Farmer
Dingqian	37	F	Senior manager	Master	Married	State-owned enterprise worker
Xiaoming	40	M	Senior engineer manager	PhD	Married	Farmer
Haidong	41	M	Uni lecturer	PhD	Married	Farmer
Wangfeng	45	M	Lawyer	Master	Married	Farmer
Wangjiufeng	34	M	Doctor	Master	Married	Farmer
Wangxia	40	F	Business owner	BA	Married	State-owned enterprise worker
Yangjiu	38	M	Associate professor	PhD	Married	Carpenter
Yaoqianqian	27	M	Project manager	Master	Single	Teacher
Wangjia	38	F	Business owner	BA	Married	State-owned enterprise worker
Yifei	25	F	Project manager	BA	Boyfriend	Civil servant
Daijun	40	M	Business owner	College	Married	Farmer
Daipan	36	M	Salesman	BA	Married	Farmer

reluctant to expose emotions and share private information. However, given sufficient time, the first author was able to observe life events and to collect stories of past experiences. In order to build trust, she also invited a local helper during interviews. The local helper is the village secretary of the Houbanmiao Village and played an important role in producing a closer relationship between researcher and interviewees in a short time. He also served as a cultural translator for the local experiences. The ethnographic field notes were audio recorded and transcribed for analysis.

Shanghai Marriage Market in People's Park helped to understand upper-middle-class city women and their families. Parents of singles flock to the park every weekend from noon to exchange information about their children, and some of them were already familiar with each other in the open-air Marriage Market. Single urban women's parents were interviewed through snowball sampling. The selection criteria for middle-class families in China require that at least one parent has a higher education and be employed in a position with a certain income, the standard of living, and tasteful lifestyle (China Power Team 2017; Lareau 2002).

We conducted unstructured interviews. All interviews were audio recorded and transcribed (Saunders, Lewis, and Thornhill 2009). The researcher and interviewees share the same cultural background and ethnicity, which helped facilitate rapport. In addition, past research has indicated that participants often feel more comfortable discussing feelings and emotions with female researchers (Padfield and Procter 1996). Other steps that would help participants feel relaxed during interviews include starting with asking broad questions and avoiding interrupting, confrontation, or appearing judgmental (Spradley 1980). The purpose is to gain a richer understanding of gift-giving behavior in in-law family relationships through the lens of urban women and their parents. In particular, we paid attention to family tensions related to interclass marriages, and how gifts are used to bridge the sociocultural differences. Different gift-giving practices were categorized in the three stages of prekinship gifts, establishing kinship gifts and sustaining kinship gifts. Gift-giving plays different roles at each of the stage.

Analysis and Findings

Prekinship Gift-Giving: Dating and Romantic Gift

Prior to marriage, romantic gift exchanges between male *phoenix* and their potential marriage partners are often attempts to negotiate a different style. Inappropriate gifts may lead to the dissolvement of the relationships, *Liangxiao* describes what happened in great detail:

> In her opinion, my gift for her is a test of true love and evidence of attention to her. She was very concerned about the meaning of gift. For example, in the "520" day ("I love you" special day for young in

China), I just send her a bunch of flowers, not a unique gift. When she received the flowers, she was not as happy. She told me she didn't like to receive a gift that seemed to be the token gift that was purchased for anyone. As a return gift, she gave me a famous-brand computer support frame. Because I unintentionally told to her that my neck was sore during my work. There were other special gifts like socks and underwear. It's true that I didn't seem to pay much attention to her desires. When I saw the gifts she gave, I felt ashamed, it was really the gift I needed. I didn't make she feel special. After that she tried to break up with me. I then bought an above-3000-RMB high heel shoes on her birthday, she was so happy because she thought I finally know her needs and lifestyle.

Huqiang: Sometimes she asks me to go shopping, to be honest I rarely want to go with her. The clothes she bought cost between 1,000 and 2,000 yuan. I felt I had to pay if I went with her because I don't want to lose face. I really do not have so much money, and I am afraid of such awkward situation. For girls in Shanghai like her, they pay more attention to brands, which I don't think it is necessary. For example, last birthday she wanted to buy a LV handbag, I tried to buy it for her, but it cost my 3 months of living expenses. It is understandable to buy a luxury handbag, but there must be a limit. She always figured out that line. My parents taught me to be frugal all the time, but I feel obliged to adapt to my girlfriend's affluent lifestyle to maintain our hard-won relationship.

As seen in these quotes, the key issues are the cost of gifts and many *male phoenixes* shared such experiences. At this stage, *male phoenixes* often struggle to adapt to the upper-middle-class lifestyle and gifting rituals. There is a strong sense of ambiguity and confusion. As a material bond, when the gifts fail to bridge the class gaps, the relationships would be unstable. Here, brands are an important evidence and test for love. As a result, girls from upper-middle class prefer costly gifts, as a sign of the relations. To avoid the unexpected, *male phoenixes* would give expensive gifts; however, sometimes they felt this would put intolerable financial pressure on them. Romantic relationships are here dominated by a balanced reciprocity. In premarriage relationships, the value and thoughtfulness of the gifts play an important role in bridging class disparity between the couple.

Establishing Kinship: Marriage Negotiation and Wedding Gifts

Discussing Marriage is an important stage that involves gift exchange with partner's extended family. It includes meeting the parents, bride-wealth, and wedding gifts. Gift-giving plays an important role in managing conflicts and differences. For instance, when meeting parents, an intimate knowledge of family background is important for a successful gifting ritual. *Male phoenixes* do their best to please urban partner's parents. Gift-giving in this stage is based on generalized reciprocation in order to express the respect and sincerity. Such gifting helps to bring the potential kinship relationship closer. Parents' usually do not give return gifts. *Yangjiu* explains his gift experiences at such meetings:

> At the first time I met her parents, I brought two bottles of hometown's famous wine and two cartons of cigarettes (one of the most popular brands), because her father smokes and drinks. In northern China, gifts as a bridge were usually given to build the relationship with the father and only need please to him. After that first meeting, she told me that her mother got overlooked because she didn't receive any gifts. For the second time I went to her home, I also bought donkey-hide gelatins (*ejiao*) for her mom. Since then her mom obviously tried to communicate with me. The gift expressed and showed I respected her mom as well.

Here, the Confucian norms between the young and the old also influence gift-giving, and gifts help to establish kinship hierarchy (Bell 2000; Joy 2001). Initial gifts often recognize the patriarchy of family relationships in some parts of China. Gifts emphasize the values of harmony and filial piety in Chinese culture. Gift-giving is the formal step of entering into future spouses' families.

Bride-wealth

Bride-wealth refers "the property transferred from the groom's family to the bride's family and it is often used by senior men to establish future marriages for the male siblings of the bride" (Yan 1996, 179). In contemporary China, bride-wealth is often "jointly usable gifts" to the new family from both sides of the extended families. Such gifts include both money and material goods (Jiang and Sánchez-Barricarte 2012). Two types of gifts are common: some parents may demand expensive bride-wealth, and this is referred to as "selling the daughter"; the other is to "marry out a daughter," in which bride's parents give all the received bride-wealth to the new family (Yan 1996). However, male phoenixes' parents have to compete to give more gifts than bride-wealth, as reflected in Wangfeng's experiences:

> In-laws asked us to buy a flat with 200,000 yuan. How could we get 200,000 yuan in the countryside? Even if we sold our house and land, it still wouldn't be enough even 13 or 14 years ago. We borrowed 100,000 from relatives and friends in our village, such as my

112   *Jia Cong and Xin Zhao*

son's uncle, aunt and from the relatives in my wife's mother's family, probably three aunts and two uncles. . . . The bride's father still did not want this marriage because my son was rural while their family was from the big city. Her father tried to stop their relationship and said his family could use their apartment for marriage if we didn't buy one, but the next generation should take their family name instead of my family name. After the whole family discussed this together, we decided to borrow money to pay the down-payment, and we must buy a house in Nanjing as the wedding gift. You know in the countryside, changing surname meant to forget our ancestors. We spent four or five years to pay back all the borrowed money. My daughter-in-law told me that if she married a guy in Nanjing, at least he would buy a car for her. I said that the countryside could not be compared with Nanjing.

For upper-middle-class urban family, class status is also regarded as a gift given to male phoenixes and the gift is the chance to pursue upward social mobility. As a result, bride wealth is seen as a necessary return gift. When the gifts fail to impress, other forms of compensation is demanded. In this case, the offspring's name is also decided by the value of bride-wealth, and if the groom's family can't afford the expensive bride-wealth, the off-spring may be named after the bride's family. This is considered a serious face-losing act for the male family in the rural area. Here, bride-wealth suggests a challenge to rural patriarchy value systems.

Wedding Gifts

Gift exchange is common in weddings. Weddings are also important times for two extended families to exchange gifts. It gives expression to social face, which reflects other's expectations, rather than meeting one's own wishes (Ho 1975; Hsu 1985). Therefore, "doing face work" and "seeking personal relations" are reflected in the wedding gifts. Gift-giving here is influenced by fears relating to the loss of face. Wedding ceremonies have become a battlefield which decides the family's right to dominate. More importantly, the wedding ceremony itself is a gift that plays an important role in shaping marriage and later the relationships between extended families. Dingqian describes her wedding ceremony:

Our wedding ceremonies were different from the ordinary marriage, and it was regarded as *"Liangtouguafan"* (neither married nor be married). Because my husband is the eldest son, his family didn't want him to marry into my family, and our family only has one child. My mother was quite satisfied with this arrangement and she gave wedding ceremony as a gift. Since then, I always play a dominant role within our marriage.

Wedding ceremonies are highly valued events in the relationships. In rural China, traditionally, it is often the groom's family that pays for the wedding ceremony, after which the bride moves to live with the groom's family. In rare cases, groom may move into the bride's family, and this is referred to as *Daochamen*. The notions of Liangtouguafan and Daochamen (married into the bride's family) are almost unacceptable in Chinese patriarchy norms. However, due to the rural–urban disparity, male phoenixes and their extended family often have to compromise. In this case, the bride's family pay for the wedding as a gift and the bride does not need to move into the groom's family as a result.

Sustaining Kinship Through Gift-Giving

According to Fei: "As the family in our society is a corporative group, its central axis lies between the father and the son, between the mother-in-law and the daughter-in-law. This axis is vertical rather than horizontal. The conjugal relation becomes secondary" (Fei 1947/1992, 42). Class status continue to influence couple's different gift-giving practices (Watson 1985).

Gifts to Male Phoenixes' Extended Family

The male phoenix is a tie between his own extended family and new urban lifestyles. There are conspicuous signals of the pecuniary and social distance between urban and rural families. But male phoenixes are obliged to give gifts to reduce frictions and balance the relations between his and his wife's family. The relationship between the mother-in-law and the daughter-in-law is complicated and delicate to balance. Gift-giving may take place without the wife's notice, as noted by Xiaoming:

> I bought this electric fan, which was more than one hundred yuan, for my parents. My wife never knew it and she believed it was bought by my brother, which save me a lot of trouble. Otherwise, it would be extremely terriblesome! My wife has always wanted to live separately from my parents in this house, as she is used to being independent, but my family's financial conditions do not allow her to do so, which makes her very dissatisfied. If I could, I would do something or buy gifts for my parents in secret, and wouldn't let her know. In order to avoid more conflicts, we also eat separately from my parents.

Male phoenixes play active roles of middleman to maintain the harmony of the extended family, and they have to adopt strategies such as white lie in gift-giving. These gifts are endowed with special values and help to reduce conflicts between the mother-in-law and the daughter-in-law.

114   *Jia Cong and Xin Zhao*

Gifts to Wives' Extended Family

On the opposite situation, gift-giving helps enhance the relationship between male phoenixes and their parents-in-law. Due to the class disparity, the wife's parents may never approve the marriage. Yet, after the couple got married, male phoenixes often engage in gift-giving to change such a situation, as seen below:

> I always buy gifts for my mother-in-law, take her and my father-in-law to travel. I asked my wife what her mother likes, and I bought her a diamond ring once I was on a business trip to Hong Kong. After all, it's as a kind of compensatory gift, she helps my wife and me to babysit. But it is really hard to find a right balance: she would refuse it if I give her too much; If I give her just a little, it would make me ashamed. For example, if I give her 500 yuan a month, I think it's too little. If I give her 1000 yuan, she will refuse to take it. I told her that she could spend more and that if I gave her the money, she wouldn't have to spend her own savings. I also think gift is an easy way to have an ideal relationship with my parents-in-law, to please my wife.

Gifts of Adjustment

After marriage, young couple's lifestyles converge over time. The gift is important in establishing a shared family identity and to establish common norms. It also helps to reinforce romantic relations but more importantly to maintain the harmony in the family, as Jiangjie describes:

> I often have small conflicts with his mom because of the trifles of life. She always wants me to follow her habits, but I have my own habits, and I'm angry that she wants me to adapt to her rural living habits. After that my husband gave me a book called "the analects of Confucius", and wanted me to face a painful readjustment. After reading this book, I do not want to dispute with them anymore. This gift uniquely suits me in this unbalanced family life relationship.

Here, the gift of the book plays a vital role to reduce in-law family's conflicts, and at the same time, it reflects an intimacy relationship. Such gifts help *male phoenix*es adopt similar sociocultural lifestyles with his wife.

Discussion

In this chapter, we seek to understand the role of gifts in bridging sociocultural differences in interclass marriage through studying male phoenixes' experiences of gift-giving from dating to marriage. We investigated how gifts are used to manage tensions and conflicts within family with regard to class mobility. We found that gift-giving practices within interclass marriages in urban China are motivated by hybrid reciprocities that combine generalized, balanced, and negative exchange. The stages from dating to marriage are complicated and emotion-laden, especially in the Chinese relational or renqing society, and they are dominated by different types of reciprocities (Sahlins 1972). Such reciprocity is not linear progression as described in previous literature, in which gift-giving practices differ according to kinship distances (Sahlins 1972). We found a mixed reciprocity existing within interclass marriage. In romantic relationships (Belk and Coon 1993), gift exchange is motivated by agapic love and differs from economic exchange (Jacoby 1985) and social exchange (Mill 1859/1991). Our findings suggest that even within family, a more nuanced and calculated gifting relationship may exist in interclass courtship and marriages.

We also found that consumers with lower social capital may seek to display higher social capital through gift-giving. Gifts allow them to reenact a new lifestyle and hence to display upward social mobility. Gifting gives expression to idealized lifestyle and helps to bridge social differences. City women and their parents believe that generous gift-giving from male phoenixes could remedy class disparity and improve family relations. On the contrary, if the male phoenix could not afford the gifts of a house and car, it will bring shame to the family and undermine their relationship. Expensive ritualized gifts are often deemed necessary to build relationship with the bride's family and to compensate for the perceived stigma associated with marrying a male phoenix (who is considered to come from a lower social class). Some city brides' families might even demand their future offspring to take the mother's last name if the male phoenix cannot afford to offer expensive ritualized gifts. Chinese men encounter stigmatization if their children assume their wives' last name instead of theirs.

Nonritualized or everyday gift-giving also appeared to be crucial in managing interclass marriages in urban China. We found that when the lifestyle and consumption habits of the male phoenix are consistent with the city brides and their families, fewer conflicts occur in their family interactions. Some male phoenixes engage in generous consumption strategies and mirror a healthy lifestyle like the middle class in order to gain acceptance and maintain family harmony, such as daily surprise, having fancy meals, and wearing fashionable clothes. These three aspects provide some initial promising evidence to demonstrate the importance of gifts in managing class divisions in the context of marriage and family relations and in a collective culture.

References

Belk, Russell (1996), "The Perfect Gift," in *Gift Giving: A Research Anthology*, ed. Cele Otnes and Richard Beltramini, Bowling Green, OH: Bowling Green State University Popular Press, 59–83.

116 Jia Cong and Xin Zhao

Belk, Russell and Gregory S. Coon (1993), "Gift Giving as Agapic Love: An Alternative to the Exchange Paradigm Based on Dating Experiences," *Journal of Consumer Research*, 20 (3), 393–417 (https://doi.org/10.1086/209357).

Bell, Duran (2000), "Guanxi: A Nesting of Groups," *Current Anthropology*, 41 (February), 132–38 (https://doi.org/10.1086/300113).

Caplow, Theodore (1982), "Christmas Gifts and Kin Networks," *American Sociological Review*, 47 (June), 383–92 (https://doi.org/10.2307/2094994).

Cheal, David (1988), The Gift Economy, London: Routledge.

China Power Team (2017), "How Well-off is China's Middle Class?" *China Power* (https://chinapower.csis.org/china-middle-class/).

Cohen, Myron L. (1976), *House United, House Divided: The Chinese Family in Taiwan*, New York: Columbia University Press.

Douban (2016), "Shanghai Girl Escaped from Jiangxi Countryside," *Douban Discussion Forum* (www.douban.com/group/topic/83637608/).

Elliott, Richard and Nick Jankel-Elliott (2003), "Using Ethnography in Strategic Consumer Research," *Qualitative Market Research*, 6 (4), 215–23 (https://doi.org/10.1108/13522750310495300).

Fei, Xiaotong (1947/1992), *From the Soil: The Foundations of Chinese Society*, Berkeley, CA: University of California Press.

Gouldner, Alvin W. (1960), "The Norm of Reciprocity: A Preliminary Statement," *American Sociological Review* (167–78), 161–78 (https://doi.org/10.2307/2092623).

Ho, David Yau-fai (1975), "On the Concept of the Face," *American Journal of Sociology*, 81 (December), 72–78 (https://doi.org/10.1086/226145).

Hsu, Francis (1985), "The Self in Cross-Cultural Perspective," in *Culture and Self: Asian and Western Perspectives*, ed. Anthony J. Marsella, George De Vos, and Francis Hsu, New York: Tavistock, 24–55.

Jacoby, Sanford M. (1985), *Employing Bureaucracy: Managers, Unions, and the Transformation of Work in American Industry, 1900–1945*, New York: Columbia University Press.

Jiang, Quanbao and J. Jesus Sánchez-Barricarte (2012), "Bride Price in China: The Obstacle to 'Bare Branches' Seeking Marriage," *The History of the Family*, 17 (1), 2–15 (https://doi.org/10.1080/1081602X.2011.640544).

Joy, Annamma (2001), "Gift Giving in Hong Kong and the Continuum of Social Ties," *Journal of Consumer Research*, 28 (2), 239–56 (https://doi.org/10.1086/322900).

Lareau, Annette (2002), "Invisible Inequality: Social Class and Childrearing in Black Families and White Families," *American Sociological Review*, 67 (5), 747–76 (https://doi.org/10.2307/3088916).

Mauss, Marcel (1925/1990), *The Gift: Essay on the Form and Function of Exchange*, London: Routledge.

Mill, John Stuart (1859/1991), *On Liberty and Other Essays*, Oxford: Oxford University Press.

Otnes, Cele, Tina Lowrey, and Young Chan Kim (1993), "Gift Selection for 'Easy' and 'Difficult' Recipients: A Social Roles Interpretation," *Journal of Consumer Research*, 20 (September), 229–44 (https://doi.org/10.1086/209345).

Padfield, Maureen and Ian Procter (1996), "The Effect of Interviewer's Gender on the Interviewing Process: A Comparative Enquiry," *Sociology*, 30 (2), 355–66 (https://doi.org/10.1177/0038038596030002009).

Sahlins, Marshall (1972), *Stone Age Economics*, New York: Aldine.

——— (2011), "What Kinship Is (Part One)," *The Journal of the Royal Anthropological Institute*, 17 (1), 2–19 (https://doi.org/10.1111/j.1467-9655.2010.01666.x).

Saunders, Mark, Philip Lewis, and Adrian Thornhill (2009), *Research Methods for Business Students*, Harlow: Financial Times Prentice Hall.

Schneider, David M. (1980), *American Kinship: A Cultural Account*, 2nd edition, Chicago: Chicago University Press.

Sherry, John F., Jr. (1983), "Gift Giving in Anthropological Perspective," *Journal of Consumer Research*, 10 (September), 157–68 (https://doi.org/10.1086/208956).

Spradley, James P. (1980), "Doing Participant Observation," in *Participant Observation*, Orlando, FL: Harcourt Brace Jovanovich College Publishers, 53–84.

Vatuk, Ved Prakash and Sylvia Vatuk (1971), "The Social Context of Gift Exchange in North India," in *Family and Social Change in Modern India*, ed. Giri Raj Gupta, Durham, NC: Carolina Academic Press, 207–32.

Watson, Adam (1985), "Social Class, Socially-induced Loss, Recruitment and Breeding of Red Grouse," *Oecologia*, 67 (4), 493–98 (https://doi.org/10.1007/BF00790019).

Wu, Xiaogang and J. Donald Treiman (2004), "The Household Registration System and Social Stratification in China: 1955–1996," *Demography*, 41 (2), 363–84 (https://doi.org/10.1353/dem.2004.0010).

Yan, Yunxiang (1996), *The Flow of Gifts: Reciprocity and Social Networks in a Chinese Village*, Stanford, CA: Stanford University Press.

Yang, Mei Hui (1989), "The Gift Economy and State Power in China," *Comparative Studies in Society and History*, 31 (1), 25–54 (https://doi.org/10.1017/S0010417500015656).

——— (1994), *Gifts, Favors and Banquets: The Art of Social Relations in China*, Ithaca, NY: Cornell University Press.

7 Solitary Death Is Elsewhere

The Making of Memorial Community in Japan

Yuko Minowa

Introduction

Dying and death is the final experience of a human. We defend against the uncertainty of death. We deal with the idea of finitude by repressing it, mythologizing death through the belief in the afterlife, and romanticizing personal immortality. The loneliness of dying may be alleviated by the presence of others at the deathbed. The anxiety about postmortem death rituals for the salvation of the soul may be assuaged by the continuance of kin relationship. In liquid modernity (Bauman 2000), however, and in super-aged societies in particular, incidents of solitary death among the single elderly are pervading. Bauman (1992, 5) writes, "the truth that death cannot be escaped is not denied . . . but each particular case of death can be resisted, postponed or avoided altogether." How can the consumer resist or avoid solitary death, as Bauman (1992) postulates?

The super-aged nation Japan faces challenges in maintaining the welfare of elderly consumers. In 2015, 26.6% of the population was 65 years or older. In 2040, its median age is expected to increase to 53.1 years, and 35.4% of the population is projected to be 65 years or older (Statistics Bureau of Japan 2018). The urban migration and loss of traditional community rituals and family ties and the growing segment of one-person elderly households have created a segment of the socially isolated elderly, further extending the problem of "solitary death" (Allison 2013; Hirata and Warschauer 2014; Tachibanaki 2016). In 2015, Japan had 21.71 million elderly households. These were private households with household members 65 years of age or over, excluding "institutional households" such as nursing homes. This was 40.7% of total private households. The number of one-person elderly households was 5.93 million. Among these, approximately two-thirds were made up of women. There were 3.03 million one-person elderly households in 2000. So, the number nearly doubled in 15 years. The study on the poverty rate based on age and gender differences reveals that about 25% of single men and over 40% of single women 65 years or older are in poverty. Furthermore, the government

DOI: 10.4324/9781003111559-10

survey found that more than one-third of those living alone were feeling threatened by solitary death (Tachibanaki 2016).

Solitary death, or dying alone at home, without a witness and unnoticed by anybody, is classified as unnatural death subject to autopsy in Japan (Kanawaku and Ohno 2019). It is nothing new. Incidents of solitary death were reported in the newspaper even in the 19th century. But the term in Japanese—*kodokushi*—began to appear in the media in the 1970s as a "symbolic phenomenon of urban loneliness" or a "problem of the elderly" (Nitta 2013, 105). Since the prolonged recession of 1990s, solitary death linked to poverty and deprivation has become a serious social problem. More recently, due to the rise of socially isolated elderlies, solitary death has been recognized as one situation for the end of life. Elderlies with no caretaker are at a high risk of dying alone in their own homes from an unexpected accident or an illness. Their bodies are often left unattended for several days or even months. In Tokyo alone, 4,777 people passed away in solitary death in 2017 (Ministry of Health, Labour, and Welfare 2020). A large number of urns that contain cremated remains of those who died in isolation are left in the public storage without death rituals because none of their kin is identified.

Under such circumstances, in order to be self-reliant and not trouble others, end-of-life activities (*shūkatsu*), which include preplanning of death rituals—funeral, burial, and memorial services—have been widely practiced among mature consumers in urban cities. To avoid solitary death and ensure postmortem memorial services, the consumer may join a memorial community (*kuyō no kai*). It consists of a group of people who prepay to be buried in a common burial site. They form a social, and often supportive, network inter vivos, call each other "tomb friends" (*haka-tomo*), and voluntarily undertake mass memorial services performed at an institution—often at a Buddhist temple—for the repose of departed souls. This chapter interrogates the development of the end-of-life activities (shūkatsu) market in Japan and the making of memorial communities in particular.

Extensive literature on death rites and rituals in general (e.g., Metcalf and Huntington 1991) as well as in Japan (e.g., Suzuki 2000, 2013; Yanagita 1946) exists within anthropology, ethnology, and sociology. Studies written from consumer culture and marketing perspectives have been relatively limited, however (Dobscha 2017). Empirical research on death-related consumption in Western (e.g., Gabel, Mansfield, and Westbrook 1996; Gentry, Kennedy, Paul, and Hill 1995; Price, Arnould, and Curasi 2000) and non-Western contexts has been growing (e.g., Bonsu and Belk 2003; Hackley and Hackley 2017; Zhao and Belk 2008). No study on contemporary death rituals in Japan and the associated consumer culture seems to exist in consumer research, however. This chapter thus addresses two questions: one is how has the market and marketing of death rituals—forces of cultural transition—been changing in Japan, particularly those targeted to the elderly without kin in urban

120   *Yuko Minowa*

cities? Another question is how have the shūkatsu market and memorial community been co-created by a network of actors—various human and nonhuman agencies, including consumers, the government, and sacralized material objects, such as human remains, and sanctified natural and religious artifacts, in which these social and natural entities mutually control who they are?

This article contributes to a body of research written from consumer and marketing theory perspectives on death culture and practice in aging society and the making of consumption community, examining the juncture at market system co-creation, super-aging, and urbanization.

The remaining part of this chapter is organized as follows: first, I provide an overview of death rituals in Japan. Then, I explain the methods and analytical approach—the actor–network theory (ANT) (Latour 2005; Mills 2018). Grounded on the ethnographic account, I discuss the making of the market for end-of-life, shūkatsu activities, which stimulate consumers to consider and shop around alternative forms of death rituals, including memorial communities. Agnostic and thanato-gnostic consumers are explored. The meanings of nonhuman agencies—remains—are explicated. I then discuss the making of memorial community by applying the moments of translation in ANT (Callon 1984), and how the heterogeneity of the community has been maintained within the shared cultural value system. The chapter ends with a conclusion.

Death Rituals in Japan

Japan has a rich history of death culture (Namihira 2004). The nation has lived closely with death because of the islands' defenseless exposure to abundant natural disasters. Traditionally, Japanese death rituals are a hybrid of Buddhism, Confucianism, and Shintoism fused with local folkloric customs, such as shamanism in Okinawa. Japanized Buddhist beliefs and death ritual practices originated in Neo-Confucianism, the doctrines of Zhu-zi (1130–1200), which was integrated into Zen Buddhism and introduced to Japan during the Kamakura period (1185–1333) (Kikuchi 2018). These beliefs include memorials (*nenki*), the spirit of the dead (*mitama*), and a mortuary tablet (*ihai*). A mortuary tablet is, in general, an approximately eight-inch-tall upright wooden plaque, lacquered in black and gold, standing on a base. The posthumous Buddhist name of a deceased person is written in gold on the plaque. It is intended to enshrine his or her spirit (Smith 1966).

The ritual process comprises wake and funeral, cremation, burial, and memorial services. Each rite represents the process of disintegration to synthesis, transforming the corpse to the deceased, and to ancestral spirits (Suzuki 2000). Although temples could handle all the services, today funeral homes market services from wake to cremation while cemeteries sell plots as well as burial and memorial services. In the early 2000s, more

Solitary Death Is Elsewhere   121

than 90% of funerals were carried out by following the Buddhist tradition (Walter 2008). While Japanese observe Buddhist tradition for funeral and other ancestor worshipping rituals, they also practice Shintoism. Many Japanese are not deeply religious. And, as Shintoism is polytheistic, both religions can coexist in their minds. The trend in the death rite is to reduce and eliminate all but the cremation that is required by law; this minimal death rite is called *chokusō* (direct cremation).

Practicing Buddhism was once legally mandated, while Shintoism was syncretized. In 1640, the government ruled by the Tokugawa shogunate enforced the temple certification system (Walter 2008). Under this system, each family must be a parishioner of an assigned local Buddhist temple and to obtain a certification as proof. The parishioner system served dual purposes: one was to prevent the nation from becoming Christian and another was to put each family under the surveillance of monks at temples. The religion served for a political scheme. As a result, many Japanese have continued to own their ancestral grave at their family temple.

The syncretic fusion of Buddhism and Shintoism officially ended with the Meiji Restoration in the 19th century. The Edict for Separation of Shintoism and Buddhism clarified that the roots of the nation in Shintoist myth and that each individual Japanese citizen was a subject of the emperor. The ideology helped the state to use death, as well as life, of the nation as a political resource of rulers. Death ideology of the superpower, often the State, was ordained as a state religion at various points in Japan's history, especially during times of war, which regulated the proper mortuary practices (Namihira 2004). Nevertheless, they were always syncretic with Japanized Buddhist tradition.

The wake reflects Japanized Buddhist tradition fused with local custom (Namihira 2004). The death rite begins at the moment of death: someone gives a last sip of water (*shi ni mizu*) to wet the lips of a dying person at the deathbed. At the wake, the surviving family used to spend all night long ceaselessly "looking after" the unstable soul of the deceased, averting the evil spirit. It was also to observe if the deceased may return to life. The family prepared for the departure of the deceased for his last journey to the netherworld in a traveling kimono and with the proper gear: a protective knife placed on the chest, a bowl of boiled rice, a cup of water, and other articles on the temporary altar setup in front of an inverted screen. Traditionally, the dead body is bathed (*yukan*) to purify death pollution and laid in the coffin for the funeral (Kim 2012). In premodern Japan, the wake was a family matter. Then, death rites became the affair of neighbor association (*tonari-gumi*) who reciprocated and solidified the bond. Today, having lost the family and community solidarity, the funeral professionals typically organize a wake as part of the death "ceremony"—their commoditized product—to be held in the funeral home on the night before the funeral.

Funerals used to be held at home. In the modern Japan, however, they largely moved to the funeral home as a prepackaged rite of farewell. With

122   Yuko Minowa

a microphone in his hand, the ceremony staff, who acts the master of ceremony, moves the funeral forward in accordance with the program. He performs with dignity. It begins with a priest's reciting of the sutra. Messages of condolence are announced. Attendees offer incense in turn. The coffin is then prepared for cremation: attendees place flowers into the coffin and close the lid by nailing it down in turn. The families carry the coffin to the cart to be delivered to the crematory. Before the cremation, a brief ceremony of last farewell is marked with the priest's chanting of the sutra. After the cremation, there is a ceremony called *kotsuage* in which the family of the deceased transfer the cremated ashes to an urn by using chopsticks. Then, the priest conducts a memorial service for the transformation of the body to ashes, which entails another chanting of the sutra and an offering of incense. The funeral ceremony concludes with a banquet at which the chief mourner rewards the priest and facilitators of the funeral for their services. The entire ceremony takes place within a day.

Similar to other rites of passage, such as wedding ceremonies, the sumptuousness of a funeral ceremony depends on the social status, the economic resources, and the extensiveness of social networks of the deceased and the surviving family. In the last 20 years, funeral ceremonies have become smaller and more private affairs kept among immediate family and close relatives. There are several reasons for this trend. For one, urban migrants during Japan's rapid economic growth in the 1960s grew old and lost ties to relatives in their hometown. Meanwhile, super-aging means more expenses are necessary to live a long life, leaving less budget for death rituals. Super-aging also means that surviving mourners may be too old to attend death rituals. Another reason is the growing diversity in ideology that has made the public consider nontraditional private death rituals, such as direct cremation, a legitimate choice.

A controversial aspect of death rituals is that a large number of religious events require priests' services. They are an important income source for the priests. They include the granting of a posthumous religious name to the deceased, for instance, which the priest announces during the funeral ceremony. The hierarchical rank of the dead in afterlife, which the posthumous precept name indicates, partly depends on the size of the donation made to the temple (Covell 2005). Another religious service is conducting memorial services at specific temporal intervals that require the "discretionary donation," which is also a source of income for the temple. To satirize their practice, Japanese temples have been called "funeral temples."

Methods

An ethnographic study, with 25 interviews, interrogated both consumers and suppliers of the shūkatsu market in the metropolitan Tokyo area. The consumers were mostly retirees, adult consumers with elderly parents, and singles without kin. The suppliers in the shūkatsu market

Solitary Death Is Elsewhere   123

are shūkatsu counselors, retailers, administrators of temples, Buddhist monks, undertakers, and representatives from the municipal government and a senior club in Tokyo. These interviews took place *in situ* at temples, a funeral home, a senior club, a cemetery, a community center, business offices, and an exhibition center. Their accounts were augmented by participant observations at Shūkatsu Festa and seminars, funeral workshops, a networking event of the senior club, and a monthly meeting of the memorial community. The fieldwork took place in Tokyo, Yokohama, and Kamakura between 2014 and 2017. The scale of these events varied. Shūkatsu Festa was the largest; it was participated by 58 shūkatsu suppliers each having a booth of varying size, staffed by 45 volunteers of shūkatsu counselors, and attended by 3,230 people (Shūkatsu Counselor Association 2014). Funeral workshops generally had a small group of participants, ranging between four and ten people. Other events were attended by 25–50 people. Published materials by the government were closely scrutinized for rhetorical analysis of their politics on death ideology (Earley 2014). The interviews were augmented by blogs posted on websites for shūkatsu, alternative burials, and seniors' lifestyles. For the analysis of the memorial community, *Moyai no kai*, its newsletters since its inception in 1990 were also utilized. The names of informants appeared in this chapter are pseudonyms. The analytical approach, ANT, is discussed in the following text.

Actor–Network Theory

The analytical approach I use is ANT. Law (2004, 157) refers ANT as an analytical approach, or tool "that treats entities and materialities as enacted and related effects and explores the configuration and reconfiguration of those relations." Latour (1999) also claims that ANT is not intended as a theory but as a means to learn from actors how and why they do what they do, without an a priori postulation of their "world-building capacities." ANT is a useful framework for researchers to interrogate the ways—process and progressions—actors join the network and become part of it; conflicts and collaborations between different players; and how human actors and material objects come to stabilize and maintain networks (Latour 2005). The concept of "network" is a metaphor for the interwoven nature of the social and the technical. Law and Callon (1988, 285) explain the raison d'être and practice of actors as they:

> define and distribute roles, and mobilize or invent others to play these roles. Such roles may be social, political, technical, or bureaucratic in character; the objects that are mobilized to fill them are also heterogeneous and may take the form of people, organizations, machines, or scientific findings.

124 *Yuko Minowa*

The fundamental principles of ANT are agnosticism, generalized symmetry, and free association (Adaba and Ayoung 2017). It is often known as material semiotics (Mills 2018). Agnosticism calls for analytical objectivity toward the human and nonhuman actors. The term actant refers to both human and other nonhuman agencies such as a person, an institution, and a regulation. In death ritual practices, it may include undertakers, Buddhist priests and temples, and government regulations, for instance. Generalized symmetry emphasizes describing conflicting, multiple perspectives in the equivalent terms. Free association entails the denial of theoretical distinctions between the technical and the social.

ANT has been applied to examine a wide range of issues in consumer research. For example, Giesler (2012) traced Botox market trajectories in North America from an ANT perspective and concluded that it provided an insight into the local and global actor networks that surrounded e-Government projects. Conceptualizing community as a network of heterogeneous actors, Thomas, Price, and Schau (2013) used ANT to examine the interplay of those actors in a conventional activity-based consumption community: the distance running community. Their study suggests that the analytical dimensions of ANT present a unique and valuable lens for assessing the continuity of the communities. On the other hand, Bajde (2013) posited ANT to explicate problematics of CCT—its epistemological and ontological challenges. He discussed that adopting an ANT approach would enable a profound understanding of how ontologies of consumption could be enacted through unstable networks of heterogeneous relations. ANT can also be used to interrogate actors who play critical roles in the making of memorial community and the end-of-life activities movement in Japan.

The Market for End-of-Life Activities (*shūkatsu*)

The word shūkatsu was coined in 2009 in the media. It means activities one needs to take care of before dying. Aside from preplanning death rituals, they include estate planning, writing a (living) will, advanced care planning, and so forth. The benefit is to become carefree. With its sensible, proclaimed rationality, the word shūkatsu subsequently came to mean activities for the enrichment of later life, repudiating the image of pollution and bad luck originally associated with death and dying. The diffusion of the end-of-life activities (shūkatsu) is partly attributed to the efforts made by ubiquitously distributed heterogeneous actors who created the market for consumers practicing shūkatsu. There are webs of networks in which economic, symbolic, and emotional capital are exchanged among the market, religious institutions, cultural eclecticism and materiality, and consumers.

One of the focal actors, a former insurance salesperson and later the president of the Shūkatsu Counselor Association, Yoshiko uncovered the

Solitary Death Is Elsewhere   125

problem and the potential for the market while she was networking with various actors, such as priests, to establish her own company.

> There are many aged people with ambiguous anxieties and questions about things related to their death. . . . Those days we considered death and funeral as ill-omened were gone. . . . I thought we could listen to their problems and solve them together, and in this way, I thought we could improve society by eliminating the aged people's anxieties.

The organization then invented a new profession, shūkatsu counselor, and its certification system. There is now the industry association for shūkatsu businesses. They sponsor shūkatsu events, such as exhibits and festivals. At these occasions, the consumer can be linked to shūkatsu agents—actors—from the funeral industry, religious institutions, and other NPOs. These pop-ups are sites of opportunities for consumers to experience simulated death rites: trying on a variety of funeral outfits and lying in eco-friendly coffins.

Buddhist monks in particular are enthusiastic players. The number of parishioners is diminishing and so is their income. Thus, the shūkatsu movement represents a potential business opportunity for them. At the Shūkatsu Festa, two priests representing temples shared their perspectives. Hōen, a priest and the general manager of one of the temples, said, "managing a temple requires business skills." Shinren, another priest, a former layman with an MBA who came to "market" their shared perpetual grave (*eitai kuyō bo*), said, "graves have become a burden for many people. But this is not supposed to be a tenet of Buddhism. So, we consider it is our mission to find a solution to this problem." His temple offers the shared perpetual grave for a flat fee of ¥600,000 bundled with a posthumous Buddhist name and annual memorial services until the 33rd-year anniversary of death. To the question of whether his temple would reduce the price to accommodate the rising segment of the poor, Shinren said:

> No. We will be maintaining the ¥600,000 fee. We are not thinking to compete on price. But we are competing on value. We are not thinking to target those in the lower social class. . . . There are people who are willing to spend millions of yen to have an individual grave. It depends on what they value. . . . We are not trying to eliminate the difference between the rich and the poor.

Meanwhile, Tomio (74), who still does not have enough to be able to retire, said cynically, "it costs five million yen to die. I'd rather use that money than paying to a temple." In Marx's parlance, money is "the universal whore." ANT emphasizes the distributed nature of moral agency, a decision-maker of moral actions. Building on Aquinas' *Summa*

126   *Yuko Minowa*

Theologica, Scott (2000) suggests that the moral quality of individual human actions can vary in five situational factors: the value hierarchy, the agent, the object, the effect, and the intention. Opportunistic discourse of impassive funeral professions and supposedly moral agents—priests—elides the welfare of the dying and bereaved. They exhibit a facet of moral degradation in society in the age of disparity and schism in Japan.

Consumers: Are They Agnostic or Thanato-gnostic?

Commoditization and commercialization of death rites, justified by the market logic, has transformed indifferent agnostic consumers into active shūkatsu practitioners. Organized shūkatsu tours explore traditional and nontraditional burial sites. Seminars on shūkatsu instill new knowledge about alternative contemporary death rites. Once regarded as ominous, death is objectified as a quotidian matter. Commercially or ideologically driven, proliferating decision-making alternatives (Boret 2014; Kawano 2010) have driven mature consumers to engage in the identity project through the preplanning of death rite at end-of-life activities, paralleling the global trend of personalized funerals (Schäfer and McManus 2017).

Mature consumers who participate in the shūkatsu movement are mentally and physically active; they are not frail elderlies. Their attitudes are generally in conflict with those toward the traditional death rituals; they tend to support the coexistence of religious and secular pluralism and syncretism. The president of a senior club in Tokyo said, "people today are happier, so that they can talk about their own death. Society has become happier." On the other hand, the president of the shūkatsu counselor association observed that "the people who make inquiries about new age death ceremonies, such as tree burial, are rather easily influenced by the media, and they tend to be not having profound religious or philosophical thoughts." In other words, shūkatsu practitioners are often perceived as blissful agnostics.

"Individuality" (*jibun rashisa*) has emerged as a leitmotif in the media that emphasizes one's ending as articulating the characteristic of the self. At Shūkatsu Festa, one informant Taro in his early 70s incisively pointed out, "The assumption is that self-criticism (*jibun no tanaoroshi*) takes place. Without understanding the self, one cannot prepare the death that expresses individuality." The "ending note" distributed by shūkatsu enterprises, often as a free giveaway, is a tool for a life review; completing it compels one to reflect on her own past, recapitulate the self, and assess the worthiness of the self to determine how much to spend for the death rite.

The individuation process creates tensions. The more disparity in society, the larger the tension. Taro's observation was attested to in another shūkatsu player's account. Michiko in her late 60s articulated her resistance to the dominant media discourse: "I am not sure

Solitary Death Is Elsewhere 127

[about the worthiness of myself,] as I didn't do anything particularly important in my life. So, I have never thought about [expressing the self through the death ritual] deeply." Nevertheless, postmortem death rituals were her concern. She recently applied for a public communal grave, for which the winners would be selected by a lottery. It is inexpensive, but more importantly, she said, the public grave site provides perpetual memorial service (*eitai-kuyō*). Her fear was partly rooted in a Buddhist belief about not being able to enter Nirvana and become a benign ancestral spirit unless necessary postmortem rituals were performed by relatives (Hackley and Hackley 2017, 95). These shūkatsu practitioners act as if they were thanato-gnostic: they are preoccupied with their own postmortem death rituals to control their imagined destiny hereafter and prevent themselves from falling into the abyss. Thus, having a contract with an entity that offers perpetual memorial service is as critical as the selection of other aspects of death rituals, such as burial.

Remains: The Meanings of Nonhuman Agencies

The individuation of death rites is materialized through a plethora of funeral and postmortem sacralization artifacts that complement moral objects. The moral object can be the self, others, or the thing with which the action is essentially concerned (Scott 2000). It may refer to the object that has "strong moral connotations" that demands "morally correct choice" when using it (Larssæther 2011). The moral objects that are significant in social practice are often culturally appropriated. A community and its members share knowledge about their genealogy and provenance. The objects can also act as memorializing death and commodifying sentiment.

Human remains are a moral object par excellence. They are an object for veneration. They occupy a unique place in Japanese culture. Dirges in *Manyōshu*, the oldest anthology of poems in Japan, compiled in the second half of the 8th century, reveal that the practice of picking up the cremated ashes and scattering them is ancient. Some parts of Japan, such as Okinawa, have a custom of washing ashes (*senkotsu*) that is equivalent to the secondary disposal prevalent in various parts in the world, including Indonesia and Melanesia. Such treatment of the ashes is traditionally considered a marker in the process for the dead spirit to transform into an ancestral spirit. Through the processing and managing of remains, it is believed that the bereaved sustain the relationship with the deceased (Yamaori 2002). When the Japanese move out of their hometown for good, they may also move the ashes of their ancestors in an urn and rebury them (*kaisō*) in the area of their destination.

Ashes are traditionally kept in the grave. But, the way of revering them has been changing. Norio, a sales rep of the Buddhist altar store

128   *Yuko Minowa*

from Shikoku Island, who had traveled to Tokyo to have a booth at the Shūkatsu Festa said:

> In the past, people revered the spirit of the deceased through the memorial tablet (ihai). But today, people revere the deceased through physical forms (*katachi*), such as placing the remains of the deceased in an urn in the household Buddhist altar. So, the ways that people revere have been changing; it may be underpinned by our obsession to material objects (*mono*).

Similar to the veneration of holy relics, the memorializing practice of the deceased at hand (*temoto kuyō*) is an economical alternative to buying a grave in the cemetery. It is a symbolic bridge to the deceased, which links the dead and the mourner. Belk (1988, 144) argues that "the prior possession of the deceased can be powerful remains of the dead person's extended self." Thus, the corporeal remains—ashes and bones—of the deceased are the extended-self par excellence. They may become inalienable wealth for some (Baker, Baker, and Gentry 2017).

Further, in Japan, the material object acquires a certain spirit/power (Daniels 2009; Ito 2007). Material objects engraved with the deceased's name and attached to the body, such as accessories, would infuse the deceased's aura; they mark the mourner's desire to remain physical and commemorate. Furthermore, ashes are not mere objects of memorialization or family heritage in Japan, since the possession of them gives entitlement to be the heir. As such, remains are both symbolic and economic capital. Therefore, the remains and their destination are a key concern for shūkatsu practitioners.

Memorial Community: Necroinstitution-Based Network Inter Vivos

The end-of-life shūkatsu practices may result in participating in a memorial community. It is established by religious or nonreligious organizations. They brand the community with a unique name to create a distinctive identity and to be marketable. One of the aims of the community is to organize memorial services performed at an institution, typically a Buddhist temple, in perpetuity for the repose of a departed soul. Those not affiliated to religious institutions may be run by ideologically driven organizations, such as ones for scattering of ashes and tree burials (Boret 2014). Nonreligious entities can be grassroots. The main benefit of belonging to a memorial community is functional: it ensures that the postmortem death rituals will be performed. Another benefit is social and emotional: it provides elderlies an opportunity to make bonds (*en*) with other members who will be buried in the same shared burial site and thus mitigate the fear of solitary death, thereby filling the gap between change and stability, and discontinuity and continuity caused by a super-aged society.

Solitary Death Is Elsewhere 129

Led by the feminist activist and politician Fusae Ichikawa (1893–1981), one of the earliest such communities was founded in 1979 by a group of single women; they formed the Association for the Women's Memorial (*onna no hi no kai*) at Jōjakkōji Temple in Kyoto. Those women remained single for their entire lives as a result of losing myriad male counterparts due to the 15-year war that started in 1931. In the temple precinct, they built a monument to commemorate the departed souls of the deceased members. As the proportion of unmarried women living alone, or *ohitorisama*, is surging (Dales 2014; Tachibanaki 2016), contemporary memorial communities targeted to single women could also be explored as a contested space of ideal or alternative practices.

Many temples today provide perpetual memorial services (eitai kuyō). A temple often has its own affiliated community for those who prepay to be buried in its shared perpetual memorial grave. The members are usually committed to having their own postmortem perpetual memorial services performed at the temple. Those members are not necessarily parishioners of the temple, believers of the sectorial creed, or Buddhists. They may include migrant consumers in urban cities who do not have their ancestral graves. As single elderlies without heirs or relations increase, the demand for communal burial (*gassō bo*) and perpetual memorial graves (eitai kuyō bo) that come with perpetual memorial services has surged.

Some communities resemble a social or networking club, with various events and activities. The temple affiliated with a community may offer lectures and forums related to religion: they attempt to control knowledge. They may foster and enhance the bonds among the members through class activities that vary from meditation to the copying of a sutra. Rather than cultural, activities may be practical in nature, such as career development for seniors. Speakers are invited to offer lectures and workshops. Leisurely activities may entail a pilgrimage to holy sites or an excursion to secular destinations. This shared experience and time becomes their co-construction of self, that "enhance[s] the sense of imagined community and create[s] feelings of group identity" (Belk 2013, 486). However, the most important activities take place around religious events, including the mass prayer at the regular memorial service for deceased members. By participating in the memorial service, they ensure the succession of the memorial service by fellow members.

The empirical focus of my investigation is the making of memorial communities. Specifically, I use the case about the association *Moyai no kai* in Tokyo (hereafter called Moyai). I selected Moyai because it is known as the pioneer of the "shared grave" concept in Tokyo and has attracted attention from the public and academia (e.g., Nakasuji 2006). The name Moyai literally means mooring (of a boat), and it in turn means to work in cooperation or share jointly. Moyai is affiliated with Kudokuin Temple, a Shingon sect of Buddhist temple in Tokyo. Originally founded in Kyushu Island during the feudal period, the temple's Tokyo branch opened in

130   *Yuko Minowa*

1988 with a cemetery but without parishioners. As such, they made the cemetery available to all regardless of their religious views. This contrasts with many other temples that require the users be patrons or at least (nominal) believers of the sect. The emphasis of Kudokuin is to provide services that meet the needs of people who live today. The concept of the temple, which they claim on their website (www.haka.co.jp), is "a new memorial community" for building relationships while alive in a contemporary fashion. As mutual aid in the regional community or among kin is disappearing, the temple claims to play a critical role for creating and maintaining human bonds. Aside from a traditional graveyard, they provide multiple types of shared perpetual graves, including the shared grave for the members of Moyai. By 2015, over 2,300 members' remains have been buried in this shared grave. By 2019, they had more than 7,000 users of the cemetery.

The Making of Memorial Community

In ANT, the "translation" refers to the stage of the general process by which an actor who joins a network experiences the identification of actors, the possibility of interaction, and the negotiation and definition of the boundaries of maneuver (Callon 1984). It is the process of establishing a corpus of human and nonhuman connections through the alignment of interests. The stages, or moments, can intersect.

The Problematization, or How to Become Critical

The first moment of translation is problematization. At this moment, the principal actor identifies and delineates the interests of other players in a way that is consonant with their own interests. In Moyai's case, there were two interest groups that had distinct problems but shared a common solution. One group was the founder of the association Moyai who was a focal player in its inception. An urban sociologist, he served as a chief of the public welfare bureau, a head of a ward in Tokyo, and after retiring from government posts, a college professor and the president of a university. He strived for social integration and human rights. Encountering lone elderlies dying alone in poverty in the urban metropolis of Tokyo, he searched for the solution to eradicate solitary death by creating new relationships. By his invitation, around ten college professors joined him as a co-founder.

On the other hand, the Tokyo branch of Kudokuin Temple was new. Although they had the land to site a cemetery, they had no parishioners. Thus, their problem was to find ways to bring in people. Building and marketing a shared grave was one solution. To promote it bundled with the perpetual memorial service, they pursued creating a community for those who would prepay to be buried in it. But, instead of founding and

Solitary Death Is Elsewhere   131

managing a memorial community by themselves, they donated part of the precinct for building a shared grave and let the prominent urban sociologist inaugurate the memorial community and run it as an independent organization. The temple appeared as its religious affiliation discreetly.

So, there were dual movements. The two groups of focal actors with divergent goals—the urban sociologist and the priests from the temple—determined a set of players and defined their roles in a way to establish themselves as indispensable points in the network of relationships they were constituting. Their alliance was indispensable.

The Interessement, or How to Solidify the Alliance

The second moment of translation is interessement. This is the time to persuade various players to accept the problematization with the use of divergent strategies. How did the temple impose and attain the alliance of other actors and stabilize the network? The shared grave, human remains, and the chief priest who practices memorial service—in other words, moral objects and the moral agent—constitute the core of the interessement device. The future destination of the remains locks the actors in place while the venue for practicing memorial service compels them to return regularly. The chief priest was instrumental in stabilizing the network.

The mastermind behind the scenes for maneuvering and solidifying the community was the father of the chief priest, who received the training to be a priest but chose a career in business with an entrepreneurial ambition. He persuaded his son, a charismatic former rock musician, to be the heir of his brother's temple and to promote its services and memorial community. After transforming into a priest, the son aggressively performed the role of a spokesperson through omnichannel communication to reach the mass market: a chaplain at community healthcare institutions, an author and editor of books, a TV persona, the director of the study group for contemporary Buddhist music, and a Buddhist musician giving concerts and marketing his own music.

On the other hand, the father of the chief priest has acted as the executive officer of Moyai. He is the innovator of valued services for the community and, in particular, for the elderly. Not everything he did was driven by a lucrative motive. Having been a student of the founding urban sociologist, he shared his vision. The innovative services he pioneered include an online memorialization site, Cyberstone, where the mourners commemorate the deceased remotely, and the daily morning prayer and sermon streamed online. The most valued service he innovated was the Living Support Service (LISS) system founded in 1993. The prepaid service was incepted to assist those who have nobody to bring their cremated remains to the shared grave. Subsequently, they expanded the service to cover both the critical and trivial roles of family, such as guardianship and

132   *Yuko Minowa*

grocery shopping. The number of contractors of the LISS system grew to over 5,000 members by 2017 (Nikkei 2017).

Enrollment, or How to Manage the Roles

The third moment of translation is enrollment. This reflects successful interessement. It entails different actors to consent to play a role in the network. The aforementioned device of interessement alone does not necessarily guarantee actual enrollment; the device is strategically utilized to define and designate a set of interrelated roles to actors who accept them. Describing enrollment thus requires explaining the entities of multilateral interests and negotiations (Callon 1984). In the case of Moyai, again there were dual movements: the founding urban sociologist advocated for "Moyai culture" and "Moyai activism" to stimulate the general public.

On the other hand, the executive officer of Moyai negotiated and coordinated the management of the remains for the increasing number of members of the community. Handling the remains, the moral object, always pertains moral controversy. At Moyai, it entailed the project of creating the forest in the remote rural mountain area. The remains were buried there to return to the soil, saving space in Tokyo, while the project appealed to advocates of the contemporary ecological sustainability movement. Additional services for a shared grave for nonmembers of Moyai, such as a hotel for the deceased, and "an electronic-brain tomb" Shōtenzuka, were integrated to enhance the attractiveness of existing services for the memorial community Moyai. A hotel for the deceased is a facility to store the corpse while the family makes decisions for the funeral. "An electronic-brain tomb" is an indoor shared tomb with a TV screen; scanning the individual mourner's ID card through the machine in front of the tomb enables him to watch the personal record and images of the deceased in the TV monitor. Meanwhile, the brand Moyai became polysemous.

Mobilization, or How to Organize Actions

The last moment of translation is mobilization. At this stage, the actor network is unified and solidified. Meanwhile, spokespeople who speak in the name of human and nonhuman actors appear. At Moyai, players shared benefits, more emotional than functional support at this stage as the ties of network became stronger, and the members perceived the ethos of the community as unparalleled. Their biannual mass memorial services take place in the municipal auditorium of Sugamo Ward in Tokyo. Monthly memorial services are held at the temple. The memorial practice provides participants a highly communal, pacifying experience and a cathartic escape from the anxiety of solitary death and the imagination of becoming a neglected spirit. The communal ethos manifests in the

Solitary Death Is Elsewhere   133

practice of sharing time among participants of the memorial service. One of the women in their late 80s I interviewed at the temple after a monthly memorial service said that she had an ancestral grave in her birthplace but preferred to be buried at Moyai.

> When my husband was gone, his nephews said that I could enter their grave. But, even if they now say that's fine, there may be a problem later time when their children succeed the grave. They may question who should be in the grave. So, I decided to not enter the same grave. Besides, I have my tomb friends to be buried together here.

The members like her are not thinking to terminate the relationship with their relatives. Instead, they are wishing not to make anyone obligated to take care of their postmortem death rituals. Sharing time while alive with people of the same ideology, as well as sharing the grave after death, is important for the community members.

On the other hand, the bimonthly newsletter *Moyai* has been utilized to share the voice of members since 1990. In the past, it served to align the displaced actors and solidify members by quoting their voices in unison (Nakasuji 2006). The published messages were selected and edited to reverberate the ideology and values of the community. Thus, the diversity of the individual member's thoughts was not necessarily revealed. But it showed how the members from diverse life courses utilized the community, and how the community shared them for their mutually beneficial relationship. The following exemplifies the polysemous nature of Moyai's position (Nakasuji 2006, 214–15):

> My parents died in Manchuria. Their remains were buried there. The family was torn asunder due to the war. . . . In the near future, I will move my brother's remains to Moyai, and bury with the mementos of my parents. . . . I will then feel relieved of my burden. Our family members will ultimately become together again under the grave of Moyai.

Her message indicates the heterogeneous nature of the network; it is not perceived as limited among actors while alive. But the network extends to nonhuman agencies: the remains and imagined spirits in the afterworld.

Conclusion

This chapter discussed the development of the market for end-of-life activities (shūkatsu) that involve preplanning of death rites and rituals. It interrogated the attempts by various actors to make the shūkatsu practice more accessible for a larger group of heterogeneous mature and senior consumers, the role of nonhuman agencies, and the consumers of the

134   *Yuko Minowa*

shūkatsu movement. In particular, I focused on examining the making of the memorial community based on the ANT.

In later modernity, Giddens contends (1990) that the premise was the "diembedding," or "lifting out," of social relations, caused by shifting "time-space distanciation," from local face-to-face to a growing dependence on impersonal mechanisms and expert systems. The commoditization of the death ceremony by funeral professionals has propelled the vanishing of traditional communal cooperation in death rituals. In the megacity of super-aged Japan, however, through the shūkatsu movement, a segment of active seniors and elderlies struggles to search for human interactions through networking in necro-based social organizations.

Why do the elderly seek a community and interaction with others in the social organization? In other words, why are there assemblages of collectives surrounding the consumer death culture? One explanation may be that, rephrasing Bauman (1992), survival is a social construct, and they are rejecting death by constantly preserving the past and inventing the future with actors in the network. For Bauman (1992, 31), death is defied through the "counter-mnemotechnic . . . of culture," meaning culture acts as a device to forget mortality. Forgetting is a strategy to repress or alleviate fear.

As death rituals are disconnected from the traditional religious and ethnological origins, death ceremonies becoming eclectic, society seems to defend itself harder against the ambivalence of death. The memorial community reflects this notion with their networking inter vivos. It is not clear, however, if those actors can ever be truly emancipated from the dominant market logic, typified by the market-driven experience of death, and commoditized by industry players of the shūkatsu movement, due partly to a plethora of business-minded self-claimed divine figures.

Acknowledgments

I would like to thank three reviewers for their invaluable feedback and Chiaki Sakae for bibliographical help.

References

Adaba, Godfried B. and Daniel Azerikatoa Ayoung (2017), "The Development of a Mobile Money Service: An Explanatory Actor-Network Theory," *Information Technology for Development*, 23 (4), 668–86 (https://doi.org/10.1080/02 681102.2017.1357525).

Allison, Anne (2013), *Precarious Japan*, Durham, NC: Duke University Press.

Bajde, Domen (2013), "Consumer Culture Theory (Re)visits Actor-Network Theory: Flattening Consumption," *Marketing Theory*, 13 (2), 227–42 (https://doi.org/10.1177/1470593113477887).

Baker, Courtney Nations, Stacey Menzel Baker, and James W. Gentry (2017), "The Role of Body Fisposition in Making Sense of Life and Death," in *Death in a Consumer Culture*, ed. Susan Dobscha, New York: Routledge, 213–27.

Bauman, Zygmunt (1992), "Survival as a Social Construct," *Theory, Culture & Society*, 9 (1), 1–36 (https://doi.org/10.1177/026327692009001002).

——— (2000), *Liquid Modernity*, Cambridge: Polity Press.

Belk, Russell (1988), "Possessions and the Extended Self," *Journal of Consumer Research*, 15 (September), 139–68 (https://doi.org/10.1086/209154).

——— (2013), "Extended Self in a Digital World," *Journal of Consumer Research*, 40 (October), 477–500 (https://doi.org/10.1086/671052).

Bonsu, Sammy K. and Russell Belk (2003), "Do Not Go Cheaply Into That Good Night: Death-Ritual Consumption in Asante, Ghana," *Journal of Consumer Research*, 30 (1), 41–55 (https://doi.org/10.1086/374699).

Boret, Sebastien Penmellen (2014), *Japanese Tree Burial: Ecology, Kinship and the Culture of Death*, New York: Routledge.

Callon, Michel (1984), "Some Elements of Sociology of Translation: Domestication of the Scallops and the Fishermen of St. Brieuc Bay," *Sociological Review*, 32 (S1), 196–233 (https://doi.org/10.1111/j.1467-954X.1984.tb00113.x).

Covell, Stephen G. (2005), *Japanese Temple Buddhism*, Honolulu: University of Hawai'i Press.

Dales, Laura (2014), "Ohitorisama, Singlehood and Agency in Japan," *Asian Studies Review*, 38 (2), 224–42 (http://doi.org/10.1080/10357823.2014.902033).

Daniels, Inge (2009), "The 'Social Death' of Unused Gifts: Surplus and Value in Contemporary Japan," *Journal of Material Culture*, 14 (3), 385–408 (https://doi.org/10.1177/1359183509106426).

Dobscha, Susan, ed. (2017), *Death in a Consumer Culture*, New York: Routledge.

Earley, Amanda (2014), "Connecting Contexts: A Badiouan Epistemology for Consumer Culture Theory," *Marketing Theory*, 14 (1), 73–96 (https://doi.org/10.1177/1470593113514427).

Gabel, Terrance G., Phylis Mansfield, and Kevin Westbrook (1996), "The Disposal of Consumers: An Exploratory Analysis of Death-related Consumption," in *NA—Advances in Consumer Research*, Vol. 23, ed. Kim P. Corfman and John G. Lynch Jr., Provo, UT: Association for Consumer Research, 361–67.

Gentry, James W., Patricia F. Kennedy, Catherine Paul, and Ronald Paul Hill (1995), "Family Transitions During Grief: Discontinuities in Household Consumption Patterns," *Journal of Business Research*, 34 (1), 67–79 (https://doi.org/10.1016/0148-2963(94)00054-I).

Giddens, Anthony (1990), *Consequences of the Modernity*, Stanford, CA: University of Stanford Press.

Giesler, Markus (2012), "How Doppelgänger Brand Images Influence the Market Creation Process: Longitudinal Insights from the Rise of Botox Cosmetic," *Journal of Marketing*, 76 (November), 56–68 (https://doi.org/10.1509/jm.10.0406).

Hackley, Rungpaka Amy and Chris Hackley (2017), "Death, Ritual, and Consumption in Thailand: Insights from the Pee Ta Kohn Hungry Ghost Festival," in *Death in a Consumer Culture*, ed. Susan Dobscha, New York: Routledge, 96–108.

Hirata, Keiko and Mark Warschauer (2014), *Japan: The Paradox of Harmony*, New Haven, CT: Yale University Press.

Ito, Abito (2007), *Anthropological Introduction to Japanese Folk Society*, Tokyo: Yūhikaku.

Kanawaku, Yoshimasa and Youkichi Ohno (2019), "Solitary Death in the Tokyo Metropolis and Labor Force Status: Characteristics of Unnatural Deaths at

136   Yuko Minowa

Home Among Persons Living Alone," *Journal of Nippon Medical School*, 86 (6), 360–63 (https://doi.org/10.1272/jnms.JNMS.2019_86-604).

Kawano, Satsuki (2010), *Nature's Embrace: Japan's Aging Urbanites and New Death Rites*, Honolulu: University of Hawai'i Press.

Kikuchi, Shota (2018), *Ihai no seiritsu: Jukyo girei kara bukkyo minzoku he* [*The Formation of a Buddhist Memorial Tablet: From Confucian Ritual to Buddhist Folklore*], Tokyo: Toyo daigaku shuppan.

Kim, Hyunchul (2012), "The Purification Process of Death: Mortuary Rites in a Japanese Rural Town," *Asian Ethnology*, 71 (2), 225–57.

Larssæther, Stig (2011), "Milk in the Multiple: The Making of Organic Milk in Norway," *Journal of Agricultural and Environmental Ethics*, 24 (4), 409–25 (https://doi.org/10.1007/s10806-010-9268-0).

Latour, Bruno (1999), "On Recalling ANT," *The Sociological Review*, 47 (S1), 15–25 (https://doi.org/10.1111/j.1467-954X.1999.tb03480.x).

——— (2005), *Reassembling the Social: An Introduction to Actor-Network-Theory*, New York: Oxford University Press.

Law, John (2004), *After Method: Mess in Social Science Research*, New York: Routledge.

Law, John and Michel Callon (1988), "Engineering and Sociology in a Military Aircraft Project: A Network Analysis of Technological Change," *Social Problems*, 35 (3), 284–97 (https://doi.org/10.2307/800623).

Metcalf, Peter and Richard Huntington (1991), *Celebrations of Death: The Anthropology of Mortuary Ritual*, New York: Cambridge University Press.

Mills, Tom (2018), "What Has Become of Critique? Reassembling Sociology After Latour," *The British Journal of Sociology*, 69 (2), 286–305 (https://doi.org/10.1111/1468-4446.12306).

Ministry of Health, Labour and Welfare (2020), *Kōsei rōdō hakusho, Reiwa 2 nen ban* [*White Paper on Health, Labour and Welfare, Reiwa 2nd*], Tokyo: Ministry of Health, Labour, and Welfare.

Nakasuji, Yukiko (2006), *Shi no bunka no hikaku shakaigaku: "Watashi no shi" no seiritsu* [*Comparative Sociology of Death Culture: The Establishment of "My Death"*], Matsudo, Chiba: Azusa shuppansha.

Namihira, Emiko (2004), *Nihon-jin no shi no katachi* [*The Formalities of the Japanese Death*], Tokyo: Asahi shinbunsha.

Nikkei (2017), "Kazoku no yakuwari wo 'daikō': Ohitorisama chakumoku no seizen keiyaku" ['Acting' for the Role of the Family: The Prepaid Contract Inter Vivos That Gains Attention by Singles] (https://style.nikkei.com/article/DGXMZO15727990V20C17A4000000?channel=DF_TBK20030509&n_cid=LMNST011).

Nitta, Masako (2013), "A Welfare Sociological Review of the Discourse on 'Kodokushi' (Lonely Death) or 'Koritsushi' (Isolated Death): For the Social Work Practices," *Sapporo gakuin daigaku jinbungaku kaikiyō*, 93 (February), 105–25.

Price, Linda L., Eric J. Arnould, and Carolyn Folkman Curasi (2000), "Older Consumers' Dispossession of Special Possessions," *Journal of Consumer Research*, 37 (September), 179–201 (https://doi.org/10.1086/314319).

Schäfer, Cyril and Ruth McManus (2017), "Authenticity, Informality and Privacy in Contemporary New Zealand Post-mortem Practices," in *Death in a Consumer Culture*, ed. Susan Dobscha, New York: Routledge, 57–74.

Scott, Elizabeth D. (2000), "Moral Values: Situationally Defined Individual Differences," *Business Ethics Quarterly*, 10 (2), 497–521 (https://doi.org/10.2307/3857888).

Solitary Death Is Elsewhere   137

Shūkatsu Counselor Association (2014), "2014 nendo shukatsu fesuta jisseki" [The Results of the Shūkatsu Festa in 2014] (www.shukatsu-fesuta.com/results/2014/index.html).

Smith, Robert J. (1966), "*Ihai*: Mortuary Tablets, The Household and Kin in Japanese Ancestor Worship," *Transactions of Asiatic Society of Japan*, 3rd Series, 9, 83–102.

Statistics Bureau of Japan (2018), *Statistical Handbook of Japan*, Tokyo: Ministry of Internal Affairs and Communications.

Suzuki, Hikaru (2000), *The Price of Death: The Funeral Industry in Contemporary Japan*, Stanford, CA: Stanford University Press.

———, ed. (2013), *Death and Dying in Contemporary Japan*, New York: Routledge.

Tachibanaki, Toshiaki (2016), *Rōrō kakusa* [*The Disparity Among Elderlies*], Tokyo: Seidosha.

Thomas, Tandy Chalmers, Linda L. Price, and Hope Jensen Schau (2013), "When the Differences Unite: Resource Dependence in Heterogeneous Consumption Communities," *Journal of Consumer Research*, 39 (February), 1010–33 (https://doi.org/10.1086/666616).

Walter, Mary Namba (2008), "The Structure of Japanese Buddhist Funerals," in *Death and the Afterlife in Japanese Buddhism*, ed. Jacqueline I. Stone and Mariko Namba Walter, Honolulu: University of Hawai'i Press, 247–92.

Yamaori, Tetsuo (2002), *Shi no minzoku gaku: Nihonjin no shiseikan to sōsō girei* [*Folklore of Death: The Japanese View of Life and Death and Funeral Rituals*], Tokyo: Iwanami shoten.

Yanagita, Kunio (1946), *Senzo no hanashi* [*Stories About Ancestors*], Tokyo: Chikuma shobō.

Zhao, Xin and Russell Belk (2008), "Desire on Fire: A Naturalistic Inquiry of Chinese Death Ritual Consumption," in *European Advances in Consumer Research*, Vol. 8, ed. Stefania Borghini, Mary Ann McGrath, and Cele Otnes, Milan, Italy: Association for Consumer Research, 245.

8 The Work of Culture in Thai Theravāda Buddhist Death Rituals

Rungpaka Amy Hackley

Introduction

Lying down in a coffin, a Thai woman has her palms pressed together in a prayer-like position holding flowers, a candle and three incense sticks. She can hear monks chanting prayers (*Ānisong Sīa Sop*: The Blessings of Disposing of Corpses) that are normally used in the Prayer for the Dead at Buddhist funerals. The monks cover her coffin with a large piece of white cloth that they normally use as shrouds for corpses in burial rites. After the chanting is over they remove the cloth from the coffin and the woman climbs out. She is participating in the *Norn-Loeng-Sa-Dor-Cro* death ritual, literally translated as lay down in a coffin and you can get rid of bad luck. She believes that this ritual will cleanse her soul and trick bad spirits into thinking that she is already dead so they will not do any more harm to her. After this ritual, it would be as if she was reborn and she could start a new life with a new identity shed of her previous bad karma.

(Extract from the author's ethnographic field notes at
Wat Phromanee Temple near Bangkok, Thailand, 2011).

This chapter extends studies of death and ritual in marketing and consumer research by reflecting on the ways in which a selection of the Theravāda Buddhist tradition of death rituals in Thailand manifests as consumption practices as they bind the living and the dead in rituals of continuity, identity, and social order. The assumption is that while Asian consumer culture is extensively studied from a Western perspective, the varied and nuanced contexts of Asian (Southeast Asian in particular) culture remain underexplored in the Western research literature and offer rich potential sources for consumer cultural insight.

Death rituals and the ritual process associated with death can contribute to our collective life continuity and the production of the "work of culture" (Bloch and Parry 1983; Lifton 1996; Obeyesekere 1990; Ricoeur 1973b, 1976). Elements in rituals communicate symbolic meanings (Gainer 1995; Rook and Levy 1983) and death rituals have played a key role in a better understanding of the symbolic aspects of consumption and consumer culture (Belk 1994; Holt 1992; Houston 1999;

DOI: 10.4324/9781003111559-11

Minowa 2008; Rook 1985; Stanfield and Kleine 1990; Wallendorf and Arnould 1991; Ustuner, Ger, and Holt 2000). Taking a broad perspective on what constitutes a death ritual, this chapter reflects on death rituals such as *Norn-Loeng-Sa-Dor-Cro* (death ritual for the living), '*Por-Tor*' and '*Pee-Ta-Khon*' (two of the hungry ghost festivals that occur annually in Thailand), and joss paper burning death rituals, variations of which occur across Southeast Asian including Thailand, as vivid examples of how traditional beliefs, myths, and death rituals connect through modern-day consumption practices. In these death rituals (Hackley and Hackley 2015, 2016; Tiwsakul and Lim 2011), both symbolic and material practices are used to connect the dead and living.

This chapter aims to connect theoretically with the extended form of Arnould and Thompson (2005, 2007, 2018)'s work on consumer culture theory (CCT). Although Moisander, Peñaloza, and Valtonen (2009) address the lack of interpretive consumer culture studies by non-Western (American) ethnic minority researchers within the CCT community, practical and theoretical problems and issues still remain. Moisander et al. (2009) suggest that consumer culture research related to the Asian consumer culture context often employs research conventions that broaden North American theoretical and methodological constructs to exemplify cultural differences, rather than starting with candidly investigating differing cultural consumption phenomena in developing theoretical constructs that might challenge established CCT and Western customs. This chapter hopes to address this issue by seeking to generate new insights on a central enigma of Southeast Asian consumption.

The approach taken uses multiple methods of data gathering including autoethnography, ethnographic field notes, observations, interviews, and videography, and the interpretation draws also on practice theory. The chosen rituals are described as examples of Thai Buddhist ritual and practice although, like much religious belief and practice in the east, they are highly inflected by influences from folk beliefs and local cultural and commercial practices as well as by Theravāda, Mahāyāna, and Tibetan Buddhism (Sino-Thais being the largest ethnic group in Thailand). Nonetheless, the practices would be described as essentially religious and Buddhist by participants as they are framed and constrained by Theravāda Buddhist structural and constitutive influence. The focus of the chapter is not what might be regarded as doctrinally correct Theravāda Buddhism, nor is it the historical provenance of the myth and folklore that intermingle seamlessly with daily religious practice in Thailand. Rather, the focus of the chapter falls on the everyday practice and experience of religious belief for Thai people as it manifests in selected ritual practices.

Below, the cultural context of Thailand and Thai Buddhism is introduced, followed by an introduction to the cultural logic of death rituals in Thailand. Subsequently, the chapter will offer an outline of the four death rituals that form the basis of the philosophical reflections in this chapter.

140   Rungpaka Amy Hackley

Next, the chapter will develop a discussion on contrasting eastern and western notions of selfhood and death as end point or juncture of continuity, before continuing with reflections on the ideas of Bloch, Ricour, and Obeyesekere in relation to Asian consumer culture and death ritual.

Theravāda Buddhism in Thailand

Thailand (formerly Siam) is one of the most strongly Buddhist countries in the world where 95% of the population practices Theravāda Buddhism (a branch of Hinayana Buddhism) (Anonymous 2001). Among Thai people, Buddhism is "a way of life, a national identity and the key to primordial Thainess" (Wattanasuwan and Elliott 1999, 151). Thais have a strong sense of national identity as the country "avoided the ideologically driven wars that decimated and impoverished their neighbouring countries" (Blandin 2003, 13). Thailand has been a constitutional monarchy since 1932, but its tradition of absolute monarchy goes back many centuries.

Thai culture has been influenced by Khmer, Mon, Chinese, and Indian cultures (Ginsburg 2000). Theravāda Buddhism emphasizes "the individual practice of meditation, the value of good social conduct, and the attainment of salvation from earthy desires thus breaking the cycle of rebirth and suffering" (Blandin 2003, 15). "*Sangha*" (Buddhist clergy), a national community of monks, embodies the ways of the Buddha and is highly involved in every aspect of life. For most Thai people, it is important to honor the Buddha and to accrue merit through virtuous activities such as, for example, offering food to monks at the temple in the early morning, releasing caged birds (they are captured to be ritually released in exchange for a price), building new temples, and presenting robes and other necessities to monks. Merit making and belief of reincarnation are important to Thai Buddhists. Buddhist holy days and ceremonies take place all year and offer many opportunities for merit making. Thai temples, therefore, are important sites of cultural, religious, and social practices.

Alongside belief in the Buddha and his teachings, in Thailand, a multitude of folk beliefs operate, especially beliefs in spirits and gods. The practice of Thai Buddhism remains animistic (Blandin 2003; Wattanasuwan and Elliott 1999). Spirits are believed to inhabit all things and these spirits must be placated. For example, spirit houses (which can be found in almost every Thai house and business premises) typically hold offerings of food, flowers, incense sticks, and candles to placate the spirits who dwell within. Thais have woven the animist and Buddhist beliefs together which create endless fascinating ceremonies and festivals.

Theravāda Buddhism (the School of the Elders) is the oldest branch of Buddhism practiced in Southeast Asia and is prevalent in Sri Lanka, Thailand, Cambodia, Laos, and Burma (Gethin 1998; Langer 2007), in contrast to later schools of Buddhism such as Mahāyāna (the great vehicle)

The Work of Culture in Buddhist Death Rituals   141

and Vajrayāna (the diamond vehicle) (Gethin 1998). Theravāda Buddhism evolved from the Buddhist canon of the *Tipiṭaka* (or the triple baskets of early Buddhist scriptures, which were written in the now-extinct Pali language) consisting of the *Vinaya* (the Book of Discipline for the monks or sangha), the *Suttanta*, Discourses, and the *Abhidhamma* (the higher teachings or exposition of realities) (Gorkom 1996). The fundamental tenets of Theravāda Buddhism are stated in the Four Noble Truths (*ariya sacca*) which were articulated by *Siddhattha Gotama* in Pali or *Siddhartha Gautama* in Sanskrit. The Four Noble Truths are existence (*dukkha—*suffering); craving/attachment (*trishna*—the cause of dukkha); the state of nirvana or *Nibbāna* (liberation, enlightenment, and the extinction of personality and personal desires which is the end of all suffering); and the way to end all dukkha and achieve nirvana. The cessation of dukkha is through the practice of the Eightfold Path (*ariya magga*), namely, right understanding, right thinking, right speech, right action, right livelihood, right effort, right mindfulness, and right concentration (Gorkom 1996).

For Buddhists, refining their practice of Buddhism can free them from the cycles of birth, death, and rebirth. Buddhists believe in *karma* (or merit) and *samsāra*. Karma is a Sanskrit word which refers to effects of actions during several lives [through the wheel of life (WOL)] which defines the destiny of an individual. Samsāra is a Sanskrit word which literally means continuous flow. Samsāra in Theravāda Buddhism refers to the idea of the cycle of rebirth and suffering due to their karma. Thai Buddhists believe that any acts done in accordance with the Buddha's teachings are to be counted as positive karma or merit (*bun* in Thai), whereas any acts against them are counted as negative karma or demerit (*bap* in Thai). Both positive and negative karma affect a person's present life, next life, and in reincarnated lives on the WOL.

The Realms of the WOL

In the cycle of the WOL, beings are born, die, reborn, die again, and reborn again while going through the six realms of life. According to Gould (1991, 1992),[1] these six realms (which are common to Theravāda and Mahāyāna Buddhism) serve as a hierarchy of desirable states of existence. The lowest realm is the hell realm, followed by the hungry ghost (preta or pret) realm, animals, humans, gods/antigods, and finally, enlightened beings. The hell realm is the least desirable as the being is in a state of misery, privation, and pain as he/she is punished for misdeeds and in the previous life. The hungry ghost realm is where the individual is full of greed and unfulfilled desire and yearning for food, love, or material goods, and he/she is reborn as a hungry ghost. The animal realm is where the individual has a miserable and ignorant life. In the human realm, the being can attain some material gratification, but he/she has to work hard to achieve it and it can be lost. Envy of the higher gods leads to the

142   *Rungpaka Amy Hackley*

antigod realm. In the god realm, the being can achieve degrees of great and constant pleasure (which can go beyond material gratification). The last realm is beyond the WOL which is the most desirable realm. This happens when the being achieves enlightenment or nibbāna (Pali or nirvāna in Sanskrit), being free from all sorrow, birth, old age, and death. He/she has gone beyond this cycle of life, birth and rebirth, leaving materialism, desire, and possessiveness behind.

Theravāda Buddhism encourages Buddhists to prepare for death in order to live a mindful and conscientious life. This contemplation of death is integrated with the practice of mindfulness. The sutta on the four Foundations of Mindfulness lists nine different contemplations on a corpse at different stages of decay (Fronsdal n.d.). In Theravāda Buddhism, Buddhists are encouraged to reflect on the four protections which are the contemplation of the qualities of the Buddha that can protect Buddhists from doubt and discouragement, the practice of loving-kindness for anger, contemplating the unappetizing aspects of the body to calm desire (especially sexual desire and the contemplation of death as a protection from laziness). The decaying corpse is perceived as evidence of the fundamental Buddhist doctrines of the moral cause and effect (karma), of impermanence of all things (anicca), of existence as suffering (dukkha), and of the absence of an eternal self (anattā). In Theravāda Buddhism, the quality of the last conscious moments at the time of death is important as it can determine the circumstances of the next rebirth. There are good and bad deaths in Theravāda Buddhism (Langer 2007). If one practices and understands the Buddha's teachings, this should lead to a good death.

Helping the Dead Achieve a Good Rebirth

Thai people believed that the *phī* (ghost) of death can be dispelled through appropriate performance of death rituals and funerary rites. These performances, chanting prayers by monks, and merit making on the behalf of the deceased assist the *dūang winñān* (the essence that survives not only death but also the disposal of the body) to have a greater chance of being reborn in a desirable state or contribute to reducing the time that he/she might spend in that state of suffering. This merit transfer is believed to ensure a good rebirth for the person who has died.

Phī: The Essence Beyond Death

"Preta" (Hungry Ghost)

The hungry ghost is a particularly significant figure in Thai Buddhist belief and folk mythology: "A preta (ghost) is one who, in the ancient Buddhist cosmology, haunts the earth's surface, continually driven by hunger—that is desire of one kind or another." (Oates 1974, in Gould

1991, 33). Those people who accumulated bad karma when they were alive may be punished by being reborn in the ghost realm as hungry ghosts. The translation of preta to refer to the myth of the hungry ghost seems to cause some confusion in the Western literature. The Sanskrit word preta is generally used to mean dead or as defined by Langer (2007) "in a more technical sense, newly dead, ghost" (17), so the word has a slightly different meaning (and different Anglicized spelling) in reference to Theravāda Buddhist death rituals in Southeast Asia. According to Langer (ibid), "the past participle from the root pra √i, preta (mfn.)," which literally means "gone away," came to mean "departed, deceased, dead, a dead person." In the course of time, the term acquired another, more specialized meaning, namely, "the spirit of a dead person (especially before obsequial rites are performed), a ghost, an evil being and a newly dead as opposed to ancestor (pitṛ, m.)" (17). In Buddhism, death rituals should be performed to help the deceased transfer from being pretas (ghosts) to pitṛ (ancestors). Holt (1981) supports this belief: "the pattern of ritual activity designed to promote the deceased from the status of pretas to pitṛ was prevalent before the emergence of specifically Buddhist conceptions" (6). Pretas, without death rituals, would retain their hunger and misery.

There are three different types of pretas according to their dwelling place and behavior: the ñati-prēteo (ñati = relative who cannot let go of his/her loved ones), the maḷa-prēteo (maḷa = dead) prefers dwelling places like cemeteries and crossroads, and the gevala-prēteo (geval = houses) are ghosts who cannot let go of their homes (Langer 2007). Pretas are always hungry and thirsty, and they cannot feed or put on any clothes themselves. They have long thin necks, tiny mouths, long arms and legs, and huge bellies. Their appearance and craving are depicted in many folk tales that are related to Thai children.

Hungry Ghosts Versus Ancestors

In Buddhism, not all the deceased will become ancestors because some will become ghosts, depending on the person's moral behavior, how they died, and whether proper death rituals were conducted for them. Langer (2007, 14), writing of Sri Lankan Buddhist practices, discussed the importance of the "quality of the last conscious moments at the time of death as determining the circumstances of the next rebirth." Buddhists believe that people who die during a natural disaster or in an unnatural death are likely to become ghosts as their bodies cannot be found, and hence, it is not possible for their relatives to conduct proper death rituals or hold appropriate funerals. In addition, if the deceased relatives have no living descendants, they are also likely to become ghosts as there is no one who cares for them by feeding them (donating food to monks or taking part in death rituals) and performing death rituals on their behalf. In Theravāda

144   *Rungpaka Amy Hackley*

Buddhism and Chinese Confusion Buddhism and Taoism, abandoned/ wandering souls and hungry ghosts seem to be the main kinds of ghosts that are related to death rituals. It is also believed that by conducting death rituals on behalf of ancestors and feeding them, the ancestors in return will offer protection and good luck for the living. The hungry ghost or pretas realm of the WOL is clearly separated from that of the living (the Human realm), but death rituals conducted at specific times and places can open the gates to an interaction between the living and the dead, as we will see in the rituals discussed below.

The Interpretation of Death in Buddhist Texts

In Thailand, when a death occurs, before the corpse (*sop*, in Thai) is cremated, it will be laid in a room for up to 100 days (or even years in the cases of some high ranking monks) in order for relatives to pay respects and offer prayers. The physical remains are no longer considered to be a person (*khon* in Thai), but the source of a potentially perilous spirit (phī) which would trouble the living until the physical remains are properly disposed of and the spirit is placated. It is believed in Buddhism that a corpse must be sent off so it can be separated from the social grouping in which it has been part of when the deceased was alive. Thai funerary rites are directed toward the disposing of a corpse (and sending off of the phī) and giving friends and family a chance to sit with the dead body which can help with their grieving process. This tainted spirit can benefit from merit made on its behalf by family members and friends of the decreased in death rituals. After this ritual process, the spirit can be further transformed through rebirth into a new being the state of which would be determined by the merit (positive karma—bun in Thai) and demerit (negative karma—kam in Thai) accumulated by the deceased during his or her lifetime and by the merit transferred to the spirit by his or her family and friends. By taking part in Thai funerary rites, the phī would become dūang winñān (the essence that survives not only death but also the disposal of the body). This essence has liminal essence, and it is linked to the Buddhist construct of consciousness. This state is not an immortal state but a link between one existence and the next on the WOL.

The phī can include the *thēwadā* (Gods or deities) who may be dangerous if their death has been sudden and violent, and their spirits have not been placated properly. Theravāda Buddhists, like Western counterparts, are unwilling to accept death as signifying the finality of life. The phī can be sent off through the performance of appropriate death rituals and funerary rites, but the idea of dūang winñān shows that the deceased and his or her identity goes beyond death and has a new existence.

This chapter will now outline the method and describe the four death rituals chosen for this study by the author.

Methodology and Data Collection

This research is framed within a social constructionist ontology to imply that human beings are interactional beings who construct knowledge not in isolation or solely as a result of external variables but in engagement with the social world. Practice theory (Bourdieu 1977; Ortner 2006; Skålen and Hackley 2011) was adopted in this study in tandem with ethnography, videography, autoethnography, reflexive field notes, and observations. The theoretical perspective of practice theory informed the analysis of ethnographic data and tentative interpretations of some of the cultural meanings of the chosen four death rituals. The author sought an ethnomethodologically informed rich description (Geertz 1973) by contextualizing this insight with her first-hand knowledge of ghost mythology, Theravāda Buddhism, and Thai death rituals and language.

Four Thai Death Rituals

Por Tor Hungry Ghost Festival in Phuket Province

Hungry ghost festivals are celebrated in many East and Southeast Asian countries. In the Chinese calendar, the ghost festival is on the 15th night of the 7th lunar month. This day is considered to be a ghost day, and the 7th lunar month is a ghost month. It is believed that ghosts and ancestors will move from the lower realm of the WOL (hell being and hungry ghost realms) to the human realm. On this particular period, Buddhists believe that the gates of the realms of hell are opened, and the living and the dead can intermingle. The ghosts are invited to the human realm and offered food to placate them. Rituals would typically include singing and dancing, praying, ritualistic food offerings, burning incense sticks, and burning joss paper money.

Por Tor derives from the Chinese heritage in Southern Thailand when the first immigrants from China and Malaysia came to work in the mines of Phuket. In this ritual, unique red turtle-shaped cakes that are symbolic of long life and good fortune are offered and consumed. Food is offered to Por Tor Kong, who is the Devil spirit in charge of the hungry ghosts' realm on the WOL and to other hungry spirits who have been released from their realm by the goddess Gwan Yin to return to their former homes. In return for the food, it is hoped that the hungry ghosts will give local people and the town blessings.[2] One distinctive aspect of this ritual is that the ghosts are assumed to be physically present, and seats are left empty at the site of the ritual for the ghosts to occupy. When singing or dancing is taking place on the stage, some visitors lean over as if they are trying to see around the bodies of the ghosts. This ritual is closely linked to local cultural identities and community.

146 *Rungpaka Amy Hackley*

Pee Ta Khon Hungry Ghost Festival in Dan-sai District, Loei Province

The Pee Ta Khon hungry ghost festival is held annually for three days between March and June in Dansai district in the north-central Loei province. Dansai is regarded as a sacred place, and this hungry ghost festival is unique to this province. Its history goes back further than local memory. It is one of the most important merit-making ceremonies in the Heed Sib-Song Klong Sib-Si tradition of the Theravāda Buddhist calendar. It doubles as a fertility ritual calling on the relevant spirits to bless the forthcoming harvest. It is, like the Por Tor festival, central to the identity of the local people, and it also acts as a tourist attraction. Pee Ta Khon is part of the larger event called Bun Luang. This event consists of the Pee Ta Khon festival (hungry ghost festival), Prapheni Bun Bung Fai (rocket festival), and Bun Pra Wate (a merit making ceremony). This hungry ghost festival was originally known as Pee Tam Khon, which is literally translated as ghosts follow the living. It is based on an old folklore tale of the last and tenth incarnation of the Buddha, Prince Mahavejsandon Chadoh who left his banishment in the forest to return to the village.

The first day of the festival is called Wan Ruam, which literary means an assembly day. The ritual starts in the early morning; the town's residents invite the spirit known as Phra U-Pakut from the Mun River to protect the area where the festival is held. There is a small parade at this stage. Later in the morning, the parade goes to the house of the black magician or witch, called Ban Chow Guan in order to perform the ritual Bai Sri Soo Kwan (the ritual of bringing back spirits). When this is finished, Chow Guan (the black magician who takes care of a ghost named Pee Hor Luang), Nang Tieam, Kana San, and Nang Tang (the black magician's helpers), a dancing group of Pee Ta Khon, and some local residents would be invited to join the parade. The parade then moves to Phon Chai temple.

The second day of the Pee Ta Khon festival is the occasion of the centerpiece, a colorful and ribald march of hungry ghosts, portrayed by locals in fierce masks and elaborate homemade ghost outfits, who drink, dance, and tease people along their way, occasionally prodding tourists and local people with giant phalluses. Much food and drink are offered and consumed on the route of the parade. The parade continues until the afternoon when they welcome the Buddha Mahavejsandon and his family back to the town (this part is called Hae Phra). The third day of the festival is the day of virtue, with no ribaldry or dancing. Local people attend a grand sermon and follow Buddhist precepts.[3]

Norn-Loeng-Sa-Dor-Cro Death Ritual for the Living

This is the ritual described in the opening passage of this chapter. It earned popularity locally as a way of getting rid of bad luck but when it was featured in a Thai horror film called The Coffin (2008) directed by Ekachai

The Work of Culture in Buddhist Death Rituals   147

Uekrongtham and distributed by Arclight Films, it achieved a national presence. Some temples such as Wat Phromanee near Bangkok offer this death ritual for the living on a rather commercial basis and hundreds of people queue to take part for a fee of US$5. It is not unusual for Thai monks and temples to offer what are essentially commercialized spiritual services, and the death ritual for the living has become a significant brand. The participants to this ritual partake in a mock funeral rite, laying in real coffins and undergoing much of the ceremony and prayers that are conducted in real funeral rites. It is a dramatic and visually enchanting ritual undergone in all sincerity by devotees and conducted with gravitas by the monks.

Joss Paper Burning Ritual

The Joss paper burning ritual is a Chinese/Thai ritual that originally used mock money, but in recent years, it has become highly commercialized with paper versions of branded goods, houses, cars, handbags, wrist watches, laptops, mobile phones, cigarettes, and Viagra tablets (often tagged with the name of the intended decreased recipient), each of which is burned so that the deceased may enjoy them in their ghostly realm. The act of merit making can be seen as a moral obligation and an expression of respect and gratitude for what the ancestors and the deceased relatives had done for the living. Where paper mock-ups of branded goods are burned in such rituals, it seems evident that the memories of the deceased's favorite brands that once constituted their identities can carry on and attain immortality. A more recent innovation of this ritual for Thai people is an iPhone app that they can download to virtually burn ghost money for their ancestors.

The chapter will now discuss some of the philosophical issues arising from these ritual practices, drawing on the work of various theorists. Importantly, the discussion will focus on the contrasts and commonalities between Western and Eastern notions of death.

Discussion: Bloch's Rebounding Violence, Ricoeur's Cultural Hermeneutics, and Obeyesekere's Work of Culture

Bloch (1992) extended and challenged Van Gennep's theory of rites of passage. One of the key limitations of Van Gennep's work, Bloch thinks, is that it focused too much on status acquisition and does not quite explain the power of ritual in people's lives. Ritual, for Bloch (1992) acts "as though humanity interrupts the natural process of birth, growth and death, replacing it, in a symbolic way, with a process of ritual death and ritual rebirth" (Davies 2002, 19). He refers to this process as the rebounding violence or rebounding conquest. This process is mediated through

148　Rungpaka Amy Hackley

religious rituals which are performed so participants can become who they are meant to be, and the process involves the transformative energies of the human being and life cycle (ibid).

In Theravāda Buddhism, the idea of the consciousness, mind, or life force (*Vijñāna* in Sanskrit or *viññāna* in Pali) that links the life of a person who dies with the life of a person who is born (Keyes 1987). The viññāna is one of the five constituents or aggregates (*skhandha* in Sanskrit *or khandha* in Pali) that constitute the person. The four other aggregates are materiality or form (*rūpa*), feeling or sensation (*vedanā*), perception (*sañña*), and coefficients of consciousness (the formation that condition consciousness or *sankhārā*) (ibid). The Path of Purification (Visuddhimagga, VIII) is important in Theravāda Buddhist doctrine written by Buddhaghosa in Sri Lanka that these five aggregates should not have any permanence because if they did the doctrine of anattā (the eternal or non self) could not be sustained. Buddhaghosa repeated reference to rebirthconsciousness (*paṭisandhi viññāna*) as being which links one existence with the next and anattā is maintained by denying that consciousness is an absolute entity (Keyes 1987). In Thailand, the concept of consciousness (viññāna) has been linked with the term dūang winñān (it has a liminal existence beyond death that links between one existence and the next on the WOL).

In Buddhism, it is believed that life and our experience in the world are not permanent; henceforth, Buddhists should be released from dukkha which can be translated as suffering and attempt to attain nibbāna (Pali or nirvāna in Sanskrit), being free from all sorrow, birth, old age, and death. Nibbāna is the end of the cycle of birth and death. The Buddha said, "Birth is dukkha, decay is dukkha, death is dukkha; likewise sorrow and grief, woe, lamentation and despair. To be conjoined with things we dislike, to be separated from things we like, that also is dukkha. Not to get what one wants, that also is dukkha" (Gorkom 1996, 80). In Visuddhimagga (the Path of Purification), the life moment of living being is really short, "the life of living beings lasts only a single conscious moment. . . . Life, person, pleasure, pain—just these alone. Join in one conscious moment that flicks by. Ceased khandhas of those dead or alive. All are alike, gone never to return. No (world is) born if (consciousness is) not. Produced, when that is present, then it lives; when consciousness dissolves, the world is dead" (Gorkom 1996, 82). Death can remind us the impermanence of each life moment. This is rather similar to Ricoeur's work on *Oneself as Another* (1992) as he remarked on a correlation between acting and suffering. He writes, "For my part, I never forget to speak of humans as acting and suffering" (320).

Obeyesekere (1990) construes the work of culture in much the same way as does Ricoeur (1913–2005). The work of culture refers to "the process whereby symbolic forms existing on the cultural level gets created and recreated through the minds of people" (Obeyesekere 1990, xix).

The Work of Culture in Buddhist Death Rituals 149

It focuses on the formation and transformation of symbolic forms. The work of culture (symbols, signs, and texts) forms the central core of Ricoeur's understanding of selfhood which is equated with the linguistic reflection on existence. Telling and retelling rituals and narratives, for example, reenact our symbolic connection to our world and existence. Death rituals entail a form of the symbolic connection with existence. Ricoeur emphasized a priority of meaning over self-consciousness (Ricoeur 1975). Before we can reflect on questions of being, the detour of a hermeneutics of symbols must be undertaken (Ricoeur 1973a). The task of hermeneutical discovery of selfhood is to recover the self from the vast diversity of symbols, signs, and texts by the interpretation of various forms of semiotic meaning. Death rituals can be understood as part of this process of recovery.

Ricoeur's work on a cultural phenomenological-hermeneutics (1975) emphasizes practical life as action. For Ricoeur, the enduring interconnections of phenomenology and hermeneutics helped us understand our lived experiences, giving us a sense of belonging and being-in-the-world (1992). He discussed several layers of the social and ideological imaginary of the human structures of being-in-the-world and hermeneutical experience itself (ibid). Our being and self, for Ricoeur (1992), is a respondent to a call that comes from the other, "this Other, the source of injunction, is another person whom I can look in the face or who can stare at me, or my ancestors for whom there is no representation, to so great an extent does my debt to constitute my very self, or God—living God, absent God—or an empty place" (355). The death rituals of Thai Buddhism connect consumerism, folklore and superstition, and religious belief, and they also operate on the plane of this injunction to invest ancestors with life and to elaborate on the sense of being-in-the-world of the living.

For Ricoeur, the meaning of being is mediated in a continuous process of interpretations. He believed that meanings were not solely produced by the subject of consciousness, and the subject did not constitute the world. Instead, the object (the world or culture) also intends meanings toward the subject. Human existence is dependent on cultural meanings, "existence arrives at expression, at meaning, and at reflection only through the continual exegesis of all the significations that come to light in the world of culture" (Ricoeur 1974, 26). It "becomes a self—human and adult— only by appropriating that meaning which first resides outside, in works, institutions and cultural monuments in which the life of the spirit is objectified" (Ricoeur 1965, 26). In order to achieve proper self-consciousness, one must go through cultural meaning where one receives from another the opinion of worth as an end in oneself by means of language.

In the Theravāda Buddhist world, meaning is projected through the use of various symbols in Norn-Loeng-Sa-Dor-Cro (death ritual for the living), Por-Tor and Pee-Ta-Khon (hungry ghost festivals), and joss paper burning ritual that carry many connotations. In the production and reproduction

150   *Rungpaka Amy Hackley*

of Buddhist texts and the ritual language around these four death rituals, Thai cultural meaning and identity emerge and continue from the existential awareness of death and the quest for continuity beyond death. For Thai people, reflecting Ricoeur's and Obeyesekere's cultural hermeneutics (1965) and the work of culture (1990), death rituals can help the bereaved and Thai society move away from the brute fact of death to the acceptance of death and create a sense of continuity after death. The memory of a person, a multitude of signs (such as paper representations of things that belonged to the deceased, vividly portrayed hungry ghost figures, coffins in which the living assume a symbolic state of death, red turtle-shaped cakes as offerings), and the repeated memory of the deceased can create a strong sense that the deceased is still present in the world of the living. This supports Hertz (1960/2009)'s remark on death, "the brute fact of physical death is not enough to consummate death in people's minds. The image of the deceased is still part of the system in this world . . ." (81). The death ritual process leads the living to the sense of immortality and self-consciousness by maintaining collective cultural identities linked to those who are now dead. Death would be inconceivable if it were not related to a form of being in some way or another. Such meaning takes place in the process when one moves away from the direct confrontation with death toward one's acceptance that the deceased no longer lives in this world but has achieved a new state of being on the WOL.

For Thai people, death is a result of the transformation of a living person into a phī (the tainted spirit of the deceased before death rituals are performed on their behalf). A ghost is a liminal entity in Buddhism as it is in a transitional state toward other incarnations on the WOL. As noted earlier, when loved ones die, the living have a duty to take part in death rituals that will assist the transition of the deceased spirits from tormented, yearning ghost to happy and placated ancestors. During the process of sending off the phī when death rituals are performed, it can be transformed into the surviving essence dūang winñān (the liminal essence that survives not only death but also the disposal of the body), guided by Buddhist monks through delivering sermons (thēt) and chanting traditional ritual texts from ānisong texts at various points in the process.

As discussed previously, Thai people believe that one's current existence is conditioned by his or her previous karma (Pāli kamma; positive karma Thai *bun* and negative karma bāp). As Tambiah (1970) explains the effect of karma, "Bap has clearly evident results in everyday life in the form of illness, death, misfortune and the pervasive existence of evil spirits . . . the results of bun are vaguely formulated as a desirable state of mind or a better rebirth" (56). Thus, moral action in terms of making merit in the context of death rituals and consumption has been extended to ongoing events of everyday life for Thai people. Merit making through ritual is an essential part of Thai culture and way of life. For Thai people, partaking in the rituals maintains psychological security (their continual

The Work of Culture in Buddhist Death Rituals 151

existence, self-consciousness, and identity) and solidarity in his/her community and family, while also helping to build a peaceful state of mind,
accumulate merit and shift the responsibility to karma (leading to a better
rebirth and eventually nibbāna, the end of the cycle of death and rebirth).
Death rituals can also be seen to provide a means of behavioral control,
social order, stability, and incentives for good behavior in Thai society and
communicating respect and gratitude for parents, elders, and ancestors.
Finally, such rituals also act as a means of social mobility within the very
hierarchal Thai social system, since merit can lead to improved status,
power, and wealth.

The Por Tor hungry ghost festival in Phuket province, for example, is
intended to earn merit for the living by offering food to the Devil spirit
Por Tor Kong and to other spirits from the hungry ghost realm thereby
increasing the well-being of the local villagers. The ritual is essentially
spiritual, but it has a material implication for devotees, many of whom
are not economically secure and believe that correct observance of such
rituals can assist them in achieving better social status, power, and wealth,
while also ameliorating the negative forces of the ever-threatening mali-
cious angry spirits. In performing these death rituals, the living acknowledge their own and the ghosts' liminal state as temporary beings on the
WOL. There is no ontological discontinuity between the death and living.
The work of culture, the continuing existence of the dead, death rituals,
and the ritual language and chants used during these death rites allow
Thai people to restore social order in the face of the rupture caused by
death. The symbolic and material consumption can be enacted during
these death rituals is important to the maintenance of the social order and
also to maintaining the shared cultural identities and hierarchies between
the living and the dead. Driver (2018) refers to gifts of order: rituals and
their material components act as gifts to bestow order on community
and society.

Conclusion

There are potential tensions in applying concepts such as Ricoeur's and
Obeyesekere's cultural hermeneutics (1965) and the work of culture
(1990) to local ritual practices such as Thai death rituals. While acknowl-
edging that there is not a neat or seamless basis for their application, in
this chapter, I have attempted to draw out elements of conceptual resonance that are intended to deepen the understanding of Thai death rituals
not merely unknowable events (to Westerners) or as taken-for-granted
everyday practices (to Thais) but as socially functional phenomena that
can assist in our understanding of consumer culture. Thai people, like
their Western counterparts, are unwilling to accept death as absolute
finality, but their response to this dilemma is very different to that of
the West. The different ways in which Western and Eastern death rituals

152 *Rungpaka Amy Hackley*

intersect consumer culture can be enlightening as they speak to human commonalities in the psychological, social, and spiritual dilemmas raised by the stark reality of death. The brief ethnographic descriptions of death rituals on this chapter highlight how the essential continuity of life and death in Thai Theravāda Buddhism is evoked in symbolic exchanges that are inflected with folklore and local cultural practices. Consumption practices articulate and facilitate these symbolic exchanges, of food, money, offerings, and the material benefits that derive from ritual merit making. Death rituals challenge human identity as our self-consciousness is challenged by mortality. Consumer culture, hence, should not be seen as one variable among others, but a central and autonomous element of this transformation.

Notes

1. See the wheel of life in Gould, S. (1991) on page 39 for further detail.
2. This information is based on a special report on "Por Tor" Hungry ghost festival in Phuket on Andaman News NBT FM 90.5 radio in Thailand at 8.30 AM, a repeat on a local cable TV Channel 1 broadcasted in Phang Nga, Krabi and Phuket provinces, http://thainews.prd.go.th/newsenglish, and personal experience.
3. The information in this part is based on Ruangviset, P. (1996), "Heed Sib-song Klong Sib-si" of Loei people at www.thaifolk.com/doc/phitakhon_e.htm and personal experience.

References

Anonymous (2001), *Thailand: A Traveller's Companion*, Singapore: Editions Didier Millet.

Arnould, Eric J. and Craig J. Thompson (2005), "Consumer Culture Theory (CCT): Twenty Years of Research," *Journal of Consumer Research*, 31 (4), 868–82 (https://doi.org/10.1086/426626).

——— (2007), "Consumer Culture Theory (and We Really Mean Theoretics): Dilemmas and Opportunities Posed by an Academic Branding Strategy," *Research in Consumer Behaviour*, 11 (June), 3–22 (https://doi.org/10.1016/S0885-2111(06)11001-7).

———, eds. (2018), *Consumer Culture Theory*, London: Sage.

Belk, Russell (1994), "Carnival, Control, and Corporate Culture in Contemporary Halloween Celebrations," in *Halloween and Other Festivals of Death and Life*, ed. Jack Santino, Knoxville, TN: University of Tennessee Press, 105–32.

Blandin, Herve (2003), *The Culture, Tradition, and Beliefs of Thailand*, Bangkok: Asia Books.

Bloch, Maurice (1992), *Prey Into Hunter*, Cambridge: Cambridge University Press.

Bloch, Maurice and Jonathan Parry (1983), "Introduction: Death and the Regeneration of Life," in *Death and the Regeneration of Life*, ed. Maurice Bloch and Jonathan Parry, Cambridge: Cambridge University Press, 1–44.

The Work of Culture in Buddhist Death Rituals   153

Bourdieu, Pierre (1977), *Outline of a Theory of Practice*, Cambridge: Cambridge University Press.

Davies, Douglas J. (2002), *Death Ritual and Belief: Rhetoric of Funerary Rites*, 2nd edition, London: Continuum.

Driver, Tom F. (2018), *Liberating Rites: Understanding the Transformative Power of Ritual*, Oxon: Routledge.

Fronsdal, Gil (n.d.), "Notes on a Theravada Approach to Spiritual Care to the Dying and the Dead," *Insight Meditation Centre* (http://tibetanbuddhistency-clopedia.com/en/index.php?title=Notes_on_a_Theravada_Approach_to_Spiritual_Care_to_the_Dying_and_the_Dead_By_Gil_Fronsdal).

Gainer, Brenda (1995), "Ritual and Relationships: Interpersonal Influences on Shared Consumption," *Journal of Business Research*, 32 (3), 253–60 (https://doi.org/10.1016/0148-2963(94)00050-O).

Geertz, Clifford (1973), "Thick Description: Toward an Interpretative Theory of Culture," in *The Interpretation of Cultures: Selected Essays*, ed. Clifford Geertz, New York: Basic Books, 3–30.

Gethin, Rupert (1998), *The Foundations of Buddhism*, Oxford: Oxford University Press.

Ginsburg, Henry (2000), *Thai Art and Culture: Historic Manuscripts From Western Collections*, Chiang Mai: Silkworm Books.

Gorkom, Nina V. (1996), *Buddhism in Daily Life*, London: Triple Gem Press.

Gould, Stephen J. (1991), "An Asian Approach to the Understanding of Consumer Energy, Drives and States," in *Research in Consumer Behaviour: A Research Annual*, Vol. 5, ed. Elizabeth C. Hirschman, London: JAI Press, 33–59.

——— (1992), "Consumer Materialism as a Multilevel and Individual Difference Phenomenon—An Asian-Based Perspective," in *Special Volumes—Meaning, Measure and Morality of Materialism*, ed. Floyd W. Rudmin and Marsha Richins, Provo, UT: Association for Consumer Research, 57–62.

Hackley, Rungpaka Amy and Chris Hackley (2015), "How the Hungry Ghost Mythology Reconciles Materialism and Spirituality in Thai Death Ritual," *Qualitative Market Research: An International Journal*, 18 (2), 427–41 (https://doi.org/10.1108/QMR-08-2014-0073).

——— (2016), "Death, Ritual and Consumption in Thailand: Insights from the Pee Ta Kohn Hungry Ghost Festival," in *Death in a Consumer Culture*, ed. Susan Dobscha, London: Routledge, 96–108.

Hertz, Robert (1960/2009), *Death and the Right Hand*, trans. Rodney and Claudia Needham, London: Routledge.

Holt, Douglas B. (1992), "Examining the Descriptive Value of Ritual in Consumer Behaviour: A View From the Field," in *Advances in Consumer Research*, Vol. 19, ed. John F. Sherry, Jr. and Brian Sternthal, Provo, UT: Association for Consumer Research, 213–18.

Holt, John C. (1981), "Assisting the Dead by Venerating the Living: Merit Transfer in the Early Buddhist Tradition," *Numen*, 28 (June), 1–28 (https://doi.org/10.2307/3269794).

Houston, Rika H. (1999), "Through Pain and Perseverance: Lminality, Ritual Consumption and the Social Construction of Gender in Contemporary Japan," in *Advances in Consumer Research*, Vol. 26, January, ed. Eric J. Arnould and Linda M. Scott, Provo, UT: Association for Consumer Research, 542–48.

154   Rungpaka Amy Hackley

Keyes, Charles F. (1987), "From Death to Birth: Ritual Process and Buddhist Meanings in Northern Thailand," *Folk*, 29, 181–206.

Langer, Rita (2007), *Buddhist Rituals of Death and Rebirth: Contemporary Sri Lankan Practice and Its Origins*, New York: Routledge.

Lifton, Robert J. (1996), *The Broken Connection: On Death and the Continuity of Life*, New York: American Psychiatric Association.

Minowa, Yuko (2008), "The Importance of Being Earnest and Playful: Consuming the Rituals of the West Indian American Day Carnival and Parade," in *European Advances in Consumer Research*, Vol. 8, ed. Stefania Borghini, Mary Ann McGrath, and Cele Otnes, Duluth, MN: Association for Consumer Research, 53–59.

Moisander, Johanna, Lisa Peñaloza, and Anu Valtonen (2009), "From CCT to CCC: Building Consumer Culture Community," in *Explorations in Consumer Culture Theory*, ed. John F. Sherry and Eileen Fischer, Oxfordshire: Routledge, 7–33.

Oates, Carol J. (1974), *The Hungry Ghosts*, Los Angeles: Black Sparrow Press.

Obeyesekere, Gananath (1990), *The Work of Culture: Symbolic Transformation in Psychoanalysis and Anthropology*, Chicago: The University of Chicago Press.

Ortner, Sherry B. (2006), *Anthropology and Social Theory: Culture, Power, and the Acting Subject*, Durham and London: Duke University Press.

Ricoeur, Paul (1965), *Fallible Man*, trans. Charles Kelbley, Chicago: Henry Regnery.

———— (1973a), "From Existentialism to the Philosophy of Language," *Philosophy Today*, 17 (2), 88–96.

———— (1973b), "The Model of the Text: Meaningful Action Considered as a Text," *New Literary History*, 5 (1), 91–117.

———— (1974), *Conflict of Interpretations: Essays in Hermeneutics*, Evanston, IL: Northwestern University Press.

———— (1975), "Philosophical Hermeneutics and Theological Hermeneutics," *Studies in Religion/ Sciences Religieuses*, 5 (1), 14–33.

———— (1976), *Interpretation Theory: Discourses and the Surplus of Meaning*, Texas: The Texas A&M University Press.

———— (1992), *Oneself as Another*, trans. Kathleen Blamey, Chicago: The University of Chicago Press.

Rook, Dennis W. (1985), "The Ritual Dimension of Consumer Behavior," *Journal of Consumer Research*, 12 (3), 251–64 (https://doi.org/10.1086/208514).

Rook, Dennis W. and Sidney J. Levy (1983), "Psychosocial Themes in Consumer Grooming Rituals," in *Advances in Consumer Research*, Vol. 10, ed. Richard P. Bagozzi and Alice M. Tybout, Ann Abor, MI: Association for Consumer Research, 329–33.

Skålen, Per and Chris Hackley (2011), "Marketing-as-practice. Introduction to the Special Issue," *Scandinavian Journal of Management*, 27 (2), 189–95 (https://doi.org/10.1016/j.scaman.2011.03.004).

Stanfield, Mary A. and Robert E. Kleine (1990), "Rituals, Ritualised Behaviour and Habit: Refinements and Extensions of the Consumption Ritual Construct," in *Advances in Consumer Research*, Vol. 17, ed. Marvin E. Goldberg, Gerald Gorn, and Richard W. Pollay, Provo, UT: Association for Consumer Research, 31–38.

The Work of Culture in Buddhist Death Rituals   155

Tambiah, Stanley J. (1970), *Buddhism and the Spirit Cults in Northeast Thailand*, Cambridge: Cambridge University Press.

Tiwsakul, Rungpaka A. and Ming Lim (2011), "Death Consumption and Symbolic Exchange: Postmodern Paradoxes of the 'Hungry Ghost' Festivals in Thailand and Singapore," Paper presented at *the 6th Workshop on Interpretive Consumer Research*, Odense, Denmark.

Ustuner, Tuba, Guliz Ger, and Douglas B. Holt (2000), "Consuming Ritual: Reframing the Turkish Henna-night Ceremony," in *Advances in Consumer Research*, Vol. 27, ed. Stephen J. Hoch and Robert J. Meyer, Provo, UT: Association for Consumer Research, 209–14.

Wallendorf, Melanie and Eric J. Arnould (1991), "We Gather Together: Consumption Rituals of Thanksgiving Day," *Journal of Consumer Research*, 18 (1), 13–31 (https://doi.org/10.1086/209237).

Wattanasuwan, Kritsadarat and Richard Elliott (1999), "The Buddhist Self and the Symbolic Consumption: The Consumption Experience of the Teenage Dhammakaya Buddhists in Thailand," in *Advances in Consumer Research*, Vol. 26, ed. Eric J. Arnould and Linda M. Scott, Provo, UT: Association for Consumer Research, 150–55.

Section IV

Governance and Sustainability in Consumption Practices

9 Utopia and Dystopia

Consumer Privacy and China's Social Credit System

Eric Ping Hung Li, Guojun (Sawyer) He, Magnum Man Lok Lam, and Wing-sun Liu

In 2014, the Chinese government piloted a new surveillance system, the "social credit system" (hereafter, the SCS) in Mainland China to scrutinize the daily conduct of individuals and organizations to "strengthen the establishment of creditworthiness in government affairs, commercial creditworthiness, social creditworthiness, and judicial credibility . . . during the period from 2014 to 2020" (The State Council of China 2014). The SCS combines a reward and penalty mechanism wherein different "social credit scores" are assigned to businesses and citizens to evaluate and reflect their "trustworthiness" in Chinese society. Both state apparatuses (e.g., central and local authorities and judiciary courts [The Supreme People's Court of the People's Republic of China 2019], the People's Bank of China, and the National Development and Reform Commission [Xinhua Net 2019a]) and several private enterprises (e.g., Alibaba, Jingdong, and Tencent [Science Times China 2018]) are mobilized by the central government to develop and implement the reward and penalty system collaboratively.

This nationwide mobilization effectively integrates governmental institutions with private enterprises, rendering the SCS system to resemble Foucault's (1975) concept of "gaze," which consists of a state's exercise of power to oversee the conduct of all social actors at societal, organizational, and individual levels. At the societal level, provincial capital cities and subprovincial cities are urged to develop their region-specific SCS so that the state can score and publicly publish rankings of the trustworthiness of cities annually (Xinhua Net 2018, 2019b). At the organizational level, enterprises from all sectors are subject to the SCS's evaluation of their trustworthiness consisting of corporate social responsibilities, business ethics, and prosocial conduct (Xinhua Net 2016, 2019b). Individual citizens are subject to the SCS measurement at the personal level using dimensions such as sincerity, honesty, and integrity (Mac Sithigh and Siems 2019). Across all three levels, cities, organizations, and individuals with high trustworthiness scores are awarded tax reduction, easier public service access, and so on, while those with low scores are subject to sanctions such as the state's public condemnations, the deprivation of business

DOI: 10.4324/9781003111559-13

licenses, and the limited individual access to public services in education and medical care (Liu 2017; Nanfang Metropolis Daily 2018). Powered by the punishment and reward mechanism applied at different levels in the entire Chinese society, the SCS empowers the state to constantly track and shape the conduct of not only organizations but also individual citizens.

While the SCS intended to create a more socially responsible market and a more ethical and ordered society, it raised a number of concerns related to consumer privacy. First, personal and transaction-related data collected by private firms are expected to be hoovered up by the government without notifying the users. Second, while both the state and private enterprises are now using sensor networks to real-time monitor and analyze citizens' behaviors (usage, brand preferences, etc.) and mobilities, the underlying analytic mechanism remains opaque to the public. Third, the new technologically mediated surveillance platform may substantially influence citizens' consumption behavior and marketing/business practices.

In this chapter, we adopted Foucault's conceptualizations of power, panopticism, and governmentality (Dean 2010; Foucault 1975, 1979, 1991) to unveil the new age of digital panopticism forged by the SCS. We argue that the Internet of Things (IoT) and big data analytics technologies now acts as a one-way mirror that monitors citizens' behavior and interactions in the public space. While it is questionable whether such a high technology-enabled approach erodes our human rights or not, governments and businesses are, in fact, keep collecting and piling up our information and activities, making individuals and organizations fully trackable subjects with permanent records and documentation stored in the "cloud" server. Mareike Ohlberg, a research associate at the Mercator Institute for China Studies, once shared his concerns about the new digital governmentality of China's SCS: "that's a lot of data being collected with little protection, and no algorithmic transparency about how it's analyzed to spit out a score or ranking, though Sesame does share some details about what types of data is used" (Kobie 2019). While it is inevitable for us to shift to a more technology-mediated society, it is crucial for us to remain vigilant in living under digital governmentality in the era of digitalization. For this very purpose, this chapter seeks to probe the evolution of the SCS as a representative of digital governmentality.

Consumer Privacy in the Age of Digital Surveillance

While there are many different conceptions of privacy, Solove (2008) classified these conceptions into six general types: (1) the right to be let alone—the right to privacy; (2) limited access to the self—the ability to shield oneself from unwanted access by others; (3) secrecy—the concealment of certain matters from others; (4) control over personal information—the ability to exercise control over information about oneself; (5) personhood—the protection of one's personality, individuality, and dignity; and (6) intimacy—control over, or limited access to, one's intimate relationships or aspects of life (12–13). At the same time, privacy management is considered an essential (social) skill found in cultures around the world (Petronio 2002).

In the age of digital society, the study of consumer privacy and digital surveillance experienced various stages of transformation. In the 1990s and early 2000s, the study of online consumer privacy primarily focused on consumers' ability to control access to and use of their personal information (Culnan 2000; Milne 2000; Milne and Culnan 2004; Phelps, Nowak, and Ferrell 2000) and their ability to withdraw from unwanted interactions with marketing activities initiated by companies (Petty 2000). In the late 2000s and early 2010s, the increasing popularity of social media triggered various consumer researchers to explore the impact of the new forms of peer-to-peer interactions and sharing on consumer privacy. Venkatesh (2016) adopted the socioanalytical perspective to feature the role of (social) media in facilitating consumers' identity transformation. He explicitly pointed out that consumer privacy has become a key concern in a highly complex environment.

The recent discussion of big data and the IoT technologies further reconfigure the notions of consumer privacy in the new age of digital surveillance. Researchers examined the interdependent privacy infringement (Kamleitner and Mitchell 2019) in the age of digital integration. Numerous online activities are no longer transactions that take place only between marketers and consumers but now also involve interactions that occur among consumers, ranging from partners and family members to friends, acquaintances, and even strangers.

Living in the age of electronic surveillance, there is literally no place for consumers to hide. At the beginning of the digital age, multiple scholars predicted the digital media would act like a panopticon where "observers" would have the power and ability to monitor and control others in an antidemocratic manner (Gandy 1993; Katz and Rice 2002). While we enjoy the free services from social media, search engines, emails, and mobile applications, many of us did not recognize the amount of information we gave away to the service providers or the digital community as a whole. Our everyday (consumption) activities are closely monitored (or tracked) by digital devices and technologies (Lyon 2007). Online banking and online shopping platforms are archiving our consumption and transaction. Companies are constantly collecting our name, address, telephone number, email address, and credit card information while we create an account and/or shop online (*Consumer Privacy 1.0 era*). Our media (e.g., Facebook, WeChat, Twitter, Instagram, LinkedIn) pretty much document all our social interactions and emotions (Fuchs 2014; Nguyen and Li 2010). The new media and "big data" society also create a new panopticon for other agencies such as employers or insurers to track

162   *Eric Ping Hung Li et al*

their employees' or clients' interactivities (Brown and Vaughn 2011; Loi, Hauser, and Christen 2020; Mellet and Beauvisage 2020) (*Consumer Privacy 2.0 era*). Our GPS and GIS systems provide real-time updates of our physical location, Amazon's Alexa and Google Home are now activated by our voices, and wearable technologies like the Fitbit and Apple watch are capturing our steps, heartbeat, and other body movements and activities (Hoffman and Novak 2018) (*Consumer Privacy 3.0 era*).

The increasing popularity of smart devices and smart appliances such as our smartphones, tablets, Google Home, Alexa, and smart TV and smart refrigerator not only create a great convenience for consumers to manage their everyday lives but also generate new sets of privacy concerns that are associated to the data tracking and integration through the new IoT technologies (Mellet and Beauvisage 2020). Kamleitner and Mitchell (2019) introduced a new interdependent privacy protection framework to realize the transfers between sharers, to recognize others' rights and ownership of shared goods, and to respect others' right to privacy. Other scholars also expressed their concerns about the limited regulatory mechanisms on corporate privacy responsibility and consumer data protection (Andrew and Baker 2021; Bandara, Fernando, and Akter 2020) in the new digital age.

While studies of consumer privacy in the digital age are fruitful, they paid much attention to studying privacy mostly in Western contexts and at an individual or organizational level. Research on precarious consumption in the new digital marketplace through the lens of governmentality is scant (Flyverbom, Deibert, and Matten 2019). To provide our probe of the intersection between consumer privacy and the SCS from the perspective of the Chinese government with a solid theoretical foundation, next, we revisited Foucauldian conceptualizations of power, panopticism, and governmentality.

Revising the Foucauldian Power, Panopticism, and Governmentality

In his seminal work, *Discipline and Punish: The Birth of the Prison*, Foucault (1975) investigated the diversity of power relations between political regimes and individuals since the 17th century and introduced two types of power: the sovereign power and the disciplinary power. Foucault referred to sovereign power to a monarchy state's use of mainly juridical apparatus to forge laws defining wrongdoings and impose sanctions such as public torture and execution on wrongdoers to make a population obedient to the monarchy. However, Foucault pointed out the sovereign power began to transform into the disciplinary power in Western societies during the 18th century. While sovereign power is often exercised by the state's use of juristic forces to make punishments spectacular in public, disciplinary power is deployed by the state's efforts in using disciplinary apparatus (e.g., prisons and schools) to identify, correct, and punish individuals who are deemed abnormal deviants according to social norms set by the state. Instead of depriving the lives of deviants, disciplinary power seeks to sustain social norms by training and rehabilitating these deviants, thus realigning deviants' conduct to the state's advocacy.

Drawing on Bentham's notion of the Panopticon, Foucault (1975) conceptualized panopticism by examining the architectural design of a ring-shaped prison complex with two layers. The outer ring-shaped layer has individual cells in which each inmate is locked to be physically and visibly separated from others. Since the panopticon only has windows pierced to face toward the cells, and it is located inside the prison and surrounded by inmates' cells, the interior space of the panopticon is significantly darker than that of cells, thus facilitating the "effect of backlighting" (Foucault 1975, 200). While celled inmates have their behaviors illuminated adequately by natural light, they can barely see guards in the dark panopticon, making inmates rather visible to guards and guards invisible to inmates. This invisibility–visibility dyad makes inmates uncertain about when or whether or not they are being watched. Since inmates have the knowledge of their full exposure to guards and of punishments of wrongdoings once spotted by guards, to avoid potential punishments, these inmates have to spontaneously behave in designated ways as if they are constantly surveilled. Accordingly, the uncertainty enabled by the invisibility–visibility dyad generates self-disciplined inmates, rendering the panopticon to become "a marvelous machine" that controls what one sees and is seen in order to produce *"a guarantee of order"* (Foucault 1975, 200) and "homogeneous effects of [disciplinary] power" (Foucault 1975, 202). In this way, panopticism becomes a light yet efficient surveillance system that can be operated by only a few guards who use the backlighting effects to surveil a large number of inmates and to produce docile and obedient bodies.

Besides prison, Foucault (1975) argued that panopticism is also established in and used by other broader social institutions such as schools, hospitals, barracks, workshops, religious groups, and charity organizations, which contribute to "a formation of what might be called in general the disciplinary society" (209). Powered by surveillance, these institutions systematically and constantly scrutinize, examine, and correct people's conduct according to state advocacies (Foucault 1975).

While both sovereign and disciplinary power manifest the repressive side of the state's exercise of power, Foucault's (1978) later works on the third type of power, biopower, unveil the productive side of power. To Foucault (1978), biopower primarily seeks not to punish or discipline deviants but "incite, reinforce, control, monitor, optimize and organize" a population (136) for "taking charge of life" (143). It refers to a state's efforts in mobilizing a variety of apparatuses, including but not limited to disciplinary ones, to produce subjectivity of a population (Dean 2018).

164   *Eric Ping Hung Li et al*

Building on biopower, Foucault coined "governmentality" to present his thoughts on modern states' governance (Lemke 2007). In governmentality, "government" is not only a political entity that exercises its sovereign and disciplinary power through mobilizing specialized state apparatus but also a state's practice of developing "the conduct of conduct" (Foucault 1982, 221), namely, "a form of activity aiming to shape, guide or affect the conduct of some person or persons" (Gordon 1991, 2).

Echoing Foucault's conception of governmentality, Dean (2010) argues the state now governs an entire population through indirect intervention into ordinary people's lives by diffusing guidance for daily conduct to societies in every possible way (Collier 2009; Dean 2010; Gordon 1991). In doing so, the state produces a self-disciplined population consisting of people who experience freedom while thinking and behaving in ways aligned to the state-advocated guidance.

The Foucauldian concept of governmentality is insightful, particularly because it diversifies states' construction and exercise of power. It illuminates states' governance through exercising the repressing juristic apparatus-operated sovereign power, the disciplining apparatus-enforced disciplinary power, and the productive biopower. However, the genealogy-enabled Foucauldian account suggests that the sovereign power, disciplinary power, and biopower are paralleled and that governmentality is more of biopower than sovereign or disciplinary power (Lilja and Vinthagen 2014; Sharp, Routledge, Philo, and Paddison 2000). Echoing this view, CCT studies also generally revealed that contemporary states often used biopower/governmentality techniques in consumer societies, as states were found to appropriate consumer goods and marketplaces to diffuse state-advocated agendas to societies (Zhao and Belk 2008) without invoking legalistic, centralized, negative, and repressive power (Giesler and Veresiu 2014). Nevertheless, as we will demonstrate in the following section, in the present era of digitalization, governmentality can be seen as a product produced by states' dynamic exercise of all sovereign, disciplinary power, and biopower in the context of consumption in general and in the realm of consumer privacy in particular.

Illustrative Case Study: The Chinese Social Credit System

In the past decade, China has experienced rapid economic growth, leading the country to become the second largest economy in the world now and be expected to surpass the United States in 2030 (Lee 2019). To better monitor the fast-changing demographics and market system and ensure efficient policy-making and enforcement, the Chinese government has explored cutting-edge technologies to address societal problems and preempt social instabilities (Kostka 2019).

At the beginning of the 2000s, the Chinese government sought to promote Confucian morality and implement a socioethical agenda to construct a "spiritual civilization" that accompanies the concomitant progress in material and economic conditions (Brady 2009; Shambaugh 2007). Since then, the government began stressing trust-keeping (诚信) as one of the core constructs of Confucian morality and the fundamental base of the future Chinese market economy (Tang, Hu, and Pan 2001; Zhou 2001).

The official initiation of the SCS dates back to 2007 when the General Office of the State Council of China issued the *Guiding Opinions Concerning the Construction of a Social Credit System* (hereafter, the Opinion) to encourage local authorities to "accelerate the construction of the Social Credit System in China in order to further improve the socialist market economy." Later in 2014, the State Council of China issued *The Notice of the State Council on the Planning Outline of the Construction of a Social Credit System* (hereafter, the Notice). The Notice argued that since "trust-keeping [in the Chinese society] is still insufficiently rewarded, and the costs of breaking trust still tend to be low," addressing the intensified social trust crisis is an urgent need that can be achieved by establishing an SCS scheme. Unlike the Opinion, the Notice directly offered specific directives of building a nationwide SCS by 2020 and explicitly commanded local authorities to "carefully implement."

Close reading on the Notice suggests that the state designed the SCS from mainly two perspectives. First and foremost, the state aimed to make the SCS an accurate surveillance system to ensure that "[there is] no place [in China] for people who does not keep trust (使失信者一处失信, 寸步难行)." The surveillance system was powered by a "Real-Name Mechanism" (实名制, hereafter, the RNM). As the Notice specified, "to establish a trust-keeping information system that different departments can share, all state departments shall work conjointly to properly use the Real-Name Mechanism." The history of the RNM dates back to 2000, when the State Council issued its Gazette No. 285, mandating the use of real names in the financial service sector (e.g., in all banking services). The digitalization allowed the state to exercise its disciplinary power to expand the RNM mandate to other sectors in the 2010s. Mobilized by the state, multiple powerful state apparatuses (e.g., the State Administration for Industry and Commerce, the Ministry of Industry and Information Technology, of Public Security, of Transport, of Construction, the Supreme Court, and the Supreme Procuratorate) to conjointly establish and implement a variety of regulations, legal bills, and laws applicable to nearly all sectors, such as telecommunications and internet communications, online/offline financial services, social media, online shopping platforms, public transportation agencies, and public health services (BBC News 2017; Global Times 2015; Pengpai News 2017). In this way, the RNM mandate becomes effective at both the organizational and individual levels in penetrating the most fundamental shield of consumers' privacy, their real names. The RNM thus serves as the infrastructure of the SCS and resembles a digital panopticon helping the state to cast gazes on people and organizations' daily activities.

166　*Eric Ping Hung Li et al*

The second perspective that the state designed for the SCS is to define it as a helpful device for exercising both disciplinary and sovereign power. The state exercised its disciplinary power by calling for establishing a Punish-Reward Mechanism (hereafter, the PRM) aiming at rewarding people with responsible conduct and punishing deviants. The Notice defined the PRM to be effective in comprehensively examining and regulating the trust-keeping behaviors from four broad sectors: governmental administrations (e.g., local government's delivery of promises they made to the public), public services (e.g., strictly implementing state-set/-advocated policies in sectors such as public health, education, labor market, and popular culture), juristic system (e.g., keeping juristic practices transparent to the public), and commercial activities (e.g., overseeing pollution produced by manufacturers, punishing providers of misleading marketing communications, scams, and frauds). Accordingly, the PRM was meant to compromise not only the privacy of consumers but also that of organizations.

To implement the PRM, the state exercised its sovereign power to call for juristic apparatuses to develop relevant sanctions and impose them on deviants. Simultaneously, it also advocated for developing point-based scoring mechanisms to serve as the basis for the measurement of sanctions. To speed up installing the SCS nationwide, the state did not promote a nationwide universal SCS scheme or a scoring mechanism but decentralized the power to local authorities. As of 2021, over 261 prefecture-level cities and 36 provincial capitals and subprovincial cities have built their localized SCS schemes (Credit China 2021) upon their region-specific scoring mechanisms.

While the state drew the blueprint of the SCS in the Notice, the operation of the SCS can be best exemplified by taking a closer look at the Sesame Credit (芝麻信用) scheme, one of the most predominant SCS schemes developed by the Ant Financial Services Group (hereafter, the AFSG). The AFSG is a subsidiary of Alipay, the most used moneyless payment platform for both online and offline payments that is owned by Alibaba, the Chinese e-commerce giant and the owner of the Alibaba wholesale website, and Taobao and T-mall, the two most visited online shopping platforms for individual consumers (Alibaba Group 2021). Backed by these Alibaba platforms covering shopping and moneyless payment services in both online and offline, the Sesame Credit collected data from all possible transactions (Sesame Credit 2019a) made through Alipay, including payments for local grocery shopping, hydro bills, mobile phone, and internet plans, and anything in between.

Once collected, all data were analyzed using an AFSG-specific point-based scoring mechanism. The scoring system assesses consumers' credibility based on personal credit history, personal preference, personal contractual capacity, the characteristics of personal identity, and interpersonal connections. The Sesame Credit scores range from 350 to 950. The

Utopia and Dystopia 167

higher the score represents, the better person's trustworthiness (Sesame Credit 2021).

Due to the state's decentralization approach mentioned earlier, any authorized city/company was empowered as the disciplinary apparatus of the SCS to configure its own scoring mechanism to speed up the construction of the PRM and the SCS. Consequently, many unstandardized and opaque scoring mechanisms have been produced and adopted by various local authorities and authorized RNM-enabled private enterprises (e.g., Jingdong, a leading online shopping platform, and WeChat Pay, a popular moneyless payment platform developed by the Chinese internet giant, Tencent).

In terms of rewards, at an organizational level, state and local departments publicly published "red lists" to praise legal persons and their organizations who have high trustworthy scores because of their records of "trustworthy" behaviors (e.g., corporate giving, volunteerism), showing organizational social responsibility, business ethics, and prosocial conduct (Xinhua Net 2016). These legal persons and organizations were then rewarded with tax reductions, low-interest loans, and fast-track access to governmental services (Kostka 2019; Xinhua Net 2019c). At an individual level, people were measured in terms of sincerity, honesty, and integrity in their daily lives (Mac Sithigh and Siems 2019). Highly scored individuals were then rewarded by authorized private enterprises (e.g., the AFSG) with services that can better their quality of lives, such as deposit-free or a discounted rate of renting umbrella, power bank, bike, cars, apartments, and easy access to or the increased credit limit of loans/mortgages (Nanfang Metropolis Daily 2018; Sesame Credit 2019b).

However, the PRM seems to emphasize more punishments than rewards. At an organizational level, state apparatuses, especially from the administrative and judicial systems, created "blacklists" for "untrustworthy" companies that have low trustworthy scores resulted from business misconduct (e.g., the violation of environmental laws, tax fraud, production of counterfeits, and deferred commercial loan payments) (MBAlib 2019). The state's legal sovereign power was then exercised through these apparatuses, which suspended blacklisted companies' business permits and licenses (MBAlib 2019).

Both state apparatuses and selected private enterprises helped the state to exercise its sovereign power at an individual level. These institutions conjointly produced "blacklists" for deviants, namely, certain legal persons of companies and individual consumers with low trustworthy scores. Sanctions were then imposed on these deviants to deprive certain types of their civil rights (Liu 2017) by constraining goods and services they can access and lifestyles they can live with. Deviants were restricted to access to first/second-class public transport tickets (e.g., flight and high-speed trains), hotels with a star rating, nightclubs, and golf clubs; banned from acquiring, constructing, and/or expanding real estates, renting luxury offices, buying premium insurances, investing financial products, booking travel and vacation packages, and purchasing any goods that were deemed unnecessary for sustaining essential lives; restrained from sending their children to private schools (CCTV News 2019; Liu 2017); limited to receive benefits from social welfare programs or removed from the government subsidies beneficiaries lists; and barred from applying for government jobs (Liu 2017).

Compared to Foucault's (1975) example of disciplining convicts through imprisoning, enforcing the SCS by punishing deviants through constraining their consumption is indeed minor and lenient. Nevertheless, for most people, these punishments deprived their freedom of consumption, thus causing inconveniences for their lives. In response, mass media outlets were seemingly proactive in publishing articles to help people avoid punishments by revealing methods useful for increasing trustworthy scores. As Souhu Finance (2019) explained, Chinese consumers can increase their scores by (1) building connections on RNM-enabled social media with users who are red-listed and thus owners of high trustworthy scores, (2) proving personal financial and contractual capabilities by making a frequent purchase on RNM-enabled e-commercial platforms, and most importantly, (3) making all payments by choosing moneyless payment platforms, installment plans, or credit cards offered by RNM-enabled private enterprises with SCS-authorized point-based scoring mechanisms (e.g., the Sesame Credit, Alipay, and WeChat Pay). By framing the use of RNM-enabled services offered by authorized SCS co-constructors as the resolution for increasing trustworthy scores, mass media essentially serves as a biopower apparatus that guides consumers to perform their daily activities in ways easy for the state to cast gazes.

Besides mass media, consumers also explored ways to increase their trustworthy scores to either fix their low scores and avoid punishments or boost up their scores for rewards. However, the sizeable nationwide number of unstandardized and opaque scoring mechanisms blinded the public to know how and what conduct would lead to how many scores of reduction. Consequently, consumers were found to experiment with their daily lives in order to identify the influences of different conduct on their scores. Experimental results were often shared and discussed on user-generated content websites such as Baidu Experience and Jianshu. On these websites, consumers mapped out behaviors leading to score increase, such as registering moneyless payment accounts on predominant RNM-enabled and SCS-recognized moneyless payment platforms (e.g., Alipay and WeChat Pay) and using predominant moneyless payment platforms to pay for as many purchases as possible in both online and offline contexts (Jianshu 2017).

Meanwhile, misconduct leading to scoring reduction was also identified and discussed, including deferring the payment of a fine, complaining about the government, neglecting to care for their elderly parents, breaking traffic rules, frauding taxes, stealing electricity, misbehaving on a train (e.g., occupying seats that are not paid for), as well as spending too much time on video/online games (Baidu Experience 2018). Consumers' spontaneous exploration and sharing of information about the impact of certain behaviors on trustworthiness scores can be considered as a result of the Foucauldian concept of the backlighting effect. On the one hand, consumers were blinded to understand the point-calculation methods used in different scoring mechanisms that were decisive in the PRM, making the state's scrutinization invisible. On the other hand, consumers were fully aware of the SCS's PRM and relevant punishments/rewards, of their compromised privacy, and their full exposure to the state's invisible gazes cast through the SCS. Under this backlighting effect, consumers became so self-disciplined that they were even proactive in experimenting with their daily lives according to the vague PRM and the opaque scoring mechanisms to calibrate their conduct carefully. In this way, the backlighting effect led to the birth of docile bodies, who behaved as if they were under constant surveillance from the state, thus aligning themselves to the state-advocated SCS.

Discussion

Orwell (2014) has foreseen that our future will be "a world of terror as much as a world of triumph" (281). It is clear that we are living in a world where utopian ideals and dystopian chaos are coexisted. In this chapter, we unveiled the recent implementation of the social credit system in China. This new governance tool integrates IoT technologies with social expectations promoted by the government. The social credit system is the largest and the most technologically advanced monitoring system in the world at the moment. It is considered a gigantic urban experiment where the new governance mechanism may move between utopia and dystopia (Caprotti and Cowley 2017). The long-standing friction and injustice between the empowered and oppressed may potentially escalate through the power of technology and algorithms (Beer 2017). Such social intervention, or "purposive intervention" (Bulkeley, Castán Broto, and Edwards 2015, 5), may also redefine the notion of human rights as well as reconfigure human experience in the context of consumer citizenship. In other words, we demonstrate the new use of power and technologies that turn the market and society into a totalitarian system. Building on the contradictory conceptions of utopia and dystopia, the following sections highlight the three themes associated with our examination of consumer privacy in China's new social credit system.

Future of Citizen-Consumer Privacy

The Chinese SCS creates an updated disciplinary gaze (Foucault 1975, 198) where every action that citizens and businesses take may eventually

170   *Eric Ping Hung Li et al*

affect what they get in the future. While citizens and companies will be rewarded for their prosocial behaviors such as donation and volunteerism, they may face criticism and loss of civil rights if they misbehave. The Chinese SCS has shifted the enforcement of laws and regulations to a more extensive evaluation system that connects to citizens' everyday activities such as consumption, social media interactions, and traveling. Business practices are monitored by the systems and society as well. As we showed in the case, the evolution of the digital surveillance of the SCS was a historical process enabled by the constant technological development that happened, especially in the past two decades. In the future, the advance of digital technologies will likely activate more comprehensive digital surveillance systems.

The digitalization of surveillance in China began with the state's mandate of RNM that revealed consumers' real names and penetrated the basis of consumer privacy. In a matter of 20 years, such surveillance is expanded to allow the state to cast gazes upon almost all social actors' activities at both individual and organizational levels. Along with the ongoing progress in technologies, consumers, enterprises, and all of their personal and business activities will be further digitized, potentially leading them to live under the state's totalitarian gazes that oversee the lives of consumers and enterprises, from their birth to death.

Digital Governance and Online Surveillance

As Starr (1997) pointed out, the three branches of the Chinese political system (legislature, executive, and judiciary) are very much operated in two ways as the judiciary functions are more or less considered a department of the executive, the Chinese system relies on negotiated relationships between and among individuals and organizations instead of on relationships fixed by law, constitutional provisions, or regulations. The new SCS has shifted the negotiation to algorithms, and the new digital-mediated monitoring systems penetrate through citizens' and businesses' everyday activities. The SCS now serves the state to forge such authoritarian governmentality, as it has the capability to mobilize many state and private institutions to work conjointly to develop sophisticated digital devices and the algorithms to situate consumers into a digital panopticon. In this sense, the new SCS could be viewed as a strategic power technique that the Chinese government adopted to create a model "citizen-consumer" (Cohen 2003) and a new "Lei Feng"[1] archetype in the 21st century to guide people's daily conduct. The publicly accessible "blacklist" and the publicly recognized good citizens and businesses reconstruct the notions of discipline and security in the Chinese political system. As Foucault (2007) pointed out, "discipline is exercised on the bodies of individuals, and security is exercised over a whole population" (11). He further argued that "discipline is a model of individualization of multiplicities rather than something that constructs an

Utopia and Dystopia 171

edifice of multiple elements based on individuals who are worked on as . . . individuals" (12). The SCS, in this sense, seeks to reinforce discipline and sovereignty through the multiplicity of people.

While the typical Foucauldian account advocates the use of biopower in governmentality over that of sovereign and disciplinary power (Lilja and Vinthagen 2014; Sharp, Routledge, Philo, and Paddison 2000), the illustrative case presented earlier affords us to theorize the CCP's nationwide establishment and installation of the SCS as a governmentality practice involving the state's exercise of the three types of power. The SCS was primarily configured as a surveillance system built upon the RNM. As a result, the RNM resembled a digital panopticon tower that oversaw the conduct of individuals and organizations by compromising their privacy.

The PRM was made as a legal sovereign and disciplinary power device that sought to enforce the trust-keeping discipline by accurately targeting and punishing deviants. To operate the PRM, the state decentralized the power to local governments and leading Chinese private enterprises, allowing them to co-develop and implement region-specific reliable scoring mechanisms that were opaque to the public. Unlike Foucault's (1975) accounts of states' exercise of legal sovereign power through public and spectacular torture in the 17th century, the opacity of the scoring mechanism made the state invisible in its exercise of such power in the digital era. Powered by the state's exercise of the legal sovereign, disciplinary power, and biopower, the SCS operated at its full throttle in China and forged what Lyon (1994) called a ceaseless surveillance society, wherein the entire population lived in ways as if they were under constant surveillance and thus in ways according to the state's advocacies.

Built on Foucault's (2007) conception of apparatuses of security, the SCS is obviously a new architect of the disciplined space where multiple regulars, including the prescribed algorithms, are actively monitoring citizen and business activities in both the digital market and social spaces. While discipline allows nothing to escape (Foucault 2007, 45) and the internet allows nothing to hide (Solove 2011), it is crucial to examine the consequences of regulating, if not delimiting, citizens' and businesses' freedom in SCS. As Solove (2008) argued, too much social control may adversely impact freedom, creativity, and self-development. Being a good citizen-consumer and a socially responsible business has become an expectation, an obligation, and a tool to achieve social credits in the new governance system. This forced us to revisit the debate between liberalism and interference under the concept of governmentality.

Distributed Versus Centralized Trust

In the case of SCS, it is arguable to say that the central concern of the whole system is which should have the right to design and approve the evaluation algorithm. While we certainly agree that many prosocial

172   *Eric Ping Hung Li et al*

behaviors such as donation and volunteering should be embraced and rewarded, it is unclear how the scoring mechanisms work to assess different types of prosocial behavior. The SCS is also a complicated system as multiple agents (governments, judicial courts, financial institutions, and private businesses) and technologies are involved in the tracking and evaluation system. Some evaluation criteria such as crossing the red light or being late for paying credit card bills are easy to track and record; other measures such as supporting parents or criticizing governments are very subjective in nature. Seidel (2018) argued that a distributed trust platform could operate in a fully cooperative structure as it transforms the boundaries of organizations and overcomes market trust coordination issues (41–42). The development of the SCS platform may represent a step to the Community Form (C-form) government (Seidel and Stewart 2011; Seidel, Whitehead, Mossman, and Sá 2017), but there may be an ongoing negotiation between issues related to ownership and leadership.

Regarding the conception of ownership, the SCS platform is a new form of shared database environment where systems are integrated digitally to provide a 360-degree evaluation. As mentioned earlier, the integrated system raises several privacy concerns. The SCS also presents challenges related to the trustworthiness and transparency of the evaluation mechanism. While the IoT technologies and algorithms are considered instruments providing "objective truth/assessment" to citizen and business practices, it is certainly unclear the details and the development and advancement of the SCS understand the government and market cooperative platform.

Conclusion

Our chapter presents a critical ontological understanding of how IoT technologies, big data analytics, and algorithms have transformed governmentality, social orders, and consumer privacy and well-being. Chinese government's ambitious and far-reaching plan to employ advanced data science and digital technologies to monitor citizens' behaviors through the social credit system presents a new form of governmentality and a new threat to consumer privacy. In this sense, the social credit system is not only a practice of government but also a practice of the self (Dean 2010).

The contributions of this chapter to marketing and consumer research are threefold. First, we argue that the SCS is a double-edged sword. It is crucial for the government and market agents to revisit policies and practices on data acquisition and management in the "big data" era. Authorized agents shall shift the focus from limiting the collection and retention of data to a more regulated mechanism to control and future usage of citizens' data. While the SCS may be welcomed by citizens who are fed up with rampant fraud, counterfeit products, and public health failures, governments should pay attention to the trust and loyalty issues as well

Utopia and Dystopia 173

as be prepared for the criticism of such an all-powered surveillance regime that may potentially violate the general conception of human rights.

Second, governments should pay attention to the primary and secondary use of technologies. For instance, citizens should have a clear idea of who, when, where, and how governments and market agents collect, retrieve, and assess the information in their everyday lives. The ownership of information may also connect to further discussion on privacy and digital copyright issues.

Finally, governments should revisit the leadership style in the new technologically mediated society and marketplace. While government-driven and market-driven policies and practices were avoidably coexisted, the negotiation of ownership of data and policy-making will become an ongoing challenge to governments and market agents.

Future research on this topic could examine the longitudinal effect of the newly implemented social credit system on consumer behavior and marketing practices in China. Multiple case studies could be conducted to compare the mechanisms and effectiveness of different credit systems. Even though the Chinese social credit system is likely the largest and the most controversial, it is crucial to point out that many countries and organizations have implemented different credit systems. In the United States, the Fair, Isaac, and the Company (FICO) has implemented the FICO Score to measure the risk of default by considering various factors in a person's financial history. COMPAS, a recidivism-prediction algorithm used in various states in the United States, was developed to help judges with sentencing by looking at defendants' criminal histories and then predicting what likelihood there was of them reoffending. In Germany, Schufa is a private company that assesses the creditworthiness of about three-quarters of all Germans and over 5 million companies in the country.

In conclusion, this chapter presents the intersectionality of privacy and governance under the state-market pendulum. While the SCS is definitely a revolutionary platform that combines the incentive and penalty mechanism in one platform, it is worthwhile for academic researchers to further explore the consequences of the SCS (or similar mechanisms). At an ontological level, the SCS is creating a new panopticon where the digital technologies and algorithms have become a new substitute, if not a replacement, of the existing laws and legal systems. Instead of exploring or debating whether the SCS is challenging human rights, future research may want to further investigate whether there is an alternative form of human rights and governance with the inspiration of the SCS.

Note

1. Lei Feng was a socialist model of self-sacrifice who was created by the CCP in 1963 in order to promote volunteerism and other prosocial behaviors.

174   *Eric Ping Hung Li et al*

References

Alibaba Group (2021), "Our Business of Alibaba," (www.alibabagroup.com/cn/about/businesses).

Andrew, Jane and Max Baker (2021), "The General Data Protection Regulation in the Age of Surveillance Capitalism," *Journal of Business Ethics*, 168, 565–78 (https://doi.org/10.1007/s10551-019-04239-z).

Baidu Experience (2018), "How to Increase the Sesame Credits," (https://jingyan.baidu.com/article/cdddd41c824c5d53cb00e1db.html).

Bandara, Ruwan, Mario Fernando, and Shahriar Akter (2020), "Addressing Privacy Predicaments in the Digital Marketplace: A Power-relations Perspective," *International Journal of Consumer Studies*, 44, 423–34 (https://doi.org/10.1111/ijcs.12576).

BBC News (2017), "Is Here Any Privacy? Chinese Netizens' Opinions on the Implementation of the Real Name System on the Internet," (www.bbc.com/zhongwen/simp/chinese-news-40056223)

Beer, David (2017), "The Social Power of Algorithms," *Information, Communication & Society*, 20 (1), 1–13 (https://doi.org/10.4324/9781351200677-1).

Brady, Anne-Marie (2009), *Marketing Dictatorship: Propaganda and Thought Work in Contemporary China*, Lanham, MD: Rowman & Littlefield Publishers.

Brown, Victoria R. and E. Daly Vaughn (2011), "The Writing on the (Facebook) Wall: The Use of Social Networking Sites in Hiring Decisions," *Journal of Business Psychology*, 26 (2), 219–25 (https://doi.org/10.1007/s10869-011-9221-x).

Bulkeley, Harriet, Vanesa Castán Broto, and Gareth A.S. Edwards (2015), *An Urban Politics of Climate Change: Experimentation and the Governing of Socio-technical Transitions*, London: Routledge.

Caprotti, Federico and Robert Cowley (2017), "Interrogating Urban Experiments," *Urban Geography*, 38 (9), 1441–50 (https://doi.org/10.1080/02723638.2016.1265870).

CCTV News (2019), "Still Ignoring the Importance of Trust-keeping?" November 21 (http://m.news.cctv.com/2019/11/10/ARTIZSW3YjQvCtkrMJTfqUGQ191110.shtml).

Cohen, Lizabeth (2003), *A Consumers' Republic: The Politics of Mass Consumption in Postwar America*, New York: Knopf.

Collier, Stephen J. (2009), "Topologies of Power: Foucault's Analysis of Political Government Beyond 'Governmentality'," *Theory, Culture & Society*, 26 (6), 78–108 (https://doi.org/10.1177/0263276409347694).

Credit China (2021), "City Credits," (https://creditcity.creditchina.gov.cn/?navPage=12).

Culnan, Mary J. (2000), "Protecting Privacy Online: Is Self-regulation Working?" *Journal of Public Policy & Marketing*, 19 (1), 20–26 (https://doi.org/10.1509/jppm.19.1.20.16944).

Dean, Mitchell (2010), *Governmentality: Power and Rule in Modern Society*, 2nd edition, Los Angeles, CA: Sage.

——— (2018), "Foucault and the Neoliberalism Controversy," in *The SAGE Handbook of Neoliberalism*, ed. Damien Cahill, Melinda Cooper, Martijn Konings, and David Primrose, Los Angeles, CA: Sage, 40–53.

Flyverbom, Mikkel, Ronald Deibert, and Dirk Matten (2019), "The Governance of Digital Technology, Big Data, and the Internet: New Roles and Responsibilities for Business," *Business & Society*, 58 (1), 3–19 (https://doi.org/10.1177/0007650317727540).

Foucault, Michel (1975), *Discipline & Punish: The Birth of the Prison*, New York: Vintage Books.

———— (1978), *The History of Sexuality: An Introduction*, Vol. 1, New York: Pantheon Books.

———— (1979), "On Governmentality," *Ideology and Conscious*, 6, 5–21.

———— (1982), "The Subject and Power," in *Michel Foucault: Beyond Structuralism and Hermeneutics*, ed. Hubert L. Dreyfus and Paul Rabinow, Brighton: Harvester, 208–26.

———— (1991), "Governmentality," in *The Foucault Effect: Studies in Governmentality*, ed. Graham Burchell, Colin Gordon, and Peter Miller, London: Harvester Wheatsheaf, 73–86.

———— (2007), *Security, Territory, Population*, London: Palgrave.

Fuchs, Christian (2014), *Social Media: A Critical Introduction*, Los Angeles, CA: Sage.

Gandy, Oscar H. (1993), *The Panoptic Sort: A Political Economy of Personal Information*, Boulder, CO: Westview Press.

The General Office of the State Council of China (2007), "Guiding Opinions Concerning the Construction of a Social Credit System," (www.gov.cn/zwgk/2007-04/02/content_569314.htm).

Giesler, Markus and Ela Veresiu (2014), "Creating the Responsible Consumer: Moralistic Governance Regimes and Consumer Subjectivity," *Journal of Consumer Research*, 41 (October), 840–57 (https://doi.org/10.1086/677842).

Global Times (2015), "The Real Name Mechanism: The Virtual World Shall Also Be Regulated by Laws," (https://tech.huanqiu.com/article/9CaKrnJH2X8).

Gordon, Colin (1991), "Governmental Rationality: An Introduction," in *The Foucault Effect: Studies in Governmentality*, ed. Graham Burchell, Colin Gordon, and Peter Miller, London: Harvester Wheatsheaf, 1–52.

Hoffman, Donna L. and Thomas P. Novak, (2018), "Consumer and Object Experience in the Internet of Things: An Assemblage Theory Approach," *Journal of Consumer Research*, 44 (April), 1178–204 (https://doi.org/10.2139/ssrn.2840975).

Jianshu (2017), "Experience Sharing: My Sesame Credit Increased to 750 Within Two Months, Enabling Me to Apply for Short-term Small Loans!" (www.jianshu.com/p/13e0934f9a3a).

Kamleitner, Bernadette and Vince Mitchell (2019), "Your Data Is My Data: A Framework for Addressing Interdependent Privacy Infringements," *Journal of Public Policy & Marketing*, 38 (4), 433–50 (https://doi.org/10.1177/0743915619858924).

Katz, James Everett and Ronald E. Rice (2002), *Social Consequences of Internet Use: Access, Involvement, and Interaction*, Cambridge, MA: MIT Press.

Kobie, Nicole (2019), "The Complicated Truth about China's Social Credit System," *Wired UK* (www.wired.co.uk/article/china-social-credit-system-explained).

Kostka, Genia (2019), "China's Social Credit Systems and Public Opinion: Explaining High Levels of Approval," *New Media & Society*, 21 (7), 1565–93 (https://doi.org/10.2139/ssrn.3215138).

Lee, Yen Nee (2019), "Here Are 4 Charts That Show China's Rise as a Global Economic Superpower," *CNBC News*, September 23 (www.cnbc.

176 Eric Ping Hung Li et al

com/2019/09/24/how-much-chinas-economy-has-grown-over-the-last-70-years.html).

Lemke, Thomas (2007), "An Indigestible Meal? Foucault, Governmentality and State Theory," *Distinktion (Aarhus)*, 8 (2), 43–64 (https://doi.org/10.1080/1600910x.2007.9672946).

Lilja, Mona and Stellan Vinthagen (2014), "Sovereign Power, Disciplinary Power and Biopower: Resisting What Power With What Resistance?" *Journal of Political Power*, 7 (1), 107–26 (https://doi.org/10.1080/2158379x.2014.889403).

Liu, L. (2017), "China Is Moving Towards the 'Trustworthy' Era," *People's Daily Overseas Edition* (http://paper.people.com.cn/rmrbhwb/html/2017-01/23/content_1745737.htm).

Loi, Michele, Christian Hauser, and Markus Christen (2020), "Highway to (Digital) Surveillance: When Are Clients Coerced to Share Their Data With Insurers?" *Journal of Business Ethics*, 1–13 (https://doi.org/10.1007/s10551-020-04668-1).

Lyon, David (1994), *The Electronic Eye: The Rise of Surveillance Society*, Cambridge: Polity Press.

——— (2007), *Surveillance Studies: An Overview*, Cambridge: Polity Press.

Mac Sithigh, Daithi and Mattias Siems (2019), "The Chinese Social Credit System: A Model for Other Countries?" *Modern Law Review*, 82 (6), 1034–71 (https://doi.org/10.1111/1468-2230.12462).

MBAlib (2019), "The Trustworthy Records of Enterprises," (https://wiki.mbalib.com/wiki/企业信用档案).

Mellet, Kevin and Thomas Beauvisage (2020), "Cookie Monsters. Anatomy of a Digital Market Infrastructure," *Consumption Markets & Culture*, 23 (2), 110–29 (https://doi.org/10.1080/10253866.2019.1661246).

Milne, George R. (2000), "Privacy and Ethical Issues in Database/Interactive Marketing and Public Policy: A Research Framework and Overview of the Special Issue," *Journal of Public Policy & Marketing*, 19 (1), 1–6 (https://doi.org/10.1509/jppm.19.1.1.16934).

Milne, George R. and Mary J. Culnan (2004), "Strategies for Reducing Online Privacy Risks: Why Consumers Read (or Don't Read) Online Privacy Notices," *Journal of Interactive Marketing*, 18 (3), 15–29 (https://doi.org/10.1002/dir.20009).

Nanfang Metropolis Daily (2018), "At Least 22 Provinces and Cities Launched Their Region-Specific Personal Social Credit Systems to Include Insurance Fraud, Marriage Fraud and Yinao (Healthcare Disturbance)," (www.sohu.com/a/280766740_161795?g=0).

Nguyen, Thuc-Doan and Eric Ping Hung Li (2010), "Online Consumer Privacy 2.0," in *Advances in Consumer Research*, Vol. 37, ed. Margaret C. Campbell, Jeff Inman, and Rik Pieters, Duluth, MN: Association for Consumer Research, 873–74.

Orwell, George (2014), *1984*, Toronto, ON: Harper Perennial Classics.

Pengpai News (2017), "The Chinese Ministry of Transportation Orders the "Real-Name Mechanism" to Be Included in Bike Sharing to Encourage the Waive of Deposits for Shared Bikes, But Not Shared Electronic Bikes," (www.thepaper.cn/newsDetail_forward_1690712).

Petronio, Sandra Sporbert (2002), *Boundaries of Privacy: Dialectics of Disclosure*, Albany, NY: State University of New York Press.

Petty, Ross D. (2000), "Marketing Without Consent: Consumer Choice and Costs, Privacy, and Public Policy," *Journal of Public Policy & Marketing*, 19 (1), 42–53 (https://doi.org/10.1509/jppm.19.1.42.16940).

Utopia and Dystopia   177

Phelps, Joseph, Glen Nowak, and Elizabeth Ferrell (2000), "Privacy Concerns and Consumer Willingness to Provide Personal Information," *Journal of Public Policy & Marketing*, 19 (1), 27–41 (https://doi.org/10.1509/jppm.19.1.27.16941).

Science Times China (2018), "Alibaba, Jingdong and Other [e-commerce] Enterprises Firmly Promise: Never Produce Counterfeit Goods and Fraud Tax," (www.sciencetimes.com.cn/dujia/keji/1613.html).

Seidel, Marc-David L. (2018), "Questioning Centralized Organizations in a Time of Distributed Trust," *Journal of Management Inquiry*, 27 (1), 40–44 (https://doi.org/10.1177/1056492617734942).

Seidel, Marc-David L. and Katherine J. Stewart (2011), "An Initial Description of the C-form," *Research in the Sociology of Organizations*, 33, 37–72.

Seidel, Marc-David L., Lorne Whitehead, Michele Ann Mossman, and Creso Sá (2017), "The Distributed Network of Cooperating Teams (DNCT): A Multi-Level Initiative for Organizational Change," (https://open.library.ubc.ca/cIRcle/collections/facultyresearchandpublications/52383/items/1.0354236).

Sesame Credit (2019a), "What Is Sesame Credit," (www.xin.xin/#/detail/1-3).

——— (2019b), "The Life With Trustworthy Credits," (www.xin.xin/#/detail/1-0-3).

——— (2021), "The Sesame Credit," (www.zmxy.com.cn/#/detail/1-2).

Shambaugh, David (2007), "China's Propaganda System: Institutions, Processes and Efficacy," *The China Journal*, 57, 25–58 (https://doi.org/10.1086/tcj.57.20066240).

Sharp, Joanne, Paul Routledge, Chris Philo, and Ronan Paddison (2000), *Entanglements of Power: Geographies of Domination/Resistance*, London: Routledge.

Solove, Daniel J. (2008), *Understanding Privacy*, Cambridge, MA: Harvard University Press.

——— (2011), *Nothing to Hide: The False Tradeoff Between Privacy and Security*, New Haven and London: Yale University Press.

Souhu Finance (2019), "Sharing a Few Experiences of How My Sesame Credit Finally Reached 750," (http://m.sohu.com/n/496672510/).

Starr, John Bryan (1997), *Understanding China: A Guide to China's Economy, History, and Political Structure*, 1st edition, New York: Hill and Wang.

The State Council of China (2014), "The Notice of the State Council on the Planning Outline of the Construction of a Social Credit System," (www.gov.cn/zhengce/content/2014-06/27/content_8913.htm).

The Supreme People's Court of the People's Republic of China (2019), "The Press Conference of the Supreme Court About the Construction of the Credit China," (www.court.gov.cn/xwzx/xwfbh/twzb/xwfbh140116/).

Tang, Weihong, Guo Hu, and Yue Pan (2001), "The Interview About the 'Guideline of the Construction of Moral Citizens'," *People's Daily*, October 30, 11.

Venkatesh, Alladi (2016), "Social Media, Digital Self, and Privacy: A Socio-Analytical Perspective of the Consumer as the Digital Avatar," *Journal of the Association for Consumer Research*, 1 (July), 378–91 (https://doi.org/10.1086/686914).

Xinhua Net (2016), "The General Office of the Central Committee of the Communist Party of China and the General Office of the State Council Issued 'Opinions Concerning Accelerating the Construction of Credit Supervision, Warning and Punishment Mechanisms for Persons Subject to Enforcement for Trust-Breaking'," (www.xinhuanet.com/politics/2016-09/25/c_1119620719.htm).

——— (2018), "The Credit China Announces the Latest Ranks of Chinese Cities' Trustworthiness Scores. Chongqing Is Ranked on the 3rd," (www.xinhuanet.com/city/2018-03/22/c_129834685.htm).

——— (2019a), "Improving the Supervisional Mechanism Centring on the Construction of Trust-Keeping Behaviors: The Two Ministries," (www.xinhuanet.com/fortune/2019-07/30/c_1210220840.htm).

——— (2019b), "Qianhai Is Constructing a Social Credit System in the Tax System in Order to Guide Enterprises to Keep Trust," March 10 (http://m.xinhuanet.com/gd/2019-03/10/c_1124215995.htm).

——— (2019c), "This Is How to Make Progress on the Big Deal That Xi Jinping Concerns," June 5 (www.xinhuanet.com/politics/xxjxs/2019-06/05/c_1124587649.htm).

Zhao, Xin and Russell Belk (2008), "Politicizing Consumer Culture: Advertising's Appropriation of Political Ideology in China's Social Transition," *Journal of Consumer Research*, 35 (August), 231–44 (https://doi.org/10.1086/588747).

Zhou, Qingli (2001), "A Review of the Five-year Campaign of 'Zero Counterfeit Goods in Hundreds of Cities and Thousands of Shops'," *People's Daily*, January 05, 4.

10 The Thanatopolitics of Neoliberalism and Consumer Precarity

Rohit Varman and Devi Vijay

Prologue

India is in the throes of the COVID-19 second wave, which has drawn international and national media attention to the event of oxygen shortage in the National Capital Region of New Delhi. This chapter refers to an ominously prophetic event nearly four years ago in one of the poorest regions in the country where 60 children died within 72 hours because of oxygen shortage during an encephalitis outbreak. Arguably, COVID-19 mainstreamed what has been occurring for decades to large swathes of the poor. Then, as now, the State directed its efforts toward suppressing the death counts and distorting the cause of death. Then, as now, the event of oxygen shortage exposes the working of neoliberal capitalism that fosters death worlds of precarious consumers by dismantling State welfare institutions and by pushing the poor deeper into the abyss of poverty.

Introduction

In recent years, scholars have examined the relationship between markets, consumer precarity, and violence (e.g., Firat 2018; Varman and Vijay 2018; Varman, Goswami, and Vijay 2018). However, they have not studied the thanatopolitics of neoliberalism. Thanatopolitics, or the politics of death, informs how the dead, "whose posthumous claims can disrupt the system" (Murray 2018, 719), must be concealed, ordered, and utilized by the current neoliberal system of profiteering. To understand the thanatopolitics of neoliberalism, in this chapter, we examine three cases of encephalitis in Gorakhpur, India, with close attention to the event of oxygen shortage in a hospital that led to 60 deaths.

For over 40 years, Uttar Pradesh in northern India has had annual encephalitis epidemics, which peak during the monsoon period of August–September (Kumar, Tripathi, Singh, and Bannerji 2006). On July 31, 2017, the oxygen supply contract between Pushpa Sales Private Limited and Baba Raghav Das (BRD) Medical College, Gorakhpur

DOI: 10.4324/9781003111559-14

180　*Rohit Varman and Devi Vijay*

(Uttar Pradesh, India) expired. The proprietor of Pushpa Sales, Manish Bhandari, had sent several notices to Ajay Bisht (popularly known as Adityanath)—the Chief Minister of Uttar Pradesh, various ministers, and the district administration informing them of mounting dues (Srivastava 2017). On August 9, Bhandari allegedly wrote again to the Medical Education Minister requesting urgent payment. On the same day, Bisht visited BRD to inaugurate a ten-bed intensive care unit and a six-bed critical care unit.

On the morning of August 10, BRD's central oxygen pipeline operators learned that the liquid oxygen stock was dangerously low and that Pushpa Sales had stopped supplies because of outstanding dues. The operators wrote a letter to BRD's authorities, informing them that oxygen supply would last only that day and that lives were at risk. At 7:30 PM on August 10, the oxygen supply to BRD ran out. Fifty-two cylinders on reserve were pushed into service. Twenty-three children, 14 of whom were infants, died. The pediatric ward physician in charge, Kafeel Khan, sought to source oxygen cylinders from facilities in and around Gorakhpur. Nurses handed out self-inflating bags—or ambu bags—to parents. By August 12, the toll rose to 60 deaths. On the morning of August 13, liquid oxygen supply to BRD was restored. By now, the city of Gorakhpur and BRD had catapulted into the eye of national and international media attention. Journalists descended on Gorakhpur, and fact-finding missions and national inquiries were constituted.

In a few days, heads began to roll in a giant dramaturgy of State action. Nine people were arrested, including Manish Bhandari and Kafeel Khan (Pradhan 2020). Gorakhpur became an important headline of the week, and usual suspects were identified—bureaucratic red tape, State inefficiencies, medical negligence, and corruption. We interpret the oxygen shortage as an event. Povinelli (2011) suggests that events are outcomes or occurrences that are noticed by the State and other agencies of modern governance because they are considered extraordinary and often result in crises or catastrophes. On the other hand, quasi-events are routine, every day, and confined to the state of ellipsis. They are naturalized and considered normal. As Povinelli (2011, 13) observes quasi-events "neither happen nor not happen."

Events are framed to present a particular interest mediated by what is made visible. We argue that the narratives of victims and popular media framing of the event of oxygen supply shortage partially conceal the structural violence against the precariat and further neoliberal capitalism. We examine three cases of encephalitis in the region that occurred over the last ten years to surface structural violence. This chapter contributes to the understanding of consumer precarity by uncovering the thanatopolitics of neoliberalism. We offer the twin processes of concealment of structural violence and advancement of profiteering as the constituting features of the thanatopolitics of neoliberalism.

Thanatopolitics, Capitalism, and Bare Life

To understand thanatopolitics, we draw on Agamben (1998), who examines how juridico-institutional and biopolitical forms of power intersect to produce lives that count. A life that does not count is a bare life of a *homo sacer*. According to the ancient Roman law that Agamben draws on, a *homo sacer* could be killed but not sacrificed. In the sovereign sphere, it is permitted to kill a *homo sacer* without committing homicide. Sovereign decides what life is worth living and what is to be cast aside as a bare life. Agamben (1998) suggests that a sovereign is the point of indistinction where violence passes into law and law passes into violence. Accordingly, the ideas of bio and sovereign powers are not contradictory but intertwined: biopolitics (which fosters and regulates life) can turn into thanatopolitics (which organizes violence and death-worlds). Such a reading of violence is particularly helpful in understanding capitalism in the Global South.

Capitalism took roots in the Global South as part of European colonialism and thus was always a violent system of extraction and exploitation that fostered death worlds (Dirlik 2002). After a forced postwar compromise with anti-colonial movements and nation-building projects for a few decades in the second half of the 20th century CE, the murderous impulse of global capitalism has been particularly sharpened by finance capital and its governance system of neoliberalism (Hudson 2015; Lapavitsas 2013; Patnaik 2018). In the last four decades, under the aegis of the structural adjustment programs prescribed by the International Monetary Fund, finance capital has established a stranglehold over most national economies in the south.

Finance capital is fundamentally predatory as it grows by diverting funds meant for public welfare into its coffers. As Hudson (2015, 15) sharply reminds, "instead of creating a mutually beneficial symbiosis with the economy of production and consumption, today's financial parasitism siphons off income needed to invest and grow. Bankers and bondholders desiccate the host economy by extracting . . . a financialized economy becomes a mortuary when the host economy becomes a meal for the financial free luncher." The reduction of the south to mortuaries by finance capital has been a gradual process that is advanced through the corrosion of welfare institutions and by diversion of public goods and commons for private gains. While destroying the already precarious lives of the vast swathes of the global population and multiplying death-worlds, financiers cover their destructive tracks by espousing the neoliberal mantras of entrepreneurship and responsibilization. With increasing inequities created by finance capital, the lines between the rich and the poor get more sharply drawn. The latter are increasingly dispossessed through processes of violent accumulation (Blakeley 2019; Patnaik 2020b).

182   *Rohit Varman and Devi Vijay*

The violent accumulation gives rise to conflicts, leading to popular dis-enchantment with liberal democratic modes of governance. As Patnaik (2020a, 36) notes, "large segments of the population, especially those belonging to the amorphous 'middle class' (and in certain circumstances 'abandoned' workers who feel betrayed by their traditional leadership), feel the need, in their desperation, for a 'messiah' who can deliver them from this cul-de-sac that is marked by their hopelessness and misery; and fascist movements thrive by projecting such a 'messiah.' . . . [T]hey prom-ise a way out through a recourse to hyperbole based on unreason." Such fascist forces of unreason and totalitarian control are also bankrolled by finance capital and corporations because they protect their interests. Thus, neofascism is a natural corollary of finance capital and its neoliberal capitalism, as in the case of India. As Patnaik (2020a, 47) further notes, "Fascism is neoliberal capitalism's 'gift' to mankind in the period of its maturity, when it submerges the world economy in a crisis, and reaches a dead end from which there is no obvious escape." In this state, the poor, as both precarious consumers and workers, are abandoned as bare lives and left to fend for themselves, and any dissent is quelled to safeguard the ruling elite's interests.

Such a state of existence steeped in coercion is routinized for the pre-cariat and becomes a part of the everyday functioning of contemporary societies in the south. While the citizenship rights are reserved for the elite, the majority of the population in the south survives in a state of exception (Chatterjee 2011). Here, Agamben's reading of the state of exception is particularly helpful. Agamben clarifies that the state of exception is not just a totalitarian rule but a space devoid of law. In this state, the distinc-tion between the use of violence and the constituted law becomes indis-tinct. Although he draws upon Nazi concentration camps to understand creation of bare life, Agamben (2005, 3) observes, "the state of exception tends increasingly to appear as the dominant paradigm of government in contemporary politics."

Drawing on Agamben and examining the Indian State, Gupta (2012, 5) observes that extreme poverty should be theorized as a direct form of killing made possible by the State rather than an inevitable situation in which the poor are "allowed to die" or "exposed to death." Gupta (2012, 17) points out that "The inevitability of the death of the poor attains a different ethical dimension if the violence in such a thanatopolitics is seen as killing rather than simply allowing to die or exposing to death." Hence, we witness structural or systemic violence that cannot be attributed to a single actor but is dispersed and hidden in the current functioning of neoliberal capitalism in India. As Gupta (2012, 21) says, it is "a crime without a criminal."

In summary, we attend to the thanatopolitics of neoliberalism that fosters death-worlds. Although several scholars have offered insights into sover-eign violence and the creation of bare life, we are particularly interested in exploring how neoliberal capitalism normalizes and utilizes death-worlds. In the following sections, we elaborate on the research context, methodology, and the contours of systemic violence against bare life in Gorakhpur.

Research Context and Methodology

Uttar Pradesh, with 18.1% of India's population, is the most populous state with nearly 200 million people. Uttar Pradesh's economy is the second largest in India, contributing over 8% of India's gross domestic product (Chatterji 2019). In 2012–2013, it was the largest food grain-producing state (Rawat 2014). However, 59.819 million people live below the poverty line (Government of India 2013). While the roots of India's agrarian distress predate the structural adjustment program in 1991, rising inequality and dispossession must be analyzed within the context of neoliberal economic growth trajectory. The gap between Uttar Pradesh's and the national per capita income has steadily increased, while human development indicators remain low compared to other states (Srivastava 2017). Under the diktats of finance capital, the State has retrenched welfare and subsidy programs, scaling back crucial programs like the Public Distribution System for food rations and public health infrastructures (Ghosh and Chandrashekhar 2003; Patnaik 2020a, 2020b). Moreover, the last decade has seen Uttar Pradesh become a frontier of communal organizing and neofascism (Chatterji 2019).

Our field site is in Purvanchal or Eastern Uttar Pradesh, one of four economic regions as per official classifications (others being western, central, and Bundelkhand) (Diwakar 2009). Eastern Uttar Pradesh districts have a high proportion of the population who lives below the poverty line (Chaudhuri and Gupta 2009), and there are greater infrastructural disparities as compared to other regions (Diwakar 2009). The highest intensity of poverty was among Muslims and Dalits (see also Chatterji 2019).

BRD is a nodal tertiary care public medical college at Gorakhpur that caters to patients from Eastern Uttar Pradesh, neighboring Bihar, and Nepal. Nehru Hospital, affiliated with BRD medical college, has three intensive care units, including a pediatric unit, a neonatal unit, and one for older patients. Since encephalitis is endemic to Uttar Pradesh, there is a separate encephalitis ward. Since 2010, nearly 18,000 cases of encephalitis were officially reported at BRD, with close to 4,000 deaths. It is important to note that the epidemic is often attributed to Japanese encephalitis (JE), a mosquito-borne viral encephalitis endemic to Uttar Pradesh, Assam, West Bengal, Bihar, Karnataka, Tamil Nadu, Andhra Pradesh, Manipur, and Goa. However, recent studies indicate that outbreaks are presumptively attributed to JE virus which is only one of the major causes of acute encephalitis syndrome (AES), other causes being rhabdovirus (Chandipura virus) and water-borne enteroviruses (Joshi, Kalantri, Reingold, and Colford 2012; Sapkal et al. 2009). AES peaks

184   *Rohit Varman and Devi Vijay*

during monsoon months (typically between August and October), when water-borne and vector-borne disease transmission increases (Kakkar et al. 2011). There are over 50,000 reported JE cases and 10,000 deaths per year. AES outbreaks have high mortality and survivors have life-long impairment with various disabilities (Joshi et al. 2012). Thus, AES constitutes a major public health concern requiring coordination between health, water, and sanitation sectors.

Our data sources comprise interview transcripts, field notes, photographs, media articles, research papers, and government reports. Secondary data helped us develop insights into the thanatopolitics in the region. We conducted fieldwork in Gorakhpur to deepen our understanding. We adopted purposive sampling to include "information-rich cases for in-depth study" (Patton 1990, 182). We interviewed a journalist, an activist, and an activist physician, who have been advocating the issue of encephalitis deaths for over a decade. In these phenomenological interviews, we sought to understand the history of the epidemic, actors' experiences, and how different institutions have responded to the deaths. We followed these interviews with field visits to Nehru Hospital, BRD Medical College, and two villages of Manbela and Jungle Ekala 2, where encephalitis cases were reported. At the hospital, we briefly interviewed a staff member and two nurses. We interviewed seven villagers from two villages, including members of three families in which children were affected by encephalitis. In these phenomenological interviews, our focus was on understanding patients' case histories and lived experiences of family members as caregivers. We also observed and inquired about the state of sanitation to understand the causes of the epidemic. Additionally, we interviewed a senior professor at BRD to understand his experience at the institution and his views about the disease. Interviews ranged from 30 minutes to three hours. All participants' names have been anonymized to maintain confidentiality.

We present our analysis in two ways. First, we spatially and temporally displace and distend the event. Concurrent with Davis's (2005, 3) point that "[i]n order, to grieve over a cataclysm, we must first personify it," we present three cases of encephalitis occurring over a decade. Second, we present a "social autopsy" (Klinenberg 2001, 123) which reveals the concealment of structural violence, privatization of public health infrastructures, and the overarching apparatus of neoliberal capitalism.

Three Cases of Encephalitis

We present three cases of encephalitis spread over a ten-year period. These cases show how precarious consumers have been reduced to bare lives and have suffered systemic violence that has been concealed by thanatopolitics in the region. The precariat voice anger and, on occasion, protest against the State for their sufferings. However, these testimonies are silent about the capitalist forces of profit responsible for their plight.

The Thanatopolitics of Neoliberalism   185

The Case of Sunaina (2007)

In October 2007, Sunaina, a three-year-old girl, suffered seizures. Her parents took her to a private clinic and brought her home after her fever subsided. At home, Sunaina could neither speak nor walk. This time, her parents rushed her to BRD. Diagnosed with AES, Sunaina was admitted on October 24, 2007, for 16 days in the pediatric ward. Her discharge card indicates that she had a fever, swelling all over her body, seizures, and "uprolling of eyeballs" for 6–7 days. According to her mother, Sunaina was also in a coma for three days during her hospitalization. Although Sunaina recovered, she lost partial vision and suffers from periodic seizures.

Now aged 13, she is in Class 4 and goes to school "a few times a month" accompanied by one of her sisters or brothers. Her regular medication, taken twice a day, costs INR 60 for five days. If she has a seizure, her family takes her for medical consultation. Her mother claims the physician takes "500 rupees to write a *parchi* (prescription)" when he prescribes a new medicine. Her uncle calculates that over the last decade, her family would have spent INR 300,000–400,000 on various hospitalizations, consultations, and medications for Sunaina. Despite exploitation by the private healthcare system, the family primarily blames the State for not offering any financial support. Such expressions of dependency are also juxtaposed with patriarchy, and her mother worries that "she is a girl. When she gets married and goes somewhere, there will be a difficulty. There are also so many expenses."

Sunaina's father rears buffaloes and sells the milk. He spends a large part of his earnings on medicines. They live in a concrete unplastered house next to a pond. Without fumigation, such water bodies are breeding grounds for mosquitos. The family had a small patch of agricultural land. The Gorakhpur Development Authority (GDA) acquired this land 15 years ago, and now the family purchases grains for household consumption. The house has no is clean drinking water supply. Villagers state that 95% of residents do not have toilets. A villager told us, "There is no land. Where will we get it done?" Around Sunaina's house, there are puddles of stagnant water. Sunaina's uncle, Arvind, notes, "If the sunshine is less, you cannot sit here because of the cloud of mosquitoes. Whether night or not, mosquitoes will not spare you. While the State authorities promise fumigation, they do not do anything." This family expects the State to perform such functions and blames it for corruption and incompetence, while there is no testimony against private or corporate forces responsible for the suffering.

The Case of Dilwar (2012)

When two-and-a-half-year-old Dilwar first suffered a seizure in June 2012, his family took him to the private clinic of a physician employed at BRD. The physician directed the family to BRD with the reassurance that

186   *Rohit Varman and Devi Vijay*

"we will contact someone there; you will get good treatment." Dilwar was admitted at BRD for 18 days. Dilwar's father worked as a laborer in Saudi Arabia. Dilwar's uncle, who took care of the hospitalization, recollected:

> If we felt the child looked unwell and went to the doctor or compounder, they would shoo us away, scold us, and send us outside. They would say, "We are there. We are doing what we can." What were they doing? Every day, one child would expire. Some days, five children. We would get anxious when we saw that. That was the environment there. We would go to them when we sensed he didn't look alright. Doctors did not give us any response. They wouldn't tell us what they were doing. Only instructions—do this test from here, do that test from there.

A day's expense, not including diagnostic tests directed to private laboratories, was a minimum of INR 1,500. For diagnostic tests within the hospital that should have been free, patients' families had to pay INR 150. Dilwar's uncle recollected, "if they draw the patient's blood, then also, INR 150." If he protested about the rates and enquired why they were being charged, he was told, "Have you come here to be a politician. Are you here to become a *neta* (leader) or to give money?" He rued, his voice heavy with the memory of the traumatic experience, "*Majboori thi* [We were helpless]. We gave money." On the 18th day, the holy day of Shab-e-Baraat for this Muslim family, Dilwar died. Upon Dilwar's death, his father returned, and stricken by grief, has not gone back to Saudi Arabia. As with Sunaina's family, the GDA land acquisition affected Dilwar's family as well.

Sunaina and Dilwar are from the village of Manbela that is situated two kilometers from BRD. In a region home to some of the poorest in India, between 2004 and 2005, the GDA forcefully acquired over 475 acres of land from the villages of Manbela, Pokhar Bhinda, Salempur, Fatehpur, Hamirpur, Mirzapur, Mughlaha, Hamidpur, and other neighboring villages to develop residential colonies by corporate real estate developers (Hindustan Times 2017). As Harvey (2003) reminds us, neoliberalism is marked by accumulation based on dispossession and financialization of spheres that were outside the ambit of corporate control. Farmers protesting the land acquisition were brutally lathi-charged, and their leaders were arrested. The State used violence to force farmers to part with their land for a paltry compensation of INR 10 per square foot (Hindustan Times 2017). The acquired land was sold for constructing private houses.

When we visited Manbela, residents had organized a meeting to protest the land acquisition. The local Congress leader Rahul Rana Singh addressed the meeting, and there was palpable anger against the state government. The aggrieved farmers had organized under the banner of Kisan Mazdoor Sangharsh Samiti (KMSS) to contest the nominal rates of land acquisition. They were also demanding to free 10% of the acquired land and to leave the land belonging to a temple, cemetery, and *madrasas*. These farmers were demanding the prevailing circle rate of INR 1,200 per square foot (Hindustan Times 2017). Dilwar's uncle shared:

> The government says, "do not come in the way of *vikas* [development]." You destroy us and keep talking about vikas. This is the state of the poor. This is our *dukh-dard* (pain). By destroying farmers, you are not going to do any vikas. If you are the government, then vikas is for everyone—for the poor, the farmers, the rich.

In the 2014 central government elections, the Bharatiya Janata Party (BJP) pitched Narendra Modi as their "vikas purush" or development man, who would chart a neoliberal economic growth path for India as he gave a call for "minimum government, maximum governance." Dilwar's uncle's ire betrays the anger against this economic model that has dispossessed farmers, casting the poor aside as homo sacer. However, the anger is primarily directed at the State. The farmers discovered that the compensation they initially received was grossly inadequate. Dilwar's family informed us that they received INR 6 lakhs as total compensation. The money was divided among four brothers, each getting INR 1.5 lakhs. However, the money did not last long, and land as their livelihood source was taken away. Dilwar's uncle lamented,

> In the name of vikas, they are killing us, telling us, "you are not letting us develop." If our livelihood has been snatched from us, then is it not death for us? We have lost everything. We have been destroyed. Either you kill us and bring about vikas, or you give us what is rightfully our share and then develop. No government listens to us—neither the previous one nor the current one.

The idea of development creates a divide between developed and underdeveloped, modern and primitive, and fosters, as Fanon (1990, 40) suggests, a "Manichaeastic world" of them and us. The resulting alterity makes it easier to cast the precariat as bare life. Despite protests by farmers against the State, GDA was willing to pay only INR 65 per square foot. Further, GDA was threatening to charge interest for the compensation that was paid in 2005 or 2009. However, the agitating farmers contend that because of not being able to cultivate their land, they have faced losses. If the equivalent of the harvests were to be accounted for, they should be getting more money from GDA. On September 17, 2017, when farmers were protesting near the Town Hall in Gorakhpur, the police beat them up, and six farmers were arrested. Bhaduri (2008) referred to this neoliberal process of capital accumulation based on the transfer of property and land use from the poorest to the richest through economic means and state violence as "predatory growth."

188 *Rohit Varman and Devi Vijay*

A sense of despondency and betrayal prevails in the village, and residents believe that after making promises to get their votes, politicians have reneged on their promises. Nitesh Singh, a Gorakhpur-based journalist, observed:

> People are so poor, and they have had so many tragedies. A woman has a child's corpse in front of her, but she needs to think of cooking for the child that survived. Their tears dry up. But this becomes a wound. From outside, we see the people here [of Purvanchal]. They look sad, they do not look normal. You see, 10000 people have died if you just look at the medical college statistics. 10000 is just JE. Neonatal is triple this—30000. Purvanchal is sitting on 50000–60000 children's corpses. Think about the effect on each house for life. No one forgets these things.

Despite these conditions, little has changed for these villagers, and people continue to suffer from violence and dispossession. Moreover, the anger of the precariat is primarily directed at the State and not against the concealed rationalities of the capitalist order.

The Case of Dilip (2017)

Jungle Ekala No. 2 is eight kilometers from Gorakhpur. The village is spread across different hamlets interspersed with agricultural fields. We were directed to the Nishad hamlet in Bichla Tola marked by a cluster of semiconstructed unplastered houses. Nishads constitute around 14% of Gorakhpur district population and are low caste. The narrow unmetalled path that leads to the hamlet was waterlogged at several places, with mosquito larvae easily visible in stagnant water puddles.

Four-year-old Dilip Nishad from this village died on August 10, 2017. Dilip's grandmother described him as a healthy, "naughty and playful" child. On August 9, Dilip started vomiting and developed high fever. His family took him to a private clinic a kilometer from home. The clinic was locked. By now, Dilip had repeated seizures, and his body became limp. He was rushed to BRD. Although Dilip was admitted to the hospital at 2 PM, according to his grandmother,

> Doctors did not attend to him until late evening. Doctors and the medical staff were busy attending to Baba (Chief Minister Adityanath, who was visiting BRD). My son, Bahadur, repeatedly requested them to examine the child, telling them, "*Babu* (sir), my son is suffering from repeated seizures, his condition is deteriorating, please come and examine." They didn't listen and kept telling him to wait, saying, "we are coming, sit there, be with your son." It was only late in the evening, at

The Thanatopolitics of Neoliberalism 189

around 6 p.m., after Baba left that doctors came to attend Dilip. Now tell me, whose fault is it? Is it the fault of the government, or is it the fault of Baba?

Dilip, who was suffering from encephalitis died the next day. BRD issued a death certificate that stated the cause of death as a cardiopulmonary failure and did not mention encephalitis. Dilip's parents were in shock. While Dilip's mother went to her parents, his father had a high fever and was hospitalized at a nearby private nursing home. The family's anger was directed at the State leadership for its failures. Simone (2010) compares the temporalities of marginalized life worlds to "injury time" in football—that window in the game when players have limited time to set the rules or when the conventional rules may be suspended for a brief time period. This hospitalization is then that injury time when the family has recourse to save their child's life, knowing that the clock will soon run out. The entire game, however, has been set up to violently inflict wounds on them.

In front of Dilip's house was a large ditch filled with stagnant water that was breeding mosquitos. The civic authorities had not attempted to fumigate this ditch. The three handpumps installed by the State for drinking water were dysfunctional. A villager told us, "the water from one of the pumps stinks and cannot be used." Villagers took us to a missing water pipe that was supposed to provide drinking water. The State installed India Mark II handpumps in the region a few years back. However, local activist Somesh Mani shared that in his survey of high-risk villages, 51 of 140 installed India Mark II handpumps were dysfunctional. Although surface water is highly contaminated and deeper handpumps are needed, villagers construct shallow handpumps with available resources. If the area around a handpump is not cemented, stagnant water accumulates and becomes a breeding ground for mosquitoes. Besides, the installation of India Mark II handpumps is mired in regional caste politics, with government handpumps often installed in upper-caste hamlets. Oppressed castes were either denied access to the pumps or reluctant to go to upper-caste hamlets to fetch water because of the humiliating arrangement.

Moreover, there are no public toilets in the village. When asked about any government support to build a toilet at her place, Dilip's grandmother caustically remarked, "you think they will support the poor to build toilets." Another villager told us, "the government asks us to first dig a hole of 1 × 1.25 ×1.25 meters, take its picture to get two installments of INR 6000 each. People are talking about it, but nobody has got the money so far." Dismissing the idea and reflecting the distrust in the region for the government's welfare schemes, Dilip's grandmother added, "we dig a hole in front of our house, and at night in the darkness, somebody's child falls in it. Who is going to pay the compensation?" These villagers believe that the proposed idea would exacerbate rather than alleviate their miseries. A public toilet built 15 years ago was now in dilapidated disuse. Another

190   *Rohit Varman and Devi Vijay*

toilet built four–five years back was kept locked by the village *pradhan* [elected representative] and was not in use. The villager told us, "they inaugurated it, took pictures, made a video film, and after that locked it for good. . . . There is no MLA, pradhan interested in our welfare. There is no support from anyone in this village." The people's ire is directed at the flawed model of electoral democracy, and the way governments are elected. The grandmother further lamented, "Before elections, they come and say, *chachi* [aunt] what do you want? We will get it done for you. Once they get the votes, they don't come back." Therefore, the family and villagers do not merely see Dilip's death as a biological event. Instead, they attribute it to their poverty and hold the State responsible for the death.

In summary, the three cases that occurred over ten years show that the villages around Gorakhpur city continue to be sites of structural violence that are rarely reported as part of the thanatopolitics of neoliberalism. Moreover, the precariat primarily holds the State responsible for the tragedies without identifying or implicating privatization or corporate capital. As Mani states, "Oxygen issue came to surface. . . . Many things are still concealed. No one comes to know." We turn to these facets of concealment and privatization of healthcare without which the thanatopolitics of neoliberalism cannot be understood.

The Thanatopolitics of Neoliberalism

Concealing Structural Violence

With an event like oxygen shortage, media focuses on sites such as BRD, where death-world is emplaced. However, other sites of violence are ignored. Encephalitis disproportionately affects the poor who are cast aside as bare lives (Singh 2017a); 92% of Uttar Pradesh's hospitalization cases are because of infectious and parasitic diseases indicating poor water quality and absence of sanitation and basic hygiene that affect the poor (Mehrotra 2008). A deprivation index that captures deprivation in quality of housing, access to drinking water, sanitation, and domestic electricity indicated that most Eastern Uttar Pradesh districts had a deprivation index of 50% and above (Diwakar 2009). Open defecation rates in rural households, a cause of water contamination that in turn contributes to encephalitis, are as high as 78% (Coffey et al. 2014), and the share of rural households owning a latrine is barely 16% (Mehrotra 2008). Open defecation practices are also associated with various facets of neoliberal capitalism, such as malnutrition, diarrheal deaths, and stunting among children (Coffey et al. 2014; Walker 2008).

Moreover, successive Indian governments' health expenditures have been low and was about 3.5% of GDP in 2018 (in comparison, China spent 5.35%, Brazil 9.51%; World Health Organization 2020). Primary and Community Health Centers (PHC and CHC) that were systematically

The Thanatopolitics of Neoliberalism 191

created after India's independence increasingly have a shortfall of medical personnel and facilities (e.g., medicines, equipment) that would enable available personnel to work. Chronic absenteeism among physicians and paramedical staff at the PHCs and CHCs in Uttar Pradesh is higher than in other Indian states (Mehrotra 2008). According to Milind Gore at the National Institute of Virology, "It is safe to say that most PHC workers are insufficiently trained to manage these symptoms (of encephalitis), especially when they occur simultaneously. Also, PHCs are not equipped with respiratory support machines" (Indiaspend 2017). Consequently, when the previous Uttar Pradesh government announced the upgradation of 100 PHCs and CHCs to Encephalitis Treatment Centers (ETC) with four–six beds for encephalitis patients with round-the-clock care, it was a move without significant impact. Mani commented on the scheme,

> There are no doctors there. CHCs and PHCs are usually closed. They may have to rely on a pharmacist there. People have no faith in PHCs and CHCs. Why will they go there?

Thus, despite the physical infrastructure, PHCs and CHCs remain underutilized. It is no surprise then that people have no faith in PHCs and CHCs and come directly to tertiary hospitals like BRD. These crumbling decentralized layers have disrupted the referral mechanisms to tertiary centers like BRD, resulting in an overburdened medical staff. The State's withdrawal from public health expenditure must be seen alongside the "discipline" imposed by financial markets that serve the affluent classes; financial institutions exercise considerable influence in the formulation of government policies (Bhaduri 2008).

The event of the deaths between August 10 and August 12 due to oxygen supply disruption came to be reified as "Gorakhpur Deaths" (e.g., Rashid 2017; Sharma 2017). For a fortnight, media houses made scoops and breaking news over body counts: "120 kids die at Gorakhpur Medical College in 10 days," "14 kids die over a span of 24 hours," and "300 kids died in the month of August" (e.g., Deccan Herald 2017). Such journalistic representations are not merely simple information and views; they are at once cultural products, political instruments, and commodified objects within a competitive industry for the consumption of primarily urban middle-/upper-class consumers (Bourdieu 1998; Klinenberg 2001). Moreover, this media spectacle must be understood within the context of the corporatization of Indian media houses, which transforms journalism into what veteran journalist P. Sainath described as "stenography to corporate power" (Franklin and Shankar 2014). In the event of oxygen shortage, media images frame dead bodies as signifiers of something out of the ordinary and as another sign of corrupt and inefficient State apparatus, necessitating either privatization of public infrastructure or control by a totalitarian leader who can make the State work for the people.

192   *Rohit Varman and Devi Vijay*

Media attention on the event conceals structural violence. Mani an activist, working for over a decade on preventive aspects of encephalitis, narrates the typical staging of the spectacle,

> This has become a "seasonal show" for the government. In June, monsoons will arrive, and till November-December, [it is expected] there will be some deaths. Some decisions will be taken; some minister will come and visit BRD.

For activists, such spectacles distort reality and distract attention from some of the structural causes of these deaths. For example, every year, primary school teachers, based on State directives, conduct a rally with school children to spread awareness about encephalitis. Mani ridicules such spectacles, but these visible actions earn some support from voters, and the State garners media attention. For instance, until the event of oxygen disruption, there were 11 warmers for nearly 70 infants in BRD's neonatal ward. During our field visit, we found that the State had arranged for 40 additional warmers after the event. This move was promptly reported by local dailies as the State taking action. Responding to this move, Nitesh Singh commented, "this is like digging a well after the fire has spread." Long-term activists like Arvind Singh question the State's "eventful" actions instead of developing a year-round program targeted at preventive and public health initiatives (e.g., one toilet for two houses, India Mark II handpumps, routine sanitation measures).

Unlike media representations about the event and the State's preoccupation with BRD, the precariat and activists in Gorakhpur partially realize the significance of different sites of violence. However, as discussed in the previous section, they primarily hold the State responsible without recognizing the role of the broader capitalist relations through which state actions are controlled. Dilwar's uncle broods that "There is *durdasha* (ill-fate) here from all four sides," referring to the loss of land, the encephalitis epidemics, the state of healthcare, and state authorities' widespread apathy. Mani called Purvanchal a site of genocide. For Arvind Singh, the official numbers of about 500 patients a year at BRD is just the "tip of the iceberg." He reminded us that nearly 200 nursing homes, four big hospitals, and around 1,000 private practitioners in Gorakhpur city were also likely to treat encephalitis patients and for which no official figures were available. Moreover, patients outside the city were likely to visit *jhola chhaps* (quacks) and then try CHCs and PHCs. Arvind Singh concluded,

> My guess is, every year, 2500 patients are dying only in Gorakhpur district. The problem is big. A minimum of 4000 to 5000 people die every year only in Eastern Uttar Pradesh. Is this good governance?

The Thanatopolitics of Neoliberalism 193

Therefore, the region is marked by thousands of deaths every year, and these deaths remain concealed in a state of ellipsis. There are no testimonies against the profiteering that creates these deaths, and a bare life can only achieve the status of a speaking subject against some failures of the State. These deaths are either massified under some statistical figure and labeled as a normal occurrence and hence a quasi-event, or never recorded, as a bare life can be killed without any consequences.

Deepening Neoliberalism

The attention to the event focuses on corruption and negligence as the main causes of deaths. It furthers the very systemic force of neoliberal capitalism that creates bare life by labeling the State as corrupt and negligent. In step with neoliberalism and the imperative of finance capital, there is a withdrawal of the welfare state, and despite investment in equipment and buildings, tertiary hospitals like BRD have been systematically hollowed out. Nitesh Singh told us,

> Things were not always like this. The number of staff needed proportionate to the students was always there. Earlier doctors used to have a private practice. But they would come every day to the OPD [Out-Patient Department] between 9 a.m. and 2 p.m. In the evening, for a few hours, they would open a private practice at home. If they needed admission, patients were referred to the medical college.

Physicians employed in government institutions cannot practice privately as per service rules. Singh shares that in recent years, private practice is rampant, and it is a common understanding that government doctors have their private chambers or are also affiliated with private hospitals. Nitesh Singh elaborated,

> Nowadays, new doctors will not even come to OPD. They send patients to some outside practice or hospital—[they are] constantly in the money-making zone. Doctors who don't even have a name [reputation], will start something in a rural area. The dream for every MBBS is to start her nursing home.

A senior professor at BRD justified the neoliberal agenda, stating, "How can we expect medicine to be a noble profession?" When we asked about the state of PHCs and CHCs, he acknowledged that they were in a poor state and blamed the State for failing to provide necessary incentives for doctors to work. He further argued that doctors are at par in status with engineers, managers, and bureaucrats, and it was unfair to expect them to serve in places that did not provide adequate facilities and quality of life. Moreover, physicians spent large amounts on their education, and

194   *Rohit Varman and Devi Vijay*

it was "natural" for them to do private practice to get returns on their investment in education. Indeed, private healthcare had mushroomed in Gorakhpur. Private pharmacies surround BRD. Unlike in the past, when public hospitals were expected to supply medicines, patients had to purchase most medicines from outside. Rao (2017) reports:

> Since it is funded by the state government, the hospital is meant to provide free treatment and medicines to patients, but relatives complained that they had to purchase syringes, cotton, and medicines outside the hospital. Taj Mohammed, whose 7-year old son is admitted in the paediatric ICU with fever and seizures, said he had spent more than INR 11000 on his treatment. Anil Kumar, whose four-year-old daughter has pneumonia and is admitted to the ICU, said: "Doctors write a *parchi* [a small note] for everything from cotton to syringes."

At BRD, we observed a case of one such "parchi" written by a doctor for a diagnostic test to be done from an external private pathology laboratory instead of using the in-house laboratory. However, the patient brought it to the counter for tests done within the hospital. While we were talking to the person in-charge of the registration desk, he showed us the slip and told us how some doctors directed patients outside to private laboratories for a commission. In this case, instead of sending the patient to a private laboratory, he charged the nominal registration fee and directed the patient to the in-house pathology laboratory.

Such neoliberal forces of profiteering have deeply corroded health infrastructure. Under the National Health Mission provisions, there are three categories of medical staff: permanent, contract, and outsourced. Despite a Supreme Court ruling in December 2016 that contract and permanent employees must earn equal pay for equal work, a violation of which is tantamount to exploitative enslavement, BRD's permanent employees earn wages several times that of outsourced or contract employees with the same workload. These intraorganizational disparities are coupled with delayed wage payments for an overburdened workforce. A nurse at BRD complained to us that she was getting one-third of the salary for the same amount of work as compared to another nurse who had a permanent position. She felt discouraged because of this unequal remuneration but did not have a choice and had to work.

In a neoliberal context in which profit imperative dominates, hospitals like BRD are trying to reduce costs by downsizing permanent staff. Contract workers reduce financial liabilities and have limited bargaining power when their salaries are delayed. It is under this weight of the profit imperative that the public health apparatus is being dismantled across the region. Nitesh Singh further told us that the Composite Regional Centre for Persons with Disabilities setup at BRD (necessary because the majority of encephalitis survivors suffer from permanent disabilities) by

The Thanatopolitics of Neoliberalism   195

the National Institute for Empowerment of Persons with Multiple Disabilities, Chennai remains understaffed due to a dearth of funds. Salaries of several staff members had been delayed, some for over 27 months (Singh 2017b). Local actors informed that the staff had sent multiple letters to authorities and had directly requested the Principal Secretary of Health and Family Welfare, Prashant Trivedi, during his visit to BRD on July 24, 2017. Further, the District Magistrate had visited BRD on several occasions, while the Chief Minister and the Secretary of Health Education had visited twice within the span of July–August. However, salaries were still delayed.

In the thanatopolitics of neoliberalism, the very condition of bare life is used to usher in a regime that creates further death-worlds. The region is labeled as underdeveloped and not industrialized. This is seen as an outcome of the old logic of the State that failed to create private incentives and profit imperative. Development discourse in the neoliberal era looks at privatization as a panacea (Patnaik 2007). It pathologizes the victims as underdeveloped, inadequate, and holds them responsible for their problems. In this vein, a senior BRD professor told us that the people are illiterate and do not take precautionary measures that are needed to avoid encephalitis. He blamed the victims for their plight. Moreover, breakdowns within the public health apparatus are used to pave the way for further privatization. Union Minister, Nitin Gadkari, lost no time in stating that public hospitals are in no position to provide "professional healthcare" and that solutions rested with partnering with social institutions and entrepreneurs on government lands (Indian Express 2017). This statement echoes NITI Aayog's (India's planning body) proposals to privatize services at government hospitals (NITI Ayog 2020; see also Nandi 2020).

Summing up, the thanatopolitics of neoliberalism is constituted by the twin emphases of using the event to conceal systemic violence and to further privatization of public healthcare. The private healthcare sector is unregulated, engaging in malpractices during diagnosis, unnecessary investigations, procedures, operations, surgeries, questionable qualifications, inflated bills, and profit-driven drug prescriptions (Gadre and Shukla 2016). Private health expenditure in Uttar Pradesh is already as high as 92%, and any further privatization will further exacerbate the condition of bare life, pushing it deeper into the abyss of poverty, violence, and death.

Conclusion

The poor in and around Gorakhpur exist as bare lives who can be killed without a crime being committed. We reveal concealment of systemic violence against the precariat as part of the thanatopolitics of neoliberalism. We found that everyday deaths of bare lives are quasi-events that

196   *Rohit Varman and Devi Vijay*

are concealed through ellipsis about the forces of private profiteering. Agamben (1999, 63) observes a bare life is not human, unable to testify or speak, and "is a limit figure of a special kind, in which not only categories such as dignity and respect but even the very idea of an ethical limit loses its meaning." While the precariat identify and blame the State, there are no testimonies against private corporations and proponents of neoliberal capitalism. As a result, these deaths of the precariat go unaccounted, with the State and mainstream media merely reporting "the tip of the iceberg." Indeed, reducing events to body counts "massify death" beyond our emotional comprehension (Davis 2005, 3). The thanatopolitics of neoliberalism with concealment of structural violence against the precariat shows, as Davis (2005, 3) notes, "The afflicted, as a result, die twice: their physical agonies are redoubled by the submergence of their personalities in the black water of a mega tragedy. . . . No one mourns a multitude or keens at the graveside of an abstraction."

In uncovering the thanatopolitics of neoliberalism, we offer a different reading of thanatopolitics from that of Murray (2018, 719), who interprets it as, "what is intolerable to the state is less the living, who can be administrated, but the dead, whose posthumous claims threaten to disrupt the system." The thanatopolitics of neoliberalism does not threaten to disrupt the system. Unlike Murray's (2018, 719) "dead rising up to speak" and disaffirming the regime of neoliberal biopolitics, the dead in Gorakhpur help the neoliberal agenda of discrediting the State and advancing the interests of private capital.

Enumeration and statistics are critical techniques of concealment that surface when specific events are identified. We found that an extraordinary occurrence like the oxygen shortage becomes an event that gets included in media reports and is noticed by the State. Instead of the event signifying a state of exception that has become a rule in the setting and the oxygen shortage illuminating the systemic death world that pervades the poor in Gorakhpur, the spectacle is used to render BRD as a catastrophic site of negligence and corruption that must be corrected through State intervention and privatization (see Povinelli 2011). In so doing, it removes all traces of the lethality of the disease in its everydayness and ordinariness outside BRD. We are thus shown the familiar likeness of crumbling public health, individual corruption, and state failure. Thus, the event furthers privatization as part of neoliberal thanatopolitics.

The everyday deaths are naturalized as consequences of underdevelopment and poverty. In this *vikas* (development) rhetoric, the precariat are undernourished, illiterate, and weak bodies that must develop to overcome their problems. Neoliberal capitalism, which creates this very condition of precarity, uses discourse of development in which privatization becomes necessary to ameliorate the situation. Such a discourse of development hinges on two mutually reinforcing mechanisms. On the one hand, the public medical system is seen as corrupt with the problem

The Thanatopolitics of Neoliberalism   197

of commissions and kickbacks that hamper its functioning. The arrest of various officials at BRD and attendant media attention reinforce this carceral feature of thanatopolitics in the region. Simultaneously, in the name of development, farmland acquired for a private residential complex will provide the privileged the necessary infrastructure for entrepreneurial lives. Additionally, NITI Aayog proposes privatization of government hospitals to create a more efficient healthcare system. Therefore, in the thanatopolitics of neoliberalism a death-world of the precariat is used to create opportunities for private capital to flourish and in the process, conceal the state of crisis that the poor in Gorakhpur find themselves in.

In his examination of how violence is normalized, Gupta (2011, 2012) develops two points of departure from Agamben. First, he argues that the poor in India, unlike Agamben's homo sacer, are not cast away or excluded. Rather, they are killed despite their centrality and inclusion in democratic politics. Second, unlike Agamben's "'strong' theory of sovereignty and a powerfully unified state apparatus," Gupta (2011, 418) conceptualizes "fragmented, dispersed, or overlapping sovereignties, and a state that is pluricentered, multileveled, and decentralized." Gupta then asks, "What begs explanation in our case is the widespread acceptance of the violence being done to the poor in postcolonial India at the same time that popular sovereignty is constituted through them."

On the basis of our findings in Gorakhpur, we offer an addition to Gupta's reading of the poor's inclusion and constitution of popular sovereignty. We contend that the violence against the poor is used to further the very apparatus of neoliberal capitalism that injures them. Media plays a role in this process by concealing systemic violence and by blaming public institutions or officials for "events" that create visible injuries such as the oxygen shortage. Finance capital and the working of corporations are rarely discussed in the presentations of such events; finance dominates "through the structure, anonymously, a stealth form of oppression" (Prashad 2018, 13). Moreover, the precariat are unable to locate the role of such forces in creating systemic violence and primarily blame the State. Popular resentment and anger among the precariat then find a home in totalitarian right wing regimes that point at the weak and vulnerable—such as migrants or religious and ethnic minorities (Prashad 2018). Simultaneously, at the behest of financiers, right-wing regimes claim to overhaul the corrupt public institutions and privatize them in the name of efficiency. Patnaik (2019) labels such a tendency as the "fascification of society." Thus, the thanatopolitics of neoliberalism makes popular sovereignty inflict violence on itself.

In conclusion, we examine the event of oxygen shortage at BRD medical college as a catastrophe that morphs into a media event. To break this cycle of violence and death, the precariat will have to collectively rise against the prevailing corporate order. This will require the bare lives to disrupt the prevailing thanatopolitics and to create a new frontier that ruptures the hegemony of finance capital and its neoliberal order. Until

198   *Rohit Varman and Devi Vijay*

then, tragically, precarious consumers in the Global South and their dead bodies will continue to be used by the forces of profit as the weapons of violence against themselves.

References

Agamben, Giorgio (1998), *Homo Sacer: Sovereign Power and Bare Life*, Palo Alta, CA: Stanford University Press.
———— (1999), *Remnants of Auschwitz: The Witness and the Archive*, New York: Zone Books.
———— (2005), *State of Exception*, trans. Kevin Attell, Chicago: University of Chicago Press.
Bhaduri, Amit (2008), "Predatory Growth," *Economic and Political Weekly* (www.epw.in/journal/2008/16/commentary/predatory-growth.html).
Blakeley, Grace (2019), *Stolen: How to Save the World from Financialisation*, London: Verso.
Bourdieu, Pierre (1998), *On Television*, trans. Priscilla Parkhurst Ferguson, London: New Press.
Chatterjee, Partha (2011), *Lineages of Political Society: Studies in Postcolonial Democracy*, New York: Columbia University Press.
Chatterji, Angana (2019), "Remaking the Hindu/Nation: Terror and Impunity in Uttar Pradesh," in *Majoritarian State: How Hindu Nationalism Is Changing India*, ed. Angana Chatterji, Blom Hansen, and Christophe Jaffrelot, New Delhi: Oxford University Press, 397–418.
Chaudhuri, Siladitya and Nivedita Gupta (2009), "Levels of Living and Poverty Patterns: A District-wise Analysis for India," *Economic and Political Weekly*, 44 (9), 94–110 (www.epw.in/journal/2009/09/special-articles/levels-living-and-poverty-patterns-district-wise-analysis-india).
Coffey, Diane, Aashish Gupta, Payal Hathi, Nidhi Khurana, Dean Spears, Nikhil Srivastav, and Sangita Vyas (2014), "Revealed Preference for Open Defecation," *Economic & Political Weekly*, 49 (38), 43 (www.jstor.org/stable/24480705).
Davis, Mike (2005), *The Monster at Our Door: The Global Threat of Avian Flu*, New York: Henry Holt and Company.
Deccan Herald (2017), "No Let Up as Over 120 Kids Die at Gorakhpur Medical College in Ten Days," September 16 (www.deccanherald.com/content/633436/120-children-died-gorakhpur-hospital.html).
Dirlik, Arif (2002), "Rethinking Colonialism: Globalization, Postcolonialism, and the Nation," *Interventions*, 4 (3), 428–48 (https://doi.org/10.1080/13698 01022000013833).
Diwakar, D.M. (2009), "Intra-Regional Disparities, Inequality and Poverty in Uttar Pradesh," *Economic and Political Weekly*, 44 (26–27), 264–73 (www.jstor.org/stable/40279790).
Fanon, Franz (1990), *The Wretched of the Earth*, trans. Constance Farrington, New York: Grove Weidenfeld.
Firat, A. Fuat (2018), "Violence in/by the Market," *Journal of Marketing Management*, 34 (11–12), 1015–22 (https://doi.org/10.1080/0267257X.2018.1432190).
Franklin, Cynthia and S. Shankar (2014), "Against Stenography for the Powerful: An Interview with P. Sainath," *Biography*, 37 (1), 300–19 (https://doi.org/10.1353/bio.2014.0005).

The Thanatopolitics of Neoliberalism 199

Gadre, Arun and Abhay Shukla (2016), *Dissenting Diagnosis*, Gurgaon: Random House India.

Ghosh, Jayati and C.P. Chandrashekhar (2003), *Work and Well-Being in the Age of Finance*, Tulika: New Delhi.

Government of India (2013), *Press Note on Poverty Estimates, 2011–2012*, New Delhi: Government of India Planning Commission.

Gupta, Akhil (2011), "National Poverty and Global Poverty in the Age of Neoliberalism," *Cahiers d'études Africaines*, 51 (202–203), 415–26 (https://doi.org/10.4000/etudesafricaines.16712).

———— (2012), *Red Tape: Bureaucracy, Structural Violence, and Poverty in India*, Durham: Duke University Press.

Harvey, David (2003), *The New Imperialism*, Oxford: Oxford University Press.

Hindustan Times (2017), "Cops Lathicharge Protesting Farmers in Gkp, Several Injured," *HT Media Limited*, September 18 (www.pressreader.com/india/hindustan-times-lucknow/20170918/281779924299571).

Hudson, Michael (2015), *Killing the Host: How Financial Parasites and Debt Destroy the Global Economy*, Dresden: ISLET.

Indian Express (2017), "Difficult to Provide Professional Healthcare to Patients at Govt Facilities: Union Minister Nitin Gadkari," August 13 (https://indianexpress.com/article/india/difficult-to-provide-professional-healthcare-to-patients-at-govt-facilities-union-minister-nitin-gadkari-4795327/).

Indiaspend (2017), "Vaccination Failures, 'Mediocre' BRD Hospital, Claim Lives of Eastern UP's Children," (www.indiaspend.com/cover-story/vaccination-failures-mediocre-brd-hospital-claim-lives-of-eastern-ups-children-94520).

Joshi, Rajnish, S.P. Kalantri, Arthur Reingold, and John M. Colford (2012), "Changing Landscape of Acute Encephalitis Syndrome in India: A Systematic Review," *National Medical Journal of India*, 25 (4), 212–20.

Kakkar, Manish, Elizabeth Rogawski, Syed Shahid Abbas, Sanjay Chaturvedi, Tapan Dhole, Shaikh Shah Hossain, and Sampath Krishnan (2013), "Acute Encephalitis Syndrome Surveillance, Kushinagar District, Uttar Pradesh, India, 2011–2012," *Emerging Infectious Diseases*, 19 (9), 1361–67 (https://doi.org/10.3201/eid1909.121855).

Klinenberg, Eric (2001), "Bodies that Don't Matter: Death and Dereliction in Chicago," in *Commodifying Bodies*, ed. Nancy Scheper-Hughes and Loïc Wacquant, London: Sage, 121–36.

Kumar, Rashmi, Piyush Tripathi, Sudhakar Singh, and Gopa Bannerji (2006), "Clinical Features in Children Hospitalized During the 2005 Epidemic of Japanese Encephalitis in Uttar Pradesh, India," *Clinical Infectious Diseases*, 43 (2), 123–31 (https://doi.org/10.1086/505121).

Lapavitsas, Costas (2013), *Profiting Without Producing: How Finance Exploits Us All*, New York: Verso Books.

Mehrotra, Santosh (2008), "Public Health System in UP: What Can Be Done?" *Economic and Political Weekly*, 43 (49), 46–53 (www.epw.in/journal/2008/49/perspectives/public-health-system-what-can-be-done.html).

Murray, Scott J. (2018), "Thanatopolitics," in *Bloomsbury Handbook to Literary and Cultural Theory*, ed. J.R. Di Leo, London: Bloomsbury, 718–19.

Nandi, Sulakshana (2020), "Central Government's Move to Privatise District Hospitals Spells Disaster for India's Poor," (https://en.gaonconnection.com/central-governments-move-to-privatise-district-hospitals-spells-disaster-for-indias-poor/).

200 *Rohit Varman and Devi Vijay*

NITI Ayog (2020), "Public Private Partnership for Non-Communicable Diseases (NCDs) in District Hospitals," (https://niti.gov.in/writereaddata/files/document_publication/Draft%20Guidelines%20on%20PPP%20in%20NCDs_0.pdf).

Patnaik, Prabhat (2007), "The State Under Neo-liberalism," *Social Scientist*, 35 (1–2), 4–15 (www.jstor.org/stable/27644193).

——— (2018), "The Imperialism of Finance Capital and 'Trade Wars'," (www.thetricontinental.org/wp-content/uploads/2018/08/180803_Dossier-7_EN_Final_Web.pdf).

——— (2019), "Shadow of Fascism," *Monthly Review* (https://mronline.org/2019/04/08/the-modi-years/).

——— (2020a), "Neoliberalism and Fascism," *Agrarian South: Journal of Political Economy*, 9 (1), 33–49 (https://doi.org/10.1177/2277976019901029).

——— (2020b), "Restructure Capitalism by Controlling Finance, or Let the Tendencies Towards Very Coercive Forms of Fascism Grow," (https://gpenewsdocs.com/government-under-finance-there-is-no-easy-exit/).

Patton, Michael (1990), *Qualitative Evaluation and Research Methods*, London: Sage.

Povinelli, Elizabeth A. (2011), *Economies of Abandonment: Social Belonging and Endurance in Late Liberalism*, Durham: Duke University Press.

Pradhan, Sharat (2020), "Did Dr. Kafeel Pay a Heavy Price Because His Name Is Khan," *The Wire* (https://thewire.in/rights/did-dr-kafeel-pay-a-heavy-price-because-his-name-is-khan).

Prashad, Vijay (2018), *Strongmen*, New Delhi: Leftword.

Rao, Menaka (2017), "The Entire Corridor Was Filled With Cries: The Night When Oxygen Ran Out in Gorakhpur Hospital," *Scroll.in*, August 15 (https://scroll.in/pulse/847253/the-entire-corridor-was-filled-with-cries-the-night-when-oxygen-ran-out-in-gorakhpur-hospital).

Rashid, Omar (2017), "Gorakhpur Hospital Deaths: Documents Show That Minister Was Briefed on 'Irregularities'," *The Hindu*, August 16 (www.thehindu.com/news/national/documents-show-minister-briefed-on-brd-irregularities/article19504380.ece).

Rawat, Virendra (2014), "UP Clocks Maximum Food Grain Production in India," *Business Standard* (www.business-standard.com/article/economy-policy/up-clocks-maximum-food-grain-production-in-india-114030700676_1.html).

Sapkal, Gajanan N., Vijay Bondre, Pradip Fulmali, Pooja Patil, V. Gopalkrishna, Vipul Dadhania, Daya Gangale, K.P. Kushwala, A.K. Rathi, Shobha Chitambar, Akhilesh Chandra Mishra, and Milind Gore (2009), "Enteroviruses in Patients With Acute Encephalitis, Uttar Pradesh, India," *Emerging Infectious Diseases*, 15 (2), 295–98 (www.cdc.gov/EID/content/15/2/295.htm).

Sharma, Sanchita (2017), "Gorakhpur Deaths: Why India's Poor Public Health Delivery System Is a Killer," *Hindustan Times*, August 28 (www.hindustantimes.com/india-news/gorakhpur-deaths-why-india-s-poor-public-health-delivery-system-is-a-killer/story-ts9FxktlcUCXHgHrM3FS0I.html).

Simone, Abdoumaliq (2010), "Urban Geography Plenary Lecture—on Intersections, Anticipations, and Provisional Publics: Remaking District Life in Jakarta," *Urban Geography*, 31 (3), 285–308 (https://doi.org/10.2747/0272-3638.31.3.285).

The Thanatopolitics of Neoliberalism   201

Singh, Manoj (2017a), "Encephalitis: One Hospital, 40 Years, and 9733 Deaths," *Gorakhpur Newsline* (http://gorakhpurnewsline.com/इंसेफेलाइटिसि-एक-असपताल-40/).

———— (2017b), "How Gorakhpur's BRD Medical College Struggled With Money and Manpower for Years," *The Wire* (https://thewire.in/167498/gorakhpur-children-death-brd-medical-college-up-government/).

Srivastava, Piyush (2017), "Nothing, Nothing, Nothing—The Response to Repeated Reminders on Oxygen Dues," *Telegraph*, August 15.

Varman, Rohit, Paromita Goswami, and Devi Vijay (2018), "The Precarity of Respectable Consumption: Normalising Sexual Violence against Women," *Journal of Marketing Management*, 34 (11–12), 932–64 (https://doi.org/10.1080/0267257X.2018.1527387).

Varman, Rohit and Devi Vijay (2018), "Dispossessing Vulnerable Consumers: Derealization, Desubjectification, and Violence," *Marketing Theory*, 18 (3), 307–26 (https://doi.org/10.1177/1470593117753980).

Walker, Kathy Le Mons (2008), "Neoliberalism on the Ground in Rural India: Predatory Growth, Agrarian Crisis, Internal Colonization, and the Intensification of Class Struggle," *The Journal of Peasant Studies*, 35 (4), 557–620 (https://doi.org/10.1080/03066150802681963).

11 Cold Chains in Hanoi and Bangkok

Changing Systems of Provision and Practice[1]

Jenny Rinkinen, Elizabeth Shove, and Mattijs Smits

Introduction

It comes as no surprise to learn that habits are changing in fast growing cities like Hanoi and Bangkok that per capita energy consumption is rising and that diets are becoming more "Westernized" and resource intensive, especially among the middle class. In analyzing the emergence of new forms of distinctly urban demand, this article characterizes changing relationships between systems of food provisioning and related practices of shopping, cooking, and eating. It concentrates, in particular, on the pivotal roles of fridge freezers, arguing that these appliances are situated at the intersection of households and more extensive supply chains, including "cold chains" which enable distant forms and sources of food supply and which have simultaneously become an essential part of the urban infrastructure and of variously shared interpretations of "proper" provision. Comparing experiences from Bangkok and Hanoi allows us to identify some of the different trajectories involved in constituting and reconstituting such arrangements. More abstractly, this exercise shows how household practices, patterns of consumption, and systems of food provisioning connect and change.

Consumption, Systems of Provision, and Practice

Although it is fair to say that consumption is an outcome of practice, this is to scratch the surface of a much more complex set of relationships. As Warde (2005, 2016) explains, everyday practices such as eating, shopping, provisioning, cooking, and storing food reflect and reproduce conventions of convenience and care and are, in turn, bound up with related systems and technologies of food retailing, manufacturing, and provision. In so far as consumption is an outcome of practice, understanding changes in the demand for energy or for different types of food, like those observed in Hanoi and Bangkok, is essentially a matter of understanding how configurations of practices, infrastructures, appliances, and systems of provision cohere and evolve, especially in contexts of rapid urbanization.

DOI: 10.4324/9781003111559-15

Cold Chains in Hanoi and Bangkok 203

In taking this approach, we build on the suggestion that technologies and appliances are not only critical for the conduct of specific practices, but they are also part of bundles of practice that extend across different scales and periods of time (Hui, Schatzki, and Shove, 2017; Shove 2017). These ideas suggest that studies of domestic consumption cannot be separated from and are in fact constitutive of more extensive systems of provision. As developed by Fine and Leopold (1993) and Leslie and Reimer (1999), the concept of "systems of provision" characterizes connections between sites of production, distribution, retailing, design, marketing, and final consumption. For example, a local system of provision might only involve movement from farm to shop to home. By contrast, a more extended system might entail movements between sites of production and processing around the world before reaching shops and homes.

Our challenge is to show how changing systems of urban food provisioning in Hanoi and Bangkok sustain and are sustained by also changing practices of shopping, cooking, and eating, and how all of these depend, in one way or another, on freezers and the "cold chain."

The cold chain is a term used to describe an unbroken sequence of spaces and processes through which foods are maintained in a frozen or chilled state "from farm to fork." The cold chain depends on a network of domestic fridges and freezers, along with refrigerated transport and storage. Once in place, these infrastructures facilitate the geographical separation of food production and consumption and the distribution and circulation of foods that "need" chilling. The fridge freezer, which is crucial to these processes, is situated at the intersection of domestic and commercial systems of provision. Analysis of what these appliances contain and how they are used consequently promises to provide distinctively revealing insight into the ways in which familiar practices are maintained or transformed in new and changing circumstances and into how new diets and/or patterns of consumption take hold within, despite or alongside changing systems of provision.

Previous research suggests that freezers[2] link households to global networks of frozen food provisioning and to discourses and ideologies of care, convenience, health, well-being, and family life (Hand and Shove 2007; Shove and Southerton 2000). In addition, as Goodman et al. explain, freezers have a special role within food systems that reflect and are defined by the problem of supplying major conurbations (Goodman et al. 2012). They are also implicated in dietary trends including the consumption of imported food or food which is out of season. Fridge freezers consequently contribute to the production and configuration of what are becoming increasingly distant and distinctly resource-intensive systems of food provisioning. But as we explain below, this is not their only possible role. Fridge freezers are also used to sustain much more local systems of provision, helping to preserve "traditional" diets and sources of supply and to bypass, if not subvert, the commercial cold chains that they also enable.

204　*Jenny Rinkinen et al*

Investigating Fridge Freezers

In this article, we analyze the contents of a selection of fridge freezers and the practices of those who use them, doing so as a means to better understand the dynamics and the ironies of fridge freezer dependence. In detail, we compare the uses of fridge freezers in Bangkok (Thailand) and Hanoi (Vietnam) as part of a broader project examining trends in domestic energy demand. Bangkok and Hanoi are instructive sites in terms of changing patterns of both food and energy consumption. The number of domestic refrigerators in use is expected to rise from 10.8 million to 18 million in Thailand and from 11 million to 21.8 million in Vietnam between 2016 and 2030 (Green Cooling Initiative 2016). In addition, Bangkok and Hanoi are experiencing rapid population growth accompanied by related changes in food supply (Dixon et al. 2007; Wertheim-Heck 2015), and in both cities, there is evidence that aspects of a more "Western" diet (for instance, dairy products and ready-meals) are gaining ground.

In detail, our research shows how the double-door fridge freezer—which is the most common format for new fridge freezers in both countries—links households to changing forms of food supply. We discovered that diets were altered in ways that generated new demands for keeping food cool and that meanings of freshness and quality were renegotiated sometimes in opposition but always in relation to the affordances of commercial cold chains. This is not a uniform process. In describing how fridge freezers figured in multiple social practices and in the making of dependencies and needs within the home and beyond, we detect the ongoing co-evolution and hybridization of concepts like those of "tradition" and "modernity" and the intertwining of global and local arrangements.

This article begins with an overview of when and how fridge freezers have become "normal" home appliances and of related trends in food provisioning and consumption. We then consider how fridge freezers figure in changing food systems such as those that are developing in Bangkok and Hanoi. Drawing on household interviews in both cities, we go on to review first-hand accounts of fridge freezers in use and of how practices of shopping and cooking are shaped by freezer-related forms of storage and provisioning and associated themes of food quality and safety. In the last part of the article, we highlight tensions and ironies in how fridge freezers are embedded in urban life and how their role evolves.

What Are Fridge Freezers for?

There is no one answer to this question. Instead, responses reflect differences in how households and appliances are positioned within historical and cultural trajectories of provisioning and practice (Shove, Watson, and Spurling 2015). It is consequently impossible to provide a single history of the fridge freezer in use. Instead and as studies of domestic appliances in the United States, United Kingdom, and India indicate, fridges and freezers have "arrived" and been integrated in different countries and food systems at different moments in time.

In the United States, household refrigerators were initially acquired by relatively affluent households and became quieter, more reliable, and less expensive through the 1920s. According to Rees, the first stages of refrigerator diffusion were marked by a clear division between homeowners and tenants who were unwilling to invest in a kitchen they might soon leave. In 1935, the US government offered loans for "household modernization," which could include the purchase of appliances, and by 1944, 85% of American homes had a refrigerator. Stand-alone freezers came later, only becoming popular when the infrastructure for frozen food developed in the 1950s. In 1953, there were around 3 million home freezers (in the United States), a figure which rose to 14 million by 1965. Although the frozen food industry promoted home freezing, it was the possibility of buying ready-frozen food that prompted many households to get a freezer. As Americans became accustomed to cheap and convenient (often frozen) food, fridges and freezers quickly became indispensable (Rees 2013).

In the United Kingdom, refrigerators became available somewhat later than in the United States, with the first freezers appearing in the 1960s. At this point, there was little or no commercial frozen food provision, meaning that freezers were mostly used for preserving gluts of home produce and beating the seasons. From the 1970s onward, arguments about the "need" for a freezer reflected arguments about efficiency and economy and were clearly related to the development of a frozen food industry and opportunities for people to buy in bulk. Since the 1990s with the development of an even wider range of ready-frozen foods, the freezer (now a fridge freezer) has been repositioned as an instrument of convenience and coordination: it helps households manage busy lives while maintaining valued standards of catering and care (Shove and Southerton 2000).

In other countries, fridges and freezers have been adopted, as standard, in different decades, entering radically different worlds of food consumption and production, and having correspondingly diverse consequences for shopping, cooking, and eating. For example, although refrigerators were introduced in India in the 1960s, it took another 40 years before they were in widespread use (Wilhite 2008). As Wilhite explains, traditional aversions to eating or reheating leftovers and to consuming cold drinks and food had to be overcome before refrigeration "made sense." In effect, it took a whole new generation before refrigerators and the food practices associated with them became normal.

These examples underline the point that fridge freezers are introduced and embedded in strikingly different complexes of practice. The process of becoming normal, and of falling into use, is not simply a matter of reinventing forms of cooking and eating that already exist elsewhere (Shove

206 *Jenny Rinkinen et al*

and Pantzar 2005). Instead, and as Hand and Shove (2007) also argue, the normalization of the freezer is an ongoing, situated achievement: not a matter of sociotechnical closure and not simply an outcome of increasingly extensive diffusion.

At the same time, there is something of a sequential process. The viability and significance of the commercial cold chain and the market for ready-frozen foods change as more and more people acquire a fridge freezer and as the last link into the home is completed. These are important processes, but further steps are required to show how fridges and practices interconnect. DuPuis' (2002) account of the normalization of milk consumption in the United States provides some clues as to how an analysis of related shifts of habit, diet, and consumption might proceed. As her subtle and insightful study shows, grasping the "making" of milk as indispensable part of the American diet depends on understanding the relation between urban centers and rural farms, the politics of regulation, systems of packaging and distribution, education, and ideology. This is not only a matter of understanding different "levels" of influence or of detailing ordered chains of action: instead, DuPuis' method is to represent and describe the circulation and conjunction of interconnected flows of materials, knowledges, and discourse (Leslie and Reimer 1999). This approach is consistent with the suggestion that fridge freezers simultaneously figure as instruments of household provisioning (Shove, Pantzar, and Watson 2012; Shove and Pantzar 2005) and also as essential features of changing systems of provision (Freidberg 2015).

In the rest of this article, we draw on these ideas using them to help reveal the fridge freezer's not only pivotal but also ambivalent role in the food system and in daily life at times of rapid urbanization and as differently experienced in Bangkok and Hanoi. In pointing to similarities and differences between these two cases, our aim is to learn more about how fridge freezers mediate responses to the various challenges of managing diets and food supplies in these fast changing urban environments. While the details of the cases are not generalizable—different arrangements apply in other cities and at other times—our research reveals what are likely to be generic trends in urban diets and frozen food provisioning and in related but ambivalent responses and adaptations in practice.

Fridge Freezers and Cold Chains in Bangkok and Hanoi

Bangkok and Hanoi have expanded significantly in the last 40 years, and there have been major changes in transport, housing, urban planning, economic growth, and systems of food provision. In general, the pattern is one in which local food supplies have been supplanted or augmented by those grown or manufactured elsewhere and distributed through supermarkets rather than small stores and markets. However, there are relevant differences of scale and in when and at what rate these two cities have developed.

Cold Chains in Hanoi and Bangkok   207

In brief, Bangkok, which is in any case larger, expanded faster and earlier than Hanoi. In 2010, Bangkok was home to 8.2 million people, some of whom had lived in an urban environment for two or more generations (Baker and Phongpaichit 2014; National Statistical Office Thailand 2013). Bangkok's population continues to rise and is predicted to grow from 9.3 million to 11.0 million people (18.2%) in the period 2015–2025 (United Nations (UN) 2014). By contrast, the population of greater Hanoi has grown from 1.4 million in 1975 to 6.6 million in 2010 (General Statistics Office of Vietnam (GSO) 2011). Meanwhile, the number of people living in the urban agglomeration of Hanoi itself is expected to increase from 3.6 million to 5.0 million (37.5%) between 2015 and 2025 (UN 2014). In general, as cities develop and as supply chains get longer, new challenges of food storage and preservation arise (DuPuis 2002). But as our two cases illustrate, the nature of these challenges varies.

Bangkok's high-rise apartment buildings, shopping centers, hotels, and offices define it as a modern metropolis, enabling forms of urban living that are in stark contrast to more rural ways of life (Evers and Korff 2000). Since the late 1960s, Thai businesses have been willing and able to respond to consumers' enthusiasm for Western goods, including food, and many new products have entered the market (Baker and Phongpaichit 2014). Following rapid industrial and urban development, eating in public has increased, and in Bangkok, small-scale street vendors are considered to be part of an efficient and affordable system of food distribution that has, to some extent, displaced cooking at home (Higman 2011; Yasmeen 2006). At the same time, the role of street vending is changing: snacks and meals are also sold in privately owned indoor shopping centers, air-conditioned restaurants, and food courts.

In Hanoi, similar processes (westernization of the diet, supermarkets, mass-produced, and distributed food) are in evidence, but less extensive than in Bangkok. In Vietnam, as in Thailand, there are also concerns about the safety of mass-produced food. Wertheim-Heck (2015), who writes about vegetable shopping in Hanoi, explains that increasingly distanced relationships between production and consumption combined with an intensification of agriculture and cultivation "altered the characteristics of Vietnam's food insecurity from historic food shortage to contemporary food safety concerns" (p. 7). There are now widespread and well-documented anxieties about health risks associated with natural toxins, biological pathogens, and chemical agents such as pesticides, antibiotics, and preservatives.

In response, the government has sought to regulate food production (Van Hoi, Mol, and Oosterveer 2009) and promote the "modernization" of the food retail system by encouraging the development of supermarkets (Wertheim-Heck 2015). On this point, it is important to note that it was not until 2009 that Vietnam allowed foreign-owned companies to operate. Not surprisingly, this shift of policy led to an expansion of international

208   Jenny Rinkinen et al

retail. Despite this opening up and the proliferation of supermarkets, cities in Vietnam retain strong links to (relatively) nearby sites of small-scale agriculture and food production (Phuc 2012). Many consumers still buy food from market traders they know and trust (Wertheim-Heck 2015).

The role of fridge freezers in Bangkok/Thailand and Hanoi/Vietnam reflects and relates to these different narratives of development. In detail, fridge freezers were available in Thailand in the 1960s (as in the United Kingdom), but a study by Pongsapich and Wongsekiarttirat (1994) suggests that they were not in widespread use until the 1970s. By contrast, in 1970s Vietnam, fridge freezers were high-end luxury devices used for storing food but more importantly for making ice. They only came into use on any scale after the economic reforms of 1986 (Wertheim-Heck 2015). Partly because of these contrasting histories, different patterns of fridge freezer ownership and use remain today.

National figures are a bit patchy, but in 2002, only 10.9% of Vietnamese households owned a refrigerator while in 2006, in Thailand, the rate of ownership was already at 86%. By 2014, 91% of Thai households had a fridge (National Statistical Office Thailand 2015) compared to 49% of Vietnamese households in 2012 (GSO 2012). These figures do not distinguish between fridges, freezers, and fridge freezers, but in both countries, double-door fridge freezers are now the dominant form, at least of new appliances.[3]

In the next part of this article, we focus on the changing roles of fridge freezers within and also as part of evolving food systems. Our analysis is based on interviews with middle-class households (26 interviews in Bangkok, Thailand, and 26 interviews in Hanoi, Vietnam), all conducted in 2016. Social class is a complex concept but in Southeast Asia, what have been described as significant "consumer" classes are emerging as more people acquire more purchasing power (Asian Development Bank (ADB) 2010; Guarín and Knorringa 2014; Nguyen-Marshall, Drummond, and Belanger 2011; The Economist 2009). Given our interest in explaining how consumer needs develop in practice, it made sense to focus on this population. We therefore selected respondents from distinctively "middle-class" areas as defined by our research partners in Vietnam and Thailand. Interviewees were recruited through the professional and social networks of our local research assistants and included people living in privately owned houses, town houses, and condominiums. In all, 28 of the 52 interviews were with women, 18 with men and in 6 cases a man and a woman were both present. A total of 14 of those with whom we spoke were aged between 25 and 38, 23 were aged between 39 and 60 and 15 were 61 or over. We have used pseudonyms to maintain anonymity.

The interviews were semistructured, lasted from 45 to 90 minutes, and most took place in respondents' homes. A Vietnamese- or Thai-speaking research assistant helped translate in the interview situation, but some people chose to have the interview in English. We discussed the use of household appliances with special emphasis on fridge freezers and asked

Cold Chains in Hanoi and Bangkok 209

about present and past routines and practices. In most cases, interviewees showed us around their home, allowing us to photograph their appliances, the contents of their fridge freezer, and the room in which it was located.

It is important to be clear about the status of this material. In conducting this research, our aim was not to identify factors (such as family composition or working hours) that led households to acquire a freezer or to use it in a certain way, nor did we want to quantify the prevalence of one form of freezer-use over another, or compare the uses of freezer in different types of household (e.g., with or without children). Rather, our ambition was to establish how practices of shopping, cooking, and eating hang together and change, and how the freezer and its contents figured in these dynamic processes. Photographs of the freezers' contents, combined with accounts of where items were sourced from, and of how and when they might be used allowed us to detect the webs of materials and meanings which constituted practices of shopping and cooking and which in various ways bridged between households and urban systems and chains of provision. Our analysis focuses on these points of interconnection.

Evolving Forms of Fridge Freezer Dependence

The interviews reveal different and also dynamic interpretations of the need for a fridge freezer. As detailed below, the role of the fridge freezer is shaped by (a) changing forms and sources of supply and diet entwined with practices of shopping, cooking, and eating and (b) closely related notions of taste, quality, freshness, and safety. In discussing the contents of their fridge freezers in these terms, our respondents provided first-hand accounts of how systems of urban provisioning have reconfigured household practices and the forms of consumption that follow.

What Is in the Fridge Freezer and Where Does It Come From?

Despite the different histories of urban development outlined previously, the fridge freezers we investigated contained many of the same sorts of food. In Bangkok and Hanoi, interviewees routinely stored vegetables, fruits, drinks, eggs, condiments, milk, and cooked food in the fridge and kept meat and ice in the freezer.

But in discussion, and on closer inspection, various differences emerged. For example, Mai's fridge, in Bangkok, contains packs of eggs bought from the nearby supermarket and laid by imported chicken stock. Duc's fridge, in Hanoi, also contains eggs. But in this case, there is an entire crate of unpackaged eggs "imported" to the city from his home village by bus. As this example illustrates, the contents of fridge freezers are indicative not only of the combination of what were seen as traditional diets and new foods but also of the sources and supply chains through which necessary ingredients and products are procured.

210   *Jenny Rinkinen et al*

In Bangkok, supermarkets have had a noticeable impact on how food is supplied and how shopping and cooking figure in the sociotemporal order of urban life. According to Mrs. Pam (Bangkok), her fridge freezer became indispensable as early as the mid-1970s, a time when she and her husband were both in full-time work and when her extended family gave up the family farm located outside the city and until then a reliable source of home-grown food.

A few years ago, Mrs. Pam, now retired and living with her family in a big concrete house, upgraded to an even larger fridge freezer. She attributed this change to the fact that her neighborhood was becoming gentrified and that the food for sale in the local market was consequently becoming more expensive. She now travels to a more distant but cheaper supermarket, doing so when her son is free to take her there by car. Since these are infrequent trips, she likes to stock up, hence the big fridge freezer (Interview 2.4, Bangkok, woman aged 60+, private house).

While the possibility of storing cold or frozen food at home has released people like Ms. Nat from the task of shopping on a daily basis, there are more demands in terms of planning ahead:

> In the past, you just picked it up from the garden and cooked it. Now you need to go to the supermarket, and you need to think in advance.
> (Interview 1.11, Bangkok, woman aged 40–50, town house)

Ms. Nat uses her fridge freezer to store the ingredients needed to cook what she thinks of as proper food. At the weekend, she prepares dishes for the week ahead, making sure she has meals ready for her retired mother, and making cooking easier given her own erratic working hours.

For other people, and especially for some of the younger interviewees, the fridge freezer is an essential device in transforming rather than maintaining what they see as a traditional diet. For example, Muk and Pon are a young working couple living in a condominium in Bangkok. Unlike their parents, they don't cook at home: instead, they buy ready-made meals from the local street markets, order take-aways, eat out in restaurants, or reheat frozen food at home. For breakfast, they purchase egg sandwiches (freshly made each day) from the 7/11 supermarket. In their small fridge freezer, they store milk and frozen foods from the 7/11. They sometimes buy fresh fruit and vegetables from the local market, which they consume as snacks (Interview 3.1, Bangkok, couple, aged 30–40, condominium).

When Muk and Pon moved into the condominium, they adapted their shopping and cooking habits to take advantage of the services provided in their new surroundings (supermarkets, restaurants, and take-away food outlets). By contrast, other respondents looked for ways of preserving established practices, despite living in an urban environment. In Hanoi, experiences of leaving the countryside and moving into the city tended to be more recent and also more memorable. Those who had made this

Cold Chains in Hanoi and Bangkok 211

switch explained what it meant for shopping. While some found it easier to buy what they wanted, others said it was much more difficult.

Mr. Dung, who now lives in Hanoi with his younger sister, is of the latter view. He and his sister interact regularly with the rest of their family who live 80 km away. As he explains, the chance to bring food back to the city is an important part of his "home" visits:

> Relatives still live in the rural areas in a traditional way. People who live in the city live far from the hometown but whenever they return to their home villages they bring things from the local producers. They bring this [food] to the city because those items in the city are expensive and hard to find.
>
> (Interview II.18, Hanoi, man aged 30–40, condominium)

Mr. Dung's fridge freezer included items that are part of a typical Vietnamese diet (usually from the village) alongside yoghurt and milk bought from the supermarket. Ms. Lien, who lives in a condominium in Hanoi, also talks positively about the chance to combine the convenience and variety on offer in the city along with fresh, and in her view, "good" and reliable produce from the countryside:

> Every weekend I go to the countryside to buy food and vegetables to store in the fridge. I only buy fruits and small things [cookies, candies, yoghurt and snacks, milk] in the minimarket nearby here but main things like meat, fish, I buy from the countryside.
>
> (Interview II.13, Hanoi, woman aged 30–40, condominium)

The contents of Ms. Lien's and Mr. Dung's fridge freezers and the shopping and cooking practices they reveal demonstrate the existence of parallel systems of provision and competing but also coexisting ideas about the nature of good quality food. For Ms. Lien, as for some of the other younger people in our sample, the result is a hybrid diet the ingredients for which are sourced in very different ways and then stored together in the same fridge freezer.

The details of what is in the fridge freezer and where it comes from show how households have adapted or retained specific practices in response to the urban cold chains and food systems amidst which they now live. These responses are not simply about the availability, or otherwise, of different foods. They are also shaped by shifting ideas about quality and safety which are in turn related to changing features of urban food supply.

Taste, Freshness, and Food Quality

It is difficult to chart changing tastes or pin down what Pingali (2007) refers to as the diffusion of a "Westernized" diet, but in Bangkok and

212   *Jenny Rinkinen et al*

Hanoi, it is easy to detect the arrival and consumption of what our respondents referred to as "new" foods. For example, Mr. Ming described his interest in so-called "international" food, which he buys online and has delivered to his home or office (Interview 4.2, Hanoi, man aged 40–50, condominium). More ordinarily, and in both cities, the widespread availability of fridge freezers is closely linked to the introduction of novel products, many of which need to be kept cool. In this context, the increasing popularity of milk in Southeast Asia is especially interesting, particularly because it has such a central place in the Western diet (DuPuis 2002). In Thailand, Vietnam, and most other Asian countries, "milks" made from fresh vegetable or soy have been preferred to actual dairy products (McLeod and Nguyen 2001), but there is evidence that this is changing. Average per capita milk consumption in Thailand rose from 2 to 23 L a year between 1984 and 2007 (Food and Agriculture Organization (FAO) 2011; Suwanabol 2005), and in Bangkok and other cities, there are high-end milk bars and national advertising campaigns promoting milk. Fridge freezers are part of this story: they enable the distribution and consumption of dairy products, and they allow people to store other ready-frozen convenience foods at home. However, their role is surely not defined by these new foodstuffs alone.

In the city environments we studied, lengthening supply chains have had an impact on respondents' interpretations of freshness, quality, and safety, and on the practices through which these discourses are carried and reproduced.

Friedberg suggests that meanings of freshness have shifted such that they depend more on the technology used to preserve and retain specific qualities and less on the passage of time as such (Freidberg 2009). This is consistent with the view that interpretations of "fresh" in the urban setting are not the same as those applied to food "freshly" picked from the garden. This shift of meaning and the greater reliance on "technology" (broadly defined) has to be understood in light of other changes in where and how people live, and in how they deal with perishable food.

The suggestion that urban reinterpretations of freshness and quality emerge alongside and via new forms of food supply is supported by Mrs. Lat's account of her cooking and eating practices and by what she keeps in her fridge freezer. Mrs. Lat lives in Bangkok with her husband and two children and works in the city center. Unlike her mother, who used to make all her own meals from scratch, Mrs. Lat very rarely cooks and hardly ever buys food that is fresh in the sense of being raw or unprocessed. Although she sometimes prepares eggs and bread for breakfast, her family mostly relies on ready-meals bought from the supermarket (Interview I.21, Bangkok, woman aged 40–50, private house).

In Mrs. Lat's family, freshness is not equated with cooking and eating meals made at home with basic ingredients. Instead, freshness is treated as a taken-for-granted quality—a feature embedded in food that is made to last and designed to be stored (or frozen) for use at a moment's notice.

Cold Chains in Hanoi and Bangkok   213

In this regime, the fridge freezer is a necessary part of the ready-meal scenario and of Mrs. Lat's busy urban life.

Whereas Mrs. Lat trusts in the quality of the prepared foods that she buys, Mr. Wat, who lives in Bangkok with his wife and two school-age children, values his fridge freezer because it allows him to avoid these foods and the risks he associates with them. Mr. Wat's fridge freezer is consequently stocked with meals he has made himself, cooked in batches, and stored for future use. As he explains, this arrangement means his family can avoid eating out and refrain from buying foods that are ready-made or highly processed (Interview I.3, Bangkok, man aged 40–50, private house).

Mr. Wat was something of an exception among those with whom we spoke in Bangkok. By contrast, in Hanoi, many respondents were deeply anxious about food quality and contamination. Major scandals like those concerning contaminated fish have been widely covered in the media (Thanh Nien News 2016) and clearly add to a generic sense of unease. These fears help explain why Mr. Dung and others make regular trips to get food supplies from sources they trust:

> It is for the food security why we go home. My parents prepare the meat and the fish. They bought a pig, fed by local people, and get fish from their own pond. We take the vegetables from our own garden so all of that is considered as clean origin, safe and fresh. We bring it here and rice also we normally bring in twice a month, each time like 10kg. My mother takes it from my aunty as she has rice field. That is process to provide food for us. I guess every family whose parents live in the rural/ suburban and they live in the city, they will do all the same that way.
> (Interview II.18, Hanoi, man aged 40–50, condominium)

It is difficult to estimate the scale of this informal economy or the extent of self/family provisioning, but it is clear that Mr. Dung's reliance on rural supplies is directly related to his distrust of the urban alternative. He was not alone. Other interviewees talked about getting vegetables, chicken, eggs, and fish from relatives in the countryside, either imported in person or sent to the city by bus. For example, those quoted below describe making special efforts to get seafood fresh from the sea, to buy organic produce directly from the farmer, and even to grow their own food in the city:

> [B]efore we just bought fresh food from the local market but recently there have been so many news on food security—they talk about unsafe food—and that is why we should protect ourselves. . . . Of course sometimes we also have to buy from the local market but now we prefer buying from the local people and also [get food] from our garden.
> (Interview II.1, Hanoi, woman aged 40–50, private house)

214   *Jenny Rinkinen et al*

We shop for beef or pork twice a week. We go to a place which is quite far away from here to buy good quality meat. We know the farmer who raises the pigs. Three or four years ago we started to do this because pork from the local market is not clean and we got a bit scared.

(Interview II.14, Hanoi, woman aged 40–50, private house)

Again, having a fridge freezer made it very much easier to manage changing food systems and respond to dilemmas about quality and safety—dilemmas which are, ironically, associated with lengthening food chains themselves made possible by the domestic fridge freezer and its commercial equivalent. In such situations, forms of self or family provisioning created the need for still more frozen space. Here, Mrs. Ngon who lives in Hanoi with her husband, two children, and her mother-in-law explains why she bought a bigger fridge freezer:

We needed more space so we bought a bigger fridge freezer. Maybe 5 years ago we bought a bigger one. The new one is very convenient for us because now we have more space. Because you know now there is a lot of unsafe food so, for example, if I go to the countryside, I can buy some pork from where I know they raise the pig without chemicals put in their food. We buy 7–10 kg at once and we can store it.

(Interview II.1, Hanoi, woman aged 40–50, private house)

It is important to catch the subtleties of provisioning strategies and the tensions within. For example, although it is thought "safer" to get food direct from the countryside, there are some residual concerns about freezing and storing, as in the following extract. This means that for some people living in the city, "really" fresh becomes an unachievable ideal:

But now things have changed a lot, and we try to buy a lot of safe and organic food to store in the fridge. But even now there are some people who still keep their ideal that they want fresh food, and don't want to freeze food in the fridge freezer. They don't want to be like Westerners, sorry.

(Interview II.1, Hanoi, woman aged 40–50, private house)

Similarly, there are grades of risk to be negotiated. Hence, Mr. Ming, who lives in a condominium in Hanoi, thinks that the quality of food is better and more reliable in the supermarket. He avoids buying from street vendors because he is worried about pesticides and diseases (Interview 4.2, Hanoi, man aged 40–50, condominium). Meanwhile, Mr. Trang comes to the opposite conclusion:

We can find everything from the supermarket but the price of it is higher than in the local market. And it is not really fresh compared

to local market. . . . But we shop there because it saves time. And for the normal daily food it is ok. But if we have a party . . . we will go out [to the local market] to buy food. . . . But normally we go to the supermarket twice a week and then we store the food in the fridge.
(Interview 4.5, Hanoi, man aged 30–40, condominium)

Others described making strategic choices about where and what they eat. For example,

Some people don't want to go to the very big restaurants because they think that the big restaurants store food. It is not fresh. But we go to the small ones; they sell out every day, they can get fresh food.
(Interview II.1, Hanoi, woman aged 40–50, private house)

Such anxieties appear to be more pronounced in Hanoi than in Bangkok, perhaps because complex and extended supply chains, including those that depend on refrigeration, are a more recent phenomenon. Whatever the reason, the fridge freezer appears to be a vital tool in managing "safe" food provisioning in both Bangkok and Hanoi, however, that is interpreted. It is essential for families who seek to bypass modern food chains and rely on links of their own, and for those who make use of "modern" foods, frozen ingredients and ready-meals bought from supermarkets. As is always the case, practices are infused with judgments of quality. In the situations we describe, these judgments are in flux not randomly but in ways that are evidently linked to the somewhat different development of urban food systems in the two cities we studied.

Fridge Freezers in Action: Urbanization, Consumption, and Practice

Whether we focus on the United States, the United Kingdom, Vietnam, or Thailand, there is a clear connection between the diffusion of fridge freezers, the availability of ready-frozen food (typically mass-produced and often sold in supermarkets), and less frequent patterns of shopping. In simple terms, the proliferation of domestic fridge freezers appears to be a precondition for urban forms of provisioning-at-a-distance. Going full circle, urban systems of provision (and resistance to them) generate what seem to be unavoidable and widespread reliance on the fridge freezer. For consumers caught up in processes of rapid urbanization, fridge freezers are "needed" to avoid what are seen as the risks of processed food, or food from unknown sources, just as they are needed by those who consume mass-produced ready-meals, or who do a bit of both. This observation goes a long way toward explaining why fridge freezers, and the energy demands they generate, have become so deeply embedded in so many different lives.

216 Jenny Rinkinen et al

In thinking further about how practices of shopping, cooking, and eating interact and change, it is clearly important to consider personal and collective histories and to take note of stages and forms of urbanization alongside other more global transformations in food manufacturing and diet. The contents of fridge freezers in Bangkok and Hanoi (or in the United Kingdom and the United States) are evidence of different moments in what seems to be a longer-term narrative of urbanization entailing the progressive disconnection from rural origins, foods, skills, and practices. While respondents' interpretations of the need for a fridge freezer were varied and often ambivalent, the widespread adoption of these appliances establishes what amounts to a common infrastructure: enabling (but not requiring) production-at-a-distance, the circulation of new foodstuffs, the outsourcing of (parts of) cooking and food preparation, and the spatial and temporal reconfiguration of shopping, cooking, and eating.

The detail of what fridge freezers contain and how they are used depends on coexisting systems of provision and co-productive responses to, or within those systems. As Goodman reminds us, the significance of maintaining "traditional" systems of provision can only be understood alongside and in relation to the emergence of extended commercial cold chains of the kind that characterize "modern" urban life (Goodman et al. 2012). Recognizing that fridge freezers in use are defined and constituted not in the abstract but always in relation to the surrounding and also changing systems of diet and provision helps makes sense of differences between the contents and the roles of the fridge freezers we examined in Bangkok and Hanoi.

In explaining how and why middle-class urban households have come to need a fridge freezer, we have described the emergence of systems of food provisioning that are in various ways freezer-dependent. These arrangements underpin escalating energy demand (freezers need powering in homes and in supermarkets, and chilled transport is essential). Whether they like it or not, the practices of those with whom we spoke are enmeshed within these systems. In addition, and in showing that such practices are multiply interlinked, we have underlined the point that changes in consumption are not simply situated within the home, nor are they defined by seemingly private habits and routines or by increases in gross domestic product (GDP) (Cold Commission 2013).

Along the way, we have also explored connections between what are at first sight more diffuse concepts of taste, risk, and safety. In showing how meanings of quality and anxieties about contamination inform and are in a sense reproduced via multiple practices—shopping, but also selecting, preparing and managing food—we show how these concerns are in turn anchored in organizational changes in systems of provision including those enabled by fridge freezers. Thus, food scares are not "merely" discourses: they are of necessity enacted at all scales, by households, supermarkets, and local providers alike. By implication, the scope for scares of

Cold Chains in Hanoi and Bangkok   217

this kind is wired into contemporary forms of food supply. In that sense, it is virtually impossible to escape the grip of urbanized systems of food provisioning, even for those who resist them.

In conclusion, we are certainly not the first to characterize eating and shopping as social practices (Halkier, Katz-Gerro, and Martens 2011; Halkier and Jensen 2011; Paddock 2015; Warde 2016). In adding to this line of research, our analysis makes three quite distinctive contributions. One is to provide an account of the ongoing reconfiguration of practices of provision (retailing and distribution) and consumption (sourcing, shopping, and cooking), in situations of rapid urbanization. We have consequently conceptualized consumption as an outcome of multiple, intersecting, and always changing social practices. Second, we have shown how notions of quality and discourses of risk, modernity, safety, and tradition are quite precisely anchored in the details of supply and provision, including arrangements enabled by freezer technology. This suggests that far from being free floating, matters of meaning and judgments of significance and quality are materialized and grounded in what some might see as economic or technological processes. Last but definitely not least, we have provided a means of bridging between urban studies and theories of consumption and practice. In showing how practices of eating and shopping are bound up with and defining of seemingly extensive but also dynamic processes of urbanization, Westernization, and globalization, we have provided new insight into the constitution of what Schatzki (2011) describes as "large" social phenomena. Bringing these threads together, we have developed an account of how practices change and how consumer needs emerge within and as part of urban life. This approach has wider implications, arguing for more situated understandings of consumption and of the extent to which increasingly resource-intensive ways of life are inextricably and perhaps unavoidably embedded in urban development.

Data Statement

Information about the data on which this article is based and conditions for access is available at the Lancaster University data archive: http://dx.doi.org/10.17635/lancaster/researchdata/112.

Declaration of Conflicting Interests

The author(s) declared no potential conflicts of interest with respect to the research, authorship, and/or publication of this article.

Funding

The author(s) disclosed receipt of the following financial support for the research, authorship, and/or publication of this article: this work was

218 *Jenny Rinkinen et al*

supported by the Engineering and Physical Sciences Research Council (grant number EP/K011723/1) as part of the Research Councils UK Energy Programme and by Electricity de France (EDF) as part of the R&D ECLEER Programme.

Notes

1. This chapter was originally printed in:

   Rinkinen, Jenny, Elizabeth Shove, and Mattijs Smits (2019), "Cold Chains in Hanoi and Bangkok: Changing Systems of Provision and Practice," *Journal of Consumer Culture*, 19 (3), 379–97 (https://doi. org/10.1177/1469540517717783). (This paper was published Open Access with Creative Commons License: www.creativecommons.org/licenses/ by/4.0/.)

2. There are important differences between fridges and freezers. Freezers make it possible to store food for months, not days, and are essential for the production and circulation of frozen food. Fridges merely keep food cool. For the most part, we write about fridge freezers—that is, appliances which combine a freezer and a refrigerator: these being the most common form encountered in our research. However, some of the topics we discuss are specifically about freezing.

3. Stand-alone freezers have a very small market share (Foran, du Pont, Parinya, and Phumaraphand 2010; McNeil, Letschert, and Wiel 2007). In the last few years, some fridge freezers (in Hanoi and Bangkok) feature multiple sections set at different temperatures to help keep a variety of different foods fresh.

References

Asian Development Bank (ADB) (2010), *The Rise of Asia's Middle Class: Special Chapter in Key Indicators for Asia and the Pacific*, Manila, Philippines: Asian Development Bank.

Baker, Chris and Pasuk Phongpaichit (2014), *A History of Thailand*, Melbourne, Australia: Cambridge University Press.

Cold Commission (2013), *Doing Cold Smarter*, Report, Birmingham Energy Institute Policy Commission, University of Birmingham, Birmingham (www. birmingham.ac.uk/research/activity/energy/policy/cold/policy-commission-launch.aspx).

Dixon, Jane, Abiud M. Omwega, Sharon Friel, Cate Burns, Kelly Donati, and Rachel Carlisle (2007), "The Health Equity Dimensions of Urban Food Systems," *Journal of Urban Health*, 84, 118–29 (https://doi.org/10.1007/ s11524-007-9176-4).

DuPuis, Melanie (2002), *Nature's Perfect Food: How Milk Became America's Drink*, New York: New York University Press.

The Economist (2009), "Who's in the Middle? It's a Matter of Definition," *The Economist*, February 12 (www.economist.com/node/13063338).

Evers, Hans-Dieter and Rüdiger Korff (2000), *Southeast Asian Urbanism: The Meaning and Power of Social Space*, Münster: LIT Verlag Münster.

Fine, Ben and Ellen Leopold (1993), *The World of Consumption*, London: Routledge.

Cold Chains in Hanoi and Bangkok   219

Food and Agriculture Organization (FAO) (2011), "Milk Consumption—Excluding Butter (Total, kg/capita/yr)," *FAO Statistics Division 2011* (http://faostat.fao.org/site/610/DesktopDefault.aspx?PageID1/4610#ancor).

Foran, Tira, Peter T. du Pont, Panom Parinya, and Napaporn Phumaraphand (2010), "Securing Energy Efficiency as a High Priority: Scenarios for Common Appliance Electricity Consumption in Thailand," *Energy Efficiency*, 3 (4), 347–64 (https://doi.org/10.1007/s12053-009-9073-7).

Freidberg, Susanne (2009), *Fresh—A Perishable History*, Cambridge, MA: Harvard University Press.

——— (2015), "Moral Economies and the Cold Chain," *Historical Research*, 88 (239), 125–37 (https://doi.org/10.1111/1468-2281.12076).

General Statistics Office of Vietnam (GSO) (2011), "Population and Employment: Average Population by Province," (www.gso.gov.vn).

——— (2012), "Household Living Standards Survey 2012," (www.gso.gov.vn).

Goodman David, DuPuis Melanie and Michael Goodman (2012), *Alternative Food Networks: Knowledge, Practice, and Politics*, London: Routledge.

Green Cooling Initiative (2016), "Number of Appliances in Use of Domestic Refrigeration. Country Data," (www.green-cooling-initiative.org/country-data/).

Guarín, Alejandro and Peter Knorringa (2014), "New Middle-class Consumers in Rising Powers: Responsible Consumption and Private Standards," *Oxford Development Studies*, 42 (2), 151–71 (https://doi.org/10.1080/13600818.201 3.864757).

Halkier, Bente and Iben Jensen (2011), "Methodological Challenges in Using Practice Theory in Consumption Research. Examples From a Study on Handling Nutritional Contestations of Food Consumption," *Journal of Consumer Culture*, 11 (1), 101–23 (https://doi.org/10.1177/1469540510391365).

Halkier, Bente, Tally Katz-Gerro, and Lydia Martens (2011), "Applying Practice Theory to the Study of Consumption: Theoretical and Methodological Considerations," *Journal of Consumer Culture*, 11 (1), 3–13 (https://doi.org/10.1177/1469540510391765).

Hand, Martin and Elizabeth Shove (2007), "Condensing Practices: Ways of Living With a Freezer," *Journal of Consumer Culture*, 7 (1), 79–104 (https://doi.org/10.1177/1469540507073509).

Higman, Barry W. (2011), *How Food Made History*, Chichester: John Wiley & Sons.

Hui, Allison, Theodore R. Schatzki, and Elizabeth Shove, eds. (2017), *The Nexus of Practices: Connections, Constellations, Practitioners*, London: Routledge.

Leslie, Deborah and Suzanne Reimer (1999), "Spatializing Commodity Chains," *Progress in Human Geography*, 23 (3), 401–20 (https://doi.org/10.1177/0309 13259902300304).

McLeod, Mark W. and Thi Dieu Nguyen (2001), *Culture and Customs of Vietnam*, London: Greenwood.

McNeil, Michael, Virginie E. Letschert, and Stephen Wiel (2007), *Reducing the Price of Development: The Global Potential of Efficiency Standards in the Residential Electricity Sector*, Report, EEDAL, London, January.

National Statistical Office Thailand (2013), "The 2010 Population and Housing Census," (http://popcensus.nso.go.th/upload/census-report-6-4-54-en.pdf).

——— (2015), "Major Findings of the 2014 Household Energy Consumption," (http://web.nso.go.th/en/survey/data_survey/580923_energy_ Full.pdf).

220 Jenny Rinkinen et al

Nguyen-Marshall, Van, Lisa B. Welch Drummond, and Danièle Belanger, eds. (2011), *The Reinvention of Distinction: Modernity and the Middle Class in Urban Vietnam*, Vol. 2, Dordrecht: Springer.

Paddock, Jessica (2015), "Household Consumption and Environmental Change: Rethinking the Policy Problem Through Narratives of Food Practice," *Journal of Consumer Culture*, 17 (1), 122–39 (https://doi.org/10.1177/1469540515586869).

Phuc, To Xuan (2012), "When the uai Gia (Urban Rich) Go to the Countryside: Impacts of the Urban-fueled Rural Land Market in the Uplands," in *The Reinvention of Distinction: Modernity and the Middle Class in Urban Vietnam*, ed. Van Nguyen-Marshall, Lisa B. Welch Drummond, and Danièle Belanger, London: Springer, 143–55.

Pingali, Prabhu (2007), "Westernization of Asian Diets and the Transformation of Food Systems: Implications for Research and Policy," *Food Policy*, 32 (3), 281–98 (https://doi.org/10.1016/j.foodpol.2006.08.001).

Pongsapich, Amara and Wathana Wongsekiarttirat (1994), "Urban Household Energy Consumption in Thailand," *Energy*, 19 (5), 509–16 (https://doi.org/10.1016/0360-5442(94)90047-7).

Rees, Jonathan (2013), *Refrigeration Nation: A History of Ice, Appliances, and Enterprise in America*, Baltimore, MD: Johns Hopkins University Press.

Schatzki, Theodore R. (2011), "Where the Action Is (on Large Social Phenomena Such as Sociotechnical Regimes), Sustainable Practices Research Group," *Discussion Paper* (www.sprg.ac.uk/uploads/schatzki-wp1.pdf).

Shove, Elizabeth (2017), "Matters of Practice," in *The Nexus of Practices: Connections, Constellations, Practitioners*, ed. Allison Hui, Theodore R. Schatzki, and Elizabeth Shove, London: Routledge, 155–68.

Shove, Elizabeth and Southerton Dale (2000), "Defrosting the Freezer: From Novelty to Convenience. A Narrative of Normalization," *Journal of Material Culture*, 5 (3), 301–19 (https://doi.org/10.1177/1469540505049846).

Shove, Elizabeth and Mika Pantzar (2005), "Consumers, Producers and Practices Understanding the Invention and Reinvention of Nordic Walking," *Journal of Consumer Culture*, 5 (1), 43–64.

Shove, Elizabeth, Mika Pantzar, and Matt Watson (2012), *The Dynamics of Social Practice: Everyday Life and How It Changes*, London: Sage.

Shove, Elizabeth, Matt Watson, and Nicola Spurling (2015), "Conceptualizing Connections: Energy Demand, Infrastructures and Social Practices," *European Journal of Social Theory*, 18 (3), 274–87 (https://doi.org/10.1177/1368431015579964).

Suwanabol, Issara (2005), "School Milk Programme in Thailand," Paper presented at *the 3rd International School Milk Conference*, Kunming, China.

Thanh Nien News (2016), "Mass Fish Deaths Provoke Widespread Worry in Vietnam," (www.thanhniennews.com/society/mass-fish-deaths-provoke-widespread-worry-in-vietnam-61418.html).

United Nations (UN) (2014), "The United Nations 2014 Revision of World Urbanization Prospects," *Department of Economic and Social Affairs* (https://esa.un.org/unpd/wup/).

Van Hoi, Pham, Arthur P.J. Mol, and Peter J.M. Oosterveer (2009), "Market Governance for Safe Food in Developing Countries: The Case of Low-pesticide Vegetables in Vietnam," *Journal of Environmental Management*, 91 (2), 380–88 (https://doi.org/10.1016/j.jenvman.2009.09.008).

Warde, Alan (2005), "Consumption and Theories of Practice," *Journal of Consumer Culture*, 5 (2), 131–53 (https://doi.org/10.1177/1469540505053090).
———— (2016), *The Practice of Eating*, Cambridge: Polity Press.
Wertheim-Heck, Sigrid (2015), "We Have to Eat Right? Food Safety Concerns and Shopping for Daily Vegetables in Modernizing Vietnam," Unpublished Dissertation, Wageningen University, The Netherlands.
Wilhite, Hal (2008), *Consumption and the Transformation of Everyday Life: A View from South India*, New York: Palgrave Macmillan.
Yasmeen, Gisèle (2006), *Bangkok's Foodscape: Public Eating, Gender Relations and Urban Change*, Bangkok, Thailand: White Lotus.

Section V

Body, Technology, and Mass-Mediated Marketplace Ideologies

12 Market Versus Cultural Myth

A Skin-Deep Analysis of the Fairness Phenomena in India

Anoop Bhogal-Nair and Andrew Lindridge

Introduction

As a gender group, women encapsulate and embody cultural, economic, and social capital dynamics, often manifesting through inequality, in terms of education, employment, wages, and status, while prone to violence and fewer life opportunities (The United Nations 2017). Within this dynamic, women may often feel judged in terms of their beauty solely from the perspective of the more powerful dominant male as embodied in the male gaze. Considering this difference and how skin color may emphasize gender differences, it can be argued that organizations through the market not only perpetuate, manipulate, and tell us what feminine beauty should look like but also offer the very means to achieve that beauty. For example, the FMCG multinational Unilever uses its Dove brand in Western markets to perpetuate an image of female beauty owned by women, while equally telling women in India via its skin lightening cream brand—"Fair and Lovely"—that fairer skin equates to heightened female beauty. A beauty Hindustan Unilever is willing to help dark-skinned women achieve through "Fair and Lovely."

The role of the beauty industry, its key players, and the brands consumed have been well documented. Indeed, feminists such as Bartky (1990), Bordo (2003), Brand (2000), and Wolf (1991) have noted how the beauty industry creates and perpetuates existing women's fears of inadequacy. Bordo (2003) goes further arguing that women's physical bodies are sights of cultural and political struggles, where political, religious, and nationalistic agendas are acted out and through. Indian film industry representation of the beautiful Indian woman having fair skin appears to have fed into wider Indian media through television programs and marketing communications. Indeed, Herring, Keith, and Horton (2003) and Maddox (2004) note how darker-skinned individuals are presented as less intelligent, less trustworthy, and less attractive than their lighter skinned counterparts. While the market may perpetuate ideas of female beauty, other researchers have rightly focused not so much on the market per se but how the market perpetuates society's wider sociocultural and

DOI: 10.4324/9781003111559-17

226   *Anoop Bhogal-Nair and Andrew Lindridge*

economic discourses. For example, Bonillo-Silva (2006) distances ideas of female beauty based upon skin color from an individual level to being indicative of society's wider inherent racism. A racism originating from historical narratives of internal colonialism, racial assimilation policies, and capitalism.

Indeed, Hall (2013, 4) goes further arguing that "skin-colour ranking is primarily derived from European histories of racism where white skinned people from the United States and Europe are viewed as being at the highest state of civilisation followed by different shades of skin colours" It is this perspective of beauty as defined through skin color, originating from associations to colonialism, that forms the basis for this chapter. Thus, our research question looks to examine how these inherited memories inform female beauty in India as defined by one's skin color. Specifically, memories based upon a combination of the market and internal colonial narratives drawing upon, distorting, and reimagining ancient Hindu religious texts.

Commodity Skins

Skin, the largest organ of the body, mediates, translates, scars, and protects. It is adorned and decorated yet held in contempt. Skin is constantly at work and is often overlooked as a formidable force in the construction of one's identity. As noted by Philips (2004, 255), "phenotype variations within the human species have no meaning except the social constructions that humans put on them." Skin, then, becomes not only the site for self-reflexive identity articulation (Bjerrisgaard, Kjeldgaard, and Bengtsson 2013, 5) but also, in the Indian context, bestows one with a permanent marker of status and class identification, of purity or impurity, coupled with the power to determine an individual's fate. As a "materially and metaphorically contested terrain [skin emerges as a] site wherein agency, freedom of choice and individual empowerment conflates with the pressures of cultural power and tensions of social control" (Farber 2006, 20). Patterson and Schroeder (2010, 4) arguing from the perspective of consumer research studies, note how research on the skin as "the body's largest and most visible organ remains peripheral." Understanding skin beyond its "container" metaphor challenges the conception of consuming bodies as being relatively self-contained and responsible for their own identity construction (Patterson and Schroeder 2010, 21). If skin is also understood through Prosser's (2001) notion of skin memories, it is then further burdened with the detailed specificities of life histories as a site for registering trauma and cultural unconscious. Skin, therefore, is the "concrete boundary between the self and other, the individual and society" (Turner 2012, 503) simultaneously recipient and transmitter of cultural histories. Few, if any feature of the human body imbibes so much conflicting meaning (Jablonski 2012) as does skin.

Market Versus Cultural Myth 227

Whiteness has become a worldwide commodity (Glenn 2009; Hunter 2011). The burgeoning market in products promising to lighten, whiten, and brighten speaks to the "corporate capital's desire to sell the dream" (Harris 2009, 2) that individuals can transcend oppressive systems through the consumption of creams as alchemic agents of self-transformation (Nadeem 2014). The perpetuation of lighter skin color preference through cultural, historical, and religious contexts perpetuated in Indian media requires a solution. A solution provided by western FMCGs in India through the mass consumption of skin lightening creams, evident in Unilever's "Fair & Lovely." Launched in 1978, Fair & Lovely artificially suppresses melanin to make skin tones lighter (Garcia 2012), it now accounts for 80% of skin lightning cream sales in India (ibid) in a market valued at over £200 million. Furthermore, skin lightening creams account for 46% of the Indian subcontinent's retail facial care market (Srivastav 2017). However, Hindustan Unilever also faces competition in India from other FMCGs, including: "Garnier Natural White," "Revlon Touch and Glow," "Olay White Radiance," and "Pond's Flawless White" to name but a few. A Hindustan Unilever internal marketing memo from 2008, presented as part of Nadeem's (2014, 232) analysis of skin lightening advertisements in India, makes for interesting reading:

> Our portrayal of women was taken as an insult to many who saw it. Our campaign was called insulting, unethical, racist, and an inaccurate portrayal of women in India . . . women have a need for this product and as long as they continue to, we will continue to supply them with Fair & Lovely. Speaking from a cultural standpoint it doesn't seem that these needs will change any time soon. The most beautiful Bollywood actresses are always fair skinned and families searching for a bride for their son always request that she be fair skinned. This cultural standard for coveting fair skin is a strength for Fair & Lovely because it has created a desire for our product within our target market.

From the aforementioned memo excerpt, it becomes clear how perpetuating a social stigma was considered a viable marketing strategy, furthermore, positioning these social stigmas as a particular strength for a brand. Most recently, and as a response to social pressure resulting from the global Black Lives Matter movement and antiracism rallies, Unilever pledged a change to the brand name, looking to disassociate itself with a singular ideal of white beauty. The new name, "Glow and Lovely," looks to "embrace a more inclusive vision of beauty . . . to celebrate the diversity of beauty in India and other countries" (Unilever 2020). The song launch for the rebranding campaign features Indian feminist rapper, Dee MC, and models with notably darker skin tones—as compared to their predecessors—miming to feminism-fueled lyrics "glow ko na roko" (don't stop the glow) and "mere rang ko na dekho" (don't look at my color).

228   *Anoop Bhogal-Nair and Andrew Lindridge*

Although the advertising rhetoric among some contemporary brands of fairness creams is substituting the mention of "whiteness" with words such as "brightness" and "glow," some of the product names continue their legacy of promoting the hegemony of whiteness. This is demonstrated in the recent Pond's campaign for their White Beauty™ facewash. The campaign is titled #SeeWhatHappens, encouraging women to follow their passions and overcome their inner hesitations. The most recent advertisement presents a young woman who each day continues to tell her mother that she is late returning home because she has been studying in the library. However, she has in fact training to become a boxer and has been using concealer to cover her bruises before heading home. After deep introspection, the young woman washes her face with Ponds White Beauty facewash, exposing her scars, and plucks up the courage to tell her mother the truth. The mother responds positively asking if the other girl's face is worse than hers. Zacharias (2003, 10) claims that there is a new kind of cultural citizenship that symbolizes India's post-liberalization transformation, arguing that "whiteness, whitened bodies, and hybrid foreign bodies," signify consumer empowerment and global capitalist progress. Fundamentally, these purpose-driven campaigns of progress and limitless potential become well-intentioned distractions from the unspoken, glossed-over associations with the product's true intentions.

Contextualizing Darkness

The preference for whiteness requires an understanding that is rooted within a culture's own historical trajectories as opposed to being analyzed exclusively through westernized ideals about race (Wagatsuma 1967, 407). As noted by Hall (2009), individuals do not perceive of skin color objectively, it is always read in the context of gender, age, dress, and national identity. Dark-skin stigma does not owe its origins to Europe and the Americas, although the colonial period has often been considered a starting point for discussions of whiteness in the subcontinent. It has a much longer precolonial history which has been "exacerbated by colonialism and global capitalism" (Jha 2016, 54) through a form of layering. To consider the fetishization of fair skin as nothing more than a mere preference for aesthetic would overlook the lasting legacies of history and colonial power. Although it is beyond this chapter to dissect the conceptual heritage of "race" as canonized in western thought, Hesse's (2007) concept of the onto-colonial emphasizes the continued sustenance and preservation of colonial ideologies and taxonomies in former non-west/non-white societies which were once part of the colonial project (see Jaywardene 2013).

Colorism, as the process of discrimination that privileges light-/white-skinned individuals over their darker-skinned counterparts, is a deep-rooted and complex phenomenon within the subcontinent. Despite the

Market Versus Cultural Myth   229

obvious linkages between colorism and racism, the two form a distinct criterion of othering which can be seen to inform one another while remaining independent elements. Demonstrated through the work of Telles (2004), discussions of race in Brazil were seen to be difficult to conduct, yet respondents were more open to the discussions of skin color. Skin color assumes a particular significance, a significance which is prone to change as societies evolve. In the Indian context, religion, culture, and history perform important roles in the understanding of how skin has come to be, and it is through these important historical narratives that we are able to unearth important markers of significance which continue to manifest themselves within contemporary society.

The earliest documentation of distinction and social hierarchy based upon color in India appears in the Rigveda (circa 1,500–1,200 BC), which refers to a social stratum that would become the Indian caste system—the Varna, consisting of Brahmins (priests and scholars), Kshatriyas (rulers and warriors), Vaishyas (agriculturalists and merchants), and Shudras (laborers and service providers). These distinguishing characteristics have also been documented in the Dharmasutra and Law Code of Manu (Manu Smriti), with the latter establishing a legal basis for characterizing purity and impurity. According to Dumont (1998), the opposition of pure (fair) and impure (dark) was the structural logic through which the caste system, a form of social stratification which one is born into, was developed. Bougle (1958, 9) notes the importance of the caste system reflected an inherent need for repulsion, noting how "different groups . . . repel each other rather than attract, that each retires within itself, isolates itself, makes every effort to prevent its members from contracting alliance or even from entering relations with neighbouring groups." Thus, taken together, purity, impurity, and repulsion are a central feature of the caste groups. Indeed, Bougle (1958) notes how the Dharmasutra reinforces the association of low caste status and impurity with color in the following two verses: (i) "It takes three years of bathing at every fourth meal-time to remove the sin a Brahmin commits by serving the Black class for one day" (Dharmasutra of Baudhayana—2.2.11) and (ii) "A wife belonging to the dark class is only for pleasure, not for the fulfilment of the law (Dharmasutra of Vasistha—18.11)." Although the early references to color form part of the varna identification, skin color alone was not considered a characteristic through which groups of individuals were distinguished. Furthermore, references to "black" and "dark" may not be literal descriptions of an individual's skin color but a reference to negative traits, impurity, or stigma.

India has never been an ethnically homogenous society often experiencing frequent invasions leading to further social division. One such invasion, although historical evidence cannot completely identify the invading group, led to the historical classifications of "Aryans" and "Dravidians." Lal (1974, 201) notes the Aryans were historical invaders of the Northern

230   *Anoop Bhogal-Nair and Andrew Lindridge*

Indian subcontinent who were considered cultivators and the "Dravidians" the "aboriginal of the land was a non-cultivator." While over time the "Aryans" acculturated into Indian society taking on the Hindu religion and using India's higher caste classifications to identify themselves with and legitimize their power through land ownership. A consequence of this acquisition of Hindu beliefs was the further perpetuation of skin color as a determinant of caste difference. As Sharma (2002a) notes the "Aryans . . . on occasions set fire to settlements of the dark hued people. . . . The Aryan deity Soma is described as killing people of black skin [And] at one place [the god Indra] is credited with the slaughter of fifty thousand 'blacks.'" It is within this religious cultural context that the Imperial European countries, in establishing trading posts in India, took great interest. None more so than the British.

Part of the colonization and control of India lay in the British use of the caste system and skin color. Sharma (2002b, 8) notes "the British took the existence of caste very seriously. Successive censuses of India attempted to classify the entire population by caste . . . on the assumption that castes were real identifiable groups. As a result, this objectification of caste actually made it more real and liable to rigidification." Although it is still contested whether the early Varna distinctions were entirely normative, British occupancy soon turned caste into a substantive category (Jodhka 2012), where differentiation was interpreted through the lens of race. Isaacs (1968, 76) argues one of the prime tools of power used by European Imperialists were the "racial mythologies built around differences in skin colour" (1968, 76). The development of essentializing qualities born out of the need to justify a hegemonic order became a colonial preoccupation (see Cohn 1996). Risley's (1915) account of skin color in India demonstrates the British eugenic perspective of skin color in Imperial India distinctions: "the somewhat brighter black of the Dravidians of southern India, which has been aptly compared to the colour of the strong coffee unmixed with milk . . . the flushed ivory skin of the typical Kashmiri beauty and the very transparent brown-wheat coloured is the common vernacular description . . . of the higher castes of upper India." Nor did the British discourage skin color associations with caste difference being equated to feminine beauty. As Rothfeld (1928, 80) noted, Davidian women, overall, were considered "dark, stunted, hardly attractive," whereas their upper-caste Brahmin counterparts were considered as those with a "straight nose and sensitive nostril, fair skin . . . [and] self-restraint in every gesture" (ibid). Colonial rule in India worked to perpetuate an existing system of color-coded social stratification. As Europeans encountered new territories and people, they were renamed, remapped, and reordered into what Trouillot (1990) calls an international hierarchy of races, colors, religions, and cultures. Indeed, Imperialists' need to justify their own imperial conquests based on civilizing others, manifesting through skin color, found fertile ground in India.

Market Versus Cultural Myth 231

It is from this perspective of ancient religious texts and British colonial rule, dependent upon a system of divide and rule made feasible through reimaging the Hindu caste system, that we argue, skin color became a means to define and identify societal status. Once this connection between skin color and status was made, it took the market to communicate and associate this with female beauty. In particular, the active involvement of the Indian film industry—commonly referred to as Bollywood. How these historical narratives embed themselves into the present-day consciousness as mobilized through advertising, and the culture industries more broadly, requires some dissection. As a set of consensually held beliefs and cultural ideologies, myths allow for the seamless transition from cultural norm into activated storytelling, reinforcing society's entrenched value systems.

Legitimizing Myths

Discussed widely through the theory of social dominance by Sidanius and Pratto (2001), legitimizing myths consist of attitudes, morals, beliefs, values, and ideologies "that provide moral and intellectual justification for the social practices that distribute social value within the social system" (ibid, 45). The endorsement of societal discourses based upon a form of social ordering is considered under one of the two categorizations—hierarchy enhancing or hierarchy attenuating—where the former looks to support group-based social inequality (sexism, classical racism, and classism) and the latter looks to provide justification for equality between social groups (protected rights and egalitarianism). The innocence and neutrality offered by the myth allows it to postulate a memory as a naturalized intention (Barthes 1957) through decontextualizing its history for the purpose of a particular gain. What is interesting about the notion of the legitimizing myth is the degree to which individuals in society accept certain beliefs as true. Myths that are "firmly tied to the basic values and points of view of their culture" (Sidanius and Pratto 2001, 104) are difficult to change, yet the degree to which a legitimizing myth is seen to be effective is dependent upon a number of factors including "consensuality" and "embeddedness." Sidanius and Pratto (2001) provide the example of classical racism to demonstrate how a legitimizing myth can be embedded into ideological, religious, or aesthetic components of a culture. They note

> While the colour black is most often associated with implications of evil, filth, depravity, and fear, the color white is most often associated with notions of purity, truth, innocence, goodness, and righteousness. These two contrasting color symbols permeate a great deal of Western culture and can be discerned in everything from classical fairy tales to popular film and literature.
>
> (ibid, 47)

232 *Anoop Bhogal-Nair and Andrew Lindridge*

Myths are reassuring anchors in a sea of uncertainty; they have an ability to reassure through "telling tales that explain . . . phenomena and provide acceptable answers" (Bird and Dardenne 2009, 206).

The notion of purity and impurity manifesting through skin color is further reinforced within Indian mythology, through the depictions of gods and goddesses. Artistic representations of Hindu religious epic tales, most notably the Ramayana and the Mahabharata, typically depict the purity of deities through skin tones. As Pattanaik (2009) notes, "on the body of the Goddess, black is about wild nature. On the body of God, black is about worldliness. On the body of the Goddess, white is about domestic culture. On the body of God, white is about ascetic transcendence. Perhaps in our desire to be cultured and in our aspiration to be otherworldly, we choose white over black." The Hindu deity—Krishna—according to scripture was understood to be dark in color (Krishna is Sanskrit for "black"), yet the depiction of him in popular, specifically North Indian media, and other cultural forms is that of a fair-skinned or lightly blue-tinted being. Hence, from a historical religious perspective, Hindu mythology extols and perpetuates the importance of skin color not only from a legal religious perspective but also as a daily lived sociocultural framework where one's skin color is associated with social status.

The ability of a legitimizing myth, through its power of consensuality, to induce self-demeaning ideologies is of particular importance considering advertising rhetoric surrounding fairness creams. These ideologies are not driven through their supposed truth value, but through the associated cultural scripts which underpin their legitimacy. How these legitimizing myths are embedded, received, and understood by intended audiences is where we now turn our attention.

Methodology

Respondents were recruited from an all-women's college in New Delhi, India. A total of 27 respondents between the ages of 18 and 25 were recruited. These young women were sent qualitative questionnaires to complete as introspective accounts. Questions covered a range of open-ended topics that ultimately focused on skin color, self-identity, and well-being, for example, the representation of beauty in popular media in India and the approaches to advertising skin lightening creams. This approach was chosen to allow for informants to offer deep insights into a highly personal topic and to allow for a level of organic introspection and engagement with deeper thinking. It was felt by the authors that other data collection methods involving face-to-face interactions would inhibit informants' true thoughts and expressions. Respondents shared information about their daily lives, the pressures of being a young woman, cultural and societal expectations surrounding marriage, and the role of women in a modernizing India. Questionnaires were written in the informant's preferred choice of language, which was English, producing a total of 20 pages of handwritten data.

Transcribed interviews and written documents were analyzed using Spiggle's (1994) seven analytical stages. Transcripts were read and then reread producing preliminary codes, with coded sheets annotated to identify comparisons, metaphors, and tropes (Meamber and Venkatesh 2000). Finally, the findings were considered with the literature providing a more informed understanding, while subjecting the findings to further empirical scrutiny.

Findings

Three key findings emerged from the data: (i) the role of the market and culture industries in perpetrating the myth of fairness, (ii) history and colonialism as potent forces for the establishment of the beauty hierarchy, and (iii) resistance to cultural discourses of fairness.

The Market and Culture Industries

Responses to fairness cream advertising centered upon racist undertones, normalization of whiteness, and regressive narratives. Several participants found skin lightening advertisements "racist," perpetuating the belief that dark-skinned women were less attractive and unsuccessful: "this skin whitening trend is racist in nature. In our country educational qualifications are of no value but emphasis is more on the skin tone. Being tagged as GORA (white) is the ultimate compliment a girl can get" (Manisha). Other participants felt these advertisements shared a "regressive, sexist narrative" (Sheena) reinforcing a "very unhealthy psychological ideology" (Leena). Critical of the fact that the desirability of women rests solely on their complexion, negating all her other intellectual qualities, Leena considered such advertisements as a "huge setback to feminism and everything sensible and progressive." What is interesting in Leena's comment, and echoed among a few other participants, was the rejection of skin lightening advertising as a feminist position. While we do not dispute these respondents' intentions, we do question the origins of these intentions. While a modernizing India may be encouraging female empowerment and agency, equally such narratives reflect a subtle shift in skin lightening cream's marketing communications. Consider Ammu's conception of skin fairness: "I never thought of complete fairness as beautiful. Just a good impression of fairness. She must be well-kept and have a clear skin (not too fair)." Having "just enough" fairness reflects the contemporary advertising discourse presented in fairness cream advertising. As noted earlier, countering the social media-backlash against fairness creams and the growing concern for young Indian women's self-esteem and confidence, brands such as Fair & Lovely have adopted alternative

234 *Anoop Bhogal-Nair and Andrew Lindridge*

approaches in their storytelling. Inner beauty and bringing out one's "inner glow" have become attempts to overwrite the narratives of the fairness cream market. However, a significant number of respondents noted how the social ideologies presented in the advertising of fairness creams was a reinforcement of a self-demeaning ideology. Take Leena's analysis of the dominant advertising imagery: "brands like 'Fair and Lovely' help furthering this unhealthy ideology. Often, they portray that a woman is low on self-confidence if she is not fair, and she would only find her standing and success in life if she decides to use the brand to lighten her complexion." This transformative potential in being able to align one's beauty to socially scripted ideologies is also echoed by Vaibhavi who notes that "advertisements show a woman depressed or anxious because of her skin and this product acts as a miracle hand which magically transforms the skin tone thereby restoring the girl's happiness and confidence."

Participants were keen to demonstrate their rejection of colorist attitudes toward standards of beauty; however, they also accepted the societal attitudes toward fairness, as reflected through the culture industries in televisual dramas, the Indian film industry, advertising (irrespective of product category), and music. When considering brands such as Fair & Lovely, women demonstrated a complex range of emotions. Manisha's understanding of these images placed a heavy emphasis upon manufactured inequalities and the fracturing of women's self-confidence:

> Inequality being manufactured on a large scale advertised by revered personalities. It promotes the superiority of white skin and makes it a casual norm . . . such things brainwash the tender minds to conform to the hypocritical views of society. This is symbolic of the glossy version of the world where one can earn happiness with brightening of the skin tone. These are unfair ways to earn profits. Why is even there a need to sell such stuff which fractures one's dignity and self- confidence?

Although highly revered and popularized by many young women, the Indian film industry was presented as another site for registering the hegemony of fairness. It was considered a well-accepted norm that actresses, and to some degree actors, would require fairness as a passport of access into the industry. Malini comments upon the preference for "foreign bodies" in popular Indian cinema, commenting: "Indians are somewhat obsessed with 'firangs' or Foreigners. If actresses like Katrina Kaif come in Bollywood, then obviously there is a sense of attraction amongst Indians because well . . . she is foreigner, a white skin, speaks fluent English and hence perceived as more civilised." What is interesting to note from her response is the subtle reference to the civilized ideals of beauty and whiteness, almost as a nod to imperialist motivations. In a similar vein, Kiran adds that the appeal of "foreign" actresses in Indian cinema is subject to

Market Versus Cultural Myth 235

"their 'white' and Anglo-Indian appearances which became a highly desirable trait amongst the major 'brown' population of the country." Her emphasis on white and brown positions them as binaries of contradiction. This appeal of non-Indian actresses was considered by Devika as a form of fetishization "women admire these actresses and have even romanticized them. We think that foreigners are pretty due to their fair complexion." Fairness as understood through its associated traits and attributes was something discussed by most of the young women. Ammu was one such critic who felt strongly about the associated connotations of fairness which inadvertently had seeped into popular marketing imagery of these products "the glorification of fair skin which is pervasive throughout Indian society and goes far beyond implications of beauty- it is associated with greater intelligence, greater status and greater privilege."

History and Colonialism

Many young women identified colonialism as an ailment, one reflected in the preferences for fairness today. Farah makes this profound point by noting how there is evidence "of not having fully 'decolonised' the mind. Fairness is correlated with virtuosity and beauty." The notion of a "colonial hangover" (Sheena) was one which was shared by many of the respondents where the concept of whiteness was understood to be entrenched in the histories of invasion. Devika commented:

> I feel that Indian society values fair skinned women over darker skinned women because of the idea still prevalent in Indians' mind-set which was left behind by western invaders of having racial discrimination on the basis of one's colour. The rulers of India, the Mughals, the British, all were fair skinned, the latter much fairer than the former, and seizing control from the former. This reinforced the thought process that fairness relates to power. The desire for people to be like the ones who ruled over them, led to a preference for fair complexion.

This power-fueled imagery of whiteness was shared by a significant number of respondents who felt that India's history of being subordinated through layers of colonialism has resulted in a preference for fairness which is now considered a legacy of the subcontinent: "All thanks to British colonialism, because they often equated higher castes and higher power status with lighter skin" (Roopa). The broader issues of race and colonialism was further demonstrated in Payal's response; she notes the difficulty in being able to justify a behavior which she understands as an "import" to Indian ideals:

> The craze of Indians to follow the west is completely a well hatched plan which the British still operate on even after leaving India in the

236   Anoop Bhogal-Nair and Andrew Lindridge

form of 'colonial hangover'. The Indian mentality has undergone a great change. Dark skinned women have become an easy object to comment on and for no valid reason are underestimate in their capabilities. Not only India but even America had followed the similar practice of placing the whites above the blacks.

Indeed, most participants recognized the wider cultural, historical, and religious context of skin lightening, in particular the depiction of gods and goddesses "[Religious paintings] reduce women to their appearance and being fair has archetypal associations of purity and innocence" (Asha). Janki gave a common narrative comparing an imagined ancient sense of feminine beauty with modernity:

There is a huge difference between traditional Indian beauty ideals and modern beauty ideals. The Ajanta cave paintings tell a different story altogether from modern social networks . . . from the day she is born a modern Indian woman is taught to maintain her skin as fair and lovely as it gets. The thriving cosmetic industry plays a huge role in this difference and also the prolonged period of colonisation set the trend of fair and beautiful.

Participants noted how modern images of Hindu deities had been subject to "white-washing," with the beauty and purity of the Goddesses being preserved through the fairness of their skin. Except for Kali (the Goddess of destruction), depictions of goddesses in popular media have followed the trend of skin fairness.

Resistance

The role of the market in borrowing and perpetuating this social stigma was noted as a consistent theme among a vast number of the respondents. Jyoti reinforced the perceived potency of advertising rhetoric in over-throwing any form of problematization of the issue of skin lightening "I don't think the demand for fairness creams will be interrupted any time soon. This is because the idea of this obsession with fair skin has not been presented as a problem to the masses at all." What was interesting to note was the uptake of these creams among the respondents during their early teenage years, with some commenting that it had become a normalized routine. Behavior as normalized is something which Aasha also comments upon: "the early childhood conditioning of most of has been such that there is an inherent unconscious favourableness towards fair skin." Her reference to the unconscious presents the subtlety with which the hegemony of whiteness is now embedded within the everyday. Considered as a product which is demanded in the same way individuals "crave food" Kiran notes that consumers not only want these products but they "worship these products [with consumers] spending thousands on these creams." This product devotion is considered further by Sheena who is critical of the position women place themselves in, putting the onus on both the marketing of the products but also the lack of reflexivity on the part of young women to actively resist such discourses: "self-worth is yet to take shape in a realistic way as far as Indian women are concerned, and it is complicated by the capitalist forces that sell insecurity in many packages for people to consume."

Consequently, most of the participants ultimately criticized and rejected the very cultural, historical, and religious values embedded in skin lightening creams while simultaneously complying with the very societal demands they rejected through their early or present use of skin lightening creams. The resistance to these narratives was apparent from the responses with Manisha vehemently insisting on a critical debate: "these products should be openly criticised and must be discussed on a larger level. The high demands of such products symbolise the obsession with fair skin in our country." Furthermore, Sheena aptly described the constant tug-of-war between ethical considerations and the alluring market presence of brands such as Fair & Lovely:

> Quite recently there was much debate about this on Twitter with actor Abhay Deol calling out all leading actresses for endorsing fairness creams. While a conversation has started about it, Fair and Lovely probably sells a lot of product in tier two and tier three cities. In villages, it is perhaps the only cosmetic young girls know of. Their constant advertising and new yearly variants (including an ayurvedic fairness cream) show their enduring market presence and dominance. Indian society does largely reduce women to their appearance and being fair has archetypal associations of purity, innocence, etc. While certain regions are dominated by darker skinned women, a fairer version among the dark is always more valued. All film actresses and models testify to this.

To consider such narratives and actions as hypercritical would be at best unfair and at worst a harsh colonial narrative rejecting individual and their family needs for betterment in a society where skin color is valued. Quite simply, the young women demonstrate being caught in a wider societal system they have little influence over and little scope or possibility of rejecting on a large scale.

Conclusion

A key finding of the study was not only how the young women had been socialized into the belief that paler skin tones were indicative of female beauty but also how they reluctantly or ignorantly engaged in this belief.

238   *Anoop Bhogal-Nair and Andrew Lindridge*

The young women clearly articulated the narratives of fairness and demonstrated an understanding of its origins through the lens of colonialism; however, there was limited understanding of an inherently Indian history of fairness as distinct from colonial rule. In highlighting this behavior, we challenge previous perspectives that have equated paler skin with an inherent sense of westerness (such as Hall 2013; Russell, Wilson, and Hall 1992). Indeed, modern Indian narratives appear to perpetuate these values not only through the market but also through the media and the marital market where one's children are prepared for marriage. What is evidenced clearly through the responses is how the legitimacy of the myth of fairness rests largely in India's collective history as represented in a shared unconscious. Fundamentally, collective memories are understood to help define relations between the individual and the community to which they belong (Nieger, Meyers, and Zandberg 2011). The effectiveness of the legitimizing myth is in part dependent upon consensuality and embeddedness (Sidanius and Pratto 2001); the former demonstrated through the shared social meanings and the latter demonstrated through an understanding of shared social practices which serve to reconstruct group histories and group relations (Pratto et al. 2000).

Young women are not seen as passive consumers, their agency lies within their ability to critically examine the discourses surrounding these products. While we cannot generalize the findings to be representative of all young women in India, what can be inferred is that pockets of resistance are emerging as critical narratives in the rewriting of skin. However, the culturally embedded scripts in allowing the rewriting of the narrative are seen to inhibit a complete rejection of the preference for fairness, indicating the embedded hegemonies of whiteness. Like Bonillo-Silva (2006), the ideas of female beauty based upon skin color were viewed within the frame of society's wider inherent racism. A racism originating from historical narratives of internal colonialism, racial assimilation policies, and capitalism.

We accept Bartky (1990) and others' argument that the beauty industry perpetuates women's sense of inadequacy through a sense of impurity and imperfection. However, these values lie not solely in a market-created narrative but in the culmination of India's evolution as a state. Indeed, this perspective supports and extends further Bordo's (2003) perspective that women's physical bodies are sights of cultural and political struggles, where political, religious, and nationalistic agendas are acted out and through. Yet, the young women's ability to fight and resist who owned their skin tone was ultimately one lost to wider societal pressures where society dictated the need for a paler skin (e.g., marriage). In this study, Farber's (2006) cultural power and tensions of social control drew upon deeply embedded societal narratives which manifest themselves through a collective unconscious. India's consumption of skin fairness lies partially within a postcolonial perspective. Data indicated that the evolving

Market Versus Cultural Myth 239

iconography of mythology aides the reinforcement of a national, collective memory where womanhood—as a representation of the fair, chaste, dutiful wife, mother, and daughter—had developed into the collective memory through the penetration of historical text, significant events in history (colonialism) as further reimagined and perpetuated through the marketplace.

Limitations

The study is not without its limitations which we would like to address here. Although the sample group of participants were forthcoming in their narratives, as a sample group they were inherently well educated, English speaking, urban, and middle class. Quite possibly, another sample group with a differing socioeconomic status and education level may have revealed contrasting findings. Furthermore, incorporating the views of male consumers may also shed new light on an understanding of fairness. Therefore, we would strongly encourage future work to widen the scope of this research and seek out more critical voices. Additionally, the focus of this research has been upon the discourses surrounding fairness through the inherited memories that consumers hold; again, further research into the practice of engaging with the phenomena would provide valuable insight into the behavioral aspects of consuming fairness.

References

Barthes, Roland (1957), *Mythologies*, Paris: Éditions du Seuil.

Bartky, Sandra Lee (1990), *Femininity and Domination: Studies in the Phenomenology of Oppression*, London: Psychology Press.

Bird, Elizabeth and Robert W. Dardenne (2009), "Rethinking News and Myth as Storytelling," in *The Handbook of Journalism Studies*, ed. Karin Wahl-Jorgensen and Thomas Hanitzsch, New York: Routledge, 205–17.

Bjerrisgaard, Sofie, Dannie Kjeldgaard, and Anders Bengtsson (2013), "Consumer-brand Assemblages in Advertising: An Analysis of Skin, Identity and Tattoos in Ads," *Consumption, Markets and Culture*, 16 (3), 223–39 (https://doi.org/10.1080/10253866.2012.738067).

Bonillo-Silva, Eduardo (2006), *Racism without Racists: Color-Blind Racism and the Persistence of Racial Inequality in America*, New York: Rowman & Littlefield.

Bordo, Susan (2003), *Unbearable Weight: Feminism, Western Culture, and the Body*, Berkeley, CA: University of California Press.

Bougle, Celestin (1958), "The Essence and Reality of Caste System," *Contributions to Indian Sociology*, II (1), 7–30.

Brand, Peg Zilin (2000), *Beauty Matters*, Bloomington: Indiana University Press.

Cohn, Bernard (1996), *Colonialism and Its Forms of Knowledge: The British in India*, Princeton, NJ: Princeton University Press.

Dumont, Louis (1998), *Homo Hierarchicus: The Caste System and Its Implications*, Delhi: Oxford India Paperbacks.

Farber, Leora (2006), "Skin Aesthetics," *Theory, Culture & Society*, 23 (2–3), 247–50 (https://doi.org/10.1177/026327640602300252).

Garcia, Alma M. (2012), *Contested Images: Women of Color in Popular Culture*, New York: AltaMira Press.

Glenn, Evylyn Nakano (2009), *Shades of Difference: Why Skin Color Matters*, Stanford, CA: Stanford University Press.

Hall, Catherin (2013), *White, Male and Middle Class: Explorations in Feminism and History*, London: John Wiley & Sons.

Hall, Ronald E. (2009), "Implications of Eurocentrism for Social Work Education: Trivialization vis-à-vis Skin Color," *Asian Social Work and Policy Review*, 3 (3), 175–86 (https://doi.org/10.1111/j.1753-1411.2009.00032.x).

Harris, Angela P. (2009), "Economies of Color," in *Shades of Difference: Why Skin Color Matters*, ed. Evelyn Nakano Glenn, Stanford, CA: Stanford University Press, 1–5.

Herring, Cedric, Verna Keith, and Hayward Horton (2003), *Skin Deep: How Race and Complexion Matter in the "Color-Blind" Era*, Chicago: University of Illinois Press.

Hesse, Barnor (2007), "Racialized Modernity: An Analytics of White Mythologies," *Ethnic and Racial Studies*, 30 (4), 643–63 (https://doi.org/10.1080/01419870701356064).

Hunter, Margaret L. (2011), "Buying Racial Capital: Skin-Bleaching and Cosmetic Surgery in a Globalized World," *The Journal of Pan African Studies*, 4 (4), 142–64 (www.jpanafrican.org/docs/vol4no4/HUNTER%20Final.pdf).

Isaacs, Harold (1968), "Group Identity and Political Change: The Role of Colour and Physical Characteristics," in *Colour and Race*, ed. John Hope Franklin, Boston: Houghton Mifflin, 75–97.

Jablonski, Nina G. (2012), *Living Color: The Biological and Social Meaning of Skin Color*, Berkeley, CA: University of California Press.

Jaywardene, Sureshi (2013), "Pushing the Paradigm: Locating Scholarship on the Siddis and Kaffirs," *Journal of Black Studies*, 44 (7), 687–705 (https://doi.org/10.1177/0021934713508781).

Jha, Meeta Rani (2016), *The Global Beauty Industry: Colorism, Racism, and the National Body*, London: Routledge.

Jodhka, Surinder (2012), *Caste: Oxford India Short Introductions*, New Delhi: Oxford University Press.

Lal, Parmanand (1974), "The Tribal Man in India: A Study of the Ecology of the Primitive Communities," in *Ecology and Biogeography in India*, ed. Mahadeva Subramania Mani, The Hague: Springer, 281–329.

Maddox, Keith and Stephanie Chase (2004), "Manipulating Subcategory Salience: Exploring the Link Between Skin Tone and Social Perception of Blacks," *European Journal of Social Psychology*, 34 (5), 533–46 (https://doi.org/10.1002/ejsp.214).

Meamber, Laurie and Alldi Venkatesh (2000), "Ethno-consumerist Methodology for Cultural and Cross-cultural Research," in *Interpretive Consumer Research: Paradigms, Methodologies and Applications*, ed. Suzanne C. Beckmann and Richard H. Elliott, Copenhagen: Copenhagen Business School Press, 87–108.

Nadeem, Shehzaad (2014), "Fair and Anxious: On Mimicry and Skin Lightening in India," *Social Identities*, 20 (2–3), 224–38 (https://doi.org/10.1080/13504630.2014.881282).

Nieger, Moti, Oren Meyers, and Eyal Zandberg (2011), *On Media Memory: Collective Memory in a New Media Age*, Basingstoke: Palgrave Macmillan.

Market Versus Cultural Myth 241

Pattanaik, Devdutt (2009), "The Ancient Story of Goddess Lakshmi—Bestower of Power, Wealth, and Sovereignty," (https://qz.com/india/545655/the-ancient-story-of-goddess-lakshmi-bestower-of-power-wealth-and-sovereignty/).

Patterson, Maurice and Jonathan Schroeder (2010), "Borderlines: Skin, Tattoos and Consumer Culture Theory," *Marketing Theory* 10 (3), 253–67 (https://doi.org/10.1177/1470593110373191).

Philips, Amali (2004), "Gendering Colour: Identity, Femininity and Marriage in Kerala," *Anthropologica*, 46 (2), 253–72 (https://doi.org/10.2307/25606198).

Pratto, Felicia, James H. Liu, Shana Levin, Jim Sidanius, Margaret Shih, Hagit Bachrach, and Peter Hegarty (2000), "Social Dominance Orientation and the Legitimization of Inequality Across Cultures," *Journal of Cross-Cultural Psychology*, 31 (3), 369–409 (https://doi.org/10.1177/0022022100031003005).

Prosser, Jay (2001), *Thinking Through the Skin*, London: Routledge.

Risley, Herbert (1915), *The People of India*, Delhi: Oriental Books Reprint Corporation.

Rothfeld, Otto (1928), *Women of India*, Bombay: D.B. Taraporevala Sons.

Russell, Kathy, Midge Wilson, and Ronald Hall (1992), *The Color Complex (Revised): The Politics of Skin Color in a New Millennium*, New York: Anchor.

Sharma, Ram Sharan (2002a), *Sudras in Ancient India: A Social History of the Lower Order Down to Circa A.D. 600*, Delhi: Motilal Banarsidass Publishers.

Sharma, Ursula (2002b), *Caste*, New Delhi: Viva Books Private Limited.

Sidanius, Jim and Felicia Pratto (2001), *Social Dominance: An Intergroup Theory of Social Hierarchy and Oppression*, Cambridge: Cambridge University Press.

Spiggle, Susan (1994), "Analysis and Interpretation of Qualitative Data in Consumer Research," *Journal of Consumer Research*, 21 (3), 491–503 (https://doi.org/10.1086/209413).

Srivastav, Taruka (2017), "Skin Whitening Cream Sales Sill Boom in India Despite Rules Against Ads Deriding Darker Skin," (www.thedrum.com/news/2017/09/15/skin-whitening-cream-sales-still-boom-india-despite-rules-against-ads-deriding).

Telles, Edward E. (2004), *Race in Another America: The Significance of Skin Color in Brazil*, Princeton, NJ: Princeton University Press.

Trouillot, Michel-Rolph (1990), "Culture, Color, and Politics in Haiti," in *Race*, ed. Steven Gregory and Roger Sanjek, New Brunswick, NJ: Rutgers University Press, 146–74.

Turner, Terrence (2012), "The Social Skin," *HAU: Journal of Ethnographic Theory*, 2 (2), 486–504 (https://doi.org/10.14318/hau2.2.026).

Unilever (2020), "Glow and Lovely," (www.unilever.com/brands/personal-care/glow-and-lovely.html).

The United Nations (2017), "Worlds Apart," (www.unfpa.org/swop).

Wagatsuma, Hiroshi (1967), "The Social Perception of Skin Color in Japan," *Daedalus*, 96 (2), 407–43 (www.jstor.org/stable/20027045).

Wolf, Naomi (1991), *The Beauty Myth: How Images of Beauty Are Used Against Women*, London: Vintage.

Zacharias, Usha (2003), "The Smile of Mona Lisa: Postcolonial Desires, Nationalist Families, and the Birth of Consumer Television in India," *Critical Studies in Media Communication*, 20 (4), 388–406 (https://doi.org/10.1080/0739318032000142034).

13 Haptic Creatures
Tactile Affect and Human–Robot Intimacy in Japan

Hirofumi Katsuno and Daniel White

While Japanese popular media, manga, and science fiction have long inspired fantasies of a future society for human–robot coexistence in the global imagination, and while Japan's government has even developed specific programs to realize possible versions of this future (Robertson 2018), the current reality of human–robot relationships is far more conflicted and complex. As we aim to show in this chapter, it is consequently critical to ground perspectives on consumer robot culture in Japan in recent historical considerations and ethnographic data in order to facilitate understanding of emerging human–robot relationships and evaluate how different stakeholders (consumers, corporations, marketers, artificial intelligence (AI) researchers, and government facilitators and regulators) variously benefit from these increasingly intimate partnerships.

Nowhere is this more important than in the emerging field of social robotics, where mass-marketed robots built for entertainment and companionship are being equipped with increasing capacities for artificial emotional intelligence. Combining advances in computing with market explorations in technologies of care and companionship, the most recent of these robots, such as SoftBank's "emotional robot" Pepper or Sony's latest pet robot aibo, can—so the companies claim—stimulate, respond to, and in some cases even detect human emotions. These companies reason that robot companions can fill a deficit in interpersonal intimacy in the face of attenuating social bonds, the increase of social and economic insecurity due to Japan's three decades of economic stagnation, and the rising costs associated with an affluent middle-class family life. Concurrently, robot and AI researchers, long supported by generous grants from a government that has demonstrated a preference for technological solutions to shortages in care-sector labor rather than increase visas for foreign workers (Robertson 2007), have joined this effort to advance their research interests in automation and AI (Fujita 2001). As a result, these corporate-research collaborations have increased attention to, investment in, and the production of emotionally

DOI: 10.4324/9781003111559-18

evocative social robots, incorporating nonhuman entities into a social network of intimate human–robot relationships in Japanese society.

While an increasing number of studies have focused on the capacities for emotional bonding that these robots generate in Japan's elderly care sectors (Stevens 2011; Wright 2018) and clarified how human emotion-recognition software plays a key role in this (White 2019; White and Katsuno 2021), we want to explore a more recent and far less-studied breed of robot companions that we call *haptic creatures*. Unlike other robots with artificial emotional intelligence, these new robots do not focus specifically on reading human emotion based on psychological theories of ubiquitous and universal affective states, often referred to as the "basic emotions" paradigm (Ekman 1999); rather, these robots are more experimental. Instead of reading human emotion, although some of them can, they invite human–robot interaction through increasingly sophisticated tactile sensors. These include features such as contact-responsive wagging tails and touch-sensing furry bodies (Qoobo, Figure 13.1), and skin warmed to the body temperature of a newborn baby (LOVOT, Figure 13.2). Instead of delivering care through simulated models of human-to-human emotion, these robots generate experiments with the unknown potential of human–robot affect.[1]

We define haptic creatures as robot companions designed to deliver a sense of comforting presence through a combination of animated

Figure 13.1 Qoobo, by Yukai Engineering
Photo by Hirofumi Katsuno.

Figure 13.2 LOVOT, by Groove X
Photo provided by Groove X.

movements and healing touch. We argue that making this distinction between emotionally intelligent robots and haptic creatures allows us to answer the question of how the experimental capacities these robots engender are being newly leveraged to research, develop, and maximize profit within an economy of mass-consumer robot care in Japan. Such findings hold significance for revealing how robotics technologies in Japan not only facilitate social change but also embody and mediate it through aspects of design.

We illustrate this process in three steps. The first section of the chapter explores the recent history of the ways social robots have developed not only within the domain of robotics engineering but also in partnership with an emerging market of technologically based forms of care, or "techno-intimacy" (Allison 2006), which is closely linked to the amusement industry. By placing social robots in the context of a sociotechnical lineage of virtual and machinic creatures, most specifically with the rise of virtual and digital pets since the 1990s, we address how relationships with artificial creatures are shaped through a form of affective modulation and experimentation. The second section links this historical discussion to a growing market for companion robots, in which haptic creatures have emerged as a particularly evocative tool for generating human–robot intimacy as well as profit. In the third section of the chapter, we document the rise of the most recent haptic creatures and offer ethnographic examples of one in particular to illustrate precisely how haptic creatures are being integrated into the human social ecosystem as a new type of companion species. In particular, we focus on how new imaginaries and stories of intimate relationships with machines emerge through affective experiences produced at sites of haptic contact between human and robot. We explore this process primarily through the case of Qoobo, a headless robotic cat-like cushion designed by Yukai Engineering to elicit comfort through tail movements and touch. (Because such haptic interaction elicited by these robots is key to their evocative appeal, but difficult to communicate in text, we also intersperse images of the robots we discuss to supplement this point.) By linking these historical, market, and ethnographic segments of the chapter, we aim to demonstrate that techno-social developments in Japan elicited at the level of the body generate powerful stories about social, emotional, and interpersonal renewal through novel forms of machine-inclusive multispecies sociality.

Contextualizing Companion Robots, Techno-Intimacy, and Haptic Creatures

Companion robots are a form of social robotics technology, which is a field focused on building agents that can communicate with humans and assist them in their daily lives. While the idea of "social robots" has been explored in Anglophone literature by prominent robotics engineers, such as Cynthia Breazeal (2002), who have helped turn social robotics into a formal discipline, the notion of building robots that interact with and support human flourishing has a longer history in Japan (see White and Katsuno 2021). Most characteristic of this history of social robot engineering in Japan is a concern with designing robots not only for specific tasks but, more importantly, as socially capable robotic persons that can act as partners in daily life, assert a sense of autonomy, and facilitate a mutual recognition of each other's presence. While variously referred to as "entertainment robots" (*entāteimento robotto*), "communication robots" (*komyunikēshon robotto*), and "personal robots" (*pāsonaru robotto*) throughout the course of their development, as the market for this type of robot expands, these robots are converging into a category we think can be most aptly termed *companion robots*.[2] While still limited in their capacities (Robertson 2018, 175–92), these companion robots have made notable progress, especially with the advancement of machine learning systems that enable the robot to learn from patterns of interacting with humans and even in some cases integrate emotion recognition through signals such as vocal inflections or facial expressions.

However, the development of the social and relational capabilities of such robots cannot be viewed merely within the framework of techno-logical accumulation in the scientific fields of robotics and AI research. Rather, these capacities have also been shaped by a broader entertainment

246　*Hirofumi Katsuno and Daniel White*

marketplace in which human emotional needs and desires are tested within technologically mediated feedback loops between producers and consumers through different robotic platforms.

In this sense, social robots participate in shaping a lineage of "techno-intimacy" (Allison 2006; Galbraith 2019)—the intimacy formed between human and technologically constituted entities that has developed out of experiments in entertainment fields such as video games and toys. Within this historical trajectory, companion robots have appeared as platforms that can expand possibilities for intimacy beyond the purpose of pure amusement and create new opportunities for care and comfort. Realizing such opportunities depends on advancements in information and data science, communication technologies, mechatronics, robotics, and the field of AI, as well as the fields of "post-functionalist design" (Sicart 2014, 42), sense engineering (*kansei kōgaku*), and cute engineering (Okura 2017), which aim to appeal directly to socially conditioned bodily senses, or what we refer to as *affect*.

This trajectory of techno-intimacy can be traced to the digital companion *Tamagotchi*, released by the entertainment company Bandai. The first series of Tamagotchi was launched in 1996, exploding in popularity and creating a social phenomenon. Bandai eventually sold 40 million units worldwide (20 million in Japan and 20 million outside Japan) (Nikkei Sangyo Shimbun 2005). This first generation of Tamagotchi was modeled on the idea of "raising pets," with Tamagotchi described as "an egg-shaped portable pet whose personality and appearance changes depending on how the player raises it." The player feeds, cleans up after, and plays with the character, which appears on the screen of the egg-shaped watch and evokes a sense of biological life. If the player communicates with the virtual pet frequently, it will be in a good mood; but if the player forgets to feed or fails to clean up after it, it will be in a bad mood—or, in the worst case, even die. After a certain amount of time, Tamagotchi will develop into various characters, each reflecting the character and mood fostered by its player-carer.

By modeling the "biological rhythms involved in the care of a flesh-and-blood pet" (Allison 2006, 169), Tamagotchi incorporated not only cuteness but also labor, duty, and the responsibility associated with pet-raising into the game setting, bringing a new reality to gameplay. In turn, this blurring of the boundary between virtual space and everyday life allowed gameplay to unfold in the player's lived reality and time. Tamagotchi's continuous growth and demand for attention at all hours of the day, regardless of the player's circumstances, facilitated an affective attunement between player and virtual creature by dynamically connecting the game's rhythmic algorithm to the player's biorhythms in daily life.

We suggest that this technologically mediated form of affective intimacy that Tamagotchi enables between human and digital creature sets an important precedent in Japan for experimenting with and building subsequent "companion species" (Haraway 2008) that engender social transformation. This transformation is marked by a shift from time spent in interpersonal relationships to relationships increasingly mediated and occupied by digital technologies and the evocative agents in which they are embedded. Such increases in techno-intimacy serve as a metric for evaluating not only the rapid growth of mobile computing in Japanese public culture but also of a transition to forms of care served increasingly by digital technologies and the data infrastructures (mobile internet providers, wi-fi and cable networks, and cloud services) that support them. From this perspective, such technologies do not merely address declining forms of human-based intimacy and increasing socioeconomic precarity that characterize post-bubble Japan (Allison 2013) but also create opportunities for new forms of intimacy through technological forms of experimentation.

Since the spread of Tamagotchi, a variety of virtual pets and mechanical creatures—from communication toys for children to expensive social robots introduced to care homes—have been developed as friendly interactive partners. And while there are a variety of social robots in existence in Japan today with different capacities for connecting emotionally with humans, we want to trace one particular development particular to the field of haptic interaction. "Haptic interaction" refers to interactive experiences by which human–robot contact points are created through external stimuli, such as rounded, cute designs that invite touching or holding, soft and warm materials that stimulate comfort through touch, and cute (*kawaii*) voices that activate the auditory system. By delivering external stimuli to users through theories of evocative design and experimental techniques of trial and error, producers aim to induce feelings of joy, pleasure, comfort, and even healing (*iyashi*) through people's interactions with the machine. To put it another way, the efficacy of techno-intimacy is cultivated and enhanced through experiments with techniques and technologies of affective attunement between people and machines.

To illustrate this developmental process, consider another two examples from the same period as Tamagotchi: the video game *Pikachu Genki Dechu* (Hey You, Pikachu!), released for the Nintendo 64 in 1998, and *Seaman: The Forbidden Pets*, produced for the SEGA Dreamcast in 1999. Both games allowed players to interact with the characters through a voice recognition system. In the case of *Pikachu Genki Dechu*, Pikachu performs various expressions depending on the words the player speaks to it. In *Seaman*, the player could not only talk to the virtual character but also pick it up to observe it with a virtual hand linked to the controller or tap the virtual tank with a finger cursor to call or tickle it. This virtual mechanism for tactile interaction anticipated future possibilities for physical interaction with robots equipped with tactile sensors that appeared later.

Another example of companion creatures emerging during this period was Furby, which hit the market first in the United States in 1998 and then

248   *Hirofumi Katsuno and Daniel White*

in Japan in 1999. With Furby, the habitat of emerging virtual creatures expanded from two- to three-dimensional space. Furby was a talking electronic plush toy in the form of a small furry pet. While similar in many ways to traditional battery-operated stuffed animals, Furby's distinctiveness was found in the combination of tactile and algorithm-based developmental capacities to form relationships with owners. Furby was programmed to grow by being cared for. When hugged, played with, and fed, Furby grew in four steps and spoke about 800 words, including Furby-language, Japanese (in the version sold for the Japanese market), and onomatopoeia. It was also able to sing and dance.

In its haptic capacities, Furby was different not only from previous toys but also from virtual creatures that operate on a screen. Although it was not equipped with voice recognition technology, Furby did have a sound sensor that responds to voices and music, stimulating ear and eye movements. It also had a light sensor that could distinguish between day and night to determine when to "wake up" and when to "sleep." It also had tactile sensors on its tongue, belly, and back that respond to being stroked. In the genealogy of techno-intimate design, the emergence of its multiple modes of communication and interaction made Furby into the first significant mass-produced multimodal interface, expanding possibilities for intimate interactions between people and future haptic creatures.

Roughly a year after the appearance of Furby, multimodal companion toys began to come equipped with not only behavioral but also emotional models. Poochi, a dog-shaped robot toy released by Sega Toys in 2000, was equipped with a program called the heart circuit (*kokoro kairo*), in addition to its more conventional sound, light, and tactile sensors. The heart circuit consists of an algorithm that mimics human biorhythms linked to good and bad moods. The frequency of communication by the user, such as petting the head or talking to the robot, changes the cycle of the artificial biorhythms, which is reflected in the emotional expressions and actions of Poochi. This algorithmic model integrating human interaction and robot development found its most sophisticated embodiment at the time in Sony's pet robot AIBO (Figure 13.3), released in 1999. AIBO's degree of technological sophistication and hefty price tag (US$2,500) blurred the line between toys and robotics, ushering in a new period of development that expanded the market for companion robot pets into broader, and older, segments of the population.

The boom of the commercialization of virtual organisms in the late 1990s thus serves as an important moment that carried over into the later development of AI-equipped companion robots in Japan. Most importantly, these early experiments in human–robot interaction reveal that what equips these creatures with a sense of vitality is not only the technological system that models the behavior of living things, nor is it merely the philosophical questions these agents inspire about the sufficient ontological conditions for life. Rather, as Sherry Turkle addresses, it is the

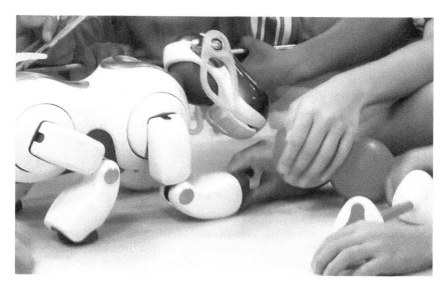

Figure 13.3 AIBO, by Sony
Photo by Hirofumi Katsuno, used by permission of Sony Electronics Inc. All Rights Reserved

"value of the interface" (Turkle 2011) that makes an agent seem alive and affectionate, and capable of diverse and unpredictable social interactions. The key component in cultivating a connection between human and robot is thus the affective attunement established within a human–robot relation. Haptic feedback, designers discovered, played a critical if difficult-to-qualify role in this process.

A distinction that emerges in Japanese robotics between emotion modeling and haptic interaction is important for understanding how experimentation increasingly drives collaborations between entertainment robotics corporations and robotics researchers. In the 1990s, several researchers were endeavoring to create artificial emotions in robots, such as in Sugano Shigeki's WAMOEBA (Waseda Artificial Mind on Emotion BASE) and Tosa Naoko's Neurobaby.[3] The goal of these projects was to build a scientifically universal model of emotion, which ironically remained only demonstrable in an experimental environment. On the other hand, the market for virtual creatures for children, which appeared in succession during the 1990s, served as productive platforms through which to explore the design features and conditions that foster opportunities for positive affective attunement. In contrast to robotics development in academic institutions, which is top-down, collective, linear, institutionalized, abstract, and theory-oriented, product development of artificial organisms for general consumers took the form of "tinkering" (Katsuno 2011),

250 *Hirofumi Katsuno and Daniel White*

which is rather bottom-up, experimental, concrete, object-oriented, and potentially endless. What is most critical for our discussion here is that the importance of the sense of touch in the construction of techno-intimacy was discovered not in laboratory settings but in the tinkering process of experimentation linked to people's lives navigated and negotiated within capitalist mass markets and then reimported into robotics development. The 1990s boom in virtual creatures thus uncovered the potential of a market for intimate relationships with virtual and machinic companions and became the driving force behind the blossoming of haptic creatures that helped integrate technological development, human–robot affect, and the growth of entertainment robotics.

Virtual Pets and Capital Accumulation

While in the previous section, we contextualized the emergence of haptic creatures and emphasized the importance of affect in this process; in this section, we want to show how haptic creatures link affect to capital accumulation. As noted previously, Sherry Turkle has argued for the importance of assessing the value of the interface between humans and machines in order to critique the quality of these relationships. In the context of haptic creatures, however, Turkle's point on the interface can be viewed in another light. In short, the virtual creatures we discussed earlier and that are precursors to haptic creatures serve not only as new companions but also as new modes of production in the digital age that multiply capital by animating *things*. One concept that helps illustrate this process is "capitalist-animism" (Imamura 2014; Shaviro 2012; Taussig 1997), which refers to a practice by which commodities are made economically productive through spiritual characteristics. According to Steven Shaviro (2012), capitalist-animism designates a "set of ritual practices, stances, and attunements to the world, constituting the way we participate in capitalist existence. . . . The 'naive' consumer, who sees commodities as animate beings, endowed with magical properties, is therefore not mystified or deluded. He or she is accurately perceiving the way that capitalism works, how it endows material things with an inner life." In other words, people's animistic sensitivities are cultivated and channeled through consumer goods that inscribe and animate capitalist logics.[4]

Viewed through the lens of capitalist-animism, virtual and robotic creatures appear as a new animist medium that can be leveraged to capitalist growth, where capitalism aims to convert uncharted regions of interior life toward accumulation. In these exploratory affective mining operations, maintaining consumer attention and interest is paramount. The lifespan of a virtual pet as a product is usually very short. Consumers are initially fascinated by the interaction, but they quickly become bored. In the case of Tamagotchi, Bandai, the manufacturer and distributor of the product realized too late that the boom was over and ended up with

Haptic Creatures 251

a large excess inventory, resulting in the company's largest loss since its inception. The social robotics industry faces a similar problem. Human interest in new robots is commonly said to be easy to heat up and easy to cool down (*nesshiyasuku sameyasui*). Industry executives also formulate this problem of maintaining a human–robot connection as the "three-month barrier" (*sankagetu no kabe*). How to overcome this short lifespan—that is, how to keep "re-animating" the product—is a major focus of consumer robot development. This is where haptic creatures can help discover new means by which consumers' attention can stay connected with products through affect, thus both augmenting and demonstrating the profit-generating potential of capitalist-animism.

Where comforting forms of affect generated by stimulating interactions between human and artificial agent sustain that connection, it also serves as a platform for extracting capital. This process has been accelerated with the emergence of cloud computing technologies and subscription payment models. For technically simple products such as Tamagotchi and Furby, companies can bring them back to life by working on new versions with relatively simple software updates (Tamagotchi has already been sold in three series). For the latest social robots powered by cloud AI, "updating" takes a different form, as interactions with human users are converted into data that are fed back to the robot to help it learn and grow. In this sense, it is not the character that is updated but rather the *relationship*, binding human and robot together in an increasingly compatible fit. Within this feedback loop, the robot's capacity for adaptability is supported by a monthly user fee for data management and maintenance, monetizing the developmental process of human–robot intimacy.

Although capitalist-animism illustrates animacy's capacity for commodifying the human–robot bond through technology, this capacity, which we also refer to as techno-animacy, shows itself capable of playing both with and against capitalist logics. When Anne Allison described the concept of techno-animism in her 2006 study of the globalization of Japanese games and toys, she offered an analytical means to link consumer desires to human–machine relationships that were cultivated through capitalist logics. Focusing on the social obsession with Tamagotchi and other early Japanese digital and robotic pets in the late 1990s and early 2000s, Allison explored how players' labor of care "gives 'life' to the virtual pet and intimacy to the bonds formed between people and their machines/Tamagotchi" (2006, 166). Here, Allison (2006, 12) uses "techno-animism" to explain "an aesthetic proclivity, a tendency to see the world as animated by a variety of beings, both worldly and otherworldly, that are complex, (inter)changeable, and not graspable by so-called rational (or visible) means alone." Most importantly, Allison sees techno-animism as a form of techno-materialist fantasy, which was formed in response to a series of social changes that Japan experienced from the postwar turmoil to the late capitalist era. According to Allison, techno-animism is "a style that

252   *Hirofumi Katsuno and Daniel White*

is deeply embedded in material practices of commodity consumerism" (Allison 2006, 13). It reconfigures intimate attachments by mapping "the desire to find meaning, connection, and intimacy in everyday life onto commodified apparatuses (goods/machines)" (ibid) in a period characterized by heightened flux, individualization, and isolation. In this sense, according to Allison, while Tamagotchi is a tool for play, it also has an educational role in life and for raising children and is useful as a communication companion in a society that is becoming increasingly lonely. As a result, these human–technology interactions help people reimagine the world by recuperating sociality and intimate attachments, which have been attenuated in the advancement of technologically mediated late-stage capitalism on a global scale.

Much of the power of Allison's argument, as partially based upon Donald Winnicott's psychoanalytic theory, comes from its framing of the real and the imaginary world as linked via virtual and mechanical organisms, which function as a medium that bridges the two worlds for the recuperation of social and psychological instability. In this view, imagination maintains a privileged position in smoothing over the different affordances of humans and machines, so that material objects are only seen to the extent that they appear to model human forms of care. However, the latest social robots we call haptic creatures, equipped with advanced sensors to register affective interactions, are designed not to model human emotion but to discover new possibilities for comforting human–robot affective presence. We believe that the term *haptic creatures* helps critics evaluate how emotional connections between human and machines have become more complex and dynamic since the time of Allison's study and less strictly dependent on the kind of animistic imagination debated in the wake of Allison's work (Jensen and Blok 2013). From our point of view, our interlocutors seem increasingly invested in situations where the increasingly interactive and perceptive abilities of digital technology and human imagination are intricately intertwined, resulting in the constant transformation of humans' imaginative capacities for fostering intimacy with artificial beings. In our final section, we illustrate how human–robot bonding can build not only on narrative imaginations cultivated in gameplay but also through a history of somatic contact and comfort underlying these imaginations.

The Rise of Haptic Creatures

To develop our argument on the important role that haptic feedback plays in linking companion robots to capital accumulation, we draw on Donna Haraway's concept of "companion species" (Haraway 2008). Haraway's concept illustrates the dynamic entanglements of human and nonhuman actors. Through the figure of companion species, Haraway describes the co-evolving process of humans, animals, and other nonhuman objects into

Haptic Creatures   253

separate but intimately connected entities. Such a process is not one in which each interacts with the other as a stable and autonomous species or being; rather, each is mutually dependent but in complex and asymmetrical ways. As the environment of the Anthropocene (although Haraway has at times preferred the "Capitalocene" and "Chthulucene" [2016]) is rapidly permeated by the information revolution, recent scholarship has shed light on how companion species are not limited to organisms but increasingly include artifacts and even data (Lupton 2016), shaping a multilayered ecosystem articulated with media, capitalism, and nature.

We add to this discussion the proposition that social robots too are becoming part of this sociotechnical ecosystem whereby machines prove increasingly capable of evoking, registering, and shaping human emotions with degrees of agency not previously possible. In this sense, we understand techno-intimacy as the very process of forming a co-constitutive and co-evolving relationship between technology and human emotion. Within this relationship, haptic contact zones become a critical site where human affect and technological affordance are encountered, transduced, and reconstituted, shaping new stories and relationships. For Haraway, most of the "transformative things in life happen in contact zones. . . . The point is that contact zones are where the action is, and current interactions change interactions to follow" (Haraway 2008, 219). In analyzing the contact zone between social robots and humans, mechanisms for tactile contact, sensing, and exchange become the primary components of the interface that enable a critical next step in techno-intimacy.

We use the term "haptic creature" to identify these new companion species with increased abilities to exchange and modulate affect. Perhaps the most important of these that marked a critical turning point from virtual pets to haptic creatures was AIST's (National Institute of Advanced Industrial Science and Technology) seal-like robot Paro (Figure 13.4). Paro was released in 1999 and extended interaction with artificial life into the realm of care by enhancing its capacity for tactile interaction. Since 1993, the creator of the robot, Shibata Takanori had been working on the development of an "artificial emotional creature," a robot that provides mental stimulation such as enjoyment and comfort (Shibata 2016). Paro's soft fur and heavy body, depicted in the figure below, generate a sense of presence that is gentle enough to invite warmth and affection but substantial enough to suggest the sense of a living body deserving of care. While Shibata anticipated such a value of haptic intimacy in the early stage of Paro's development, he also continually updated Paro's materiality through several versions, using the robot as a means of both intervening in and exploring the affective capacities mutually engendered through human–Paro interaction.

Robotic therapy using Paro bore fruit in "neurological therapy" (Shibata 2016), a biofeedback method in which the sensations of physical interaction with Paro stimulated the human brain to evoke past memories

Figure 13.4 Paro, by AIST
Photo by Hirofumi Katsuno.

and emotions effective for therapy, specifically emotions people feel when interacting with animals as well as their own various past experiences and pleasant memories of family, friends, and colleagues. By measuring the cerebral blood flow of people's brains in this practice, Shibata found that it increased in the prefrontal cortex and temporal language area. According to Shibata, this led to the innovation of nonpharmacological therapy for dementia and mental health (Shibata 2016). By using biofeedback devices to visualize information otherwise invisible to human consciousness, interaction with haptic creatures becomes an opportunity to redefine human consciousness, the senses, and even human beings themselves.

The results of Paro's robotic therapy have had a ripple effect in the use of social robots for therapy and emotional education of children. As a result, social robots, and those robots we call haptic creatures, have become platforms for experimentation in the reorganization of technologies related to care and therapy, including tactile technologies. In particular, the practical application of tactile technology has also expanded the scientific understanding of touch. In fact, recent developments in haptic technology, such as haptic interfaces on touchpads and virtual reality videogames, tactile feedback systems for surgeons in teleoperation, and artificial tactile sensations on prosthetic limbs have made engineering an influential field for defining the ontology of tactility. A leading scholar in this domain, Nakatani Masashi (2016), points out that the tactile (*shokkan*) approach aims to capture touch perception in close connection with human affects and emotions. According to Nakatani, tactile impression is a multimodal and subjective experience, shaped not only through skin sensation but also through coordination with other senses (visual, auditory, olfactory, and taste), as well as through higher-level cognitive functions such as language and memory.

In a similar vein, Watanabe Junji (2014), another haptics scholar, points out that shokkan design combines texture (*shitsukan*), sensation (*jikkan*), and emotional sensation (*jōkan*) in order to evoke particular emotions through tactile sensation. This analytical framing of the haptic field has inspired the operationalization of technology by engineers toward experimenting with and in some cases even influencing or "hacking" human perceptions via tactile sensation.

Of all the social robots released in recent years, Qoobo is one of the most popular examples of a haptic creature created with shokkan design in mind. Illustrating the distinction between haptic creatures and emotionally intelligent companion robots, Qoobo's robotic functions are simple. Most of these are concentrated in the tail movement. When the user touches the robot, internal sensors read the intensity and speed of the touch, which are then reflected in the movement of the tail. Qoobo also wags and curls its tail on its own to ask for additional interaction. What is most distinctive is that this robot has no face, consisting only of a torso and tail (Figure 13.5). However, this seemingly simple and

Figure 13.5 Tactile interaction with Qoobo, by Yukai Engineering
Photo by Hirofumi Katsuno.

256 *Hirofumi Katsuno and Daniel White*

incomplete appearance is strategically designed to stimulate humans to complement its imperfections with their feelings and imagination through tactile interaction.

In the remainder of this section, we illustrate how tactile interaction elicits affective impressions that stimulate the imagination of new possibilities for human–Qoobo relationships. These accounts of human–robot first encounters took place within a focus-group-format discussion with 20 participants on reactions to Qoobo, as well as in interviews, which were conducted after three of the group's participants spent a week with the robot. Among the participants, we focus our analysis on two female students whose narratives were thematically typical but particularly evocative of the affective potential of haptic creatures.

In June 2019, one of the authors (Katsuno) held a workshop on social robots at the university where he works. None of the participants had seen Qoobo before. Upon their first encounter with Qoobo, some of the students started to touch the fluffy body of the robot as soon as they saw it, while others looked puzzled as if viewing an "unknown creature" for the first time. Ichikawa Hikari, a 21-year-old female university student, was one of those who were most drawn to the robot. Hikari grew up with a cat until she entered university, and she now misses living with cats as her apartment does not allow them. When she saw Qoobo for the first time she expected that it would be a substitute for her cat. When she arrived home with Qoobo, Hikari immediately switched it on. Then, according to her, "I instantly remembered my cat at home. I naturally smiled and couldn't resist tossing its torso from side to side as I always did to my own cat." For the next few days, the reality of the relationship between Hikari and Qoobo was formed as a mixture of the robot's artificiality and her memories of the cat. She explained:

> For the first few days, I was always touching Qoobo and comparing it to my cat at home. When I put this robot on my lap while working on my computer, memories of my cat came back to me. On the other hand, after a few more days, I also realized that it doesn't get warm on my lap or get close to me. Also, cats purr and rebel, but Qoobo is too obedient. As such differences gradually became clear, it brought me back to the reality that this is a machine. However, memories of my real cat come to life in unexpected moments. For example, at the moment when its tail touched my arm, I felt like, "Oh, it reminds me that contact with a cat was indeed like this!" I felt comforted at that moment.

Hikari's interactions with Qoobo's materiality, tactile sensations, and mechanical behavioral responses are experienced through repeated partial connections and disconnections with her past experiences of her "home cat" (*jikka no neko*). The intense affective attunement she experienced with Qoobo upon her first contact was no longer sustainable, but the

Haptic Creatures 257

occasional unexpected physical contact with the haptic creature became an opportunity to evoke fragmented memories of her family's pet. Hikari is aware that Qoobo cannot be a substitute for her original cat, but she nonetheless cultivates intimacy with it by enjoying the memories and feelings of the cat that temporarily emerge when her body and the machine unexpectedly come into contact. In this contact zone, the relationship between human and robot is not something that can be freely controlled by Hikari's autonomous will, nor is it something that can be created merely by her active imagination. Rather, the relationship is supported by the contingency of contact and the ambivalence of tactility, which consists of the sense of touching and being touched at the same time. Most importantly, Hikari's affect-generated imagination, or what has been called the "affective imagination" (Cook 2020; De Antoni 2018), emerges first and foremost through the sense of touch, illustrating how physical contact can create a somatic archive of socially meaningful impressions on the body.

Another participant, a 21-year-old female student named Gotō Kaori, also insisted on taking Qoobo home with her and ended up living with the robot for about three months. She never had pets (except goldfish) due to allergies, and she hardly had any experience touching cats and dogs. When seeing Qoobo for the first time at the workshop, she hoped the robot would give her the feeling of keeping a pet, which she characterized as "healing" (*iyashi*). As soon as she brought Qoobo home, she called her mother via Skype and told her about her new robot pet. "What is it?! It's so creepy!" her mother exclaimed upon seeing the headless creature on the screen. Kaori elaborated on this reaction:

> Some of my friends at the seminar showed similar reactions to Qoobo as my mother did. Someone said, "What is this? It looks like a monster!" But I did not feel too uncomfortable myself with its appearance, maybe because I was filled with high expectations about finally having a pet. And when its tail actually responded to my touch, I delightedly felt that the feeling of a real cat may be like this. . . . I was especially happy when getting its hair on my T-shirt. I felt like, "Oh, this is the experience I have been yearning for."

Kaori's lack of experience with "real" pets makes her interaction with Qoobo quite different from Hikari's. For Hikari, her interaction with Qoobo was constructed through the negotiation of her lived memory and her artificial feeling of a cat. On the other hand, Kaori's experience with Qoobo was shaped in a feedback loop between Qoobo's *shokkan* design and its elicitation of her imagined expectations of what it is like to have a real cat. Such forms of the imagination emerge not merely from an association of creative narrative scenes but rather from a somatic encounter that makes simultaneously material and semiotic *sense* through bodily and affective understanding.

258   *Hirofumi Katsuno and Daniel White*

Most interestingly, as Kaori grew accommodated to life with Qoobo, she began to further define and personalize her relationship with the robot by discerning its qualities from other simulated objects, such as robotic characters from animated films and AI agents on smartphones. According to Kaori,

> In the first couple of days I was really excited about Qoobo and lost myself. However, after spending about a week together, I finally settled on the understanding that Qoobo can't be a substitute for pets. For example, some people say "I'm home!" to their pets. I want that kind of feeling, but I haven't said this to Qoobo. The main reason for this is that this robot doesn't approach me. Even if it is a machine, it could be a real pet if approaching me like Baymax [a robot from a Disney animated film]. . . . Also, a few minutes ago, Hikari said, "Qoobo is not warm." I realized it for the first time when she pointed it out. If I could get such as sense of warmth from Qoobo, I might have had another feeling. . . . Still, it became clear to me that the robot can comfort me easily. It certainly doesn't come close to me but I can probably find a convenient sense of healing from it. Recently I became addicted to the video game Splatoon, and when I was frustrated from losing a game, I naturally stretched my hand to Qoobo and was relieved by receiving a response. I thought this was robotic healing [*robotto ni yoru iyashi*]. . . . Before, when I felt lonely, I sometimes talked to iPhone's Siri. But, words convey meanings relatively clearly. As a result, when I didn't get the response I expected, I became disappointed and realized it is a program after all. However, in the case of Qoobo, because the sense of touch is direct, you can communicate without thinking about anything. Feelings appear unconsciously in how we touch, and there is always a response. I think this feeling of relief and intimacy is something only a robot can do.

The ways in which Kaori perceives Qoobo's existence not in association with real animals but rather in relation to imaginary characters and AI agents provide insight into how companion robots as new haptic creatures become incorporated into a machine-inclusive multispecies society. Just as anthropological encounters with human–animal relations incorporated sociality into what was previously seen as a "natural" world distinct from humans (Kirksey and Helmreich 2010), these human–machine encounters similarly situate sociality among an arrangement of beings whose form of personhood is not clearly distinguishable from the point of view of affective impact, resonance, and attunement. What matters in this world of animated relations (Gershon 2015; Manning and Gershon 2013; Nozawa 2013; Silvio 2010) is not the differences between inanimate and animate beings but the different affective intensities and valences of various animated arrangements (Slaby, Mühlhoff, and Wüschner 2019).

Haptic Creatures 259

Importantly, as we have aimed to show in the first sections of our chapter, these arrangements have a historical context from which they draw their capacity to affect. Robots in the early days of social robotics tended to be modeled after real animals such as canine-type (AIBO) and seal-type (Paro) robots, which simulated intimate relationships with pets and the healing experience of animal therapy, respectively. However, as the commercialization of robots has expanded, creating a market for testing the efficacy and desirability of techno-intimate design, the meaning and value of robots have taken shape not only in comparison with the original living model but also with other artificial creatures and agents. In this sense, social robots are not mere substitutes for relationships with other people and species (even if that is how they are sometimes understood); rather, they influence how human imagination and emotions foster new relationships that have never existed before: Kaori's "robotic healing." In fact, Kaori does not define her relationship with Qoobo in the conventional perceptions of organic versus inorganic life, by which the organic is understood as authentic and warm and the inorganic as counterfeit and cold. Rather, in her view, Qoobo's shokkan becomes a hub for multiple dimensions of reality, in which her relational network expands through the integration of robots, AI agents, and imaginary characters. In this way, she fosters the formation of a new mode of intimacy through her relationship with Qoobo. Here, the techno-social relationship induced in the haptic contact zone becomes a generative site of powerful new narratives of social, emotional, and interpersonal renewal through novel forms of machine-inclusive multispecies sociality.

Conclusion

The cases of Hikari and Kaori illustrate how a new form of comfort and intimacy emerges in relation with haptic creatures. Importantly, this intimacy is not shaped purely through the narrative memory of closeness and credibility felt by humans toward pets but rather through mediated contact points which evoke the recalling of somatic histories that integrate affect, technological affordance, materiality, tactility, and human imagination. Despite its extremely simple and homogenous design (a cushion with a tail) and irrespective of the similar themes that emerged in conversation about Qoobo's lifelike touch, each of our robot users, like Hikari and Kaori, also expressed different experiences and impressions. Such differences in user experience indicate how dynamic the affordances of relationships between robots and users can be and illustrate how increasingly sophisticated technological systems can amplify the effects of visual and tactile design elements while also stimulating diverse memories to which they are connected. Here, the robot's haptic design invites human–robot interaction in a personal and intimate space within a resonant loop of technological affordance and emotional bonding based upon the affects of tactile sensation.

260 *Hirofumi Katsuno and Daniel White*

Accordingly, as haptic creatures continue to increase in number, robot-user experiences of tactile sensations are likely to be increasingly incorporated into robotics design as targets of capital generation, serving as the next dimension of humans' ongoing transformation into sources and resources of information processing for companion robot corporations. Through this chapter, we have introduced the concept of haptic creatures in order to draw attention to this process, to ground it in a history of collaborations between the entertainment robotics industry and robotics and AI researchers in Japan, and to demonstrate how technological experimentation can build new service industries that drive social, emotional, and interpersonal renewal through affect modulation. While it is too early to say to what extent consumers will continue to seek comfort in haptic creatures, and what visions of human–robot sociality will crystalize as a consequence, it is clear that haptic creatures will play an important role in shaping the future, ethics, and politics of Japan's machine-inclusive multispecies society.

Acknowledgments

The authors gratefully acknowledge the financial support of Doshisha University, the University of Cambridge, The Leverhulme Centre for the Future of Intelligence, Freie Universität Berlin, and the funders of a JST RISTEX Grant (number JPMJRX19H5) for this research.

Notes

1. Social scientists distinguish "emotion," feelings that have clear sociolinguistic labels like happiness and sadness, from "affect," sensations that are generated between people, objects, and environments and that, although socially conditioned, may not crystalize into prefigured emotion terms (Massumi 2002; White 2017).
2. In the Euro-American market, the term "social robot" is more commonly used for general consumers in the same way as "companion robot" is used in Japan. Meanwhile, in Japan, the expression "social robot" is used rather more preferably by researchers and developers.
3. Japanese names appearing in the chapter are written in the customary Japanese order, family name first.
4. Animated film is a quintessential example. As early as his 1941 publication, Imamura Taihei had already argued that Western animation appropriates animist desires toward the interests of capitalism.

References

Allison, Anne (2006), *Millennial Monsters: Japanese Toys and the Global Imagination*, Berkeley, CA: University of California Press.
——— (2013), *Precarious Japan*, Durham, NC: Duke University Press.
Breazeal, Cynthia (2002), *Designing Sociable Robots*, Cambridge, MA: MIT Press.

Haptic Creatures 261

Cook, Emma E. (2020), "Embodied Memory, Affective Imagination, and Vigilance: Navigating Food Allergies in Japan," *Culture, Medicine, and Psychiatry*, 1–21 (https://doi.org/10.1007/s11013-020-09689-z).

De Antoni, Andrea (2018), "A Vision Softly Creeping, Left Its Seeds While I Was Weeping: Spirit Becomings, Exorcisms, and Affective Imagination Skills in Italy and Japan," Paper presented at *the Skills of Feeling with the World Third Workshop*, Kyoto, Japan.

Ekman, Paul (1999), "Basic Emotions," in *Handbook of Cognition and Emotion*, ed. Tim Dalgleish and Mick Power, Chichester: John Wiley & Sons, 45–60.

Fujita, Masahiro (2001), "Robotto entāteimento to jinkō chinō" [Robot Entertainment and Artificial Intelligence], *Jinkō Chinō Gakkai* [*Journal of Japanese Society for Artificial Intelligence*], 16 (3), 399–405 (https://doi.org/10.11517/jjsai.16.3_399).

Galbraith, Patrick (2019), *Otaku and the Struggle for Imagination in Japan*, Durham, NC: Duke University Press.

Gershon, Ilana (2015), "What Do We Talk About When We Talk About Animation," *Social Media and Society*, 1 (1), 1–2 (https://doi.org/10.1177/2056305115578143).

Haraway, Donna (2008), *When Species Meet*, Minneapolis, MN: University of Minnesota Press.

——— (2016), *Staying With the Trouble: Making Kin in the Chthulucene*, Durham, NC: Duke University Press.

Imamura, Taihei (2014), "Japanese Cartoon Films," trans. Thomas Lamarre, *Mechademia*, 9, 107–24 (https://doi.org/10.1353/mec.2014.0002).

Jensen, Casper Bruun and Anders Blok (2013), "Techno-animism in Japan: Shinto Cosmograms, Actor-network Theory, and the Enabling Powers of Non-human Agencies," *Theory, Culture & Society*, 30 (2), 84–115 (https://doi.org/10.1177/0263276412456564).

Katsuno, Hirofumi (2011), "The Robot's Heart: Tinkering With Humanity and Intimacy in Robot-Building," *Japanese Studies*, 31 (1), 93–109 (https://doi.org/10.1080/10371397.2011.560259).

Kirksey, Eben and Stefan Helmreich (2010), "The Emergence of Multispecies Ethnography," *Cultural Anthropology*, 25, 545–76 (https://doi.org/10.1111/j.1548-1360.2010.01069.x).

Lupton, Deborah (2016), "Digital Companion Species and Eating Data: Implications for Theorising Digital Data—Human Assemblages," *Big Data & Society* (January–June), 1–5 (https://doi.org/10.1177/2053951715619947).

Manning, Paul and Ilana Gershon (2013), "Animating Interaction," *HAU: Journal of Ethnographic Theory*, 3 (3), 107–37 (https://doi.org/10.14318/hau3.3.006).

Massumi, Brian (2002), *Parables for the Virtual: Movement, Affect, Sensation*, Durham, NC: Duke University Press.

Nakatani, Masashi (2016), *Shokuraku nyūmon: Hajimete sekai ni fureru toki no yō ni* [*Introduction to Tactile Pleasure: Like When You First Touch the World*], Tokyo: Asahi Shuppansha.

Nikkei Sangyo Shimbun (2005), "Tamagotchi Plus (Interview with Hongo Takeichi, Bandai)," June 6, 18.

Nozawa, Shunsuke (2013), "Characterization," *Semiotic Review*, 3, online, https://semioticreview.com/ojs/index.php/sr/article/view/16.

262   Hirofumi Katsuno and Daniel White

Okura, Noriko (2017), *Kawaii kōgaku* [*Cute Engineering*], Tokyo: Asakura Shoten.

Robertson, Jennifer (2007), "Robo Sapiens Japanicus: Humanoid Robots and the Posthuman Family," *Critical Asian Studies*, 39 (3), 369–98 (https://doi.org/10.1080/14672710701527378).

—— (2018), *Robo Sapiens Japanicus: Robots, Gender, Family, and the Japanese Nation*, Oakland: University of California Press.

Shaviro, Steven (2012), "The Pinocchio Theory," *Shaviro Blog* (www.shaviro.com/Blog/?p=414).

Shibata, Takanori (2016), "Mentaru-komitto-robotto 'Paro' no kaihatsu to fukyū: Ninchishō nado no hi-yakubutsu chiryōhō no inovēshon" [Development and Spread of Therapeutic Medical Robot, PARO: Innovation of Non-pharmacological Therapy for Dementia and Mental Health], *Jōhō Kanri* [*Journal of Information Processing and Management*], 60 (4), 217–28 (https://doi.org/10.1241/johokanri.60.217).

Sicart, Miguel (2014), *Play Matters*, Cambridge, MA: MIT Press.

Silvio, Teri (2010), "Animation: The New Performance?" *Journal of Linguistic Anthropology* 20 (2), 422–38 (https://doi.org/10.1111/j.1548-1395.2010.01078.x).

Slaby, Jan, Rainer Mühlhoff, and Philipp Wüschner (2019), "Affective Arrangements," *Emotion Review*, 11 (1), 3–12 (https://doi.org/10.1177/1754073917722214).

Stevens, Carolyn S. (2011), "Touch: Encounters With Japanese Popular Culture," *Japanese Studies*, 31 (1), 1–10 (https://doi.org/10.1080/10371397.2011.559898).

Taussig, Michael (1997), *The Magic of the State*, London and New York: Routledge.

Turkle, Sherry (2011), *Alone Together: Why We Expect More From Technology and Less From Each Other*, New York: Basic Books.

Watanabe, Junji (2014), *Jōhō o umidasu shokkaku no chisei: Jōhō shakai o ikiru tame no kankaku no riterashī* [*Tactile Intelligence that Generates Information: Sensory Literacy for Living in an Information Society*], Kyoto: Kagaku Dōjin.

White, Daniel (2017), "Affect: An Introduction," *Cultural Anthropology*, 32 (2), 175–80 (https://doi.org/10.14506/ca32.2.01).

—— (2019), "The Mechanics of Fear: Re-envisioning Anxiety Through Emerging Technologies of Affect," *TG Technikgeschichte* [*History of Technology*], 86 (3), 245–64 (https://doi.org/10.5771/0040-117X-2019-3-245).

White, Daniel and Hirofumi Katsuno (2021), "Toward and Affective Sense of Life: Artificial Intelligence, Animacy, and Amusement at a Robot Pet Memorial Service in Japan," *Cultural Anthropology*, 36 (2), 222–51 (https://doi.org/10.14506/ca36.2.03).

Wright, James (2018), "Tactile Care, Mechanical Hugs: Japanese Caregivers and Robotic Lifting Devices," *Asian Anthropology*, 17 (1), 24–39 (https://doi.org/10.1080/1683478X.2017.1406576).

Index

Note: Page numbers in *italics* indicate a figure and page numbers in **bold** indicate a table on the corresponding page.

918 Day 75

Aayog *see* NITI Aayog
Abhidhamma 141
actor-network theory (ANT) 123–124
acute encephalitis syndrome (AES) 183–185
Adityanath *see* Bisht, Ajay
affective attunement between people and machines 247, 249
affective presence 252
affective states and experiences 243–246
AFSG *see* Ant Financial Services Group (ASG)
Agamben, Giorgio 8, 9; on "bare life" 196; *homo sacer* 8, 197; on "state of exception" 182; "strong" theory of sovereignty 197; thanatopolitics and 181–182
AIBO 242, 248, *249*, 259
Alexa (Amazon) 162
Alibaba Group 159, 166
Alipay 73, 76, 166, 168
Allen, C.T. 67
Allison, Anne 252
Amazon 162
Andhra Pradesh 183
anti-Japanese boycotts 25
animal realm 141
animal therapy 259
animated movements *see* Furby; LOVOT; Qoobo; robotics
animation (Disney) 258
anime 12
animism 140, 250–252

Ant Financial Services Group (ASG) 166–167
Anthropocene 253
Aquinas, Thomas 125–126
Arnould, Eric J. 3, 139
artifacts: Chinese 70, 75; as companion species 253; Indian 66; postmortem sacralization 127; religious (Japanese) 120
"artificial emotional creature" 253
Aryans 229–230
"Asianization of Asia" 12
"Asianization of the World" 12
Assam 183
Association for the Women's Memorial (*onna no hi no kai*) 129
autonomous women 84–86
autonomy of women (India): collective family decision making and 94; database consulted for study 97–99; definition of 84–85; educational expenditures and 86–89; education of children, importance of 91–92; equality and empowerment factoring into 94–95; financial concerns impacting 93–94; four dimensions of 87–88, 90; future research into 97; homemaker 67; safety concerns impacting 92–93

Baba Raghav Das (BRD) Medical College 179–180, 183–186, 188–197
Baidu Experience 168
Bajde, Domen 124

264 *Index*

Bandai 246, 250
Bandyopadhyay, Ranjan 68
Bangkok, food provisioning in 202–218
"bare life" 181–183
Bartky, Sandra Lee 225, 238
Basu, Alaka 90
Baudrillard, Jean 66
Bauman, Zygmunt 118, 134
beauty *see* female/feminine beauty
beauty hierarchy 233
beauty industry 238
"behavioral culture" 34
behavior, commodification of 35
Beijing 22, 64
Belk, Russell W. 20, 66, 67, 128
belt (*obi*) 41, 44
Belt and Road Initiative 12
Bengal 183
Beti Bachao, Beti Padhao Save the Daughter, Educate the Daughter 2015 campaign 83
Bhandari, Manish 180
Bharatiya Janata Party (BJP) 187
big data 160, 161, 172
Bihar 183
biofeedback 253, 254
biological life 246
biological pathogens 207
biopolitics 8; neoliberal 196
biopower 163–164, 168, 171, 181
biorhythms 248
Bisht, Ajay 180
Blanc, Ann K. 85
Black class 229
black (colour) 231
blacklists (China) 9, 167, 170
Black Lives Matter 227
black magic 146
black people 236
black skin 230, 232
Bloch, Maurice 140, 147–151
Bonillo-Silva, Eduardo 226, 238
book publishers (*shomotsu-don'ya*) 48
BOP *see* bottom of the Pyramid (BOP)
Bordo, Susan 225, 238
bottom of the Pyramid (BOP) 2, 8
Bougle, Celestin 239
Boxer, Charles R. 30n9
Brahmins 229, 230
brand communities 10, 106, 128
branding and national identity (China) 77

Brand, Peg Zilin 225
brand preference 160
brands: death ritual for living as 147; experiential consumption and 67; foreign 64; skin cream 225, 227–228, 233–234, 237
bride wealth: China 111–112
Breazeal, Cynthia 245
Brook, Timothy 19
brothels 50, 52
Bucy, Erik P. 97
Buddha 140, 141, 142, 146, 148
Buddhaghosa 148
Bundelkhand 183
Bun Luang 146
Bun Pra Wate 146

Callon, Michel 123
Canton System 22, 27, 30n10
capitalism: dominance of 33; global 228, 252; late-stage 252; neoliberal 179–184, 190, 193, 196–197; racism and 226, 238; thanatopolitics and 181–183
capitalist-animism 250–251
Capitalocene 253
caste system: female beauty and 230; gift giving (India) and 106; Hindu 231
Cayla, Julien 10
CCT *see* consumer culture theory (CCT)
Chatterji, Sangeeta 90
Chen Yao 19
chic (*iki*) 39, 47, 52
China: 1980s anti-Japanese boycotts 25; Beijing 22, 64; commodity in 19–29; consumer culture and international tourism in 64–65; consumer identity projects in 66–67; consumerism, arrival of 27–28, 63–64; Dynastic Era (China) 20, 21–23; as "factory of the world" 19; Guangzhou 27; Houbanmiao Village 107, 109; Japan and 76; "male phoenix" (male rural migrants) in 105–115; "National Humiliation Day" 75; national humiliation discourse (*bainian guochi*) 63; Patriotic Education and Central Leading Group for Propaganda and Ideology 64; politics of consumption 28–29;

Index 265

Qing dynasty 19, 20, 22–23; Republican era 20, 23–25; Republic of China, creation of 21; Shang dynasty 20; Shanghai 31, 64, 105, 107, 110; Shanghai Marriage Market 107, 109; "Sick Man of East Asia" 63, 76, 77; single-child consumer 29; special economic zones, creation of 27; Sun Yat Sen 24; *xiaokang* 28–29; Tiananmen massacre 63, 76; United States and 75, 76; *see also* Chinese national identity; Confucianism; Cultural Revolution; Deng Xiao-ping; gift giving in China; humiliation discourse; Mao era; social credit system

Chinese Communist Party (CCP) 27; ideological agenda of 76; national discourse and consumer culture 77; "National Humiliation Day" 75; social credit system and 171

"Chinese Dream" 29, 31n14

Chinese national identity 2, 63–77; modern 75; nationalist perspective on 63; postmodern crisis in 65–68; identity negotiation in Chinese tourists 69–77; racist discrimination encountered during travel 75; theme "rising from past humiliation" 69, 70–71, 74; theme "rising from the ashes 69, 71–73; theme "surpassing the former enemy" 69, 73–75, 76; victimhood narrative and 63, 76, 77

chokusō (direct cremation) 121

Chthulucene 253

citizen-consumer privacy, future of 169–170

Clunas, Craig 22, 23

cold chains *see* fridge freezers

colonialism: ailment of 235; beauty hierarchies built by 233, 235–236; British 231, 235; European 181; Hong Kong impact on 68; ideologies of 228; internal 226, 238; postcolonial India 197, 239; racist mythologies underpinning 230

colorism 228–229

commodification: definition of term 33; of Japanese food 40, 52

"commodification of behavior" 35

commodity: authentic 4; capitalist-animism and 250; China 19–29; death ceremony as 121, 126–127, 134; death spectacle as 191; fetishization of 33; hybridized 4; independence as 84; Japan 33–34; of leisure 35; *see also* consumerism

commodity consumerism 252

commodity skins and beauty industry 226–228

Community Form government (C-form) 172

COMPAS algorithm 173

Complete Book of Soba Noodles (Soba Zensho) 36

Confucianism: association with wealth and privilege 24; central tenets of 22–23; Chinese social conduct scores and 164–165; consumerism in China and 20–25; Deng's encouraging of 27–28; gift giving influenced by 111; Hu's pursuit of language of 29; in Japan 48, 120; Mao's ban of 25–27; wealth, understanding of 23; rebranding of 27

"Confucian values" 27

consumer behavior 106

consumer culture: Asian 138, 139, 140; China 63–77; escapist 4; Japan, development of 53; postmodern 6; Third World 5

consumer culture theory (CCT) 2, 11, 65–66, 164; gift giving and 106; problematics of 124, 139

consumer death culture: Japan 134; Thailand 140, 151–152

consumer education 96

consumer identity projects (China) 66–67

consumerism: China 19–29, 64; in early modern Japan 33–35, 40–47; in Japanese commercialized publication 47–52, 53; identity enacted via 34; in Japanese culinary culture 35–40, 53; in Japanese fashion (kimono) 40–47, 52–53

consumer precariousness 2, 3

consumer privacy in China 159–173; citizen-consumer privacy, future of 169–170; digital governance and 170–171; digital surveillance 160–162; distributed versus centralized trust 171–172; power and panopticism 162–164; social credit system 164–169

266 *Index*

consumer research 84; ANT applied to 124; on death culture 119, 120
consumer rituals 5, 103
consumers: agnostic 126; China 64; Chinese 71; elderly 118, 133; male 239; mature 119; migrant 129; *shūkatsu* agents linked to 125, 126–127, 133; social capital and 115; three-tiered class structure of (Japan) 34; vulnerable 83
consumer society 107
consumption, politics of 28–29
consumption practices 157
cotton (Japan): ease of dyeing 44; ginned 33; restricted by class 42
Covid-19 12, 179
cultural hermeneutics 147, 149–151
cultural myth, market versus 225–239; *see also* mythology; racism; skin color and skin creams
Cultural Revolution (China) 19, 20, 28, 73, 77
cycle of death and rebirth 140–144, 147

Dalits 183
Davis, Mike 184, 196
Dean, Mitchell 164
dead, hierarchical rank of 122
death *see* cycle of death and rebirth; solitary death
death rituals in Japan 118–134; agnostic and thanato-gnostic consumers of 119, 126–127; commodification and commercialization of 126, 134; history of 120–122; ideology of 123; "individuality" and individuation of 126, 127; market and marketing of 119–120; market for end-of-life activities (*shūkatsu*) 124–128; memorial communities 128–133; perpetual memorial service 127; preplanning of 126, 133; private 122; remains and nonhuman agencies 119, 127–128; simulated 125; *see also shūkatsu*
death-worlds: 181, 182, 183, 190, 195, 197
de Guignes 21
de Mendoza *see* Mendoza, Juan Gonzales de
dementia 254
Deng Xiao-ping 4; Confucianism and Maoism used by 20; death of 28;

economic reforms led by 19, 27–29, 64; *xiaokang* (term) used by 29
Deol, Abhay 237
Dharmasutra 239
diaspora tourism 68
digital governance 170–171
digital surveillance 160–162
Dikötter, Frank 24–25
distributed versus centralized trust 171–172
Dixon-Mueller, Ruth B. 85
docile bodies 9, 163, 169
Dong, Lily 10
Douban Discussion Forum 105
Dravidians 229–230
Driver, Tom F. 151
dūang winñān 142, 144, 148, 150
Du Halde 21
dukkha 141, 142, 148
Dumont, Louis 229
DuPuis, Melanie 206
Dynastic Era (China) 20, 21–23
Dyson, Tim 84

Echigoya (now Mitsukoshi Department Store) 42
Edict for Separation of Shintoism and Buddhism 121
Edo 34; kimono fashion trends 44; kimono shops 42; publishers based in 47–52; soba noodle restaurant 36–39, 52; sushi restaurant 40, 52; teahouse 35; Tsuruya Kiemon 48, 49; *see also* Tokyo
Edo-native publisher (*jihon-don'ya*) 48
Edoite (*Edokko*) 39, 52
Edo-style (*Edomae*) 40, 53n3
Eightfold Path (*ariya magga*) 141
encephalitis 179, 180, 183–198; Dilip 188–190; Dilwar 185–188; structural violence of 190–193; Sunaina 185; three cases of 184–190
Encephalitis Treatment Centers (ETC) 191
encyclopedias: *Morisada Mankō* 35–38, 40
Encyclopedists 21

Fair & Lovely skin cream 225, 227
fairness of skin *see* skin color and skin creams
Fan, Ruiping 23

Fanon, Frantz 187
Farber, Leora 238
fashion: Mao era 26; mass (kimono) 33, 42; Qing dynasty 19; thrift ordinances and sumptuary laws (Japan) 34, 40, 42–44, 47; trickle-down model in 34, 47
fashion trends: kimono 40–44, 53; patterns inside kimono linings 44–47
fast moving consumer goods (FMCGs) 225, 227
Fei, Xiaotong 113
female/feminine beauty 225–228; caste differences and 230; colorist attitudes towards 234; "inner" 234; impurity/imperfection and 238; modernity and 236; representations of 232; skin color and social status and 231; socialization of beliefs regarding 237–238; socially scripted ideologies of 234; see also colorism
FICO Score 173
Fine, Ben 203
Finnane, Antonia 19
First Opium War 64; see also Opium Wars
First Sino-Japanese War 63, 74
FMCGs see fast moving consumer goods (FMCGs)
Foucault, Michel 7; backlighting effect, concept of 169; discipline, understanding of 168, 170–171; "docile bodies" 9, 163, 169; gaze, concept of 159; on power, panopticism, and governmentality 160, 162–164
Fournier, Susan 67
four dimensions of autonomy see autonomy
Foundations of Mindfulness 142
Four Noble Truths (Buddhist) 141
four protections (Buddhist) 142
fridge freezers 202–206; cold chains in Bangkok and Hanoi 206–209; dependence on 209–215; India 205; purpose of 204–206; urbanization and 215–217; United Kingdom 205, 208, 215, 216; United States 205, 206, 215, 216; see also milk; milk consumption
Furby 247–248, 251

Gao Lian 30n12
Genroku Culture 53n2
George the Third (king of England) 22
Gerth, Karl 20, 24–25
ghost see hungry ghost
Giddens, Anthony 134
Giesler, Markus 124
gift-giving in China 105–115; bride wealth and 111–112; conflict and difference managed by 110–111; kinship making and 106–107; loss of face connected to 112; sustaining kinship via 113–114; wedding gifts 109–113
gifts of adjustment 114
gifts to male phoenixes' extended family 113
gifts to wives' extended family 114
Goa 183
Goldsmith 21
Gonzelez de Mendoza see Mendoza, Juan Gonzales de
Goodman, David 203, 216
Gorakhpur 179–180, 183–197; Baba Raghav Das (BRD) Medical College 179–180, 183–186, 188–197; protests 187; Pushpa Sales 179–180
'Gorakhpur Deaths' 191
Gorakhpur Development Authority (GDA) 185, 186, 187
Gore, Milind 191
Gotō Kaori see Kaori, Gotō
Gould, Stephen J. 141
governmentality: authoritarian 170; consumer precariousness and 2, 3; neoliberal 8; violence involved in 8; social credit system (China) and 160, 162–164, 170, 171, 172
Great Leap Forward (GLF) 72
green food consumption 2
green tea 35
Gregson, Kimberly S. 97
Gries, Peter H. 65
Guangzhou 22, 27
Guo, Yingjie 65
Gupta, Akhil 182, 197

haiku 39
Hall, Catherin 226
Hall, Ronald E. 228
Hall, Stuart 65
handcraft markets 3
Hand, Martin 206

268   *Index*

handpumps 189, 192
hand-to-mouth existence 93
hankō 47
Hangzhou 21
Hanoi, food provisioning in 202–218;
  anxiety regarding 213, 215; "cold
  chain" in 203, 207–209; contents
  of fridge freezers 209–216; fridge
  freezers in 206–209; "new" food"
  212; rapid population growth in
  204; Westernized diets in 202
haptic creatures 242–260; rise of
  252–259; techno-intimacy and
  245–250; techno-sociability of 259;
  virtual pets and 250–252
Haraway, Donna 252–253
Harunobu Suzuki *see* Suzuki,
  Harunobu
Harvey, David 186
Heed Sib-Song Klong Sib-Si tradition
  146, 149
Henderson, Joan 68
Herring, Cedric 225
Hertz, Robert 150
Hesse, Barnor 228
Hikari, Ichikawa 256
Hindu religion 89, 230; caste system
  231; deities 232, 236; epic tales
  232; mythology 232; religious
  texts 226
Hindustan Unilever 225, 227
hiragana 47, 48, 50, 51
Hirschmann, Nancy J. 84
Hishikawa, Moronobu 43
Holt, Douglas B. 143
holy day (Muslim) 186
holy days (Buddhist) 140
holy relics 128
holy sites 129
homo sacer 8, 181, 187, 197
"*hongs*" 22, 27
Horton, Hayward 225
Houbanmiao Village 107, 109
Hua Guofeng 30n6
Hudson, Michael 181
Hu Jintao 29
human-robot sociality *see* haptic
  creatures
Humble, Richard 21
Hume, David 21
humiliation (China) 26, 63
humiliation discourse (China)
  64; Patriotic Education linked

to 75; theme "rising from past
  humiliation" 69, 70–71, 74; United
  States and Japan as common
  enemies of China 76; victimhood
  narrative in 63, 76, 77
Hummon, D.M. 67
hungry ghost 142–145, 150
hungry ghost festivals 139, 147,
  149, 151
hungry ghost realm 141, 143, 147

Ichikawa, Fusae 129
Ikegami, Elko 42, 47
iki 39, 47, 52
Imamura, Taihei 260n4
India: Buddhism 140; children's
  education in 82–98; Covid-19 179;
  fairness and beauty industry 225–239;
  gift giving and caste hierarchy
  in 106; Gujarat 91; history and
  colonialism 235–237; *see also* Uttar
  Pradesh
Indian Human Development Survey
  97–98
individual human actions, five
  situational factors impacting moral
  charge of 126
"individuality" 126
internet 171; China 166, 167
internet communications 165
Internet of Things (IoT) 160, 161
internet providers (Japan) 247
intimacy 114, 161; affective 246;
  human-based 247; robot (Japan)
  242–259; techno- 244, 246–248,
  250, 253, 259; virtual 251
intimidation 8
Isaacs, Harold 230
Issei Miyake 53
iyashi 12, 247, 257, 258

Jameson, Fredric 24
Janki 236
Japan: Buddhist beliefs 120, 121;
  China compared to 74, 76; China,
  invasion of 75; consumerism in
  33–53; disparity and schism in
  126; national culinary culture 53;
  temples 122; urban migrants 122;
  see also death rituals in Japan; Edo;
  First Sino-Japanese War; haptic
  creatures; kimono; Kyōto; Osaka;
  shūkatsu; soba noodles; solitary

death in Japan; sushi; Tokyo; udon
noodle restaurants
Japanese encephalitis 183–184
Jiangjie [pseudonym] **108**, 114
Jianshu 168
Jingdong 159, 167
Jōjakkōji Temple 129
joss paper burning ritual 139, 145,
147, 149

kabuki theater 35, 44, 49
Kali 236
Kamleitner, Bernadette 161
kanazōshi 48
Kanbun pattern book 41
kanji 47, 48
Kaori, Gotō 257–249
karma 141–144, 150–151
Karnataka 183
kawaii 247
Kenzō 53
Khader, Serene 96
khandha 148
kimono 33, 40–47; early fashion
trends 40–42; lining and hem
patterns in 44–47, 52–53;
sumptuary laws and 42–44;
traveling 121
Kimura, Yaeko 52
kinship: definition of 106;
symbolic 106
kinship distance 107; negative
reciprocity based on 106
kinship-making in China: establishing
kinship through wedding gifts
110–113; gift giving and 106–107;
prekinship gift-giving 109–110;
sustaining kinship through gifts
113–114
kinship network 107
Kiran 234, 236
Kisan Mazdoor Sangharsh Samiti
(KMSS) 186
Koolwal, Gayatri 90
Kōrin Ogata 43, *43*
Kōrin's patterns 43
K-pop 12
Krishna 232
Kudokuin Temple 129–131
Kumar, Anil 194
Kuomintang (KMT) 30
kusa-zōshi 50–52
Kyōden Santō 51–52

Kyōto 34; boxed sushi popular in 39;
Kanbun pattern book published in
41; publishers based in 47–48; soba
sauce 38

Lal, Parmanand 229
Lamont, Michèle 65
Langer, Rita 143
Latour, Bruno 123
Law Code of Manu 229
Law, John 123
"Lei Feng" archetype 170
Leopold, Ellen 203
Leslie, Deborah 203
Li Conghua 29
Lloyd, Cynthia B. 85
loss of face 112
LOVOT 243, *244*
Lu Xun 30n13
Lyon, David 171

Maddox, Keith 225
Mahabharata 232
Mailer, Greig 66
Malaysia 69, 75, 145
"male phoenix" (male rural
migrants)105–115; *see also* gift
giving in China
manga 52, 53, 242; *see also*
kusa-zōshi
Manipur 183
Manu Smriti 229
Manyōshu anthology 127
Mao era 19, 20, 25–28; Cultural
Revolution 77; Great Leap Forward
72; "national humiliation"
discourse 76
Marco Polo 21
Marx, Karl 26, 125
McCartney Embassy 21–22
McCartney, George 21
Mehta, Raj 66
Meiji Restoration 4, 52, 121
Mendoza, Juan Gonzales de 21
migrants *see* "male phoenix"
milk: refrigeration of 209, 210; sale of
185; supermarket 211
milk consumption 206, 212
Miller, F. 67
millet 107
Ming dynasty 22; manuals 30
Mitchell, Vince 162
Miyake, Issei *see* Issei Miyake

270   *Index*

Mizukami, Kayoko 47
Modi, Narendra 187
Moisander, Johanna 139
Moore, Mick 84
Morisada Mankō 35–38, 40
Moyai no kai 129–130, 132
Murray, Scott J. 196
Muslims: India 183; mothers 89; poverty
   among 183; Uttar Pradesh 185
mythology: folk 142; ghost 145;
   Hindu 232; iconography of 239;
   Indian 232; racial 230

Nadeem, Shehzaad 227
Nakatani, Masashi 255
"National Humiliation Day" (China) 75
national humiliation discourse
   (*bainian guochi*) 63
National Institute for Empowerment
   of Persons with Multiple
   Disabilities, Chennai 195
National Institute of Virology, Uttar
   Pradesh 191
Nazi concentration camps 182
Nehru Hospital 183, 184
neocolonial development paradigm 3
Neo-Confucianism 120
neofascism 182
neoliberal biopolitics *see* biopolitics
neoliberal capitalism *see* capitalism
neoliberal governmentality
   see governmentality
neoliberalism: deepening of 193–195;
   dispossession and 186; finance
   capital and 193; profiteering and
   194; thanatopolitics of 179–198
nibbāna 141, 142, 148, 151
nigirizushi 39, 40
Nihon Ukiyoe Kyōkai 48
nishikie 47
Nishiyama, Matsunosuke 34–35
NITI Aayog 195, 197
Norn-Loeng-Sa-Dor-Cro death ritual
   146–147

Oakes, Tim 75
Obeyesekere, Gananath 140,
   147–151
obi 41, 44
ohitorisama 129
opium crisis (1839–1842;
   1856–1860) 23
Opium Wars 30n11, 63, 74

Orwell, George 169
Ōsaka 34; boxed sushi popular in 39;
   publishers in 48; soba sauce in 38

Palmer, Catherine 68
Paro 253, 254, 259
Path of Purification 148
Patnaik, Prabhat 181, 182, 197
Pattanaik, Devdutt 232
Pax Tokugawa 4
'*Pee-Ta-Khon*' hungry ghost festival
   139, 146, 149
phenotypes 226
phī 142–144, 150
Philips, Amali 226
Phuket Providence 145–146, 151
Piacenti, Marla 66
Pikachu Genki Dechu (Hey You,
   Pikachu!) 247
Pingali, Prabhu 211
plant milks 212; *see also* milk
Pliny the Elder 21
Pond's White Beauty 227, 228
Pongsapich, Amara 208
Por-Tor hungry ghost festival 139,
   145, 146, 149, 151
Povinelli, Elizabeth A. 180
power, panopticism, and
   governmentality *see* Foucault,
   Michel; governmentality
pradhan 190
Prapheni Bun Bung Fai (rocket
   festival) 146
Pratt, Michael G. 65
Pratto, Felicia 231
precariat: anger of 184, 188, 190,
   192; bare life of 187; death-world
   of 197; violence against 180,
   195–197; *see also* death-worlds;
   neoliberalism
preta and *preta* realm 141,
   142–143, 144
privacy management 161
privacy protection framework 162
privacy: compromised 169, 171;
   corporate 162; six general types of
   160; *see also* consumer privacy
private basic writing schools
   (*tenaraijo*) 47
private schools (Gujarat, India) **91**
PRM *see* Punish-Reward Mechanism
   (PRM)
Prosser, Jay 226

Punish-Reward Mechanism (PRM) 166–167, 169, 171
purity and impurity 226, 229, 232; white and black associated with 231
purity and innocence 236–237
Pushpa Sales 179–180

Qianlong (Emperor) 22
Qing dynasty 19, 20, 22–23
Qoobo 243, 245–259

racism 226–229; classical 231; colonial narratives and 238; colorism and 228–229
rakugo 39
Rao, Menaka 194
rebirth 150; *see also* cycle of death and rebirth
rebirth consciousness 148
rebounding violence 147
Rees, Jonathan 205
refrigeration *see* fridge freezers
Republic of China, creation of *see* China
rhabdovirus 183
Ricci, Matteo 21
Ricoeur, Paul 147–151
"Rinpa" art school 43
Risley, Herbert 230
RNM-enabled services 168, 170–171
robotic healing 259
robotics 246, 248; *see also* social robotics
robotics corporations 249–250, 260
robotics development in academia 249–250
robotics engineering 244, 245
robotics technology 244
robotic therapy 253–254
Rothfeld, Otto 230
Rousseau, Jean-Jacques 21

Sahlins, Marshall 106–107
Saikaku Ihara 48
Sainath, P. 191
samsāra 141
Schatzki, Theodore R. 217
Schrift, Melissa 19
Scott, David 63
Scott, Elizabeth D. 126
Seaman: The Forbidden Pets 247
Seidel, Marc-David 172

Sen, Amartya 84
Sesame Credit 160, 166–168
Shab-e-Baraat 186
Shang dynasty 20
Shanghai 31, 64, 105, 107, 110
Shanghai Marriage Market 107, 109Sharma, Ram Sharan 230
Sharma, Ursula 230
Shibata, Takanori 253–254
Shikoku Island 128
Shove, Elizabeth 206
shūkatsu and *shūkatsu* market 119–120, 122–128, 133–134
Shūkatsu Festa 123
Sidaneus, Jim 231
Shang dynasty 20
Shanghai 31, 64, 105, 107, 110
Shanghai Marriage Market 107, 109
"shared grave" concept 129
Shaviro, Steven 250
Shintoism 120–121
shūkatsu 119–120, 122–128, 133–134; market for 124–126
Shūkatsu Counselor Association 124
Shūkatsu Festa 123, 125, 128
"Sick Man of East Asia" 63, 76, 77
Sidanius, Jim 251
Siddhattha Gotama 141
silk cloth: China 19, 21; Japan 33, 42, 44
Simone, Abdoumaliq 189
Singh, Arvind 192
Singh, Nitesh 188, 192, 193, 194
Singh, Rahul Rana 186
single-child consumer 29
sign value 67
Sigurdsson, Geir 23, 27
Sirgy, Joseph M. 67
skhandha 148
skin color and skin cream 233–234, 237; Fair & Lovely 225, 227; Hindustan Unilever Dove brand 225, 227; Pond's White Beauty 227, 228; skin lightening 225, 227, 232, 233, 236–237; *see also* purity and impurity
Small Guidebook of Famous Eating and Drinking Places in Edo 35
soba noodles 36–39, 52–53; *kakesoba* 38; "nightjar soba-sellers (*yotaka-soba*)" 38–39
soba noodle shops 40
social credit system (SCS) 159–173; Community Form government

272 Index

and 172; docile bodies under 169;
consumer privacy and 160, 162; as
governmentality practice 171; human
rights and 173; official initiation
of 165; scoring mechanism 167;
state's design of 166; surveillance of
everyday life under 170
social robotics 242, 245, 251, 259
solitary death in Japan 118–134;
anxiety of 132; eradication of
130; fear of 128; *kodokushi* 119;
memorial community as solution
119; social problem of 119
Solove, Daniel J. 160
Souhu Finance 168
Spiggle, Susan 233
special economic zones (SEZ) 27
Starr, John Bryan 170
Staunton, George Leonard 22
Stearns, Peter 23
sumptuary laws *see* fashion
Sun Yat Sen 24
Supreme People's Court of the People's
Republic of China 159, 165
Supreme Procuratorate 165
sushi, marketing of 39–40, 52, 53
Suttanta 141
suzhi 29
Suzhou 19
Suzuki, Harunobu 47

tactile affect and human-robot
interaction 242–260
tactile interaction 247, 253, 256
tactile sensors 243
tactile (*shok-kan*) approach 255
tactile sensation 259, 260
tactile technologies 254
Takada, Kenzō 53
Tamagotchi 246–247, 250–252
Tambiah, Stanley 150
Tang dynasty 19
Taobao 166
Taoism 144
"techno-intimacy" 244, 246–248,
250, 253, 259
Telles, Edward, 229
temple schools (*terakoya*) 47
tenaraijo 47
Tencent 159, 167
terakoya 47
Thailand: Bangkok 204, 207–208;
Buddhist death rituals 139, 144,

150–152; consciousness, concept
of 148; fridge freezers in 204, 208,
215; plant milks 212; Por Tor
145; social system 151; Theravāda
Buddhism in 140–141, 152
thanato-gnostic consumers 120,
126–127
thanatopolitics of neoliberalism
179–198; capitalism and 181–183,
197; Murray's interpretation of
196; violence of 182; *see also* death-
worlds; Gorakhpur; precariat; Uttar
Pradesh
Theravāda Buddhism 139–145;
consciousness, idea of 148; death
rituals 145–147, 149–150; Heed
Sib-Song Klong Sib-Si tradition 146,
149; joss paper burning ritual 147,
149; Norn-Loeng-Sa-Dor-Cro
Death Ritual for the Living
146–147, 149; Path of Purification
148; Pee Ta Khon hungry ghost
festival 146, 149; *viññāṇa* 148;
see also death rituals; hungry ghost;
Thailand
Thomas, Tandy Chalmers 144
Thompson, Craig J. 3, 139
thrift ordinances and sumptuary laws
(Japan) 34, 40, 42–44, 47; Tibetan
Buddhism 139
Tiananmen massacre 63, 76
Tipiṭaka 141
T-mall 166
Todorov, Vladislav 25
Tokugawa Shōgunate 40, 42, 51, 121
Tokyo 73, 74; Kudokin Temple
129–131; Moyai 132; solitary death
in 119; "shared grave" concept in
129;; shūkatsu in 122–123, 126,
128; Sugamo Ward 132
transnational imaginary Asia 10, 12
trickle-down model in Japan 34, 47
Trivedi, Prashant 195
Trouillot, Michel-Rolph 230
Tsuruya Kiemon 48, *49*
Tu Long 30n12
Turkle, Sherry 248–249, 250

udon noodle restaurants (*udonya*)
36–38
Uekrongtham, Ekachai 146–147
ukiyoe (woodblock prints) 35, *36*, *38*,
43, 47

ukiyo-zōshi (the books of fleeting world stories) 48
United Kingdom: China compared to 74; China GDP compared to 28; fridge freezers 205, 208, 215, 216
United States: China GDP compared to 28; China in dispute with 76; China's progress compared to 75; financial scoring systems in 173; fridge freezers 205, 206, 215, 216; Furby sold in 247; white skin in 226
urbanization 120; food technologies and 202, 206, 215–217
utopia: communist 26
utopia and dystopia, social credit as experiment in 159–173
Utagawa, Hiroshige 36
Uttar Pradesh 179–180; deprivation index 190; economy 183; Primary and Community Health Centers (PHC and CHC) 191, 192, 193; private health expenditure in 195; *see also* encephalitis

Van Gennep 147
Varman, Rohit 8
Vatuk, Sylvia 106
Vatuk, Ved Prakash 106
Venkatesh, Alladi 161
Vietnam 72; domestic refrigerators use in 204, 208, 211; soymilk consumed in 212; provisioning-at-a-distance in 215; *see also* Hanoi
vikas (development) 187, 196
viññāṇa 148
Vinaya 141
virtual pets 250–252
virtual reality 246, 254
Visuddhimagga 148
Voltaire 21
volunteerism 167, 173n1

Wangfeng [pseudonym] **108**, 111–112
Wang, Helen 31n14
Wangjia [pseudonym] **108**
Wangjiufeng [pseudonym] **108**

Wangxia [pseudonym] **108**
Wang, Zheng 75
Watanabe, Junji 255
Warde, Alan 202
WeChat 161
WeChat Pay 73, 76, 167, 168
Wen Zhenheng 30n12
Wertheim-Heck, Sigrid 207
wheel of life (WOL) 141; *dūang winñān* and 148; ghosts and 150, 151; *preta* realm 144; realms of 141–142; *see also dūang winñān*; hungry ghost; *phī*; *preta* and *preta* realm
White Beauty 228
white color 231–233
whiteness as commodity 227–228; hegemonies of 238; normalization of 233
white skin 226, 234–236
Wilhite, Hal 205
Wolf, Naomi 225
WOL *see* wheel of life (WOL)
Wongsekiarttirat, Wathana 208
woodblock prints (*ukiyoe*) 35, *36*, 38, 43, 47
woodblocks (*bangi*) for books 48
work of culture 147–151; definition 148
Wu Juanjuan 19, 26

Xia Dynasty 30n5
Xi Jinping 29, 31n14
xiaokang 28–29

Yamamoto, Kansai 53
Yan, Yunxiang 106
Yanfan [pseudonym] **108**
Yanjiu [pseudonym] **108**, 111
Yanyang [pseudonym] **108**
Yifei [pseudonym] **108**
yoga 12

Zacharias, Usha 228
Zhao, Xin 20
Zimmerman, Marc A. 95

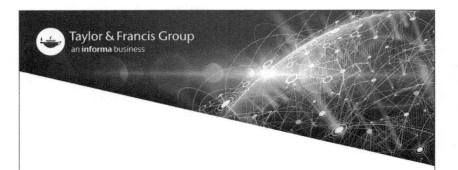